PIONEERING ECONOMIC THEORY, 1630-1980

A Mathematical Restatement

ABOUT THE AUTHOR   Hans Brems is professor of economics at the
University of Illinois. He has taught at the universities
of Copenhagen and California at Berkeley and, as a
visiting professor, at the universities of Basle,
Copenhagen, Gothenburg, Göttingen, Hamburg, Kiel,
Lund, Uppsala, and Zurich as well as the Industrial
Institute for Economic and Social Research in
Stockholm and the Stockholm School of Economics.
His books include *Product Equilibrium under
Monopolistic Competition* (1951), *Output,
Employment, Capital, and Growth* (1959; 1973),
Quantitative Economic Theory (1968), *Labor, Capital,
and Growth* (1973), *Inflation, Interest, and Growth*
(1980), *Dynamische Makrotheorie—Inflation, Zins
und Wachstum* (1980), and *Fiscal Theory* (1983).

HANS BREMS

PIONEERING ECONOMIC THEORY, 1630-1980

A Mathematical Restatement

THE JOHNS HOPKINS UNIVERSITY PRESS
Baltimore and London

The Johns Hopkins University Press
701 West 40th Street
Baltimore, Maryland 21211
The Johns Hopkins Press Ltd., London

*The paper in this book is acid-free and meets the guidelines for
permanence and durability of the Committee on Production Guidelines
for Book Longevity of the Council on Library Resources.*

LIBRARY OF CONGRESS CATALOGING-IN-PUBLICATION DATA

Brems, Hans.
  Pioneering economic theory, 1630-1980.

  Bibliography: p.
  Includes index.
  1. Economics—History.   2. Economics—Mathematical models.
3. Equilibrium (Economics)   4. Equilibrium (Economics)—
Mathematical models. I. Title.
HB75.B7845   1986   330.1   85-19819
ISBN 0-8018-2667-5 (alk. paper)

Körper und Stimme
leiht die Schrift
dem stummen Gedanken,
durch der Jahrhunderte Strom
trägt ihn
das redende Blatt.

Friedrich Schiller,
"Der Spaziergang" (1795)

Scripture lends
body and voice
to silent thought,
the articulate leaf
conveys it
through the passage of centuries.

CONTENTS

FIGURES

TABLES

PREFACE

Never before has as much economic knowledge been produced per annum as in the last two-thirds of our own century. But knowledge is more than the current flow of its output. Like capital stock, knowledge is an accumulation, i.e., an integral with respect to time of the flow of output *minus* scrappage.

Thus visualized, could the history of pioneering economic theory be an aid to a deeper understanding of our current body of theory? The objective of this book is to see it as such an aid. To meet its objective, the book will adopt three principles.

First, the book will examine pioneering economic theory the way we examine all theory nowadays, i.e., as models formulated mathematically, so their consistency may be checked, their solutions found, and their properties discussed—hence all the equations and inequalities of the book.

Second, to keep its mathematics from running wild the book will confront its mathematical premises and conclusions with the original pioneering text—hence all the page references and quotes of the book.

Third, stopping at Marshall or even Keynes will not do. We must avoid provincialism in time no less than space, carry our history all the way to our own time, and pay no less attention to late than to early pioneering. Since there is so much more late than early pioneering, inevitably the going will get slower as we approach our own time: the fifth period 1930-1980 constitutes a mere 14 percent of the period 1630-1980 covered by the book, yet will occupy 45 percent of its space.

For such a book I had the good and early fortune to find a publisher seeing no sharp break between theory and its history and seeking the advice of William J. Baumol. To Paul A. Samuelson I am grateful for an early "Right on!" and to Gottfried Haberler and E. Roy Weintraub for other early encouragement.

Parts of the book were offered during visiting professorships abroad in 1982 and 1983. For their magnificent hospitality I am grateful to Ragnar

Bentzel of Uppsala, Gottfried Bombach of Basle, Gunnar Eliasson of the Stockholm Industrial Institute for Economic and Social Research, and to Bruno Frey, Heidi Schelbert, and Helmut Schneider of Zurich.

Here at home I am indebted, first and foremost, to the University of Illinois Library, whose collection in the history of economic thought must be second only to that of the Kress Library at the Harvard School of Business Administration. Always finding what I was looking for, I wondered whether the book could have been written anywhere else than here and on Soldiers Field in Boston. For efficient word-processing and photographic assistance I am indebted to my Department of Economics and College of Commerce, and for help in locating the Schiller quote following the title page to my colleague Henri Stegemeier.

No less than its six predecessors, this book owes its existence to Ulla Brems, who read proofs, smoothed paths, provided material and spiritual maintenance, and yet endured long spells of inattention.

ACKNOWLEDGMENTS

To be both honest and successful, a mathematical restatement must confront its mathematics with the original form of the theory, thus enabling the reader to decide if the restatement is a fair one. Such original form is best rendered by direct quotes. Our quotes will be numerous but short, hence constitute a minuscule proportion of both our own book and the books quoted. Such use is believed to be fair use of copyrighted work, to be everywhere acknowledged in gratitude but not requiring explicit permissions to quote.

Material from the author's own publications in *American Economic Review, Economie appliquée, History of Political Economy*, and *Quarterly Journal of Economics* has been used in several chapters. Journal editors have assured him that such use, too, is acceptable.

Lexington Books (D. C. Heath and Company) readily granted permission to use in chapter 16 graphs and other material from chapter 9 of the author's *Fiscal Theory: Government, Inflation, and Growth*, Lexington, Mass., 1983. *Fortune* (Time Inc.) readily granted permission to use in chapter 4 data from the *Fortune 500* listing (May 1974) to draw figure 4-1, on U.S. capital intensities by industry. Harcourt Brace Jovanovich readily granted permission to reprint in chapter 9 four lines from *Collected Poems 1909–1962* by T. S. Eliot, copyright 1936 by Harcourt Brace Jovanovich, Inc.; copyright 1963, 1964 by T. S. Eliot.

PIONEERING ECONOMIC THEORY, 1630-1980

A Mathematical Restatement

INTRODUCTION Men and Ideas in Economic Theory

> *Under a powdered wig you find the usual head,*
> *like yours and mine...*
>
> Samuelson (1978: 1429)

I. MEN

1. *The Muse of Economics*

The muse of economics has dwelt in many places, great or obscure. She dwelt in the hustle and bustle of Paris and inspired a banker. In the closing decades of French absolutism she dwelt in the splendor of the palace of Versailles and inspired the physician to the king but soon left for the provinces. There, in the town of Limoges, she inspired the *intendant*, equally able as a thinker and as an administrator and destined for high office. She dwelt on the banks of the Firth of Forth, first on the hills of Edinburgh, then in rustic Kirkcaldy. She dwelt in the hustle and bustle of London and inspired a broker. She dwelt in Trinity College in Dublin and on the indifferent soil of the econometric estate of Tellow in Mecklenburg. She inspired a solitary retiree in Cologne. She dwelt in pompous "Imperial and Royal" Vienna in the closing decades of the Hapsburg Empire; in a provincial academy in Lausanne; at the oldest of all German-language universities, that of Prague; on the well-groomed banks of the River Cam; and in a small-town idyll in the shade of the cathedral of Lund. In the interwar years she came back to Vienna, now reduced and threatened, and back to the River Cam, still the same. She went farther up the River Thames to Christ Church and All Souls of Oxford.

A century after its political independence the New World declared its intellectual independence, and the muse of economics left Europe for the first time. At first she dwelt on a serene campus in New Haven; then on Manhattan and at either end of Massachusetts Avenue in another Cambridge. She liked America and went farther afield, to the drab Chicago South Side and all the way to the West Coast. She even crossed the Pacific and paid her visits to a new industrial giant.

2. *A Map*

Let us put our most important pioneers on a map. Who is important? What is importance? Importance to his contemporaries or impor-

INTRODUCTION, FIGURE 1. The Muse of Economics: Places and Authors Visited

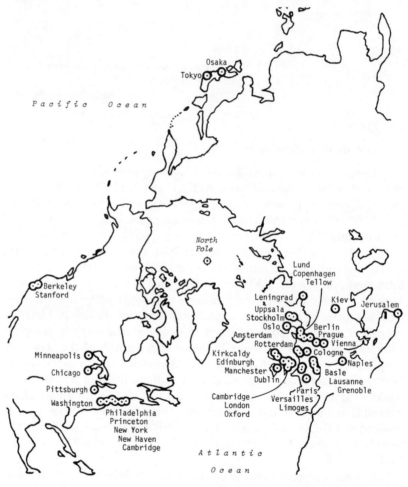

tance to us? Pioneers may have been fully appreciated in their own time, as were, say, Ricardo and Keynes. But others may have been virtually unknown and only discovered, not to mention translated, much later. Cantillon and Walras had to wait 176 and 80 years, respectively, for their English translations. The 84 pioneers put on our map in figure 1 are those who are most important to us, regardless of what their contemporaries thought of them. Our readers might prefer different subsets.

Where did our 84 pioneers do their most important work?

Cantillon divided his time among the financial markets of Amster-

Basle
Bernoulli, 1700-1782

Berkeley
Dorfman, 1916-

Berlin
v. Stackelberg, 1905-1946

Cambridge, England
Malthus, 1766-1834
Marshall, 1842-1924
Pigou, 1877-1959
Keynes, 1883-1946
Sraffa, 1898-1983
Ramsey, 1903-1930
Robinson, 1903-1983
Kaldor, 1908-

Cambridge, Massachusetts
Schumpeter, 1883-1950
Hansen, 1887-1975
Chamberlin, 1899-1967
Leontief, 1906-
Samuelson, 1915-
Solow, 1924-
Eckstein, 1927-1984

Chicago
Douglas, 1892-1976
Koopmans, 1910-1985
Friedman, 1912-

Cologne
Gossen, 1810-1858

Copenhagen
Zeuthen, 1888-1959

Dublin
Longfield, 1802-1884

Edinburgh
Hume, 1711-1776
Steuart, 1712-1780

Grenoble
Cournot, 1801-1877

Jerusalem
Patinkin, 1922-

Kiev
Slutsky, 1880-1948

Kirkcaldy
Smith, 1723-1790

Lausanne
Walras, 1834-1910
Pareto, 1848-1923

Leningrad
Kantorovich, 1912-

Limoges
Turgot, 1727-1781

London
Mun, 1571-1641
Petty, 1623-1687
Lauderdale, 1759-1839
Ricardo, 1772-1823
Mill, 1806-1873
Marx, 1818-1883
Wicksteed, 1844-1927
Edgeworth, 1845-1926
Bowley, 1869-1957
Phillips, 1914-1975

Lund
Wicksell, 1851-1926

Manchester
Jevons, 1835-1882
Hicks, 1904-

Minneapolis
Sargent, 1943-

Naples
Galiani, 1728-1787

New Haven
Fisher, 1867-1947
Tobin, 1918-
Debreu, 1921-

New York
Clark, 1847-1938
Hotelling, 1895-1973

Osaka
Morishima, 1923-

Oslo
Frisch, 1895-1973
Haavelmo, 1911-

Oxford
Harrod, 1900-1978

Paris
Cantillon, 1697-1734
Say, 1767-1832
Dupuit, 1804-1866
Bertrand, 1822-1900

Philadelphia
Klein, 1920-
Phelps, 1933-

Pittsburgh
Lucas, 1937-

Prague
v. Wieser, 1851-1926

Princeton
Morgenstern, 1902-1977
v. Neumann, 1903-1957

Rotterdam
Tinbergen, 1903-

Stanford
Arrow, 1921-

Stockholm
Cassel, 1866-1945
Ohlin, 1899-1979
Hansen, 1920-

Tellow
v. Thünen, 1783-1850

Tokyo
Uzawa, 1928-

Uppsala
Lindahl, 1891-1960

Versailles
Quesnay, 1694-1774

Vienna
Menger, 1840-1921
Böhm-Bawerk, 1851-1914
v. Mises, 1881-1973
Schlesinger, 1889-1938
v. Hayek, 1899-
Wald, 1902-1950

Washington, D.C.
Dantzig, 1914-

dam, London, and Paris. We do not know where, around 1730, he found the time to write his *Essai* (1755). But it was published in French, so our guess is Paris. Bernoulli's permanent academic base was Basle, but he must have written his "Specimen" (1738) as a visiting professor at the court in St. Petersburg. Malthus wrote his *Essay* (1798) at Cambridge but his *Principles* (1820) at Haileybury (Hertford). Dupuit wrote the first article (1844) on demand before, but the rest of them after, being called to Paris. Pareto wrote his *Cours* (1896-1897), containing Pareto's Law, while still active at Lausanne but his *Manuale* (1906) in his early retirement 27 miles farther down the lakefront in Céligny. Wicksell's permanent academic base after 1901 was Lund, where he wrote his *Föreläsningar I-II* (1901-1906), but he had laid the foundations in *Ueber Wert* (1893) and in *Geldzins* (1898) while studying abroad and in Stockholm. Wieser wrote his most important work, *Der natürliche Werth* (1889), as a professor at Prague, before succeeding Menger at Vienna. The most footloose of our pioneers was Schumpeter, who between 1906 and 1914 lived in five different places located in four countries on three continents and yet managed to publish his *Wesen* (1908), his *Entwicklung* (1912), and his *Epochen* (1914). The last two were the foundations of his *Business Cycles* (1939) and his *History* (1954), respectively, written at Harvard. Hicks wrote *Value and Capital* (1939) at Manchester but all later works at Oxford.

Having selected our 84 pioneers and drawn our map, let us classify them according to time, space, language, and use of mathematics.

3.   *Time and Space*

Our map shows a distribution of pioneers that is uneven both in its time and space dimensions. If we classify them according to the century of their birth our breakdown will be:

Sixteenth Century	1
Seventeenth Century	3
Eighteenth Century	11
Nineteenth Century	37
Twentieth Century	<u>32</u>
Total	84

And those born in the twentieth century will keep coming of age for quite some time!

If we classify our pioneers according to the continent where they did their most important work, classifying von Neumann and Schumpeter as Americans, our breakdown will be:

Europe	57
United States	24
Asia	3
Total	84

4. The Totalitarian Countries

A non-Jewish economist in Nazi Germany (1933-1945) was free to publish purely analytical work, and one of our pioneers (von Stackelberg) did. Official party ideology was racial rather than economic. But an economist wishing to keep his job had better join the party—and the best minds were rarely that type.

Soviet party ideology was and is economic. Stalin demanded unconditional adherence under penalty of loss of job or even life (Kondratief). Mathematics, engineering, and accountancy were possible shelters: the mathematician Kantorovich discovered linear programming, used it under Stalin, and won the Nobel Prize in economics for it.

As the Huguenots had done in the seventeenth century, the refugees from twentieth-century totalitarianism enriched and inspired their havens. Eight of our pioneers did: Hayek, Koopmans, Leontief, von Mises, Morgenstern, von Neumann, Schumpeter, and Wald. One could not do so: having helped others to get out while there was still time, Schlesinger did not make it and committed suicide on the morning of the Nazi invasion. Von Stackelberg became a refugee in the only neutral country friendly to a German in 1943, i.e., Spain.

5. Languages and the Language Barrier

The muse of economics spoke many languages. Let us define a pioneer's language as that in which his most important work was first published. That makes Schumpeter, Frisch, Tinbergen, Haavelmo, Debreu, Morishima, and Uzawa English-language pioneers; Wicksell, Cassel, Hayek, von Neumann, and Zeuthen German-language pioneers; and Slutsky an Italian-language pioneer, so our breakdown will be:

English	53
German	15
French	8
Italian	3
Swedish	3
Latin	1
Russian	1
Total	84

Was there a language barrier in economic theory? During his stay in Paris Smith met the physiocrats and must have been impressed by Turgot—but academic etiquette did not demand acknowledgment in those days. Ricardo and Say corresponded and visited. Each apparently wrote and spoke his own language and was understood by the other. Ricardo [1822 (1952: 243)] was favorably surprised by Sismondi and wrote home: "I am a great admirer of his talents, and I was very favorably impressed by his manners—I did not expect from what I had seen of his controversial writings to find him so candid and agreeable. M. Sismondi takes enlarged views..."

Jevons may have been the first Englishman to comment on the language barrier in terms as strong as those used in the preface to his second edition (1879) characterizing English economics as "insular narrowness" and "a fool's paradise." The only hope was "to fling aside, once and for ever, the mazy and preposterous assumptions of the Ricardian school." By contrast, Jevons paid full tribute to Cournot, Dupuit, and Gossen.

To a degree the language barrier was a one-way barrier: the Continentals did read English. Routinely Wicksell wrote his early books in German and corresponded with Böhm-Bawerk in that language, with Marshall in English, and with Walras in French.

6. The Vanishing Language Barrier

In the shrinking world of the late twentieth century economic theory has become international—and monolingual! Continental Europe never quite recovered from the exodus under Hitler, and knowing what is good for them the younger Continentals publish in English. Founded as bilingual and trilingual international journals, respectively, *Econometrica* and *Kyklos* have become virtually monolingual. So have the German *Zeitschrift für die gesamte Staatswissenschaft* and the Austrian *Zeitschrift für Nationalökonomie*. Most consistent is the Scandinavian journal; it knows no language other than English—even in its title.

But economics knew another barrier, more serious than the literary-language barrier and fortunately also vanishing.

7. The Muse of Economics and the Muse of Mathematics

Very early the muse of economics joined hands with the muse of mathematics and inspired one of the members of the Basle lineage of brilliant mathematicians, Daniel Bernoulli (1700-1782) to whom it occurred to apply his uncle Jakob's discovery of the theory of probability to economic behavior. Such theory would be consistent with observed economic behavior only if marginal utility were assumed to be diminishing, and that was what Daniel assumed it to be. Hidden behind a double language barrier of Latin and mathematics, Daniel's assumption and results remained unknown to economists for more than a century.

The muse of economics and the muse of mathematics were to meet again, in other centuries and with increasing frequency. They met in Tellow, Grenoble, Lausanne, New Haven, Lund, interwar Vienna, and Princeton. They met in three large bureaucracies well removed from market prices and hence badly in need of shadow prices: Soviet industrial planning, wartime Allied shipping administration, and the administration of the U.S. Air Force.

How many of our 84 pioneers were mathematical economists?

What is a "mathematical" economist? Let us define him as one who makes operational use of mathematics. He may be a tyro like Jevons or Walras but still qualify. Like Gossen's, Cassel's, or Sraffa's, his operations may be nothing beyond addition, subtraction, multiplication, and division but still qualify. What will not qualify is mere arithmetic like Quesnay's, Ricardo's, or Böhm-Bawerk's; mere diagrams like Clark's, Robinson's, or Chamberlin's; mere shorthand recording of a definition or an equilibrium condition like Lindahl's, Ohlin's, or Harrod's; mere extolling of mathematics like Schumpeter's; or mere training in it like Keynes's. Samuelson (1951: 49) didn't suppose Schumpeter "ever crossed the Atlantic without spoiling the trip by taking along a book on tensor calculus or partial differential equations." At school and college, Keynes distinguished himself in mathematics. But neither of them applied it himself to what Keynes (1936: 298) called "the complexities and interdependencies of the real world."

Such a definition would leave us with 53 mathematical and 31 nonmathematical pioneers among our 84. The mathematical pioneers are about evenly divided between 24 born before 1900 and 29 born after. The nonmathematical pioneers are very far from being evenly divided: 28 were born before 1900, and only 3 (Harrod, Robinson, and Friedman) were born in or after 1900. Mathematics has been gathering momentum, and it is not difficult to see why.

The momentum may be seen as a Darwinian survival of the fittest. Those coming to economics, whether to stay or merely for a brief visit, from mathematics, physics, or engineering simply had a head start and did better economic theory.

First, economists sometimes seem to be pulling rabbits out of hats. But no proof, mathematical or nonmathematical, is possible without invoking premises, so those premises had better be formulated explicitly—which was exactly what mathematics forced its users to do. Mathematical economists, then, were better protected from *non sequiturs* than were nonmathematical ones.

Second, some problems do not even allow a choice between a mathematical and a nonmathematical approach. The only practical way of solving a large-scale problem like a Leontief interindustry equilibrium was the mathematical way.

Third, economics is supposed to help us understand the world around us, but sometimes economists seem less interested in testing hypotheses than in formulating them. For centuries, lack of data was an excuse. But after the Second World War governments made a wealth of numerical data available and removed the excuse. If hypotheses were to be tested, they would have to be given the form of equations. Mathematical economists, then, were better protected from formulating nontestable hypotheses than were nonmathematical ones.

Would verbal logic never do? It would still do in problems so simple that the risk of a *non sequitur* was minimal. But that is not the point. The point is that the mathematical economist could do everything the nonmathematical economist could do. The mathematical-language barrier was always a one-way barrier: Bernoulli was fully literate in Latin, Cournot in French, von Thünen, Wald, and von Neumann in German, Fisher in English, Wicksell and Cassel in Swedish, and bilingual Pareto, for good measure, in Italian and French.

8. *Giants and Midgets*

One man's giant is another's midget. Schumpeter used to tease his monolingual graduate students by telling them that of the four greatest theorists of all time three were French, i.e., Quesnay, Cournot, and Walras. Presumably the fourth was neither Smith nor Ricardo but Marshall. As we know, with Schumpeter's (1954) choice of giants and midgets none of his reviewers agreed. Robbins (1955: 5-6) in particular censured him for placing von Thünen and Cournot above Ricardo and Walras above Marshall. Robbins applied what he called the Austrian loss principle: suppose the theoretical contributions of Ricardo and Cournot, or of Marshall and Walras, to be alternately withdrawn, then which would have been the greater loss? In his answer Robbins referred to "the relative amounts of space given to the work of these two authors," including the relative amounts given by Schumpeter himself. But isn't the very point of a reappraisal that such an inordinate amount of space is given by later writers to the writers reappraised—thus decelerating the progress of science? Such deceleration may be protracted: claiming that his "standards are those of modern economic theory," Blaug (1978: 1 and 7) still devotes 105 pages to "Marshallian Economics" versus 16 to "Walrasian General Equilibrium" and treats von Neumann in connection with neither general equilibrium nor game theory but merely in connection with cardinal utility.

Our standards, too, will be those of modern economic theory, but our giants and midgets will be more like Schumpeter's than like those of Robbins and Blaug. We shall not consider Smith our founding father but shall pay full attention to mercantilist macroeconomics and physiocrat microeconomics. Modifying Schumpeter we would, perhaps, replace the ambiguous Quesnay by the lucid Cantillon and Marshall by another brilliant synthesizer more tuned to general equilibrium, i.e., Wicksell. Behind their one-way language barrier English economists did enjoy a protection enhancing their reputation among themselves and in the United States—but after 1870 no longer justified. We shall not consider Keynes the happy ending of economics but shall pay full attention to the saddle points of general equilibria and game theory emerging in microeconomics around the same time. Accepting the risk of mistaking fads for trends, we shall venture beyond the reach of hindsight and try to include monetarism and the new classical resurgence.

Our arrangement will be this. Sixteen self-contained chapters, divided into five periods, will deal with our particular giants. Five introductions will convey the flavor of each period and restate the contributions of important pioneers not considered in the chapters. Epigones will be ignored but good space given to forerunners like Bernoulli, Galiani, Hume, Turgot, von Thünen, Longfield, Cournot, Dupuit, Gossen, Wicksteed, Cassel, and Ramsey.

II. IDEAS

1. A Core of Economic Ideas

This book is about ideas rather than men, and let us identify the core of economic ideas it is going to include.

Economic theory may be seen in three dimensions. First, its subject matter may be quantity or price. Second, its degree of aggregation may be macro or micro. The first two dimensions give us a simple two-by-two matrix shown in table 1. The third dimension, in which each of the four elements of table 1 may be seen, is the time dimension: a static model determines a stationary equilibrium level of its variables; a dynamic model determines their time path.

Reluctantly we pass up a fourth dimension, the space dimension. We shall have nothing to say about the theory of international trade and refer the reader to Chipman's (1965-1966) mathematical survey of its history.

The four elements of table 1, whether in static or dynamic vision, will

INTRODUCTION, TABLE 1. Two Dimensions of Economic Theory

	MACRO	MICRO
QUANTITY	Unemployment Theory	Allocation Theory
PRICE	Inflation Theory	Theory of Relative Prices

constitute our core of economic ideas. They are written in the order in which they were discovered.

The first element of our matrix is seventeenth-century mercantilist unemployment theory representing the first half of macroeconomics by emphasizing physical output as the equilibrating variable but ignoring price and believing that demand will always create its own supply.

The second element of our matrix is early-eighteenth-century alloca-tion theory representing the first half of microeconomics without entirely crowding out the second half, relative price. In his precise way Bernoulli saw diminishing marginal utility. In his intuitive way Cantillon saw, first, allocation in accordance with "Taste, Humours and Manner of Living" and, second, relative price in accordance with land and labor input coeffi-cients. Indeed Cantillon came closer to a general-equilibrium vision than anyone before Walras.

The third element of our matrix is Hume's mid-eighteenth-century inflation theory representing the second half of macroeconomics by em-phasizing absolute price as the equilibrating variable but crowding out the first half, physical output. Demand management was believed to be re-dundant and even harmful; supply would always create its own demand anyway.

The fourth element of our matrix is late-eighteenth and early-nineteenth-century English classical theory of relative price representing the second half of microeconomics and entirely crowding out the first half, allocation theory. Smith determined relative price by relative full cost of land, labor, and capital. Ricardo and Marx determined relative price by relative labor embodiment alone.

Not until the late nineteenth century did the two halves of microeco-nomics merge fully into a static general equilibrium, and not until the early twentieth century into a dynamic one. The existence of a dynamic general equilibrium was proved in the first third of the twentieth century and the existence of a static one with consumer preferences in it in the first half of the twentieth century. The two halves of macroeconomics came back in refined forms in the twentieth century, unemployment theory in its Keynesian form in the early twentieth century and inflation theory in its monetarist form in the late twentieth century.

Having chosen our core, we must choose our form of exposition.

2. *Mathematization of the History of Economic Thought?*

In discussing the psychological problem raised by the mathematization of economic theory, Samuelson (1954: 380) points to the history of economic thought as a possible refuge for nonmathematical theorists seeking cover. Even that refuge may no longer be safe after his own forays into Ricardo, Marx, Quesnay, and von Thünen! Should we, then, follow Samuelson's example and mathematize even the history of economic thought?

Two extreme cases have clear answers. First, pioneers who themselves used mathematics often did so for the excellent reason that they could not do without it. In that case, who are we to try to restate them in nonmathematical form? Second, at the other extreme, impressionistic writers may have provided valuable insights without saying enough to determine their equilibrating variables. Malthus, Veblen, or Galbraith are examples. In that case, who are we to try to put words, let alone equations, into anybody's mouth?

Should we use mathematics to restate pioneers who did determine their equilibrating variables but did so without the use of mathematics? We should.

The point to make is that mathematics will work, impartially as it were, not only for the few and brilliant giants but also for the rest of us. In the fourth century B.C. Plato [Bury (1926: 387, 389)] observed: "[The study of numbers] wakes up the man who is by nature drowsy and slow of wit, and makes him quick to learn, mindful and sharp-witted, progressing beyond his natural capacity."

Even the best of the nonusers sometimes failed to see what they themselves were doing. Such blindness is well illustrated by the examples of Menger, Wieser, and Böhm-Bawerk who, as Schumpeter (1954: 957n) points out, held their own system to be superior to that of Walras on the grounds that the latter was merely "functional," whereas their own system offered "causal explanations." Menger, Wieser, and Böhm-Bawerk were dealing with static general equilibria. In such equilibria mathematics—even the rudimentary mathematics used by Walras—would have taught them the lesson that a variable is neither the "cause" nor the "effect" of any other. All variables are determined on an equal footing and simultaneously, and all are the effects of the only causes found in a model, i.e., its parameters. Throughout the present volume we shall carefully distinguish variables from parameters, indeed begin each chapter and each of our five introductions with a list of symbols making that distinction.

3. *What's New?*

Some of the results of our mathematical restatements may be new. The mercantilists, Hume, Cantillon, Menger-Wieser, or even Wicksell's cumulative process may never have been restated mathematically before. Where such restatement exists, some of our details may be new, such as our inclusion of fixed capital ("machinery") in a mathematical Ricardo model, our use of present-net-worth maximization in Ricardo, Marx, Böhm-Bawerk, and Friedman models, or our replacement of Böhm-Bawerk's simple by compound interest with instantaneous compounding yielding particularly simple solutions.

We shall let Walras's counting of equations and unknowns stand as he left it but shall try to set out Menger and Wieser as they would have done it themselves had their mathematics matched their economics. We shall restate the von Neumann and the Dorfman-Samuelson-Solow-Arrow-Debreu proofs of the existence of competitive equilibria in algebra much simpler than their own. We shall restate Friedman in the long-run dynamic setting he requires, and deserves, rather than in the short-run static *IS-LM* setting into which he locked himself.

4. *Quotes*

Our mathematical form restating both premises and conclusions of our pioneers will require documentation. Because we are easily accused of putting words—or worse, equations—into their mouths, we shall use direct quotes where needed. Quotes from foreign-language originals will always be rendered in English, based on either published translations or our own.

5. *Chronology*

Away from the mainstream there have always been the independent few spiritually belonging in a different century. That century may be a later one: hindsight requires our inclusion of discoveries far ahead of their time such as those by Bernoulli or Cantillon. Or the century may be an earlier one: the last Ricardian, Sraffa, was with us until 1983. Of some we are not so sure: was Steuart a mercantilist one hundred years late or a Keynesian 170 years early?

Good historiography must proceed chronologically. Wherever our pioneers belonged spiritually we must treat them within the period in which they were condemned to live! Our only violations of strict chronology will occur *within* our five periods: we must complete our introduction to each period before we can proceed with its individual chapters.

Let us go to work!

REFERENCES

M. Blaug, *Economic Theory in Retrospect*, 3rd ed., Cambridge, 1978.

R. G. Bury (ed.), Plato, *Laws*, Book V, Cambridge, Mass., 1926.

J. S. Chipman, "A Survey of the Theory of International Trade: Parts 1-3," *Econometrica*, July 1965, *33*, 477-519, Oct. 1965, *33*, 685-760; and Jan. 1966, *34*, 18-76.

J. M. Keynes, *The General Theory of Employment, Interest, and Money*, London, 1936.

D. Ricardo, Letters, 1821-1823, reproduced in *The Works and Correspondence of David Ricardo*, P. Sraffa and M. H. Dobb (eds.) New York, 1952, volume IX.

L. Robbins, "Schumpeter's History of Economic Analysis," *Quart. J. Econ.*, Feb. 1955, *69*, 1-22.

P. A. Samuelson, "Schumpeter as a Teacher and Economic Theorist," in S. E. Harris (ed.), *Schumpeter, Social Scientist*, Cambridge, Mass., 1951.

———, "Some Psychological Aspects of Mathematics and Economics," *Rev. Econ. Stat.*, Nov. 1954, *36*, 380-382.

———, "The Canonical Classical Model of Political Economy," *J. Econ. Lit.*, Dec. 1978, *16*, 1415-1434.

J. A. Schumpeter, *History of Economic Analysis*, New York, 1954.

PART *I*   1630-1730

Mercantilism

I. THE SETTING

Our period covers the full bloom of the nation state. How did the nation state come into existence?

In the millennium between the fall of the Roman Empire and the Renaissance, coinage had become unreliable or even unavailable. Europe had reverted to a system of almost self-sufficient manors. Sharply reduced in size and significance, cities carried out a minimum of crafts and long-distance commerce. Essentially the medieval economy was a stationary barter economy. What revolutionized it was new technology.

New naval technology and scientific navigation made ocean-going vessels feasible, thus opening new trade routes to merchant-adventurers. At home, new weapons technology made artillery feasible, thus rendering the manor indefensible. Monarchs and merchants now combined against the pillars of the established order, the nobility and the church. How did they split their gains? No longer at the mercy of the nobility, Continental European monarchs became absolute. (On the periphery of Europe, parliamentary control was unquestioned—in Sweden since independence in 1523 and in England after the Glorious Revolution of 1688.) The merchants financed the monarch's wars and in return received military protection of their trade routes—hitherto blocked by toll-collecting local lords, domestic and foreign. Merchants were freed from the ban on interest imposed by the church. In Northern Europe the Reformation completed the weakening of the church.

Ocean-going commerce and the nation state had created the prerequisites for monetization of the economy. In its wake followed growing division of labor, growing productivity, and lower interest rates. Logically enough, monetization became the goal of the commercial and monetary policies of the nation states—well articulated by the economists of the day. Metal money could be provided via an export surplus. Paper money could be provided by the new central banks, the first of which were the Bank of Sweden of 1668 and the Bank of England of 1694.

The expanding nation states were bound to clash. Game theory shows that the solution to a game with more than two players lies in a coalition. Within our period, uneasy power equilibria with constantly shifting coalitions developed among the nine leading powers, i.e., Austria, Brandenburg, England (after 1707 Great Britain), France, Poland, Russia, Saxony, Sweden, and the United Netherlands. In Liddell Hart's words (1954: 91), the tension produced "the interminable series of wars between the close of the Thirty Years' War [1618-1648] and the opening of the War of the Spanish Succession [1701-1713]—in which the armies of Louis XIV faced collectively, or in turn, most of the other armies of Europe.''

Such was the setting in which seventeenth-century economists wrote. The absolute monarch wanted to know how to finance the mercenaries of his wars, the splendor of his court, the sciences and the arts, and his subsidies to new industries. But in addition to such fiscal problems there was the matter of unemployment.

In a neat piece of sector analysis Sir William Petty [1662 (1899: 30)] estimated unemployment as follows. Out of a total labor force of 1,000, on an average of good and bad years only 900 will be employed, i.e., in agriculture 100; in export 200; in luxuries (''the ornaments, pleasure, and magnificence of the whole'') 400; and in the service industries (''Governors, Divines, Lawyers, Physicians, Merchants, and Retailers'') 200. The remaining 100 would be unemployed:

> ...The question is, since there is food enough for this super-numerary 100 also, how should they come by it? whether by begging or by stealing; ... perhaps they may get either by begging or stealing more than will suffice them, which will for ever after indispose them to labour...

As a response to such a setting the first of two macroeconomic schools of thought, still alive, emerged in the mid-seventeenth century, not the least in the hands of the brilliant Petty himself.

II. NOTATION

1. *Variables*

C $\equiv$ physical consumption
I $\equiv$ physical investment
M $\equiv$ supply of money
R $\equiv$ government net receipts
r $\equiv$ rate of interest
X $\equiv$ physical output
Y $\equiv$ money national income
y $\equiv$ money disposable income

2. *Parameters*

c $\equiv$ marginal propensity to consume real disposable income
E $\equiv$ export surplus

G ≡ physical government purchase of goods and services
P ≡ price of goods and services
T ≡ tax rate

III. A MERCANTILIST MODEL

1. *Seventeenth-Century Assumptions*

Seventeenth-century and early twentieth-century unemployment theory alike see physical output as bounded by demand. Supply is no problem. There is always excess capacity; consequently demand will create its own supply. Monetary or fiscal policy may stimulate demand, and the result will be larger physical output and better utilization of resources. In its extreme form the school has ideological overtones: left to itself, capitalism is incapable of utilizing its own resources. Government action is the remedy.

Can we build an unemployment model whose solutions will possess seventeenth-century properties and permit seventeenth-century policy conclusions to be drawn? Let us try.

Consider a one-good economy with firms, households, and government in it. Consider the price of goods and services a parameter. In other words don't worry about inflation. As for fiscal policy, any model of fiscal policy must deal with three magnitudes, i.e., physical government purchase of goods and services, the fiscal deficit, and the tax rate. They cannot, all three of them, be parameters at the same time, or government could decide to buy all it cared for at low tax rates, yet run a fiscal surplus. A choice will have to be made. To fit the seventeenth century, we choose to fix physical government purchase and the tax rate as parameters and let the resulting fiscal deficit be a variable. A fiscal deficit will have to be financed by government borrowing in a capital market. Government itself can create no money: we follow Thomas Mun (1664) in assuming money to be metal of which the country has no mineral deposits of its own. As a result, money may be added to the system only by way of an export surplus.

Mercantilists did not see the rate of interest as determined by lending and borrowing in a capital market, hence could ignore the effect of a fiscal deficit upon the rate of interest. Instead they saw the rate of interest as determined by the money supply, hence could concentrate their attention on the export surplus affecting the rate of interest via its effect upon the money supply.

2.   *The Equations*

Money national income defined as the aggregate earnings arising from current production is identically equal to national product defined as the market value of physical output:

$$Y \equiv PX \tag{1}$$

Disposable income equals money national income *minus* government net receipts:

$$y \equiv Y - R \tag{2}$$

Let consumption be a function of real disposable income:

$$C = cy/P \tag{3}$$

where $0 < c < 1$.

Let government net receipts be in proportion to money national income:

$$R = TY \tag{4}$$

where $0 < T < 1$.

Thomas Mun [1664 (1949: 14)] said:

> I will take that for granted which no man of judgment will deny, that we have no other means to get Treasure but by forraign trade, for Mines wee have none which do afford it, and how this mony is gotten in the managing of our said Trade I have already shewed, that it is done by making our commodities which are exported yearly to over ballance in value the forraign wares which we consume.

Consequently, the change in the money supply equals the export surplus:

$$\frac{dM}{dt} = E \tag{5}$$

or, in Mun's own, more dramatic, words [1664 (1949: 87)]:

> Let the meer Exchanger do his worst; Let Princes oppress, Lawyers extort, Usurers bite, Prodigals wast, and lastly let Merchants carry out what mony they shall have occasion to use in traffique. Yet all these actions can work no other effects in the course of trade than is declared in this discourse. For so much Treasure only will be brought in or carried out of a Commonwealth, as the Forraign Trade doth over or under

ballance in value. And this must come to pass by a Necessity beyond all resistance.

As it was to Petty, let the rate of interest be determined by the money supply:

$$r = r(M) \tag{6}$$

where $dr/dM < 0$.

Let investment be a function of the rate of interest:

$$I = I(r) \tag{7}$$

where $dI/dr < 0$.

Goods-market equilibrium requires the supply of goods to equal the demand for them:

$$X = C + E + G + I \tag{8}$$

IV. SOLUTIONS AND THEIR SENSITIVITIES

1. *Solution for Physical Output*

For the time being ignore (5), (6), and (7) and solve for physical output X: insert (1) through (4) into (8) and find

$$X = \frac{E + G + I}{1 - c(1 - T)} \tag{9}$$

2. *Trade Policy: Encouraging Export and Discouraging Import*

Ignoring money, interest, and investment, differentiate our solution (9) with respect to the export surplus E and find

$$\frac{\partial X}{\partial E} = \frac{1}{1 - c(1 - T)} \tag{10}$$

Since $0 < c < 1$ and $0 < T < 1$, the export-surplus multiplier (10) is positive and greater than one. Subsidizing the exporters, prohibiting import, and fighting the smugglers, then, did make sense to the mercantilists. Down through three centuries comes Mun's glorification of the noble profession of the merchant [1664 (1949: 88)]:

> Behold then the true form and worth of forraign Trade, which is, *The great Revenue of the King, The honour of the Kingdom, The Noble profession of the Merchant, The School of our Arts, The supply of our wants, The employment of our poor, The*

improvement of our Lands, The Nurcery of our Mariners, The walls of the Kingdoms, The means of our Treasure, The Sinnews of our wars, The terror of our Enemies. For all which great and weighty reasons, do so many well governed States highly countenance the profession, and carefully cherish the action, not only with Policy to encrease it, but also with power to protect it from all forraign injuries.

3.   *Fiscal Policy: Public Works*

Still ignoring money, interest, and investment, differentiate our solution (9) with respect to physical government purchase G and find

$$\frac{\partial X}{\partial G} = \frac{1}{1 - c(1 - T)} \tag{11}$$

The government-purchase multiplier (11), then, is the same as the export-surplus multiplier (10), hence is positive and greater than one. Petty [1662 (1899: 29-31)] recommended public works satisfying two conditions. The first condition was high labor intensity. The works should be "works of much labour, and little art." The second condition was low import requirement: "let it be without expence of Foreign Commodities." With these two conditions satisfied, public works should preferably be productive, e.g.,

> ...making all High-wayes so broad, firm, and eaven, as whereby the charge and tedium of travelling and Carriages may be greatly lessened. The cutting and scowring of Rivers into Navigable; the planting of usefull Trees for timber, delight, and fruit in convenient places.

But to Petty, productivity was not the prime consideration. He realized that even useless public works have the multiplier (11):

> ...'tis no matter if it be employed to build a useless Pyramid upon *Salisbury Plain*, bring the Stones at *Stonehenge* to *Tower-Hill*, or the like; for at worst this would keep their mindes to discipline and obedience, and their bodies to a patience of more profitable labours when need shall require it.

So much for fiscal policy.

4.   *Monetary Policy: A Low Rate of Interest*

Public works were one way of employing the unemployed. Exports were another. But besides the direct effect of export upon output described by (10), the mercantilists saw an indirect effect via money, the rate of interest, and investment. To see it, differentiate (7) with respect to time and find

$$\frac{dI}{dt} = \frac{dI}{dr}\frac{dr}{dt} \tag{12}$$

Then differentiate (6) with respect to time and find

$$\frac{dr}{dt} = \frac{dr}{dM}\frac{dM}{dt} \tag{13}$$

Finally insert (5) into (13) and the latter into (12):

$$\frac{dI}{dt} = \frac{dI}{dr}\frac{dr}{dM}E \tag{14}$$

which has the same sign as E, because dI/dr and dr/dM were assumed to be negative.

Our correct formulation (5) of the connection between money supply and export surplus brought a derivative with respect to time into our model, hence made it inherently dynamic. The dynamics show in our result (14). A given export surplus E will set investment *in motion* by generating, via its effect upon money supply and rate of interest, a positive derivative of investment with respect to time.

Petty thought that ample money had reduced the rate of interest to six percent. Now in England money was metal, but Andrew Yarranton [1677 (1854: 38)] called attention to the practice of Dutch banks of extending credit with mortgages as collateral: "Observe all you that read this, and tell to your children this strange thing, that *paper in Holland is equal with moneys in England* ..." and believed that following the Dutch example would lower the rate of interest from six to four percent.

5.   *Were They Keynesians?*

Much of all this sounds like early-twentieth-century economics—we shall meet our very derivative (11) three hundred years later, in chapter 10 on Hansen. Indeed, Keynes (1936: 336) did not think of himself as the first Keynesian and found mercantilist reasoning compatible with his own:

> ...At a time when the authorities had no direct control over the domestic rate of interest...the effect of a favourable balance of trade on the influx of the precious metals was their only *indirect* means of reducing the domestic rate of interest and so increasing the inducement to home investment.

Was Keynes, the theorist, putting words into the mouths of the mercantilists? Heckscher (1955: 353), the historian, thought so. The real reason, he said, for the excess of currency so characteristic of the history of Western civilization was simply that governments needed money to finance wars and other state expenditures. In Heckscher's judgment, the effects on general economic life may have materialized but were generally not intended. To Keynes the mercantilists had a Keynesian model; to Heckscher they were pragmatists.

REFERENCES

E. F. Heckscher, *Mercantilism*, London, 1955.

J. M. Keynes, *The General Theory of Employment, Interest, and Money*, London, 1936.

B. H. Liddell Hart, *Strategy*, New York, 1954.

T. Mun, *England's Treasure by Forraign Trade*, London, 1664; republished Oxford, 1949.

W. Petty, *A Treatise of Taxes and Contributions*, London, 1662, reprinted in C. H. Hull (ed.), *The Economic Writings of Sir William Petty*, Cambridge, 1899.

A. Yarranton, *England's Improvement by Sea and Land. To Outdo the Dutch without Fighting. To Pay Debts without Money. To Set at Work all the Poor of England with the Growth of Our Own lands* ..., London, 1677; quoted from P. E. Dove, *Account of Andrew Yarranton*, Edinburgh, 1854.

PART *II* 1730-1770

I. THE SETTING

On the European Continent our period is the age of enlightened absolutism. Here, fate produced three roughly simultaneous wise and able rulers: Catherine the Great 1762-1796, Frederick the Great 1740-1786, and Maria Theresa 1740-1780. Their courts promoted sciences and the arts, and the nation states were trying to live with one another. Still, there were the War of the Austrian Succession 1740-1748 and the Seven Years' War 1756-1763, inconclusive in Europe but of profound consequence in North America, where it was known as the French and Indian War.

The Western European economies had become monetized. As a result, division of labor and trade had, perhaps, been carried as far as pre-industrial technology permitted.

II. MICROECONOMICS: BERNOULLI, GALIANI, CANTILLON, QUESNAY, AND TURGOT

1. *The Value Paradox*

Throughout the seventeenth, eighteenth, and three-quarters of the nineteenth century, mainstream microeconomics remained supply-side economics. What kept it from ever considering the demand side was the value paradox. Aristotle had distinguished between value in use and value in exchange. Ever since, everybody had observed that things having the highest value in use often had the lowest value in exchange and vice versa. Everybody had duly concluded that value in use could not explain value in exchange.

The value paradox is easily resolved once the derivative of utility with respect to quantity consumed is taken: water has a low value in exchange because it is abundant. Diamonds have a high value in exchange because they are scarce. For two millennia after Aristotle that derivative remained untaken—for the excellent reason that the calculus had not yet been discovered. But in 1665 Newton discovered it. And in 1684 Leibnitz beat him to print. The stage was set for the meeting of the muses of economics and mathematics.

2. Bernoulli

The derivative of utility was first taken by Daniel Bernoulli,[1] professor at the University of Basle 1733-1777 and—at the time he wrote his "Specimen theoriae novae de mensura sortis" (1738)—visiting professor at the Imperial Academy of Arts and Sciences in St. Petersburg.

Daniel Bernoulli's uncle, Jakob Bernoulli, had discovered the theory of probability in his *Ars conjectandi* (1713), and Daniel Bernoulli wanted to apply that theory to, among other things, business practices. Located where the Rhine becomes navigable, Basle was a trading and insurance center and a good place to observe business practices. Like Cantillon, Ricardo, and Keynes, Bernoulli was that rare combination of a keen observer and a born theorist.

3. Bernoulli's Differential Equation

The observer Bernoulli was struck by the fact that business decisions made under uncertainty were based on something more than the mathematical expectation of the outcome. Variance seemed to matter. Large variances were eschewed and if possible traded for smaller ones. Such trade was indeed possible: insurance companies did nothing else. But why should businessmen wish to insure themselves, i.e., wish to trade large variances for smaller ones? Almost routinely Bernoulli formed the hypothesis needed and serving his purpose. Using the notation

$a \equiv$ initial possession
$b \equiv$ a constant
$x \equiv$ possession
$y \equiv$ advantage,

Bernoulli [1738 (1896: 34)] expressed his hypothesis mathematically as

$$dy = \frac{bdx}{x} \tag{1}$$

and [1738 (1896: 27)] verbally as:

> It seems highly likely that any arbitrarily small gain will produce an advantage which will be in inverse proportion to the already existing possession. Clarifying this hypothesis I should explain

[1]In 1728 the Swiss mathematician Gabriel Cramer (1704-1752) wrote a letter to Daniel Bernoulli's uncle Nicolaus Bernoulli in which a marginal-utility function similar to Daniel Bernoulli's was used—and for a similar primary purpose, i.e., to clear up the St. Petersburg paradox. Nicolaus Bernoulli showed the letter to his nephew, to whom [1738 (1896: 56)] "the similarity appears most remarkable."

what I mean by "possession," i.e., anything which offers us nourishment, clothing, convenience, indeed even luxury and the satisfaction of any desire whatever (my translation).

4. *Bernoulli's Primitive*

Next Bernoulli wished to recover the primitive giving rise to the differential (1). Try the function

$$y = b\log_e x + K \tag{2}$$

where K is the constant of integration.

In 1748, ten years later, Euler defined his number e, and let us take advantage of it to show that the differential of (2) is indeed (1). A property of the exponential function $f(x) = e^v$ is that

$$\frac{d(e^v)}{dx} = e^v \frac{dv}{dx} \tag{3}$$

Define the natural logarithm of x:

If $x = e^v$ then $\log_e x \equiv v$ \hfill (4), (5)

Insert (4) and (5) into (3) and find

$$\frac{d\log_e x}{dx} = \frac{1}{x} \tag{6}$$

Using (6), find the derivative of (2) with respect to x to be $dy/dx = b/x$. Consequently, the differential of (2) is indeed (1). But (2) is an indefinite integral, and we must find its constant of integration, K.

Let a person's initial possession be α. Consider an event, say a shipwreck, a fire, a profit, a payment of an insurance premium, affecting the person's possession x. Our result (2) will measure his advantage from his gain $x - \alpha$. But if (2) is to hold universally, it must also hold in the case of no such event, i.e., when $x = \alpha$ and $y = 0$. Insert those values into (2) and find it collapsing into $0 = b\log_e \alpha + K$, from which we may find our constant of integration

$$K = -b\log_e \alpha \tag{7}$$

Insert (7) into (2) and write the latter as

$$y = b(\log_e x - \log_e \alpha) = b\log_e(x/\alpha) \tag{8}$$

Here is Bernoulli's primitive, and we show it in figure II-1. What is its economic meaning? Consider any event, or no event, affecting the person's possession x. The primitive (8) will measure his advantage from his gain $x - \alpha$, where α is his initial possession. The curve intersects the hori-

FIGURE II-1.
Advantage as a
Function of Possession
Shown by Bernoulli
[1738 (1896: 32)]

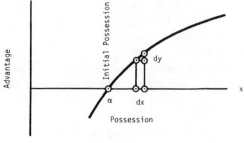

zontal axis in the point α, where there is no event, no gain, and no advantage. That the curve has the vertical axis for an asymptote is seen as follows. Let a ruinous event make the person's possession x vanish. At a given initial possession α a vanishing x means a vanishing $x/α$ and a $\log_e(x/α)$ falling beyond bounds. Consequently

$$\lim_{x \to 0} y = -\infty \tag{9}$$

In other words, a person moving leftwards along his curve is plunging into the abyss as the curve approaches the vertical axis.

5. *Bernoulli's Applications*

Probability theory as developed by Jakob Bernoulli considered games of chance consisting of events with their attached probabilities. To each of his uncle's events, Daniel Bernoulli could now apply his function (8), find the advantage of the event, find the advantage of the game as a whole, and decide if, to the person in question, the game was worth playing. An example is the following [1738 (1896: 42-44)]:

> The habits of merchants insuring their cargoes at sea deserve
> special consideration. The following example will clarify the
> matter. In Amsterdam Cajus of Petersburg has purchased
> commodities which he could sell at 10,000 Rubles if they were
> available in Petersburg. He has them transported by sea but is
> unsure whether or not he should insure them. He knows that of
> one hundred ships sailing in this season from Amsterdam to
> Petersburg five will perish. But he can find nobody willing to
> insure him at less than 800 Rubles, which seems to him a very high
> price. The problem is: Apart from the said merchandise, how large

must Cajus's possessions be in order to make him prudently dispense with insurance? (my translation).

Bernoulli's answer was that if Cajus already possessed 5,043 rubles he would need no insurance. What must the insurance company possess in order to make it worth 800 rubles to insure Cajus's cargo? The answer was 14,243 rubles.

Other examples examined by Bernoulli were spreading of risk by spreading a cargo on several ships and by portfolio diversification. The correspondence between theory and observed practice delighted him [1738 (1896: 45-46)]: "And precisely because all these results correspond so well with those of natural experience, it would not be right to neglect them for lack of proof—neglect them as resting on dubious hypotheses" (my translation).

6.   *A Single Slip*

Bernoulli slipped only once. In his section 6 [1738 (1896: 29-31)] he did make an interpersonal utility comparison. Comparing a person owning 100,000 ducats with a person owning 50,000 ducats, Bernoulli found it "perfectly clear" that the significance to the first person of one ducat would equal the significance to the second person of half a ducat. But the slip was harmless. In none of his applications did Bernoulli ever make interpersonal utility comparisons.

7.   *Galiani*

For the following one and one-third centuries the only economist who ever mentioned Bernoulli was Ferdinando Galiani [1751 (1924: 301-302)]. Galiani wanted to explain the value of money and explained it in terms of the value of gold and silver qua commodities. A born theorist, he was carried from the subject of value of money to the subject of value. Value, he said, was determined by two things, utility and scarcity. Galiani [1751 (1924: 284)] defined utility succinctly: "By utility I mean a thing's capacity to bring happiness" and [1751 (1924: 289)] defined scarcity equally succinctly: "By scarcity I mean the proportion between the quantity of a thing and the use made of it." With this, he had cleared up the value paradox and said [1751 (1924: 287)]:

A natural calf is nobler than a golden calf, but how much less its value is. I answer, that if a natural calf were as rare as one of gold, its price would be as much more than that of the golden calf as the utility and need of the one exceeds that of the other.

From Galiani's "scarcity" it would be a short step to take the derivative of utility with respect to quantity consumed. Indeed the step was so short that when Léon Walras took that derivative he *called* it "rareté"—a term he inherited from his father Auguste Walras.

We must now turn to the Physiocrats.

8. *A Glimpse of General Equilibrium*

A microeconomic consequence of the new division of labor was resource allocation via a market mechanism. Cantillon's *Essai*, written around 1730 but published posthumously in 1755, gave us the first glimpse of a general economic equilibrium.

Cantillon determined the relative prices of factors and goods, the quantities absorbed of factors and supplied of goods, the distribution of income, and the total sustainable employment in an economy, and we shall devote our chapter 1 to his determination. Cantillon saw output as bounded by the available physical stock of land. The employment the available physical stock of land could support depended on the land absorption by the necessities needed to feed labor as well as on the land absorption by the luxuries demanded by landlords. Behind demand Cantillon found preferences ("Taste, Humours and Manner of Living")—a subject that was to lie dormant for more than another century. He saw competitive price as determined by cost of production, saw labor as reproducible, and reduced labor to the land from which it was reproduced. In this sense his price theory was a land theory of value.

9. *A Numerical Intersectoral Equilibrium: Quesnay*

The lucid Cantillon is less famous than the ambiguous Quesnay. Beyond doubt, Quesnay [1759 (1972)] established an intersectoral equilibrium of a three-sector economy of farmers, landlords, and artisans, and we shall devote our chapter 2 to it. We shall read its ambiguities and omissions in a way permitting Quesnay's equilibrium, indeed his very numbers, to emerge.

10. *Diminishing Marginal Productivity: Turgot*

Turgot was the discoverer of all but the name of diminishing marginal productivity. The discovery is not found in his *Réflexions* (1769-1770) but in his earlier [1767 (1844: 418-433), (1977: 109-122)] comments on an essay by Saint-Péravy that won a competition sponsored by the *Société royale d'agriculture de Limoges*. Following Quesnay, Saint-Péravy had assumed the ratio between inputs advanced by capital and output of produce to be a fixed one. Turgot objected that "it can never be assumed that double the advances will yield double the product" and set out [1767 (1844: 420-422), (1977: 112-113)] his own analysis, pathbreaking in two respects.

First, Turgot's analysis was cast in the form of marginal, not average, product: "As the advances are increased gradually . . . each increase would be less and less productive. . . . The product will still increase, but less so, and continuously less and less until an addition to the advances would add nothing further to the produce, because the fertility of the soil is exhausted and art cannot increase the product any further."

Second, Turgot's analysis observed not only that marginal productivity is diminishing but also how far to diminish it: "Although further increments in advances do not yield as much as the preceding increments, if they yield enough to increase the *net product* of the soil, there is an advantage in making them, and it will still be a good investment." Turgot, in other words, saw an optimum in which a marginal advance would just earn its keep.

III. MACROECONOMICS: HUME, TURGOT, AND STEUART

1. *Eighteenth-Century Assumptions: Hume and Turgot*

By the eighteenth century the Western European economies had become monetized, and division of labor and trade had, perhaps, been carried as far as preindustrial technology permitted. A macroeconomic consequence was that further additions to the money supply would generate inflation rather than physical expansion. The time for the second of the two major macroeconomic schools of thought—the theory of inflation—had come. In its most lucid form the new theory emerged in the hands of Hume.

Eighteenth-century and late-twentieth-century inflation theory alike see physical output as bounded by supply. Demand is no problem: supply will create its own demand. There is never excess capacity. Monetary or fiscal policy may stimulate demand but to no use: monetary stimuli will merely generate inflation, fiscal stimuli merely crowding-out. In its extreme form the school has ideological overtones: left to itself, capitalism is fully capable of utilizing its own resources. Government action, however well meant, is the problem.

As a counterpart to our unemployment model in part I can we now build an inflation model whose solution will possess eighteenth-century properties and permit eighteenth-century policy conclusions to be drawn? We shall try.

Consider a one-good economy whose physical output is considered a parameter. In other words, don't worry about unemployment. For the sake of comparability with our mercantilist model let us use the same notation as in part I.

2. The Equations

If money is metal and if the country has no mines of that metal, then exactly as in the mercantilist model, the change in the money supply equals the export surplus:

$$\frac{dM}{dt} = E \tag{10}$$

To Petty the money supply determined the rate of interest, but to Hume the money supply determined the price level or, in his own words [1752 (1875: 333)]:

> Suppose four-fifths of all the money in GREAT BRITAIN to be annihilated in one night, and the nation reduced to the same condition, with regard to specie, as in the reigns of the HARRYS and EDWARDS, what would be the consequence? Must not the price of all labour and commodities sink in proportion, and everything be sold as cheap as they were in those ages?

> Again, suppose, that all the money of GREAT BRITAIN were multiplied fivefold in a night, must not the contrary effect follow? Must not all labour and commodities rise?

So let us write Hume's simple proportionality as

$$P = kM \tag{11}$$

where $k > 0$.

3. Inflation and the Balance of Trade

Since there is no excess capacity, output is capacity output, a parameter, and there is no point in trying to solve for it. What we must solve for to simulate Hume is inflation, and that is easy. Differentiate (11) with respect to time, insert (10), and find

$$\frac{dP}{dt} = k \frac{dM}{dt} = kE \tag{12}$$

which has the same sign as E, because $k > 0$.

Like our mercantilist model, our Hume model has in it the correct formulation (10) of the connection between money supply and export surplus. That brings a derivative with respect to time into the model and makes it inherently dynamic. The dynamics show in our result (12). A given export surplus E will set price in motion, and the motion will have the same sign as E. An import surplus will reduce price, an export surplus will raise price. For how long?

Let's examine things in Hume's order. First the case of "four fifths of all the money in Great Britain to be annihilated in one night..." A falling price will make exports more competitive and imports less competitive, hence will keep working towards the elimination of an import surplus as long as there is one—or in Hume's own words [1752 (1875: 333)]:

> Must not the price of all labour and commodities sink in proportion, and everything be sold as cheap as they were in those ages? What nation could then dispute with us in any foreign market, or pretend to navigate or to sell manufactures at the same price, which to us would afford sufficient profit? In how little time, therefore, must this bring back the money which we had lost, and raise us to the level of all the neighbouring nations? Where, after we have arrived, we immediately lose the advantage of the cheapness of labour and commodities; and the farther flowing in of money is stopped by our fulness and repletion.

According to our (12) such a downward price motion will not stop, i.e., dP/dt will not become zero, until the import surplus has disappeared and the trade balance become zero.

Next Hume's case of "all the money of Great Britain multiplied five-fold in a night..." A rising price will make exports less competitive and imports more competitive, hence will keep working towards the elimination of an export surplus as long as there is one—or in Hume's own words [1752 (1875: 333)]:

> Must not all labour and commodities rise to such an exorbitant height, that no neighbouring nations could afford to buy from us; while their commodities, on the other hand, became comparatively so cheap, that, in spite of all the laws which could be formed, they would be run in upon us, and our money flow out; till we fall to a level with foreigners, and lose that great superiority of riches, which had laid us under such disadvantages?

According to our (12) such an upward price motion will not stop, i.e., dP/dt will not become zero, until the export surplus has disappeared and the trade balance become zero.

Hume had found perhaps the first self-regulating economic equilibrium. Subsequent centuries were to find more of them and to be as fond of them as Hume was [1752 (1875: 333)] when he compared his economic equilibrium to a hydraulic one:

> Now, it is evident, that the same causes, which would correct these exorbitant inequalities, were they to happen miraculously, must prevent their happening in the common course of nature, and must for ever, in all neighbouring nations, preserve money nearly proportionable to the art and industry of each nation. All water, wherever it communicates, remains always at a level. Ask naturalists the reason; they tell you, that, were it to be raised in any one place, the superior gravity of that part not being balanced, must depress it, till it meet a counterpoise; and that the same cause, which redresses the inequality when it happens, must for ever prevent it, without some violent external operation.

In conclusion: Mun's, Petty's, or Yarranton's prescriptions would not work. Neither a positive balance of trade bringing in more precious metals nor an expansion of mortgage-backed bank credit could have any effect other than inflation.

4.   *The Rate of Interest: Hume*

To Petty and Yarranton the rate of interest was determined by the supply of and the demand for money, and so it was to Keynes. Hume disagreed. To him the rate of interest had nothing to do with the abundance or scarcity of gold and silver but was determined by the supply of funds by lenders and the demand for them by borrowers. Behind supply and demand Hume found what, in another century, Fisher (1930: title page) was to call, respectively, "impatience to spend income and opportunity to invest it." Hume [1752 (1875: 322)] put it as follows:

> High interest arises from *three* circumstances: A great demand for borrowing; little riches to supply that demand; and great profits arising from commerce: And these circumstances are a clear proof of the small advance of commerce and industry, not of the scarcity of gold and silver. Low interest, on the other hand, proceeds from the three opposite circumstances: A small demand for borrowing; great riches to supply that demand; and small profits arising from commerce: And these circumstances are all connected together, and proceed from the encrease of industry and commerce, not of gold and silver.

In other words, Hume saw a secular fall in the rate of interest as the result of "the encrease of industry and commerce, not of gold and silver." Hume [1752 (1875: 321-322)] illuminated his "real" theory of interest by his example of residential construction:

> If a man borrow money to build a house, he then carries home a greater load [of money]; because the stone, timber, lead, glass, &c. with the labour of the masons and carpenters, are represented by a greater quantity of gold and silver ... And if you lent me so much labour and so many commodities; by receiving five *per cent.* you always receive proportional labour and commodities, however represented, whether by yellow or white coin, whether by a pound or an ounce.

5. *The Rate of Interest: Turgot*

Like Hume, Turgot [1769-1770 (1922: 74)] saw the rate of interest as the equilibrating variable in a market in which borrowers and lenders met: "... When there are many borrowers who need money, the interest of money becomes higher; when there are many holders of money who offer to lend it, interest falls."

Like Hume, Turgot [1769-1770 (1922: 75-76)] did not expect a doubling of the money supply to reduce the rate of interest. Unlike Hume, Turgot even expected the doubling to *raise* it:

> ... it may on the contrary happen that the very cause which increases the money in the market, and which increases the prices of other commodities by lowering the price of money, is precisely that which increases the hire of money or the rate of interest.

Here Turgot anticipates Fisher's (1896) distinction between a nominal and a real rate of interest differing by the rate of inflation.

6. *Seventeenth-Century Assumptions: Steuart, Latecomer or Forerunner?*

Immediately before Adam Smith, seventeenth-century assumptions came to life once again: physical output is bounded by demand. Supply is no problem. There is always excess capacity; consequently demand will create its own supply. Monetary or fiscal policy may stimulate demand, and the result will be larger physical output and better utilization of resources. Taxes, said Sir James Steuart [1767 (1796: 271-272)], were expansionary, because they reduced taxpayer's demand by less than they increased government demand:

> ... In proportion ... as taxes draw money into circulation, which otherwise would not have entered into it at that time, they

encourage industry; not by taking the money from individuals, but by throwing it into the hands of the state, which spends it . . .

It is no objection to this representation of the matter, that the persons from whom the money is taken, would have spent it as well as the state. The answer is, that it might be so, or not: whereas when the state gets it, it will be spent undoubtedly.

Once again the similarity between seventeenth and early twentieth-century assumptions shows. With Steuart's distinction between the propensities to consume of taxpayers and government, the balanced-budget multiplier was ready for formalization. But the times became unfavorable to interventionist views, and the formalization had to wait for 174 years before it was accomplished by Gelting (1941) and Haavelmo (1945) within a straight Keynesian framework of a single equilibrating variable, i.e., physical output.

With his seventeenth and twentieth-century assumptions, then, eighteenth-century Steuart is at the same time a latecomer and a forerunner.

REFERENCES

D. Bernoulli, "Specimen theoriae novae de mensura sortis," *Commentarii academiae scientiarum imperialis Petropolitanae*, 1738, V, St. Petersburg, 175-192; translated as *Versuch einer neuen Theorie der Wertbestimmung von Glücksfällen* (An Attempt at a New Theory Determining the Worth of Games of Chance) by A. Pringsheim, Leipzig, 1896; translated from Latin into English as "Exposition of a New Theory on the Measurement of Risk" by L. Sommer, *Econometrica*, Jan. 1954, *22*, 23-36 and reprinted in W. J. Baumol and S. M. Goldfeld (eds.), *Precursors in Mathematical Economics: An Anthology*, London, 1968, 15-26.

R. Cantillon, *Essai sur la nature du commerce en général*, written around 1730, published 1755 referring to a fictitious publisher: "A Londres, Chez F. Gyles, dans Holborn"; reprinted, Boston, 1892; edited and translated into English by Henry Higgs, C.B., London, 1931; translated into German with an introduction by F. A. Hayek, Jena, 1931; republished in French, Paris, 1952.

I. Fisher, "Appreciation and Interest," *Publications of the American Economic Association*, Aug. 1896, *11*, 331-442.

————, *The Theory of Interest*, New York, 1930.

F. Galiani, *Della moneta*, Naples 1751, translated as "Money," in A. E. Monroe (ed.), *Early Economic Thought—Selections from Economic Literature prior to Adam Smith*, Cambridge, Mass., 1924, 279-307.

J. Gelting, "Nogle bemaerkninger om finansieringen af offentlig virksomhed," *Nationaløkonomisk Tidsskrift*, 1941, *79*, 293-299.

T. Haavelmo, "Multiplier Effects of a Balanced Budget," *Econometrica*, Oct. 1945, *13*, 311-318.

D. Hume, "Of Interest" and "Of the Balance of Trade," *Political Discourses*, Edinburgh, 1752, reprinted in *Essays—Moral Political, and Literary*, I, London, 1875.

F. Quesnay, *Tableau Economique*, third edition, Versailles, 1759, edited, with new material, translations and notes by M. Kuczynski and R. L. Meek, London and New York, 1972.

J. Steuart, *An Inquiry into the Principles of Political Economy*, London, 1767, 1796.

A. R. J. Turgot, "Observations sur le Mémoire de M. de Saint-Péravy," Limoges, 1767, in E. Daire (ed.), *Oeuvres de Turgot*, Paris, 1844, 418-433, translated as "Observations on a Paper by Saint-Péravy on the Subject of Indirect Taxation," in P. D. Groenewegen, *The Economics of A. R. J. Turgot*, The Hague, 1977, 109-122.

———, "Réflexions sur la formation et la distribution des richesses," *Ephémérides du citoyen*, Nov. 1769-Jan. 1770, reprinted in E. Daire (ed.), *Oeuvres de Turgot*, Paris, 1844, 1-71, translated as *Reflections on the Formation and the Distribution of Riches*, New York, 1922. Translated again as "Reflections on the Formation and Distribution of Wealth," in P. D. Groenewegen, *The Economics of A. R. J. Turgot*, The Hague, 1977, 43-95.

CHAPTER *1* Sustainable Population and the Land Theory of Value

CANTILLON (1697-1734)

... the time of Cantillon and Quesnay, when scientific model-building began, ...

Schumpeter (1954: 632)

I. INTRODUCTION

1. *Cantillon's Problem*

Cantillon wanted to determine the relative prices of factors and goods, the quantities absorbed of factors and supplied of goods, the distribution of income, and the total sustainable employment in an economy. Thus he came closer to formulating a general-equilibrium vision than anyone else before Walras. His model had choice in it. There was choice among crops, and input-output coefficients differed among crops. Ultimately labor could be reproduced by feeding it alternative menus, and there was choice among such menus. The choice among crops and menus forced Cantillon to consider preferences—a topic that was to lie dormant for more than another century.

2. *Cantillon's Method*

Cantillon used nothing but beautiful, lucid French bristling with precise and specific quantitative estimates. He had a clear grasp of sectoral interdependence in an economy, and abstractions came easily to him. Indeed he had a mathematical mind without mathematical training and could specify his system so well that its properties are beyond doubt.

3. *Our Own Restatement*

Because it was so lucid and well-specified, Cantillon's system lends itself well to algebraic restatement, as we shall now demonstrate. We confine ourselves to his core of a long-run, static, general economic equilibrium and ignore parts of his book having much to say about capital accumulation, growth, saving, profits, and money.

Let the notation of our restatement be as follows.

4.   *Variables*

L ≡ number of men employed in the economy
L_i ≡ number of men employed to produce ith good
N_i ≡ number of acres of land used to produce ith good
n ≡ money rent rate per acre-year
P_i ≡ price of ith good
w ≡ money wage rate per man-year
X_i ≡ physical output of ith good per year

5.   *Parameters*

a_i ≡ man-years absorbed in producing one physical unit of ith good
b_i ≡ acre-years directly absorbed in producing one physical unit of ith good
c_1 ≡ necessities absorbed in producing one man-year
N ≡ available number of acres of land in the economy

II.   A CANTILLON MODEL

Let a Cantillon economy be producing two consumers' goods, i.e., a necessity consumed only by labor and a luxury consumed only by landlords. There are no capital goods. Both consumers' goods are produced solely from labor and land in processes having fixed input-output coefficients:

$$L_i = a_i X_i \tag{1}$$

$$N_i = b_i X_i \tag{2}$$

where subscripts $i = 1, 2$ refer to the necessity and the luxury, respectively. Labor is employed, and land is used in the production of both goods, so $a_i > 0$ and $b_i > 0$. Consequently

$$L \equiv L_1 + L_2 \tag{3}$$

$$N = N_1 + N_2 \tag{4}$$

where available land N is a positive parameter.

But employment L is a variable to be determined. Like Malthus and von Neumann, Cantillon saw labor as reproducible—produced from necessities in a process having an input-output coefficient fixed, not by biology alone but also by the "Manner of Living" of labor:

$$X_1 = c_1 L \tag{5}$$

A good econometrician, Cantillon [1755 (1931: 71)] had made

... estimates of the amount of Land required for the support of a Man according to the different assumptions of his Manner of Living. It will be seen that a Man who lives on Bread, Garlic and Roots, wears only hempen garments, coarse Linen, Wooden Shoes, and drinks only water, like many Peasants in the South of France, can live on the produce of an Acre and a half of Land of medium goodness, yielding a sixfold harvest and resting once in 3 years. On the other hand a grown-up Man who wears leather Shoes, Stockings, Woollen Cloth, who lives in a House and has a change of Linen, a Bed, Chairs, Table, and other necessaries, drinks moderately of Beer or Wine, eats every day Meat, Butter, Cheese, Bread, Vegetables, etc. sufficiently and yet moderately needs for all that the produce of 4 to 5 acres of land of medium quality.

But a man cannot live on nothing, so $c_1 > 0$.

Now in long-run equilibrium let all processes break even. The two goods-producing processes will break even after freedom of entry and exit has done its work and washed away all profits over and above labor cost at the standard money wage rate w and land cost at the standard money rent rate n. As a result, in each industry revenue equals cost:

$$P_i X_i = L_i w + N_i n \tag{6}$$

The labor-producing process will break even, because [1755 (1931: 83)]"Men multiply like Mice in a barn if they have unlimited Means of Subsistence." Here, too, revenue equals cost or, in more familiar terms, the money wage bill equals the money value of labor's necessary consumption:

$$Lw = P_1 X_1 \tag{7}$$

Sum (6) over $i = 1, 2$, insert (3) and (4), subtract (7), and find that the money rent bill is spent on the second good:

$$Nn = P_2 X_2 \tag{8}$$

We may now solve our system.

III. LONG-RUN EQUILIBRIUM SOLUTIONS

1. *Real Factor Prices*

Since wages are spent on the first good only, the real wage rate is the money wage rate divided by the price of that good. Divide (7) by employment L, use (5), rearrange, and find the solution for the real wage rate

$$w/P_1 = c_1 \tag{9}$$

Since rent is spent on the second good only, the real rent rate is the money rent rate divided by the price of that good. To find it, first divide (6) by output X_i, use (1) and (2), and write the price of the ith good as

$$P_i = a_i w + b_i n \qquad (10)$$

or, in Cantillon's own words [1755 (1931: 41)]: "... the intrinsic value of any thing may be measured by the quantity of Land used in its production and the quantity of Labour which enters into it, ..."

Then write P_i for $i = 1$, insert (9), and express the price of the first good in terms of the money rent rate:

$$P_1 = b_1 n/(1 - a_1 c_1) \qquad (11)$$

Finally write P_i for $i = 2$, insert (9) and (11), and find the solution for the real rent rate

$$n/P_2 = (1 - a_1 c_1)/[b_2 + (a_2/b_2 - a_1/b_1)b_1 b_2 c_1] \qquad (12)$$

2.   *Relative Price of Necessities and Luxuries*

To see how Cantillon used his "Par between Land and Labour" to arrive at his land theory of value we form the reciprocal of (12), divide it into (11), let things cancel, and write the relative price of necessities and luxuries

$$\frac{P_1}{P_2} = \frac{b_1}{b_2 + (a_2/b_2 - a_1/b_1)b_1 b_2 c_1} \qquad (13)$$

When we expressed (10) in Cantillon's own words, the first component of the "intrinsic value of any thing" was "the quantity of Land used in its production"—our b_i. The second component was "the quantity of Labour which enters into it"—our a_i. But Cantillon reduces his second component to land [1755 (1931: 41)]: "... in other words by the quantity of Land of which the produce is allotted to those who have worked upon it."

In other words, instead of determining the intrinsic value by land and labor, Cantillon now determines it by land used directly in cultivation *plus* land used indirectly to feed the labor involved in the cultivation. That is precisely what our (13) does algebraically, and our interpretation is straightforward as follows.

Since a_i is man-years absorbed in producing one physical unit of the ith good and b_i is acre-years directly absorbed in producing that physical unit, the ratio a_i/b_i is simply men per acre in producing the ith good. Call it the "labor intensity" of the ith good and distinguish three cases.

First, if the labor intensities of necessities and luxuries are the same, i.e.,

$$a_1/b_1 = a_2/b_2 \tag{14}$$

then according to (13) $P_1/P_2 = b_1/b_2$: since necessities absorb the same labor per acre as do luxuries, they also absorb the same indirect land (to feed labor) per acre. Consequently, necessities should have a relative price expressed equally well by their relative overall or by their relative direct land absorption.

Second, if necessities have a higher labor intensity than do luxuries, i.e.,

$$a_1/b_1 > a_2/b_2 \tag{15}$$

then according to (13) $P_1/P_2 > b_1/b_2$: since necessities absorb more labor per acre than do luxuries, they also absorb more indirect land (to feed labor) per acre. Consequently, necessities should have a relative price higher than indicated merely by their relative direct land absorption.

Third, if necessities have a lower labor intensity than do luxuries, i.e.,

$$a_1/b_1 < a_2/b_2 \tag{16}$$

then according to (13) $P_1/P_2 < b_1/b_2$: since necessities absorb less labor per acre than do luxuries, they also absorb less indirect land (to feed labor) per acre. Consequently, necessities should have a relative price lower than indicated by their relative direct land absorption.

3. A Land Theory of Value?

Is (13) a land theory of value? It follows from (2) that the dimension of the numerator b_1 of (13) is acre-years absorbed in producing one physical unit of necessities. It follows from (1), (2), and (5) that the dimension of the terms of the denominator of (13) is acre-years absorbed in producing one physical unit of luxuries. Consequently, (13) expresses relative price in terms of nothing but relative acre-years absorbed and can be affected by changes in nothing else. Specifically, (13) can be affected by changes in neither the money rent rate nor the money wage rate. The money rent rate n doesn't appear in (13), because it canceled when (11) was divided by (12). The money wage rate w doesn't appear either; it disappeared when (9) was inserted into (10).

Thus, in Schumpeter's words (1954: 220), Cantillon "reduced from cost in terms of land and labor to cost in terms of land alone." Our (13) is his land theory of value.

4. Physical Outputs and Real-Income Distribution

Into (8) insert (12) and find the solution for the second output

$$X_2 = (1 - a_1c_1)N/[b_2 + (a_2/b_2 - a_1/b_1)b_1b_2c_1] \tag{17}$$

Into (7) insert (3), (1), and (9) and find first output expressed in terms of second:

$$X_1 = a_2c_1X_2/(1 - a_1c_1) \tag{18}$$

Finally insert (17) into (18) and find the solution for first output

$$X_1 = a_2c_1N/[b_2 + (a_2/b_2 - a_1/b_1)b_1b_2c_1] \tag{19}$$

Since wages are spent on the first good only and rent on the second good only, our solutions (19) and (17) for the physical outputs of the first and the second good, respectively, are at the same time solutions for the real incomes of labor and landlords, respectively.

5. Sustainable Employment

Insert (1), (17), and (19) into (3) and find the solution for sustainable employment

$$L = a_2N/[b_2 + (a_2/b_2 - a_1/b_1)b_1b_2c_1] \tag{20}$$

Does this solution for sustainable employment have the sensitivities Cantillon said it had? It has those—*plus* some he never mentioned.

IV. SENSITIVITIES OF SOLUTION FOR SUSTAINABLE EMPLOYMENT

1. Sensitivity of Employment to Land Absorption by Luxuries

Take the partial derivative of solution (20) with respect to the input-output coefficient b_2, the per-unit land absorption by luxuries:

$$\frac{\partial L}{\partial b_2} = - \frac{(1 - a_1c_1)a_2N}{[b_2 + (a_2/b_2 - a_1/b_1)b_1b_2c_1]^2} \tag{21}$$

Here the denominator is a square, always positive. It follows from (1) and (5) that $a_1c_1 = L_1/L$ or, in English, the fraction of the labor force employed in producing necessities. To guarantee that some labor is left for luxuries, we must impose the constraint that $a_1c_1 < 1$ or $1 - a_1c_1 > 0$. We have assumed that $a_i > 0$ and $N > 0$. As a result, the numerator of (21) is positive, and the entire partial derivative (21) is negative: the more land absorbed per unit of luxuries the less employment the economy will sustain.

The farmer's choice of crop of luxuries is influenced by the landlord—but not directly. Cantillon's farmers were independent and market-oriented entrepreneurs, so the landlord's influence was an indirect one exerted via the marketplace. As Cantillon [1755 (1931: 73)] put it: "The Prices [the Proprietors of Land] offer in the Market and their consumption determine the use made of the Land just as if they cultivated it themselves."

Cantillon offers two examples of such market orientation. First, transportation demand generated by absentee ownership:

> If the Proprietors of Land who live in the Country go to reside in the Cities far away from their Land, Horses must be fed for the transport into the City both of their food and that of all the Domestic Servants, Mechanicks and others whom their residence in the City attracts thither.

> The carriage of Wine from Burgundy to Paris often costs more than the Wine itself costs in Burgundy; and consequently the Land employed for the upkeep of the cart horses and those who look after them is more considerable than the Land which produces the Wine and supports those who have taken part in its production.

Second, the demand for imported luxuries:

> If the Ladies of Paris are pleased to wear Brussels Lace, and if France pays for this Lace with Champagne wine, the product of a single Acre of Flax must be paid for with the product of 16,000 acres of land under vines, if my calculations are correct.

2.   Sensitivity of Employment to Land Absorption by Necessities

Take the partial derivative of solution (20) with respect to the input-output coefficient b_1, the per-unit land absorption by necessities:

$$\frac{\partial L}{\partial b_1} = -\frac{a_2{}^2 c_1 N}{[b_2 + (a_2/b_2 - a_1/b_1)b_1 b_2 c_1]^2} \tag{22}$$

Again the denominator is a square, always positive. As for the numerator, a_2 is squared, too, and we have assumed that $c_1 > 0$ and $N > 0$. As a result, the partial derivative (22) is negative: the more land absorbed per unit of necessities the less employment the economy will sustain or, in Cantillon's [1755 (1931: 67-69)] comparison of extremes, the bison economy of the American Indian will support far fewer people than the rice economy of China:

> ... there is no Country where the increase of Population is more limited than among the Savages in the interior parts of America. They neglect Agriculture, live in Woods, and on the Wild Beasts they find there. As their Forests destroy the Sweetness and

Substance of the Earth there is little pasture for Animals, and since an Indian eats several Animals in a year, 50 or 100 acres supply only enough food for a single Indian.

By contrast:

There is no Country where Population is carried to a greater Height than in China. The common People are supported by Rice and Rice Water; they work almost naked and in the southern Provinces they have three plentiful harvests of Rice yearly, thanks to their great attention to Agriculture. The Land is never fallow and yields a hundredfold every year. Those who are clothed have generally Clothing of Cotton, which needs so little Land for its production that an Acre of Land, it seems, is capable of producing a Quantity full sufficient for the Clothing of five hundred grown-up Persons ... They look upon it as a Crime to lay Land out in Pleasure-Gardens or Parks, defrauding the Public of Maintenance. They carry Travellers in sedan Chairs, and save the work of Horses upon all tasks which can be performed by Men.

3. *Sensitivity of Employment to Labor's Manner of Living*

Cantillon [1755 (1931: 77)] described labor's supply reaction:

... If a Man is satisfied with the produce of an Acre and a half of Land he will marry if he is sure of having enough to keep his Family in the same way. But if he is only satisfied with the produce of 5 to 10 Acres he will be in no hurry to marry unless he thinks he can bring up his Family in the same manner.

Now suppose labor succeeds in raising its standard from the former to the latter level. How will such a higher "Manner of Living" affect sustainable employment? For an answer take the partial derivative of our solution (20) with respect to the input-output coefficient c_1, i.e., the per-man-year absorption of necessities by labor:

$$\frac{\partial L}{\partial c_1} = -\frac{(a_2/b_2 - a_1/b_1)a_2 b_1 b_2 N}{[b_2 + (a_2/b_2 - a_1/b_1)b_1 b_2 c_1]^2} \tag{23}$$

Again the denominator is a square, always positive. The sign, then, of (23) depends on the sign of the parenthesis $(a_2/b_2 - a_1/b_1)$. It will help us interpret (23) if we first divide (19) by (17) and find relative physical output

$$X_1/X_2 = a_2 c_1/(1 - a_1 c_1) \tag{24}$$

from which we see that the higher the "Manner of Living" c_1 the higher the ratio of physical output of necessities to luxuries. Let us now distinguish our three cases (14), (15), and (16).

First, if the labor intensities of necessities and luxuries are the same, i.e.,

$$a_1/b_1 = a_2/b_2 \tag{14}$$

then according to (23) $\partial L/\partial c_1 = 0$: the enlarged crop of necessities has the same labor intensity as the reduced crop of luxuries. Consequently, overall sustainable employment is independent of the allocation of the given land between necessities and luxuries.

Second, if necessities have a higher labor intensity than do luxuries, i.e.,

$$a_1/b_1 > a_2/b_2 \tag{15}$$

then according to (23) $\partial L/\partial c_1 > 0$: the enlarged crop of necessities has the higher labor intensity and the reduced crop of luxuries the lower one. Consequently, overall sustainable employment is raised.

Third, if necessities have a lower labor intensity than do luxuries, i.e.,

$$a_1/b_1 < a_2/b_2 \tag{16}$$

then according to (23) $\partial L/\partial c_1 < 0$: the enlarged crop of necessities has the lower labor intensity and the reduced crop of luxuries the higher one. Consequently, overall sustainable employment is lowered.

Of our three possibilities, Cantillon never mentioned the first two. He was sure that [1755 (1931: 83)]:

> The Increase of Population can be carried furthest in the Countries where the people are content to live the most poorly and to consume the least produce of the soil. In Countries where all the Peasants and Labourers are accustomed to eat Meat and drink Wine, Beer, etc. so many Inhabitants cannot be supported.

and raised the question [1755 (1931: 85)]:

> ... whether it is better to have a great multitude of Inhabitants, poor and badly provided, than a smaller number, much more at their ease: a million who consume the produce of 6 acres per head or 4 million who live on the produce of an Acre and a half.

Perhaps Cantillon took for granted that necessities would always have a lower labor intensity than luxuries. Incidentally, his answer to the question raised was modern: such a question was "outside of my subject"! Cantillon could distinguish analysis from value judgment.

V. CONCLUSION

With few but powerful strokes Cantillon, a born theorist, painted a vivid picture of prerevolutionary and preindustrial France. He offered a theory of price and a theory of output and its allocation.

Cantillon saw competitive price as determined by cost of production. Far from denying that labor is necessary for production—as (1) says it is—Cantillon saw labor as reproducible, hence could reduce it to the land from which it was reproduced. In this sense his price theory was a land theory of value.

Cantillon saw output as bounded by the available physical stock of land. The employment the available physical stock of land could support, depended on the land absorption by the necessities needed to feed labor as well as on the land absorption by the luxuries demanded by landlords. Behind demand one finds the preferences of the landlords—the "Taste, Humours and Manner of Living," as Cantillon called them in his succinct summary [1755 (1931: 81)] of his system:

> ... it therefore seems pretty clear that the Number of Inhabitants of a State depends on the Means allotted them of obtaining their Support; and as this Means of Subsistence arises from the Method of cultivating the soil, and this Method depends chiefly on the Taste, Humours and Manner of Living of the Proprietors of Land, the Increase and Decrease of Population also stand on the same Foundation.

So demand had its place in Cantillon's system.

REFERENCES

R. Cantillon, *Essai sur la nature du commerce en général*, written around 1730, published 1755 referring to a fictitious publisher: "A Londres, Chez F. Gyles, dans Holborn"; reprinted, Boston, 1892; edited and translated into English by Henry Higgs, C.B., London, 1931; translated into German with an introduction by F. A. Hayek, Jena, 1931; republished in French, Paris, 1952.

J. A. Schumpeter, *History of Economic Analysis*, New York, 1954.

CHAPTER 2   Intersectoral Equilibrium

QUESNAY (1694-1774)

> ... When Quesnay first published his famous schema,
> his contemporaries and disciples acclaimed it as the
> greatest discovery since Newton's laws. The idea of
> general interdependence among the various parts of the
> economic system has become by now the very
> foundation of economic analysis.
>
> Leontief (1941: 9)

I. INTRODUCTION

1. Quesnay's Problem

As a physician, Quesnay must have thought of the analogy between a human body and an economy. Like the organs of the body, the sectors of an economy interact: each is well only as long as the others are. The size of each is geared to the sizes of the others. All are connected through a circular flow—the discovery of the circular flow of human blood preceded Quesnay's table by 130 years.

Quesnay wanted to understand such interaction among sectors and determine the size of output and income in each sector.

2. Quesnay's Method

Quesnay's method was the numerical example with an iterative solution. His numerical example illustrated the anatomy of a healthy economy. No artery was clogged: no government interfered. No artery was leaking. There was no savings leakage, for all income was consumed. There was no import leakage, for import was matched by export. Possible tax and tithes leakages were ignored in a first approximation.

Quesnay's iterative solution reminds us of the successive rounds used by early Keynesians to work out their multiplier. The iterative method is not efficient, but Quesnay apparently knew no other. The trouble it gave him is apparent from the fact that several small and slightly different editions were run off the royal printing press. We shall use the recently discovered third edition [1759 (1972)].

Quesnay liked to see the things themselves and concentrated on "purchases at first hand, abstracting from trade, which multiplies sales and purchases without multiplying things." He decided to boil down the economy to a mini-economy with four heads of families in it. The first three, always at the center of the stage, were the farmer, the landlord, and the artisan. The fourth family head, a farmhand, was very nearly forgotten when it was time to scale up the mini-economy to a France-sized one but did receive his scaling-up in the last moment.

3. *Our Own Restatement*

Unlike Barna (1975), we disaggregate Quesnay's farm into the farmer and the farmhand and accept the resulting rise in the number of sectors from three to four.

TABLE 2-1. A Five-Sector Leontief Transactions Table

		Farmer (1)	Farm- hand (2)	Land- lord (3)	Artisan (4)	Foreign Countries (5)	Row Total
Farmer	(1)	x_{11}	x_{12}	x_{13}	x_{14}	x_{15}	X_1
Farmhand	(2)	x_{21}	x_{22}	x_{23}	x_{24}	x_{25}	X_2
Landlord	(3)	x_{31}	x_{32}	x_{33}	x_{34}	x_{35}	X_3
Artisan	(4)	x_{41}	x_{42}	x_{43}	x_{44}	x_{45}	X_4
Foreign Countries	(5)	x_{51}	x_{52}	x_{53}	x_{54}	x_{55}	X_5

Will four sectors do? Almost, but Quesnay's economy was not a closed one. However casually referred to, farm products were exported and manufactures imported. We agree with Barna (1975: 492) that "consistency required explicit entries for exports and imports." We accept the resulting rise in the number of sectors from four to five and restate Quesnay's [1759 (1972)] table as the five-sector Leontief transactions table[1] shown in table 2-1, where

$x_{ij} \equiv$ physical output of ith sector absorbed by jth sector
$X_i \equiv$ physical output of ith sector

---

[1]Phillips (1955) restated Quesnay in the form of a static closed Leontief model of three industries. Such a system of homogeneous equations cannot determine the levels of but only the proportions between outputs. Quesnay's system was not homogeneous: its autonomous part was the rent paid by the farmer to the landlord. We wish to preserve Quesnay's determination of the levels of output—indeed his very numbers—and do not go to the Phillips extreme.

Quesnay's explanation of his table did allow for the fact that production takes time. He referred [1759 (1972: iv)] to "costs provided for by the annual advances" and recorded that the sale of the finished product "regenerates," "restitutes," or "returns" such advances of which the farmer had received 600 and the artisan 300. We agree with Barna (1975: 490) that what Quesnay called "interest" was probably capital consumption allowances. But whatever it was, it made Quesnay no pioneer of capital theory and may safely be ignored. We do so by simply thinking of all production as instantaneous. Under that assumption *plus* the assumption that artisans need no land, Quesnay's numerical results will emerge. In making those assumptions, then, we may safely follow Samuelson (1982: 49 and 53).

On two other points, however, we cannot follow Samuelson (1982: 50 and 51). First, we cannot ignore the demand for artisan output by farmers and farmhands, numerically specified by Quesnay. Second, we cannot read Ricardian diminishing returns into Quesnay. As we saw, diminishing marginal productivity was discovered by Turgot on the very occasion of criticizing Quesnay's use of a fixed ratio between inputs advanced by capital and output of produce.

II. THE QUESNAY MINI-ECONOMY

1. *The Leontief Transactions Table*

An element x_{ij} of a Leontief transactions table represents the supply by ith sector demanded by jth sector. There are equal numbers of rows and columns. A row will account for all demand satisfied by a sector's supply. Consequently, in equilibrium the row total must equal the sector's supply. A column will account for all supplies satisfying a sector's demand. Consequently the column total is the sector's demand. In equilibrium a sector must break even: its revenue must equal its expenditure. In other words, its row total must equal its column total.

A five-sector Leontief transactions table has twenty-five elements in it. Fortunately in Quesnay's case many of the elements are zero. Since we like to stay as close to Quesnay as we can, we shall go through all the twenty-five elements, column by column, and describe each element in his own words.

2. *Demand by Farmer*

Farm output demanded by the farmer x_{11} consists of two parts. First [1759 (1972: iv)]: "The costs provided for by the [600 livres of] annual advances of the productive expenditure class, which are also regenerated each year, and of which one-half is spent on the feeding of livestock." Second, [1759 (1972: ij)]:

> The 300 livres of revenue . . . which are returned at the beginning of the process to the productive expenditure class, by means of the sale of the products which the proprietor buys from it, are spent by the farmer, one-half in the consumption of products provided by this class itself . . .

Consequently, farm output demanded by the farmer is

$$x_{11} = 300 + x_{13}/2 \qquad (1)$$

Farmhand service demanded by the farmer x_{21} is [1759 (1972: iv)] "the other half . . . of the costs provided for by the annual advances . . . in paying wages to the men engaged in the work carried on by this class:"

$$x_{21} = 300 \qquad (2)$$

Land use demanded by the farmer x_{31} occupies a prominent position in Quesnay's model. He opens his explanation of the table by fixing it. Land use is supplied by the landlord and paid for by rent or, in Quesnay's own words [1759 (1972: i)]:

> The sale of the net product which the cultivator has generated in the previous year, by means of the annual advances of 600 livres employed in cultivation by the farmer, results in the payment to the proprietor of a revenue of 600 livres.

Consequently, land use demanded by the farmer is

$$x_{31} = 600 \qquad (3)$$

Artisan output demanded by the farmer x_{41} is the other half [1759 (1972: ij)]:

> These 300 livres, I say, which are returned at the beginning of the process to the productive expenditure class, by means of the sale of the products which the proprietor buys from it, are spent by the farmer . . . the other half in keeping itself in clothing, utensils, implements, etc., for which it makes payment to the sterile expenditure class.

$$x_{41} = x_{13}/2 \qquad (4)$$

No import x_{51} is demanded by the farmer.

3. *Demand by Farmhand*

Although Quesnay does not say so directly, let the farmhand spend his income the same way that the farmer does. If so, farm output demanded by the farmhand x_{12} must be [1759 (1972: ij)] "one-half in the consumption of products provided by this class itself:"

$$x_{12} = x_{13}/2 \tag{5}$$

Artisan output demanded by the farmhand x_{42} is "the other half [spent] in keeping itself in clothing, utensils, implements, etc." or:

$$x_{42} = x_{13}/2 \tag{6}$$

Farmhands demand nothing else: no work of their own x_{22}, no land use of their own x_{32}, and no import x_{52}.

4. *Demand by Landlord*

How does the landlord spend his rent? In Quesnay's words [1759 (1972: i)]: "Of the 600 livres of revenue, one-half is spent by the proprietor in purchasing bread, wine, meat, etc., from the productive expenditure class ..."

Consequently, farm output demanded by the landlord is

$$x_{13} = x_{31}/2 \tag{7}$$

"and the other half in purchasing clothing, furnishings, utensils, etc., from the sterile expenditure class." Consequently, artisan output demanded by the landlord is

$$x_{43} = x_{31}/2 \tag{8}$$

Landlords demand nothing else: no farmhand work x_{23}, no land use for their mansion x_{33}, and no import x_{53}.

5. *Demand by Artisan*

Farm output demanded by the artisan x_{14} consists of two parts. The first is [1759 (1972: i)]:

The annual advances of the sterile expenditure class, amounting to 300 livres, are employed for the capital and costs of trade, for the purchase of raw materials for manufactured goods, and for the subsistence and other needs of the artisan until he has completed and sold his work.

The second is [1759 (1972: ij-iij)]:

The 300 livres of the proprietor's revenue which have passed into the hands of the sterile expenditure class are spent by the artisan, as to one-half, in the purchase of products for his subsistence, for raw materials for his work, and for foreign trade, from the productive expenditure class . . .

Consequently, farm output demanded by the artisan is

$$x_{14} = 300 + x_{43}/2 \tag{9}$$

Artisan output demanded by the artisan x_{44} is "the other half . . . distributed among the sterile expenditure class itself for its maintenance and for the restitution of its advances" or

$$x_{44} = x_{43}/2 \tag{10}$$

Import, handled by the artisan, x_{54} consists of [1759 (1972: iv)] "the purchases of the commodities and bullion which are obtained from abroad" and will equal export:

$$x_{54} = x_{15} \tag{11}$$

Artisans demand nothing else: no farmhand work x_{24} and no land use for their workshops x_{34}.

6. *Export Demand*

Only farm products enter "into external trade, either as exports or as raw materials and subsistence for the country's workers who sell their goods to other nations" [1759 (1972: iv)]:

$$x_{15} = 150 \tag{12}$$

Foreign countries demand nothing else.

7. *Market Equilibrium*

For each sector supply must equal demand:

$$X_1 = x_{11} + x_{12} + x_{13} + x_{14} + x_{15} \tag{13}$$

$$X_2 = x_{21} + x_{22} + x_{23} + x_{24} + x_{25} \tag{14}$$

$$X_3 = x_{31} + x_{32} + x_{33} + x_{34} + x_{35} \tag{15}$$

$$X_4 = x_{41} + x_{42} + x_{43} + x_{44} + x_{45} \tag{16}$$

$$X_5 = x_{51} + x_{52} + x_{53} + x_{54} + x_{55} \tag{17}$$

which is the justification for writing the row totals of table 2-1 as X_i. We are now ready to solve Quesnay's model.

III. THE MINI-ECONOMY: EQUILIBRIUM SOLUTIONS

1. *Finding the Solutions*

Set all transactions x_{ij} other than (1) through (12) equal to zero. Then insert (1) through (12) and all the zeros into the system (13) through (17), and find the solutions for all transactions x_{ij} and outputs X_i listed in table 2-2. So the farmer produces 1,500 livres' worth of produce; the farmhand works 300 livres' worth of hours; the landlord supplies 600 livres' worth of land use; the artisan produces 750 livres' worth of merchandise; and 150 livres' worth of produce exchanges internationally for 150 livres' worth of merchandise.

Notice that every sector's row total equals its column total or, in English, the value of everything supplied by that sector equals the value of everything demanded by it. The sector breaks even.

Let us illuminate our results by subjecting them to three different types of accounting: product, flow-of-funds, and income accounting.

2. *Product Accounting: Where Does Product Go?*

The farm produces 1,500 livres' worth of produce. Of this, 600 livres' worth will never reach the market but is consumed down on the farm itself: livestock consumes 300, farmhand consumes 150, and the farmer himself consumes another 150. That leaves 900 livres' worth to go to market. Here, 300 is sold to the landlord, 450 to the artisan, and 150 to foreign countries.

The artisan produces 750 livres' worth of merchandise. Of this, 150 livres' worth will never reach the market but is consumed by himself. That leaves 600 livres' worth to go to market. Here 300 is sold to the

TABLE 2-2. Quesnay's Transactions

		Farmer (1)	Farm-hand (2)	Land-lord (3)	Artisan (4)	Foreign Countries (5)	Row Total
Farmer	(1)	450	150	300	450	150	1,500
Farmhand	(2)	300	0	0	0	0	300
Landlord	(3)	600	0	0	0	0	600
Artisan	(4)	150	150	300	150	0	750
Foreign Countries	(5)	0	0	0	150	0	150
Column Total		1,500	300	600	750	150	3,300

landlord, 150 to the farmer, and 150 to the farmhand on their days off in the city.

3. *Flow-of-Funds Accounting: Where Does Money Go?*

What goes on inside the farm requires no money: livestock, farmhand, and farmer consume produce directly. But paying the landlord his 600 livres' worth of rent requires money. So do the farmer's and the farmhand's purchases of 150 livres' worth of merchandise each. That makes a total outflow of 900 livres, financed neatly by the total inflow from the 900 livres' worth of produce that went to the market and was sold there.

The landlord pays cash and is paid in it. His outflow of 300 livres for produce and 300 for merchandise is financed by his inflow of 600 livres' worth of rent.

The artisan purchases 300 livres' worth of raw materials *plus* 150 livres' worth of produce from the farmer and 150 livres' worth abroad. That makes a total outflow of 600 livres, financed neatly by his total inflow of 600 livres' worth of merchandise that went to market and was sold there: 150 to the farmer, 150 to the farmhand, and 300 to the landlord.

4. *Income Accounting: How Is Income Earned?*

The farm produces 1,500 livres' worth of produce. To the farmer, 1,200 livres' worth is cost of production: livestock consumes 300, farmhand is hired at 300, and land is rented at 600. That leaves 300 livres' worth as the farmer's net income. But what is a cost of hiring to the farmer is an income to the farmhand hired at 300 livres. Two heads of households, then, make a living down on the farm, each at 300 livres.

The landlord earns 600 livres' worth of rent. Since he has no costs of production, his rent is a net income.

The artisan produces 750 livres' worth of merchandise. To him, 450 livres' worth is cost of production: his raw materials cost 300, and his import costs 150. That leaves 300 livres' worth as the artisan's net income.

Summarizing, then, of the four heads of families found in our mini-economy three make a living of 300 livres each. The fourth, the landlord, lives better at 600 livres!

5. *"Net Product," "Productive," and "Sterile" Classes*

The mystique surrounding Quesnay's labels should by now have been dispelled. By "net product" he simply meant the value of product over and above cost of production and necessary consumption of those producing it. Only the farm produced such a net product. Having fed its livestock 300 livres' worth and having allowed farmer and farmhand 300 livres' worth of consumption each—necessary to compensate them for their toil and trouble—the farm still generated 600 livres' worth over and above such cost of production and necessary consumption. Those 600 livres constituted rent paid to the landlord but were a compensation for no toil and trouble. But weren't they a compensation for the use of his land? We would say so. The physiocrats simply saw the land as nature's precious gift to man.

The artisan, by contrast, produced no net product. Having paid for his 300 livres' worth of raw materials and his 150 livres' worth of import and having allowed himself 300 livres' worth of consumption—necessary to compensate him for his toil and trouble—the artisan had exhausted his 750 livres' worth of product. No net product left!

Quesnay's class labels now fall into place. A class producing a net product was called "productive," a class producing no such net product was called "sterile." The labels were items of Quesnay's national income accounting, that's all.

IV. SCALING-UP THE MINI-ECONOMY

1. *Multiplying by a Million*

With his income accounting, Quesnay is ready to scale up his mini-economy to a France-sized economy. At first, he forgets the farmhand [1759 (1972: iv)]:

> The proprietor subsists by means of the 600 livres which he spends. The 300 livres distributed to each expenditure class, together with the product of the taxes, the tithes, etc., which is added to them, can support one man in each: thus 600 livres of revenue together with the appurtenant sums can enable three heads of families to subsist.

Next comes the scaling-up: "On this basis 600 millions of revenue can enable three million families to subsist, estimated at four persons of all ages per family."

Only now does Quesnay remember the farmhand:

> The costs provided for by the annual advances of the productive expenditure class, which are also regenerated each year, and of which one-half is spent on the feeding of livestock and the other half in paying wages to the men engaged in the work carried on by this class, add 300 millions of expenditure to the total; and this,

together with the share of the other products which are added to them, can enable another one million heads of families to subsist.

All in all, then, there is room for four million heads of families:

1 million farmers @ 300 livres' income,
1 million farmhands @ 300 livres' income,
1 million landlords @ 600 livres' income,
1 million artisans @ 300 livres' income.

"Four persons of all ages per family" make "16 million people of all ages to subsist according to this order of circulation and distribution of the annual revenue." Add 4 million in the public sector and the church, and we have the actual population of France at Quesnay's time, 20 million.

2. *Quesnay's Policy Opinions*

Only at this point does it become clear that Quesnay's table was meant to describe what ought to be rather than what was. His table assumes large-scale cultivation using 333,334 large ploughs drawn by horses [1759 (1972: v-vi)]:

Assuming a satisfactory state of affairs in which large-scale cultivation was being carried on with the aid of horses, this portion would require the employment of 333,334 ploughs at 120 arpents of land per plough; 333,334 men to drive them; and 40 million arpents of land.[2]

He contrasts such happy circumstances with actual ones [1759 (1972: vi)], i.e.,

... small-scale cultivation carried on with the aid of oxen, in which more than a million ploughs and about two million men would be required to work 40 million arpents of land, and which would bring in only two-fifths of the product yielded by large-scale cultivation. This small-scale cultivation, to which cultivators are reduced owing to their lack of the wealth necessary to make the original advances, and in which the land is largely employed merely to cover the costs, is carried on at the expense of landed property itself, and involves an excessive annual expenditure for the subsistence of the great numbers of men engaged in this type of cultivation, which absorbs almost the whole of the product. This thankless type of cultivation, which reveals the poverty and

---

[2]One arpent was the equivalent of 51 metric ares or 1.2 acres.

ruin of those nations in which it predominates, has no connection with the order of the *tableau*.

The happy circumstances of the table, in which "a state is strong in taxable capacity and resources, and its people live in easy circumstances" may be in store for France but may also be jeopardized "for eight principal reasons" [1759 (1972: xj-xij)]:

1. A bad system of tax-assessment, which encroaches upon the cultivators' advances.
2. An extra burden of taxation due to the costs of collection.
3. An excess of luxury in the way of ornamentation.
4. Excessive expenditure on litigation.
5. A lack of external trade in the products of landed property.
6. A lack of freedom of internal trade in raw produce, and in cultivation.
7. The personal harassment of the inhabitants of the countryside.
8. Failure of the annual net product to return to the productive expenditure class.

REFERENCES

T. Barna, "Quesnay's *Tableau* in Modern Guise," *Econ. J.*, Sep. 1975, *85*, 485-496.

W. W. Leontief, *The Structure of American Economy, 1919-1929*, Cambridge, Mass., 1941.

A. Phillips, "The Tableau Economique as a Simple Leontief Model," *Quart. J. Econ.*, Feb. 1955, *69*, 137-144.

F. Quesnay, *Tableau Economique*, third edition, Versailles, 1759, edited, with new material, translations and notes by M. Kuczynski and R. L. Meek, London and New York, 1972.

P. A. Samuelson, "Quesnay's 'Tableau Economique' as a Theorist Would Formulate it Today," in I. Bradley and M. Bradley (eds.), *Classical and Marxian Political Economy: Essays in Honour of Ronald L. Meek*, London, 1982, 3-78.

PART *III* 1770-1870

English Classicism
Marginal Productivity
Monopoly-Polypoly
Marginal Utility

I. THE SETTING

Our period covers the span from the first industrial revolution to the second. The firm foundation of the first industrial revolution was the steam engine. A steam engine demanding prohibitive amounts of fuel had been known throughout the eighteenth century but could not revolutionize industry and transportation until, first, between 1763 and 1785 James Watt had sharply reduced its fuel consumption and, second, ironmaking and tooling had provided the materials and the precision, respectively, with which to build it. Only after the beginning of our period did coke smelting of iron ore and precision drilling become efficient and widespread. In 1804 Richard Trevithick put the steam engine on rails, and in 1807 Robert Fulton put it into a boat.

Large-scale reallocation of manpower accompanied the first industrial revolution. Farming released manpower to manufacturing. The use of machinery released manpower to the manufacturing of it. But capitalism was up to the task. Initial large profits of innovation were plowed back, or via the securities market channeled back, into further improvement.

Close, personal labor-capital relations gave way to distant and impersonal ones. The very efficiency of the new machinery reduced the premium on human muscle power and encouraged female and child labor—thus undermining family life and literacy. Cantillon's preindustrial class distinction between farmer and landlord seemed unimportant compared with the new labor-capital relations. Halfway through our period, between the first and third edition of his *Principles*, Ricardo decided to include a chapter on machinery—"a subject of great importance."

For all the initial human misery created by machinery, Britain's population more than doubled between 1750 and 1830. After that, the first industrial revolution spread to Belgium, the United States, and Germany.

II. NOTATION

1. *Variables*

$G \equiv$ physical government purchase of goods and services
$L \equiv$ labor employed
$N \equiv$ land cultivated
$n \equiv$ money rent rate (in Smith)

$n \equiv$ number of producers (in Cournot)
$P \equiv$ price of output
$p \equiv$ price of capital stock
$\Pi \equiv$ price of bonds
$R \equiv$ government net receipts *before* interest paid by government
$r \equiv$ rate of interest
$S \equiv$ physical capital stock
$w \equiv$ money wage rate
$X \equiv$ physical output
$Y \equiv$ money national income
$y \equiv$ money disposable income

2. *Parameters*

$a_i \equiv$ man-years absorbed in producing one physical unit of ith good
$b_i \equiv$ acre-years directly absorbed in producing one physical unit of ith good
$c_1 \equiv$ necessities absorbed in producing one man-year
$i \equiv$ interest payment per bond
$M \equiv$ supply of money
$Q \equiv$ supply of bonds: physical quantity of government bonds outstanding

III. ENGLISH CLASSICAL MACROECONOMICS: SAY'S LAW— SAY, SMITH, RICARDO, LAUDERDALE, MALTHUS, AND MARX

1. *The Two Parts of Say's Law*

Formally no part of Hume's theory of money, Say's Law was a neat supplement to it. Say's Law explained why monetary expansion was redundant: supply would always create its own demand.

Say's Law did not have to wait for Say. There are two parts to it, and Adam Smith had both. The first part is entirely noncontroversial and consists of the national product-national income identity. The second part is controversial and consists of the statement that the savings, import, and tax leakages are always stopped by investment, export, and government expenditure, respectively.

2. *The National Product-National Income Identity*

Generation of product is generation of value added, and value added is somebody's earnings. Value added by a firm is either cost or profits. To the worker, landlord, or capitalist, the cost of hiring him is his earnings. To the firm, the profits are its earnings. Thus money national income defined as the aggregate earnings arising from current production is identically equal to national product defined as the market value of physical output:

$$Y \equiv PX \tag{1}$$

The identity was seen and expressed well by Adam Smith [1776 (1805: 204)]: "The annual revenue of every society is always precisely equal to the exchangeable value of the whole annual produce of its industry, or rather is precisely the same thing with that exchangeable value."

Modern economists doubt neither that product and income are the same thing nor that income is a necessary condition for demand. But is it also a sufficient condition? Consider three possible leakages.

3. The Savings Leakage

Income saved does not demand output. Will investment stop the leakage? Will a well-functioning capital market always bring about an equality between intended saving and intended investment? Turgot [1769-1770 (1922: 74)] described such a well-functioning capital market:

I have already said that the price of borrowed money is regulated, like that of all other merchandise, by the balance of supply and demand: thus, when there are many borrowers who need money, the interest of money becomes higher; when there are many holders of money who offer to lend it, interest falls. It is, therefore, another mistake to suppose that the interest of money in commerce ought to be fixed by the laws of Princes. It is a current price, fixed like that of all other merchandise.

Adam Smith [1776 (1805: 78-79)] must have had such a Turgotian well-functioning capital market in mind when he wrote:

Whatever a person saves from his revenue he adds to his capital, and either employs it himself in maintaining an additional number of productive hands, or enables some other person to do so, by lending it to him for an interest . . .

What is annually saved is as regularly consumed as what is annually spent, and nearly in the same time too; but it is consumed by a different set of people.

Say himself [1803 (1830: 53)] was equally confident that saving would be spent and ultimately consumed: "No act of saving subtracts in the least from consumption, provided the thing saved be reinvested or restored to productive employment. On the contrary, it gives rise to a consumption perpetually renovated and recurring.''

Was the savings leakage stopped by a price mechanism? Specifically, was there a well-functioning capital market in which a flexible rate of interest served as an equilibrating variable between saving and investment, as Turgot had suggested? If this was what Say had in mind, he did not say so.

4. *The Import Leakage*

Income spent on imports does not demand domestic output. Will exports stop the leakage? Say [1803 (1830: 83)] was confident that they would:

> ... it is no injury to the internal or national industry and production to buy and import commodities from abroad; for nothing can be bought from strangers, except with native products, which find a vent in this external traffic. Should it be objected, that this foreign produce may have been bought with specie, I answer, specie is not always a native product, but must have been bought itself with the products of native industry; so that, whether the foreign articles be paid for in specie or in home produce, the vent for national industry is the same in both cases.

Was the import leakage stopped by a price mechanism? Specifically, was there a well-functioning foreign-exchange market in which a flexible rate of exchange served as an equilibrating variable between import and export? Or would import or export surpluses generate an outflow or inflow, respectively, of specie which in turn would generate deflation or inflation, respectively, thus ultimately restoring the trade balance, as Hume had suggested? If this was what Say had in mind, he did not say so.

5. *The Tax Leakage*

Income taxed away does not demand output. Will government expenditure stop the leakage? Define money disposable income as money national income *plus* interest iQ paid by government *minus* government net receipts before interest iQ paid by government:

$$y \equiv Y + iQ - R \tag{2}$$

If and only if a political process balances the budget, i.e., if government expenditure on goods and services *plus* interest paid by government *minus* government net receipts before interest paid equals zero:

$$GP + iQ - R = 0 \tag{3}$$

will the tax leakage be stopped. Say [1803 (1830: 80)] assumed it to be when he wrote:

> Should a producer imagine ... that there is a class of demand other than that of the actual producers, he would but expose the shallowness and superficiality of his ideas. A priest goes to a shop to buy a gown or a surplice; he takes the value, that is to make the purchase, in the form of money. Whence had he that money? From some tax-gatherer who has taken it from a tax-payer. But whence did this latter derive it? From the value he has himself produced. This value, first produced by the tax-payer, and afterwards turned into money, and given to the priest for his salary, has enabled him to make the purchase.

Thoughtfully, his English translator added: "The clergy of France are now part of the national establishment, and receive salaries from the public Exchequer."

While, as we saw, the savings and import leakages could be stopped by a price mechanism, a balanced budget (3) would have to be established by a political process. No price mechanism can be depended on to establish it.

6. Conclusion: Say

When all is said and done, all leakages will be stopped, and Say's Law will hold or, in his own words [1803 (1830: 78-79)]:

> It is worthwhile to remark, that a product is no sooner created, than it, from that instant, affords a market for other products to the full extent of its own value. When the producer has put the finishing hand to his product, he is most anxious to sell it immediately, lest its value should vanish in his hands. Nor is he less anxious to dispose of the money he may get for it; for the value of money is also perishable. But the only way of getting rid of money is in the purchase of some product or other. Thus, the mere circumstance of the creation of one product immediately opens a vent for other products.

7. Concurrence: Ricardo

Say's friend and colleague Ricardo [1821 (1951, I: 290)] agreed:

> No man produces, but with a view to consume or sell, and he never sells, but with an intention to purchase some other commodity, which may be immediately useful to him, or which

may contribute to future production. By producing, then, he necessarily becomes either the consumer of his own goods, or the purchaser and consumer of the goods of some other person.

Landlords and capitalists saved. Capitalists invested but, in Ricardo's view, were by no means confined to investing what they themselves had saved. They could borrow in a well-functioning capital market in which a flexible rate of interest served as an equilibrating variable between saving and investment. In *Pamphlets and Papers, 1815-1823* Ricardo (1951, IV: 179-180) elaborated:

> There is ... no danger that ... accumulated capital ... would not find employment.... There are always to be found in a great country, a sufficient number of responsible persons, with the requisite skill, ready to employ the accumulated capital of others, and to pay them a share of the profits, and which, in all countries, is known by the name of interest for borrowed money.

8. The Doubts: Lauderdale

Lauderdale (1804) saw a tax leakage and a savings leakage. The government budget constraint is usually applied to the case of fiscal deficits. But to understand Lauderdale, we must run it in reverse and apply it to a fiscal surplus. Thus applied, it says that a government surplus may be financed in two ways: the government either destroys noninterest-bearing claims upon itself called money or buys back interest-bearing claims upon itself called bonds. The government budget constraint will be of the form

$$GP + iQ - R = \frac{dM}{dt} + \Pi \frac{dQ}{dt} \tag{4}$$

Between the Glorious Revolution of 1688—establishing the rule of William and Mary—and 1804 the British public debt had grown almost a thousandfold, from 0.66 million to 556 million pounds sterling [Hansen (1951: 230)]. Debt management was widely discussed, and the government planned, upon the return of peace, to run fiscal surpluses large enough to buy back its own bonds and retire the entire debt in forty-five years. In other words, the dQ/dt part of the budget constraint (4) was under debate.

Lauderdale saw such rapid retirement in terms of what Keynesians would call the consumption function and the marginal efficiency of capital. Huge tax collections would lower the consumption function and put huge sums into the hands of bondholders. Would the bondholders be disposed to consume those sums? No way, said Lauderdale (1804: 245-246): "It would have been difficult to persuade the proprietors of stock ... all at once to spend, as revenue, that which habit had taught them to regard as capital ..."

Now if the bondholders were not disposed to consume them, the sums would become investment-seeking funds at the very moment when investment outlets were being closed by the depressed consumption (1804: 265-266): "The continued progress of accumulation ... increases the quantity of capital; whilst, far from increasing, (by ... abridging consumption), it inevitably diminishes the demand for it."

9. The Doubts: Malthus

The Malthus who doubted the validity of Say's Law was the older Malthus (1820). To Malthus, as to Ricardo, landlords and capitalists saved, and capitalists invested. But to Malthus capitalists invested little more than what they themselves had saved. Malthus did not see Turgot's, Smith's and Ricardo's well-functioning capital market. In consequence, his policy recommendations were designed to encourage either direct consumption of rent by the landlords themselves or indirect consumption of it by government via taxation.

Eltis (1984: 177-178) agrees that Malthus never referred to a capital market with an equilibrating rate of interest in it. Eltis even thinks it "anachronistic" of the reader to expect such references. But weren't Turgot, Smith, and Ricardo keen observers? Didn't Ricardo have long personal and practical experience with securities markets? Were their well-functioning capital markets really mere hallucinations?

10. The Doubts: Marx

Marx [1905-1910 (1923: 276)] expressed his doubts about Say's Law in the very general form: "Money is not merely 'the medium accomplishing the exchange' but also the medium breaking up the exchange into two acts, independent of each other and separated in space and time" (my translation).

IV. ENGLISH CLASSICAL MACROECONOMICS: SUSTAINABLE POPULATION—MALTHUS AND RICARDO

1. Malthus

The younger Malthus (1798) emphasized but did not discover two points. The first had been well expressed by Cantillon [1755 (1931: 83)]: "Men multiply like Mice in a barn if they have unlimited Means of Subsistence." Malthus agreed and cited (1798: 20-21) evidence that "in the

United States of America, where the means of subsistence have been more ample . . . and consequently the checks to early marriages fewer, . . . the population has been found to double itself in twenty-five years.''

Malthus's second point was diminishing returns on the intensive margin of cultivation. Neither Cantillon nor Quesnay knew such diminishing returns—or had needed them to determine sustainable population. Fixed land *plus* fixed input-output coefficients would do. But as we saw in our previous period, Turgot discovered diminishing returns. Did Smith know them? Eltis (1984: 107) finds no trace of them in Smith, and Hollander (1980) finds them only on the basis of a very selective choice of quotes.

Be this as it may. Malthus combined his two points and was convinced that in countries less fortunate than the United States—and eventually even there—a doubling of the population every twenty-five years would leave its majority "unprovided for." Consequently population would have to be checked by either "preventive" checks (late marriages) or "positive" ones (vice, epidemics, wars, and famine in that order).

2. *Ricardo*

The diminishing returns emphasized but not discovered by Malthus became the cornerstone of Ricardo's long-run equilibrium of sustainable population, to which we shall devote our chapter 3. Which Ricardo are we going to restate? Samuelson (1959) and Pasinetti (1960) restated a pre-1821 Ricardo. In 1821 Ricardo added "machinery . . . a subject of great importance" to his third edition. We shall restate a post-1821 Ricardo, consider his machinery a key part of his system, and fit it in snugly. Capital then takes the form of durable producers' goods such as "the plough and the thrashing machine." There are two outputs, consumers' goods and durable producers' goods. As for consumers' goods, Ricardo's macroeconomics visualize a one-crop economy, and that crop is "corn."

A "portion of capital" is one physical unit of producers' goods properly manned for operation and is the same thing as Turgot's "advance." On the given land such portions will be applied up to the margin of cultivation where the last portion just earns its keep, i.e., adds just enough produce to, first, feed labor a minimum subsistence real wage rate and, second, give the capitalist a rate of profits high enough to keep him from decumulating.

Sustainable population is the manpower needed to, first, build and, second, operate the physical capital stock of producers' goods thus applied. Our chapter 3 will examine at length the effect of technological progress upon sustainable population and find no flaw in Ricardo's macroeconomics.

V.   ENGLISH CLASSICAL MICROECONOMICS: SMITH AND RICARDO

1.   Smith's "Natural" Price

Smith is rightly credited with his rejection of the labor theory of value. He banished it to "that early and rude state of society which precedes both the accumulation of stock and the appropriation of land." Which value theory did he hold, then? His answer is found in what Schumpeter (1954: 189) called "by far the best piece of economic theory turned out by A. Smith," i.e., [1776 (1805: book I, chapter 7)]:

> When the price of any commodity is neither more nor less than what is sufficient to pay the rent of the land, the wages of the labour, and the profits of the stock employed in raising, preparing, and bringing it to market, according to their natural rates, the commodity is then sold for what may be called its natural price.

Or, algebraically, the price of the ith good equals

$$P_i = wL_i/X_i + nN_i/X_i + prS_i/X_i \qquad (5)$$

On the face of it Smith's statement is, algebraically speaking, one equation in no less than nine unknowns: four physical quantities L_i, N_i, S_i, and X_i and five prices n, P_i, p, r, and w. As for the prices, can one explain prices by prices? In Walras's words [1874-1877 (1954: 211)]:

> It still remains to be seen whether it was because 2 francs were paid out in rent, 2 francs in wages and 1 franc in interest that this bottle of wine sells for 5 francs, or whether it is because the bottle sells for 5 francs that 2 francs were paid out in rent, 2 francs in wages and 1 franc in interest.

One equation in nine unknowns will not do. What Smith needed was more equations. Did he have them?

He did, as Samuelson (1977) showed in his bicentennial article. Let us for the moment ignore diminishing returns and consider separately Samuelson's two parts, one without, the other with capital.

2.   Smith's Natural Price: Production Takes No Time

Samuelson (1977: 46-48) first considered the case that production takes no time. Here, capital will be unnecessary, and there will be neither capitalists nor profits. We are back in a Cantillon world of only two inputs, labor and land, where for the ith good Smith's equation (5) collapses into

$$P_i = wL_i/X_i + nN_i/X_i \tag{6}$$

A Cantillon world knew of no diminishing returns and assumed all goods to be produced in processes having fixed input-output coefficients:

$$L_i = a_i X_i \tag{7}$$

$$N_i = b_i X_i \tag{8}$$

Insert (7) and (8) into (6) and find

$$P_i = a_i w + b_i n \tag{9}$$

Cantillon had two goods, a necessity consumed by labor and a luxury consumed by landlords, so $i = 1, 2$, respectively. The money wage and rent rates need no subscripts, for each must be the same in both industries. Now suppose the system (9) to be satisfied by a set of four prices P_i, w, and n. If every price were multiplied by the same arbitrary constant λ (9) would still hold. So if the system were satisfied by one set of prices it would be satisfied by infinitely many, and Cantillon was up against the same difficulty encountered by Walras 140 years later: he could not solve his system for absolute prices. His way out was the same as Walras's: he would have to choose a *numéraire*, say P_2, and divide by it. So divide (9) by P_2 and write it out for $i = 1, 2$:

$$P_1/P_2 = a_1 w/P_2 + b_1 n/P_2 \tag{10}$$

$$1 = a_2 w/P_2 + b_2 n/P_2 \tag{11}$$

So we are down to two equations in three unknowns, i.e., the three relative prices P_1/P_2, w/P_2, and n/P_2. One of those relative prices Cantillon could eliminate by assuming that labor was reproducible at a minimum menu and that "Men multiply like Mice in a barn if they have unlimited Means of Subsistence." Then the long-run money wage rate would equal the money value of that minimum menu:

$$w = c_1 P_1 \tag{12}$$

Insert the money value (12) of the minimum menu into (10) and (11) and arrive at two equations in two unknowns, i.e., relative price P_1/P_2 and real rent rate n/P_2. Solve the system for its two unknowns and find our good old Cantillon solutions from chapter 1:

$$\frac{P_1}{P_2} = \frac{b_1}{b_2 + (a_2/b_2 - a_1/b_1)b_1 b_2 c_1} \tag{13}$$

$$\frac{n}{P_2} = \frac{1 - a_1 c_1}{b_2 + (a_2/b_2 - a_1/b_1)b_1 b_2 c_1} \tag{14}$$

3.   Smith's Natural Price: Production Takes Time

In considering time-consuming production, Smith went beyond Cantillon. Capital will then be necessary; capitalists and profits will emerge and with them the third term of Smith's price equation (5). Samuelson (1977: 48-49) handled this case by making two simplifying assumptions. First, let there be a minimum rate of profit below which capitalists would decumulate. Competition among them will reduce the rate of profits r to that rate, a parameter. Second, let all capital be circulating capital invested in a one-year period of production. Capital stock is then simply a wage-and-rent fund, and (9) will be $P_i = (1 + r)(a_i w + b_i n)$. Writing it out for $i = 1, 2$, dividing each of the resulting equations by P_2 as before, using (12) as before, and solving for relative price under time-consuming production, we find

$$\frac{P_1}{P_2} = \frac{b_1}{b_2 + (a_2/b_2 - a_1/b_1)b_1 b_2 c_1 (1 + r)} \tag{15}$$

Even for time-consuming production, then, Smith had the equations needed. For $r = 0$ (15) collapses into (13). For $r > 0$ the rate of interest will matter for relative price except in the special case $a_2/b_2 = a_1/b_1$, i.e., where the two goods have the same number of men per acre or "labor intensity".

4.   Smith's Natural Price: Diminishing Returns?

Cantillon did not know of diminishing returns, but Turgot did. Did Smith? In his "canonical" model Samuelson (1977), (1978) said yes and assumed Smith to share them with Ricardo, Malthus, and Mill. Hollander (1980) could find diminishing returns in Smith only by a very selective choice of quotes.

If we side with Hollander and see no canonical model, we collapse Smith into Cantillon with capital easily added and find his relative prices safe. If we side with Samuelson and see a canonical model, we expand Smith into Ricardo and find his relative prices safe only if Ricardo's were. Were they? We shall see in chapter 3.

5.   Ricardo

Ricardo's macroeconomics visualized a one-crop economy. The closing pages of our chapter 3 will turn his macroeconomics into microeconomics simply by relaxing the one-crop assumption. There will then be several margins of cultivation, one for each crop. But Ricardo may still find his several margins by saying that portions of capital will be applied to each crop until price of crop equals marginal cost of producing it. That marginal cost will be a marginal labor cost including indirect labor with compound interest as well as direct labor. Does a labor theory of value hold, then?

Well if fixed and circulating capital were applied in the same proportion to all crops, and if the fixed capital had the same durability in all crops, relative prices would indeed be "regulated by the quantity of labor realized in each." If the fixed-circulating capital proportion or the durabilities differed among crops, the labor theory of value would have to be qualified, and Ricardo was aware of it.

What Ricardo was not aware of was more serious. His marginal cost did have in it something technologically given, i.e., the labor input coefficients involved in, first, building and, second, operating a physical unit of producers' goods. But marginal cost had in it something more, i.e., the derivatives dS_i/dX_i of physical capital stock required with respect to physical output. Those derivatives were variables. If tastes changed, microeconomic margins would change and with them the relative derivatives dS_i/dX_i and marginal costs. But tastes found no room in Ricardo and had to wait for Walras.

VI. SPATIAL GENERAL EQUILIBRIUM: VON THÜNEN

1. *Von Thünen*

Judging both men as theorists, Schumpeter (1954: 465) placed von Thünen above Ricardo. Samuelson (1983: 1487n) hailed von Thünen "as one of the great microeconomists of all time, a peer of Augustin Cournot and the often over-rated David Ricardo." Von Thünen's two major contributions were separated by a quarter-century. In *Part One* [1826 (1842), (1930), (1966)] von Thünen visualized a spatial general equilibrium which was to be the background against which he formulated in *Part Two* [1850 (1930), (1960), (1966)] a simultaneous determination of wage and interest rates. Here, following Samuelson (1983), we sketch von Thünen's vision of a spatial general equilibrium under the twin assumptions of instantaneous production and a single rural product.[1]

2. *Space and Price*

Consider an economy consisting of a single city surrounded on all sides by farmland of uniform fertility. The economy produces two prod-

---

[1]Samuelson (1983) offers a rigorous reformulation of von Thünen's two-or-more-rural-products case, von Thünen's famous rings.

ucts $i = 1, 2$. The first product, called the "rural" product, is produced by applying labor to the farmland. The second product, called the "urban" product, is produced in the city by labor alone. Either product may be consumed anywhere but exchanged against the other product only in the city. At its point of consumption or exchange the ith product has a delivered price P_i equaling its f.o.b. price at its point of origin *plus* the cost of shipping it, if needed, from its point of origin to its point of consumption or exchange.

If it moves at all, then, an urban product will always move outward into the country and have a delivered price P_2 rising with the distance from the city. If it moves at all, a rural product will always move inward into the city and have an f.o.b. price down on the farm declining with the distance from the city. A farmer producing it will apply labor to his land up to the point where the money wage rate equals the marginal product of labor valued at the f.o.b. price of produce. Two results follow. First, intensity of cultivation defined as labor applied per acre of land will be declining with the distance from the city. Second, rent defined as the residual left of f.o.b. revenue after deduction of labor cost will also be declining with the distance from the city. At some distance from the city, then, the cost of shipping the rural product will become prohibitive, rent become zero, and land become not worth cultivating. Here a frontier will be reached in the form of a perfect circle with the city as its center. Beyond that frontier there will be wilderness isolating the economy from the rest of the world, hence the title of von Thünen's book.

Unlike products, labor can move without cost and will do so until it is indifferent between locations. In or close to the city the delivered-price ratio P_1/P_2 between rural and urban products is high. Consequently, the real wage rate in terms of the rural product is low but compensated by a high real wage rate in terms of the urban product. Far out in the country the delivered-price ratio P_1/P_2 between rural and urban products is low. Here the real wage rate in terms of the urban product is low but compensated by a high real wage rate in terms of the rural product.

3. *The Equilibrating Variable*

The equilibrating variable of von Thünen's spatial general equilibrium is the delivered-price ratio P_1/P_2 *in the city*. If that ratio exceeds its equilibrium value, the city terms of trade will favor rural products and raise the overall real wage rate in the country above that of the city. The resulting migration from city to country will generate negative excess demand for the rural product and positive excess demand for the urban one, putting downward pressure on the ratio P_1/P_2.

If, on the other hand, that ratio falls short of its equilibrium value, the city terms of trade will favor urban products and raise the overall real wage rate in the city above that of the country. Labor will now migrate from country to city and generate positive excess demand for the rural product and negative excess demand for the urban one, putting upward pressure on the ratio P_1/P_2.

In section XI we shall see how von Thünen formulated his capital theory against the background of his spatial-equilibrium setting.

VII. MARGINAL PRODUCTIVITY: LONGFIELD

1. *Varying Capital at Constant Labor*

Turgot had applied gradually increasing "advances," and Ricardo gradually increasing "portions of capital," to a fixed quantity of land and watched their marginal productivities diminish. Like Turgot, Ricardo varied neither his capital with given labor nor his labor with given capital. The portion was unbreakable.

The first to break it up was Longfield, who (1834: 190) imagined "a number of intelligent and industrious men, placed in a fertile country, in full possession of all the gifts of nature, but utterly destitute of capital." A capitalist then appears and starts making tools. "Suppose," Longfield (1834: 191) continues, "those tools to be spades, or any other instruments of agricultural or manufacturing labour." Then "the number of such instruments increases in the hands of the same or different capitalists." "But as the quantity of capital increases within the country," Longfield (1834: 192) concludes, ". . . causes will come into operation to diminish the profits of this kind of instrument." So when physical capital stock is increased at constant labor employed, there will be diminishing marginal value productivity of capital, and, in Longfield's own words (1834: 193):

> . . . In every case the profits of capital will be regulated by that portion of it which is obliged to be employed with the least efficiency in assisting labour, since none will be diverted to this employment as long as the owner thereof can derive a greater profit by giving it any other direction.

2. *Varying Labor at Constant Capital?*

Having so successfully broken up the Ricardian bundle of labor and capital and varied physical capital stock at constant labor employed, did Longfield then turn around to vary labor employed at constant physical capital stock? And did he then find diminishing value marginal productivity of labor?

He did not. Longfield (1834: Lecture X) made a good beginning by saying "that the wages of the labourer depend upon the value of his labour" and correctly saw that value as the discounted value of labor's contribution to the product. Longfield's discount rate was the rate of profits and his discount period the period of production. He knew that labor cannot wait and must be paid at once. In Longfield's own words (1834: 212):

> Thus, if the rate of profits is ten percent per annum, and a commodity is fabricated by the labour of ten men, each contributing equal quantities and values of labour, and each being paid his wages, on an average, a year before the sale of the article. Then the wages of each labourer must be 1/11 of what it sells for, the remaining 1/11 going as profit to the capitalist; and this must equally happen whether the article is one of luxury or necessity.

Well and good, but notice, first, the words "each contributing equal quantities and values of labour." In other words, the productivity of labor being discounted is average productivity. A marginal value productivity of labor, let alone a diminishing one, is nowhere referred to by Longfield. Notice, second, that Longfield's determination of wages presupposes a rate of profits of ten percent. Longfield used a successive rather than a simultaneous approach. He was aware of it, even proud of it. Indeed, according to his preface (1834: vii), his own contribution was: "...to shew that the only order in which a correct analysis of the sources of revenue can be carried on is—1st. Rent. 2d. Profits. 3d. Wages."

Longfield accused his predecessors of having the wrong orders of succession: Adam Smith had had wages first, profits second, and rent third. Sir Edward West had had rent first, wages second, and profits third.

VIII. POLYPOLY: COURNOT AND BERTRAND

1. *Profit Maximization*

Ahead of von Thünen (1850), Cournot [1838 (1927)] wrote the first order condition for a profit maximum by setting the derivative of profits with respect to a decision variable equal to zero. But he was not only the father of formal profit maximization, the demand curve, the theory of monopoly, and the theory of duopoly. He was also the father of the general theory of the n-producers case; let us borrow a label from Ragnar Frisch [1933 (1951: 24)] and call it "polypoly." Cournot's theory was a crescendo of market structures ranging all the way from monopoly where $n = 1$ via duopoly, triopoly ..., etc. to pure competition, where n rises without bounds. His treatment was a tribute to the power and elegance of even elementary mathematics.

2. Cournot's "Law of Demand"

To Cournot cost was incidental to his problem and might be ignored as a first approximation, and we follow him. In his chapter V ("Of Monopoly") Cournot [1838 (1927: 57)] wrote his "law of demand" as

$$X = X(P) \tag{16}$$

expressing quantity sold as a function of price. In his chapter VII ("Of the Competition of Producers") Cournot [1838 (1927: 80)] found it "convenient to adopt the inverse notation"

$$P = P(X) \tag{17}$$

expressing price as a function of quantity sold.

Cournot treated separately the cases of 1, 2, ..., n producers, but his crescendo is easily compressed into the general case of n producers, as we shall now show.

3. The General Case of Polypoly

Let there be n producers, and let the quantity sold by the jth producer be X_j. Then market demand will be

$$X \equiv \sum_{j=1}^{n} X_j \tag{18}$$

Let the jth producer maximize his profits under the assumption that the quantity sold by all his rivals will stay put:

$$X - X_j = \text{a constant} \tag{19}$$

Differentiate (19) with respect to price P and find

$$\frac{dX_j}{dP} = \frac{dX}{dP} \tag{20}$$

Selling the quantity X_j at the price P and having no costs, the jth producer makes the profits PX_j. Let him maximize it by manipulating his X_j. A first-order condition for his maximum is

$$\frac{d(PX_j)}{dX_j} = P + \frac{dP}{dX_j} X_j = 0 \tag{21}$$

Thus Cournot was the first to write what much later became known as "marginal revenue." Now divide (21) by dP/dX_j, use the rule on derivatives of inverse functions, insert (20), and find

$$P \frac{dX}{dP} + X_j = 0 \qquad (22)$$

Sum (22) over all the n producers, use (18), and write the sum as

$$nP \frac{dX}{dP} + X = 0 \qquad (23)$$

which summarizes all of Cournot's results: for $n = 1$ (23) is identical to Cournot's eq. (4) on his page 82; for $n = 2$ (23) is identical to his eq. (3) on the same page; and for $n = 3, 4, \ldots, n$ (23) is identical to his unnumbered equations on page 84.

So far so good. But Cournot's (23) is still one equation in three variables, X, P, and dX/dP. Is there a simple interpretation of it? Let us find one. Let us rearrange Cournot's form (23), divide it by dX/dP, once again use the rule on derivatives of inverse functions, and write it

$$\frac{P}{X} = -\frac{1}{n} \frac{dP}{dX} \qquad (24)$$

To interpret (24), let us draw the market demand curve shown in figure III-1. For any point on it the ratio P/X is the ratio between its ordinate and its abscissa, hence represents the slope of a line connecting the origin with that point. The derivative dP/dX is the slope of the market

FIGURE III-1.
Crescendo of Cournot
Equilibria from
Monopoly (*M*) to
Unlimited Competition
(*U*)

Quantity Produced and Sold

demand curve itself at that point. In monopoly $n = 1$, and (24) then says that the former slope should equal *minus* the latter slope. Such is the case at point M. What does (24) say about polypoly? Well, if there are two producers, the former slope should equal *minus* one-half of the latter slope. If there are three producers, the former slope should equal *minus* one-third of the latter slope. If there are n producers, the former slope should equal *minus* one-nth of the latter slope. Generally the larger the number of producers, the lower the Cournot price.

What if the number of producers rises without bounds? If so, we have what Cournot [1838 (1927: 90)] calls "unlimited" competition, and (24) has the limit

$$\lim_{n \to \infty} (P/X) = 0 \tag{25}$$

What is the economic meaning of this limit? For the line connecting the origin with the equilibrium point to have the slope zero, the line must coincide with the horizontal axis. Then the equilibrium point is the point where the market demand curve intersects the horizontal axis, i.e., the point U—standing for "unlimited" competition. This makes sense: under pure competition producers sell at cost, and cost is zero.

We may summarize Cournot's results by saying that as market structure runs the gamut from monopoly to pure competition the equilibrium point on the market demand curve moves from M to U.

4. Bertrand

After forty-five years Cournot was reviewed—and misrepresented— by Bertrand (1883). Cournot's words and equations had been unambiguous. Under the assumption that the quantity sold by all his rivals would stay put, a Cournotian polypolist maximized his profits PX_j by manipulating his quantity X_j. A Cournotian polypolist, in other words, had a quantity policy. Ascribing it to Cournot, Bertrand posed quite a different problem. Under the assumption that the price charged by all his rivals would stay put, a Bertrandian polypolist maximized his profits PX_j by manipulating his price P. A Bertrandian polypolist, in other words, had a price policy. Assuming "qualité identique" (1883: 503), i.e., absence of product differentiation, Bertrand showed that any seller who lowered his price ever so slightly below that charged by all his rivals would get the entire market to himself. That would obviously go on until the profits of one or more polypolists had become zero.

IX. MARGINAL UTILITY: DUPUIT

1. *Bernoulli Still Neglected*

It would not be right to neglect results corresponding so well to practical business experience, Bernoulli had said. Yet neglected they were—not by probability theorists, of course: Laplace referred to Bernoulli's hypothesis and used it to distinguish between "fortune physique" defined as physical assets gained by a person and "fortune morale" defined as their value to him. Poisson, too, referred to Bernoulli's "fundamental formula." Psychologists did not neglect Bernoulli's results either. In the mid-nineteenth century, Fechner (1860) replaced Bernoulli's "gain" by an external stimulus and his "advantage" by the intensity of the resulting sensation, tried to measure them in the laboratory, and even found Bernoulli's inverse proportionality confirmed by experiment.

Only economists paid no attention. Adam Smith had repeated the value paradox as if neither Bernoulli nor Galiani had existed. For another century mainstream economists would believe that value in use could not explain value in exchange.

2. *Dupuit: Marginal Utility Measured by Price*

Dupuit [1844 (1952)] was an engineer interested in pricing of the services of public utilities like bridges, canals, highways, and railroads. In such cases of natural monopolies a downward-sloping demand curve suggests itself to a practical observer. First, he may think of its ordinates as measuring in terms of money—by proxy so to speak—marginal utility. Second, he may take the definite integral of it from zero to a given quantity consumed and think of that integral as measuring in terms of money—again by proxy—the total utility enjoyed from that quantity. Dupuit did both. In deriving utility from demand, he reversed the traditional roles of utility and demand: the traditional use of a utility function is to derive a demand function from it by maximizing it subject to a constraint. That was what Gossen did. His constraint was first a time constraint, then a toil constraint, as we shall see in section XII.

X. THE HALFWAY HOUSE: MILL

1. *John Stuart Mill*

Mill published his *Principles* (1848) twenty-seven years after the appearance of the third edition of Ricardo's—now complete with chapter 31 on machinery. After another twenty-seven years, Walras's *Eléments* (1874-1877) were arriving. When Schumpeter (1954: 603) called the house

Mill built a "halfway house" he must have meant not only intertemporally but also logically. Almost consistently, Mill stopped short of consistency—in his value theory and his capital theory. Let us look at them in turn.

2. *Mill's Value Theory*

In spelling out four things more clearly than any other English classicist had ever done, Mill was off to an excellent start.

First, he [1848 (1923: 446)] spelled out the demand curve "meaning, by the word demand, the quantity demanded, and remembering that this is not a fixed quantity, but in general varies according to the value." Cournot, as we saw, had written the demand function ten years before Mill, but Mill never refers to him and would have done so had he known him.

Second, Mill [1848 (1923: 446-447)] spelled out that positive excess demand will raise price: "... let us suppose that the demand at some particular time exceeds the supply. Competition takes place on the side of the buyers, and the value rises." Vice versa in the case of negative excess demand.

Third, Mill [1848 (1923: 447)] spelled out the elasticity of demand: "some may suppose [that] if the demand exceeds the supply by one-third, the value rises one-third. ... If the article is a necessary of life, which, rather than resign, people are willing to pay for at any price, a deficiency of one third may raise the price to double, triple, or quadruple."

Fourth, Mill [1848 (1923: 448)] spelled out equilibrium value: "The rise or the fall continues until the demand and supply are again equal to one another."

Well and good, but Mill stopped short of generalizing his four beautiful insights. He [1848 (1923: 448)] confined them to irreproducible commodities, called "the small class of commodities." As far as "the large class" of reproducible ones were concerned, Mill [1848 (1923: 456)] said, "demand and supply only determine the perturbations of value," "they themselves obey a superior force, which makes value gravitate towards Cost of Production," and [1848 (1923: 451)] "the cost of production, together with the ordinary profit, may ... be called the *necessary* price, or value, of all things made by labour and capital."

What, in turn, was "ordinary" profit? Much like Ricardo, Mill saw a minimum to profits. Ricardo's [1821 (1951, I: 122)] minimum had been "an adequate compensation for their trouble, and the risk which they must necessarily encounter in employing their capital productively." To Ricardo's trouble and risk Mill [1848 (1923: 407)] added abstinence: "The lowest rate of profit which can permanently exist, is that which is barely adequate, at the given place and time, to afford an equivalent for the abstinence, risk, and exertion implied in the employment of capital."

Mill freed himself from the Ricardian straitjacket of the labor theory of value and almost returned to Smith. Summing up his theory of relative price, Mill [1848 (1923: 480)] said:

> If one of two things commands, on the average, a greater value than the other, the cause must be that it requires for its production either a greater quantity of labour, or a kind of labour permanently paid at a higher rate; or that the capital, or part of the capital, which supports that labour, must be advanced for a longer period; or lastly, that the production is attended with some circumstance which requires to be compensated by a permanently higher rate of profit.
>
> Of these elements, the quantity of labour required for the production is the most important: the effect of the others is smaller, though none of them are insignificant.

Mill almost returned to Smith, we said. What separated them was the matter of rent. To see how, we must report on Mill's two subclasses of reproducible commodities.

In the first subclass, commodities were reproducible at constant cost per unit or, as Mill [1848 (1923: 451)] put it, "could be made by [labour and capital] in indefinite quantity." Here, was Mill justified in dismissing demand in favor of his "Cost of Production"? Let a demand curve intersect a horizontal supply curve. Then the ordinate (price) of the intersection point, but not the abscissa (quantity), will be the same for all possible demand curves. Demand, in other words, matters for allocation but not for price and could be dismissed if allocation theory were considered uninteresting.

In Mill's second subclass, commodities were only reproducible at rising cost per unit or, as Mill [1848 (1923: 469)] put it, in agriculture "doubling the labour does not double the produce." Here, value would be [1848 (1923: 471)] "determined by the cost of that portion of the supply which is produced and brought to market at the greatest expense." In this case was Mill justified in dismissing demand in favor of his "Cost of Production"? Let a demand curve intersect a rising supply curve. Then neither the ordinate (price) of the intersection point nor the abscissa (quantity) will be the same for all possible demand curves. Demand, in other words, matters for price no less than for allocation, hence could not even be dismissed by a pure price theory.

Mill's second subclass consisted of agricultural commodities. Here, would the rent of land be no part of the cost of production which determined price—as Ricardo had said? Or would the rent of land simply be an additional cost of production, along with the wages of labor and the profits of capital—as Smith had said?

Once again Mill stopped short of consistency and managed to hold *both* views! Mill [1848 (1923: 472)] was, first, of the Ricardian opinion that *within* agriculture "rent . . . forms no part of the cost of production which determines the value of agricultural produce." In [1848 (1923: 479)], discussing land allocated *between* agriculture and other uses, he took the opposite view: "But when land capable of yielding rent in agriculture is applied to some other purpose, the rent which it would have yielded is an element in the cost of production of the commodity which it is employed to produce."

In our next period, Jevons would ridicule such inconsistency and ask why the rent earned of land as pasture formed no part of the cost of producing wheat or why a potato field should not pay as well as a clover field or a clover field as a turnip field.

3. *Mill's Capital Theory*

Since Smith, English classicism knew two categories of capital, fixed and circulating. Ricardo [1821 (1951, I: 31)] saw fixed capital as "buildings and machinery [which] are valuable and durable" and circulating capital as "capital . . . employed in the payment of wages, which are expended on food and clothing."

By definition, then, labor and circulating capital were complementary: more circulating capital implied more demand for labor. Capital advanced the wage bill, and the wage bill could not be augmented by labor-union action.

But labor and fixed capital were substitutes, and Ricardo in his third edition, chapter 31, was the first to see them as such. Mill [1848 (1923: 94)] agreed that "all increase of fixed capital, when taking place at the expense of circulating, must be, at least temporarily, prejudicial to the interests of the labourers." But he [1848 (1923: 97)] did not believe in an either-or: "there is probably no country whose fixed capital increases in . . . more than proportion to its circulating." Well and good! But Mill stopped short of proving that under his stationary ratio between fixed and circulating capital the complementary effect would dominate the substitution effect.

Twenty-one years later Mill [1869 (1923: 991-993)] renounced the wage-fund doctrine. But he did so neither on the grounds that after all the substitution effect might dominate nor on the grounds that after all the ratio between fixed and circulating capital might be not stationary but rising. Instead, he simply admitted the possibility that labor unions could raise wages by squeezing the capitalist's consumption: out of his accumulated means, that capitalist "advances his personal and family expenses, exactly as he advances the wages of his labourers. . . . The less he expends on the one, the more may be expended on the other."

XI. MARGINAL PRODUCTIVITY CONTINUED: VON THÜNEN

1. *Ricardo's "Portion of Capital" Fully Broken Up: von Thünen*

Like Ricardo, von Thünen distinguished between labor absorbed in producing and labor absorbed in operating a physical capital stock of durable producers' goods like buildings, equipment, tools, and implements. Also like Ricardo, von Thünen assumed his durable producers' goods to be produced from labor alone and measured by the number of man-years of such labor embodied in them.

Unlike Ricardo, von Thünen never assumed a fixed proportion between such a physical capital stock and the number of men operating it. On the contrary, von Thünen's [1850 (1930: 484-508), (1960: 249-264)] very point was to consider a growing available physical capital stock equipping every man operating it successively with a physical capital stock embodying 0, 1, 2, . . ., 10 man-years of labor. Such variation of man-years of labor would undoubtedly mean variation of the physical form and functioning of the durable producers' goods themselves.

Our figure III-2 reproduces the first few lines of von Thünen's [1850 (1930: 507), (1960: 262)] numerical example. The numbers are his; only the notation and the diagram are ours. His numbers reveal four beautiful insights into the interdependence of the rates of wages and interest. They appear as the third through sixth columns of figure III-2.

First, von Thünen had a clear conception of marginal productivity, shown in our third column, as the partial derivative of physical output per man with respect to physical capital stock per man $\partial(X/L)/\partial(S/L) = \partial X/\partial S$, where labor employed L is kept constant.

Second, von Thünen had a clear conception of the share of output per man going to the capitalists—whoever they were. Capital's share per man, shown in our fourth column, was marginal product of capital *times* capital stock per man. Von Thünen [1850 (1930: 497), (1960: 257)] carefully explained why no part of physical capital stock could receive more than the marginal product of its last part. For a physical capital stock per man of $S/L = 3$, our figure III-2 shows marginal productivity as the slope $\partial X/\partial S$ of the tangent at C, or AB/BC. Consequently, the share of output per man going to the capitalists will be $(AB/BC)BC = AB$.

Third, von Thünen saw a Wicksell Effect. The share of output going to labor was physical output per man *minus* the share going to the capitalists. Labor's share was the real wage rate w/P per man, shown in our fifth

FIGURE III-2.
Effects of Growing
Capital Stock per Man:
von Thünen

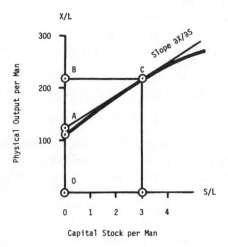

Capital Stock per Man

Capital Stock per Man	Physical Output per Man	Marginal Product of Capital	Capital's Share per Man	Real Wage Rate, w/P per Man	Interest Rate, r Percent
$S \over L$	$X \over L$	$\partial X \over \partial S$	$\partial X \over \partial S$ $S \over L$	$X \over L - {\partial X \over \partial S}{S \over L}$	$\partial X \over \partial S \Big/ {w \over P}$
0	110.0		0	110.0	
1	150.0	40.0	40.0	110.0	36.4
2	186.0	36.0	72.0	114.0	31.6
3	218.4	32.4	97.2	121.2	26.7

column of figure III-2 and as $OB - AB = OA$. At growing physical capital stock per man the point C moves to the right, the slope of its tangent declines, and labor's share OA rises. In von Thünen's [1850 (1930: 499), (1960: 258)] words "... the position of labor will become constantly more flourishing and brighter, the more machines are applied with the increase in capital."

Fourth, von Thünen clearly distinguished between the marginal product of capital, on the one hand, and its percentage rate of interest, on the other, defined as $(\partial X/\partial S)/(w/P) \equiv P(\partial X/\partial S)/w$ or simply dollars' worth of marginal product as a percentage of additional dollars invested. The rate of interest is shown in our sixth column and is declining for two reasons clearly separated by von Thünen [1850 (1930: 500), (1960: 259)]: growing capital stock per man will, first, reduce the numerator $\partial X/\partial S$ of the rate of interest and, second, raise its denominator w/P, as we just saw.

2. Does It Matter Who Hires Whom?

At the end of von Thünen's century, John Bates Clark, as we shall see later, would draw two diagrams. In his first diagram, Clark would plot variable labor on the horizontal axis and its marginal productivity on the vertical axis, keeping capital constant. Thus he would determine wages directly and interest residually. In his second diagram, Clark would plot variable capital on the horizontal axis and its marginal productivity on the vertical axis, keeping labor constant. Thus he was able to determine interest directly and wages residually. Clark would conclude that whether determined directly or residually, a distributive share would be the same. In short, it would not matter who hired whom.

Our own figure III-2 is nothing but Clark's second diagram. Did von Thünen also have Clark's first diagram? Certainly the idea of reversing variable and constant was familiar to him [1850 (1930: 584), (1960: 317)], when he suggested to "conversely consider capital as constant and the quantity of labor as growing . . ."

Euler's theorem tells us that it doesn't matter who hires whom if and only if there are constant returns to scale. Clark would overlook Euler's theorem. Did von Thünen overlook it? He never referred to it explicitly, but his intuition told him [1850 (1930: 546), (1960: 291)] to "remember that we are here talking. . . of an estate the size of the other estates of the Isolated State. Otherwise there will be a disturbing element; namely the influence of the different magnitudes of the estates on the labor product and the revenue."

Still, with all his reversal of variable and constant and with his intuitive understanding of Euler's theorem, von Thünen was to spoil his analysis of the distributive shares.

3. Who Were von Thünen's Capitalists?

Von Thünen's numerical example reproduced in our figure III-2 did not specify who his capitalists were and was safely finished before he [1850 (1930: 542), (1960: 288)] specified them and their maximands.

Since von Thünen's labor was free to move, he let a group of workers move to the frontier and set up a colony. Out there rent was zero, so wages and interest would be the only distributive shares. After arriving at the frontier, the group would split into two teams.

The first team was constructing the durable producers' goods needed by the colony: "setting up buildings, making tools." After constructing the durable producers' goods, the first team would own them, hence be entrepreneurs hiring labor to operate them.

The second team was the labor hired to operate the durable producers' goods constructed by the first team. Of their real wage rate w/P wage earners would consume their subsistence minimum c, save the rest $w/P - c$, and lend it to the first team to finance the construction of durable producers' goods. On its lending the second team would earn the rate of interest r. The second team, then, would constitute at the same time labor and capitalists of von Thünen's play.

Not only were the workers of the second team capitalists, they were the only ones. On the frontier rent was zero—which is why von Thünen moved out there. But what about inframarginal landlords, couldn't they do some of the saving? They were never mentioned. The tacit assumption necessary to confine the play to the frontier must be that unlike labor, saving could not move: the frontier colony had access to no saving other than its own. What about entrepreneurs, couldn't they do some of the saving? Because they were labor-turned-entrepreneurs, they moved with labor. But precisely because of such freedom of entry and exit, von Thünen's entrepreneurs—like von Neumann ones—would make no profits over and above their wage and interest bill. These, then, were von Thünen's actors. What were their maximands?

Clarkian capitalists hiring labor were maximizing their real interest-bill residual. So were von Thünen's labor-turned entrepreneurs: no difference between Clark and von Thünen here. But Clarkian labor hiring capital was maximizing its real wage-bill residual. Von Thünen's labor-turned-savers was doing no such thing but was asking for a real wage rate w/P which would maximize the real interest bill $(w/P - c)r$ on its saving. In von Thünen's frontier colony, then, social harmony would prevail: both teams of workers would have the same maximand!

We may object to von Thünen's model of a frontier colony on two levels, i.e., first to his choice of maximand: will labor-turned-saver really be saver first and wage earner second? Second, we may object to von Thünen's maximization of his maximand.

4. Von Thünen's Tombstone Formula

Given his odd maximand, how did von Thünen [1850 (1930: 549-551), (1960: 292-295)] maximize it? Differentiating his maximand $(w/P - c)r$ with respect to the real wage rate w/P he set the derivative equal to zero. Doing so he treated, first, his subsistence minimum a (our c) as a constant, as he should. But he also treated as constants, second, his capital stock per man q (our S/L) and, third, his output per man p (our X/L). Doing so, he found the real wage rate $w/P = \sqrt{ap}$, of which he thought so highly that he had it engraved on his tombstone!

But doing so, he also ignored his own [1850 (1930: 507), (1960: 262)] earlier numerical example (our figure III-2) with its beautiful insights into the interdependence of the wage and interest rates. As we saw in that numerical example, a volume of saving adequate to equip each man with, say, 2 physical units of capital would give the economy a physical output per man of $X/L = 186.0$ and wage and interest rates of $w/P = 114.0$ and $r = 31.6$ percent. Such wage and interest rates, and only those, would induce entrepreneurs to borrow all saving and employ all labor available to them. A different volume of saving adequate to equip each man with, say, 3 physical units of capital would give the economy a physical output per man of $X/L = 218.4$ and wage and interest rates of $w/P = 121.2$ and $r = 26.7$ percent. Again such wage and interest rates, and only those, would induce entrepreneurs to borrow all saving and employ all labor available to them.

If von Thünen's frontier colonists knew what they were doing, then, they would have noticed that different volumes of saving would go with a different physical capital stock per man S/L, a different physical output per man X/L, and a different real wage rate w/P. Having noticed that interdependence, they could not have treated S/L and X/L as constants when optimizing w/P, and von Thünen's tombstone formula would have been irrelevant to them.

5. *Still No Partial Derivative with Respect to Land Itself*

Directly von Thünen never took the partial derivative of produce with respect to land itself. But John Stuart Mill did, as we saw above, discuss alternative uses of land—if only agricultural versus nonagricultural uses. Here he correctly saw that rent in one use is an opportunity cost to other uses.

XII. MARGINAL UTILITY CONTINUED: GOSSEN

1. *Gossen: Maximize Enjoyment Subject to a Time Constraint*

Consumption takes time, and on his horizontal axis Gossen [1854 (1889: 8)] began by plotting time available for a single enjoyment ("Genuss"). On his vertical axis he plotted incremental enjoyment per incremental time and formulated his first rule [1854 (1889: 4-5)]: "The size of one and the same enjoyment served without interruption will diminish steadily until at last satiation is reached" (my translation). The resulting curve may be linear or nonlinear. Until some day the measurement of enjoyment became possible, Gossen for simplicity's sake chose a linear form.

Next Gossen considered four different enjoyments, each with its own linearly declining marginal-enjoyment curve and subject to a common time constraint. Gossen formulated his second rule [1854 (1889: 12)]:

Let enjoyment-maximizing man be free to choose among several enjoyments. Let his time not permit him to reach satiation in all of them. Before serving himself to satiation with the greatest of them, he must serve all of them partially and in such proportion that the size of his enjoyment of the moment at which his serving is being discontinued, is the same for all enjoyments (my translation).

To illustrate his second rule, Gossen added horizontally his four linearly declining marginal-enjoyment curves and found a composite marginal-enjoyment curve consisting of four linear segments. Lastly he generalized his four-segment curve into a smooth curve convex to the time axis.

2. *Gossen: Maximize Enjoyment Subject to a Toil Constraint*

Finally Gossen introduced consumers' goods produced by toil and wanted to find a unit of measurement common to all consumers' goods. To understand his unit, let us begin with a Cantillon-Leontief input-output coefficient $a_i \equiv$ man-hours absorbed in producing one physical unit of the ith good. Gossen's unit was its reciprocal $1/a_i \equiv$ physical units of ith good produced by one man-hour. With this unit of measurement common to all consumers' goods applied on the horizontal axis, equal distance would always mean equal toil.

The first few hours of daily toil may be enjoyable exercise, and Gossen added such enjoyment of toil to the enjoyment of its fruits. Soon, however, toil will be trouble ("Beschwerde"), and Gossen subtracted such trouble of toil from the enjoyment of its fruits. He could then formulate his third rule [1854 (1889: 45)]:

Enjoyment-maximizing man should allocate his time and toil among the serving of different enjoyments in such a way that the last atom of any enjoyment equals the trouble it would have caused him, had that atom been created in the last moment of toil (my translation).

3. *Gossen: Interaction Among Individuals. Market Price*

Next, Gossen [1854 (1889: 80-102)] considered interaction among individuals, first in the form of barter. Here, each individual parts with units having a low marginal utility to him and receives units having a high one. Like Bernoulli, Gossen slips once and makes interpersonal utility comparisons [1854 (1889: 85)]. But his demonstration of the gain to each individual, inherent in barter, is unaffected by his slip. The inherent gain will encourage division of labor. Money will be introduced, and barter will be replaced by trade, encouraging division of labor even more.

With money and trade, goods will have prices, and prices will equalize supply and demand. Positive excess demand will raise price and negative excess demand lower it. If at such equilibrium prices it is more rewarding ("besser belohnt") to produce one commodity than another, labor will re-allocate itself among commodities until the reward ("Belohnung") is the same everywhere.

Gossen [1854 (1889: 135-136)] used the concept if not the name of the elasticity of demand. A higher price of a good will force the consumer to save on something. If the good is a necessity, the consumer will reduce his consumption of it as little as possible and consequently have less income to spend on all other goods. But if the good is a luxury, the consumer will reduce his consumption of it so much that he has more income to spend on all other goods.

Gossen [1854 (1889: 102-133)] finally introduced the concept of rent. Working in certain locations is more rewarding than working in others. But even with freedom of entry and exit, not everybody can settle in the best locations. Competition among producers will enable owners of land in such locations to charge a rent for its use—thus increasing their own enjoyment and reducing that of their tenants.

The last half of Gossen's book discussed child labor, education, equality of the sexes, bimetallism, paper money, usury laws, socialism, and communism. The book had no chapters, sections, or headings, hence no table of contents. The mathematics was simple but tedious. Like Cinderella, the book went unnoticed, and it took a Jevons (1879: preface) to spot it—a quarter-century after its publication.

XIII. END OF AN EPOCH: MARX

Before its end, the best minds of our period had discovered the demand function, marginal utility, marginal productivity, and the general interdependence among the rates of wages, interest, and rent. To Marx such discoveries meant nothing. While Mill had freed himself from the straitjacket of the labor theory of value, Marx tightened it further around himself.

We shall devote our chapter 4 to Marx. In Marx, surplus value is generated by the application of variable capital but never by the application of constant capital. With this beginning, Marx himself had created most of the logical difficulties haunting him. We shall show that his system suffered from three *non sequiturs*: first, that rates of surplus value should be equalized among industries; second, that under technological progress the rate of profit should be falling; and third, that the real wage rate should also be falling.

REFERENCES

J. Bertrand, "Théorie mathématique de la richesse sociale," *Journal des savants*, Sep. 1883, 499-508.

R. Cantillon, *Essai sur la nature du commerce en général*, written around 1730, published 1755 referring to a fictitious publisher; edited and translated into English by Henry Higgs, C.B., London, 1931.

A. A. Cournot, *Recherches sur les principes mathématiques de la théorie des richesses*, Paris, 1838, translated as *Researches into the Mathematical Principles of the Theory of Wealth* by N. T. Bacon, New York, 1927.

J. Dupuit, "De la mesure de l'utilité des travaux publics," *Annales des ponts et chaussées*, 1844, translated as "On the Measurement of Utility of Public Works," *International Economic Papers*, 1952, *2*, 83-110.

W. Eltis, *The Classical Theory of Economic Growth*, London, 1984.

G. T. Fechner, *Elemente der Psychophysik*, Leipzig, 1860.

R. Frisch, "Monopole—polypole—la notion de force dans l'économie," supplement to *Nationaløkonomisk Tidsskrift*, Apr. 1933, translated as "Monopoly—Polypoly—the Concept of Force in the Economy," *International Economic Papers*, 1951, *1*, 23-26.

F. Galiani, *Della moneta*, Naples, 1751.

H. H. Gossen, *Entwickelung der Gesetze des menschlichen Verkehrs und der daraus fliessenden Regeln für menschliches Handeln*, Braunschweig, 1854, Berlin, 1889, translated as *The Laws of Human Relations and the Rules of Human Action Derived Therefrom* by R. C. Blitz, Cambridge, Mass., 1983.

A. H. Hansen, *Business Cycles and National Income*, New York, 1951.

S. Hollander, "On Professor Samuelson's Canonical Classical Model of Political Economy," *J. Econ. Lit.*, June 1980, *18*, 559-574.

W. S. Jevons, *The Theory of Political Economy*, London, 1871, second edition, London 1879, edited with notes and an extension of the bibliography by H. S. Jevons, London, 1931.

J. M. Lauderdale, *An Inquiry into the Nature and Origin of Public Wealth and into the Means and Causes of its Increase*, Edinburgh and London, 1804.

M. Longfield, *Lectures on Political Economy*, Dublin and London, 1834.

T. R. Malthus, *Essay on Population*, London, 1798.

————, *Principles of Political Economy*, London, 1820.

K. Marx, *Theorien über den Mehrwert*, K. Kautsky (ed.), Stuttgart 1905-1910, Berlin, 1923.

J. S. Mill, *Principles of Political Economy with Some of Their Applications to Social Philosophy*, London, 1848, 1923 edition by W. J. Ashley included later writings by Mill such as the May 1869 review article in the *Fortnightly Review* renouncing the wage-fund doctrine.

L. L. Pasinetti, "A Mathematical Formulation of the Ricardian System," *Rev. Econ. Stud.*, Feb. 1960, *27*, 78-98.

D. Ricardo, *The Principles of Political Economy and Taxation*, third edition, London, 1821, reprinted in *The Works and Correspondence of David Ricardo*, P. Sraffa and M. H. Dobb (eds.), vol. I, New York, 1951.

————, *Pamphlets and Papers, 1815-1823* reprinted in *The Works and Corre-*

spondence of David Ricardo, P. Sraffa and M. H. Dobb (eds.), vol. IV, New York, 1951.

P. A. Samuelson, "A Modern Treatment of the Ricardian Economy," *Quart. J. Econ.*, Feb.-May 1959, *73*, 1-35 and 217-231.

———, "A Modern Theorist's Vindication of Adam Smith," *Amer. Econ. Rev.*, Feb. 1977, *67*, 42-49.

———, "The Canonical Classical Model of Political Economy," *J. Econ. Lit.*, Dec. 1978, *16*, 1415-1434.

———, "Thünen at Two Hundred," *J. Econ. Lit.*, Dec. 1983, *21*, 1468-1488.

J.-B. Say, *Traité d'économie politique*, Paris, 1803; translated as *A Treatise on Political Economy* by C. R. Prinsep, Philadelphia, 1830.

J. A. Schumpeter, *History of Economic Analysis*, New York, 1954.

A. Smith, *An Inquiry into the Nature and Causes of the Wealth of Nations*, Edinburgh, 1776, "new" edition, Glasgow, 1805.

J. H. von Thünen, *Der isolierte Staat in Beziehung auf Landwirtschaft und Nationalökonomie*, Hamburg, 1826; second revised edition published as *Erster Teil*, Rostock, 1842 and *Zweiter Teil*, Rostock 1850; published jointly, Jena, 1930; partially translated by C. M. Wartenberg in P. Hall (ed.), *Von Thünen's Isolated State*, Oxford, 1966. The second part was translated by B. W. Dempsey, S.J., in his *The Frontier Wage, Jesuit Studies*, Chicago, 1960. Dempsey himself was primarily interested in the profit-sharing aspect of von Thünen's tombstone formula, but we must all be grateful for his careful translation which differs favorably from Wartenberg's, especially in von Thünen's mathematical passages.

A. R. J. Turgot, "Réflexions sur la formation et la distribution des richesses," *Ephémérides du citoyen*, November 1769-January 1770, reprinted in E. Daire (ed.), *Oeuvres de Turgot*, Paris, 1844, translated as *Reflections on the Formation and the Distribution of Riches*, New York, 1922.

L. Walras, *Eléments d'économie politique pure*, Lausanne, Paris, and Basle, 1874-1877, translated as *Elements of Pure Economics or the Theory of Social Wealth* by W. Jaffé, Homewood, Ill., 1954.

CHAPTER *3*   Sustainable Population and the Labor Theory of Value

RICARDO (1772-1823)

> *I shall enter into some enquiry respecting the influence of machinery on the interests of the different classes of society, a subject of great importance, and one which appears never to have been investigated in a manner to lead to any certain or satisfactory results.*
>
> Ricardo [1821 (1951: 386)]

I. INTRODUCTION

1. *Ricardo's Problem*

Like Cantillon, Ricardo wished to determine relative price and total sustainable employment in an economy. There were other similarities. In Cantillon and Ricardo we find the same emphasis on irreproducible land and reproducible labor. In Ricardo, too, "Men multiply like Mice in a barn if they have unlimited Means of Subsistence." Both Cantillon and Ricardo tried to explain relative price by reducing all inputs to a single one. Cantillon reduced them to land, Ricardo to labor.

What Cantillon saw around him was prerevolutionary and preindustrial France, and with few but powerful strokes he painted a vivid picture of it. His inputs were land and labor. What Ricardo saw around him was the havoc played by the new cotton machinery and the steam engine. In Schumpeter's words (1954: 693), "the results began to pour forth from 1815 on." They poured forth so swiftly and so powerfully that Ricardo had to have three inputs, land, labor, and capital, and between his first edition in 1817 and his third in 1821 had to add a new chapter "On Machinery."

2. *Ricardo's Method*

Ricardo used nothing but simple English bristling with precise and specific numerical examples. In Cantillon and Ricardo we find the same ease with abstractions, the same mathematical mind without mathematical training. The difference was Ricardo's marginalism. When he combined labor and fixed capital in his "portion of capital," Ricardo was not

94

a marginalist. But he was, when he varied his portions on a fixed quantity of land and observed the diminishing marginal productivity of the portions.

3. *Our Own Restatement*

Ricardo has been restated algebraically by Whewell, Samuelson, and Pasinetti. Whewell's (1833) premises were not consistent with Ricardo's. Neither Samuelson (1959) nor Pasinetti (1960) incorporated durable producers' goods ("machinery"). Following Brems (1970) we shall fit them in snugly and examine technological progress embodied in them.

Let the notation of our restatement be as follows.

4. *Variables*

H ≡ revenue *minus* operating labor cost
I ≡ physical output of producers' goods (investment)
J ≡ present net worth of an investment project
k ≡ present gross worth of an investment project
L ≡ labor employed
P ≡ price of consumers' goods
p ≡ price of producers' goods
S ≡ physical capital stock of manned producers' goods ("portions of capital")
w ≡ money wage rate
X ≡ physical output of consumers' goods

5. *Parameters*

α ≡ multiplicative factor of production function
a_1 ≡ labor absorbed in producing one physical unit of producers' goods
a_2 ≡ labor absorbed in operating one physical unit of producers' goods per unit of time
β ≡ elasticity of physical output with respect to physical capital stock
γ ≡ elasticity of physical output with respect to land
N ≡ land
r ≡ rate of interest or profit
u ≡ useful life of producers' goods

The symbol e is Euler's number, the base of natural logarithms. The symbol m, to be defined in eq. (10), stands for an agglomeration of parameters. The symbol t is general time. The symbol τ is present time.

II. THE MODEL

1. Fixed and Circulating Capital

Since we wish to include fixed capital in our restatement of Ricardo, let us begin with the distinction between fixed and circulating capital expressed in Ricardo's own words [1821 (1951: 31)]:

> A steam-engine will last longer than a ship, a ship than the clothing of the labourer, and the clothing of the labourer longer than the food which he consumes.

> According as capital is rapidly perishable, and requires to be frequently reproduced, or is of slow consumption, it is classed under the heads of circulating, or of fixed capital. A brewer, whose buildings and machinery are valuable and durable, is said to employ a large portion of fixed capital: on the contrary, a shoemaker, whose capital is chiefly employed in the payment of wages, which are expended on food and clothing, commodities more perishable than buildings and machinery, is said to employ a large proportion of his capital as circulating capital.

A Ricardian model including fixed capital must have at least two industries in it, a producers' and a consumers' goods industry; let us call them 1 and 2, respectively.

2. The Producers' Goods Industry

The producers' goods industry produced tools and implements used by farmers and was delightfully simple: its production function had only one input in it, i.e., labor. Let a_1 be the labor absorbed in producing one physical unit of producers' goods, then the production function is simply

$$L_1 = a_1 I \tag{1}$$

where a_1 is a technological parameter. Let there be pure competition and freedom of entry and exit in the producers' goods industry, then the price of producers' goods will equal their cost of production per unit:

$$p = a_1 w \tag{2}$$

3. The Consumers' Goods Industry

Ricardo's consumers' goods industry was farming and was less simple. Its production function had three inputs in it, i.e., land, labor, and fixed capital in the form of durable producers' goods such as "the plough and the thrashing machine." Ricardo, however, liked to think of what he called "a portion of capital." Such a portion was a bundle of labor and fixed capital: let a_2 be the labor absorbed in operating one physical unit of producers' goods per unit of time, then

$$L_2 = a_2 S \tag{3}$$

A portion of capital, in other words, is one physical unit of producers' goods properly manned for operation. By physical capital stock we shall mean a stock of producers' goods thus manned.

When farmers applied more portions of capital to a given piece of land, output would rise but by decreasing increments. Let us simulate that relationship by the linearly homogeneous production function

$$X = \alpha S^\beta N^\gamma \tag{4}$$

where $0 < \beta < 1; 0 < \gamma < 1; \beta + \gamma = 1; \alpha > 0;$ and $N > 0$. X and S are variables, α and N parameters.

4. *Desired Capital Stock*

We begin with a bit of theory of the firm. Let the firm be a farm. Let the farmer cultivate a given piece of land of size N and consider acquiring a capital stock of S new physical units of producers' goods whose useful life is u. So he must be planning for u years, not just for one year at a time. Consequently, he must maximize present net worth, not just annual profits. Let him produce an annual output of X consumers' goods to be sold at the price P. His revenue would then be PX. Since a_2 was the labor absorbed in operating one physical unit of producers' goods per unit of time, and w was the money wage rate, his operating labor cost on his entire capital stock would be $a_2 Sw$. At time t, then, his revenue *minus* operating labor cost would be

$$H \equiv PX - a_2 Sw \tag{5}$$

and per small fraction dt of a year located at time t in the future his revenue *minus* operating labor cost would be Hdt.

Let there be a market in which money may be placed or borrowed at the stationary rate of interest r. Let that rate be applied when discounting future cash flows. As seen from the present time τ, then, his revenue *minus* operating labor cost would be $e^{-r(t-\tau)}Hdt$. Define the present gross worth of the investment project as the present worth of the sum total of all future revenue *minus* operating labor cost over the entire useful life u of the new capital stock S or

$$k(\tau) \equiv \int_\tau^{\tau+u} e^{-r(t-\tau)}Hdt$$

Here H as defined by (5) is not a function of t, hence may be taken outside the integral sign. The rate of interest r was said to be stationary, hence the coefficient of t is stationary. As a result, find the integral to be

$$k = \frac{1 - e^{-ru}}{r} H \tag{6}$$

Let p be the price of a new physical unit of producers' goods. Assume the salvage value of the unit to be zero. The present net worth of the investment project is defined as the present gross worth of the investment project (6) *minus* the cost of acquisition of the new capital stock S or

$$J \equiv k - pS \tag{7}$$

Insert (2), (5), and (6) into (7) and write the present net worth of the investment project as

$$J = \frac{1 - e^{-ru}}{r} (PX - a_2 Sw) - a_1 Sw \tag{8}$$

Desired capital stock is that capital stock which maximizes present net worth (8). The first-order condition for a present-net-worth maximum is that the first derivative of (8) with respect to S be zero. Now to our farmer, the operating characteristic a_2 with which the new producers' goods come, the structural parameters α, β, and γ of his production function, the price P at which he may sell his produce, the price $p = a_1 w$ at which he may purchase his durable producers' goods, the rate of interest r at which he may place or borrow his money, the useful life u with which the new producers' goods come, and the money wage rate w at which he may hire his farmhands, are all beyond his control. So when differentiating (8) with respect to S we must treat a_1, a_2, α, β, γ, P, p, r, u, and w as constants and find the first-order condition

$$\frac{dJ}{dS} = \frac{1 - e^{-ru}}{r} \left(P \frac{dX}{dS} - a_2 w \right) - a_1 w = 0 \tag{9}$$

Use our production function (4) to carry out the derivation dX/dS and solve (9) for desired capital stock

$$S = \left(\frac{\alpha \beta}{mw/P} \right)^{1/\gamma} N \tag{10}$$

where

$$m \equiv a_1 r/(1 - e^{-ru}) + a_2$$

The second-order condition for a present-net-worth maximum is that the second derivative of (8) with respect to S be negative:

$$\frac{d^2 J}{dS^2} = \alpha\beta(\beta - 1)PS^{\beta-2}N^\gamma \frac{1 - e^{-ru}}{r} < 0 \tag{11}$$

which it is, because $0 < \beta < 1$.

So much theory of the firm. Now for aggregation. Think of our solution (10) for desired capital stock as having been derived for an individual farmer, then everything except his land N on the right-hand side of (10) is common to all farmers. So in (10) factor out all common factors, sum over all farmers, and find N to be the sum of all land under cultivation. Are the individual lots of land additive? Assume them to be of the same quality, then they are. Ricardo made no such assumption, but his realistic detail is unnecessary for his theory: he could still have his margin of cultivation if all land were of the same quality.

Having completed our aggregation, we find S to be national desired capital stock, and it is now very easy to find national desired investment.

5. *Desired Investment*

Ricardo's long-run equilibrium is a stationary economy having no net investment. But in a stationary economy with a finite useful life u of producers' goods there is replacement of retired producers' goods. Let age distribution be even, then each year $1/u$ of the physical capital stock is retired and must be replaced:

$$I = S/u \tag{12}$$

Both factor prices, the real wage rate w/P and the rate of interest r, occur in our solution (10) for desired capital stock. As we shall now see, Ricardo considered both of them to be parameters.

6. *The Real Wage Rate*

The real wage rate w/P must, in the long run, be high enough to "enable the labourers, one with another, to subsist and to perpetuate their race, without either increase or diminution" [1821 (1951: 93)]. If the real wage rate were higher than this subsistence minimum, population would rise and thus depress the real wage rate. And if the real wage rate were lower than this subsistence minimum, population would fall and thus raise the real wage rate. To Ricardo, then, while the money wage rate w and the price of consumers' goods P are variables, the real wage rate w/P is a parameter.

7. *The Rate of Interest or Profit*

Ricardo never distinguished between capitalists and entrepreneurs and consequently never distinguished between the rate of interest and the rate of profits. As for the latter, it had a minimum—as did the real wage rate. In Ricardo's own words [1821 (1951: 122)]: "The farmer and manufacturer can no more live without profit than the labourer without wages." If the rate of profit were higher than "an adequate compensation for their trouble, and the risk which they must necessarily encounter in employing their capital productively," accumulation would rise and depress the rate. And if the rate were lower than that minimum, accumulation would fall and thus raise the rate. Let our rate of interest or profit r, representing the cost of money capital to the firm, be that minimum. To Ricardo, then, the rate of interest or profit r is a parameter.

III. SOLUTION FOR SUSTAINABLE EMPLOYMENT

1. *Finding the Solution*

Aggregate employment equals the sum of labor employed in the two industries:

$$L \equiv L_1 + L_2 \tag{13}$$

Insert (10) into (3) and (12). Insert (12) into (1). Insert the results into (13) and find the solution for sustainable employment

$$L = (a_1/u + a_2) \left(\frac{\alpha\beta}{mw/P} \right)^{1/\gamma} N \tag{14}$$

where m stands for (10). Here, then, is the total sustainable employment expressed in terms of parameters alone. The employment (14) will sustain itself at the subsistence minimum as well as ensure the farmers and manufacturers a normal rate of interest on their capital. Towards the end of his chapter 5 on wages Ricardo warned against all social-security schemes:[1] if public policy tried to make the economy support a labor force in excess of the sustainable one—our (14)—only unemployment and starvation could result—a conclusion earning economics the label of "dismal science"!

Within the Ricardian system technological progress represented the only hope for a larger employment and with it, a larger population. How sensitive is our solution (14) to technological progress? Ricardo made a clear distinction between disembodied and embodied technological progress.

---

[1]Social security was pioneered in an atmosphere not contaminated by classical—or any other—economic theory, i.e., the atmosphere of Bismarck's *Reich*.

2. *Sensitivity of Sustainable Employment to Disembodied*
    Technological Progress

Ricardo [1821 (1951: 80-81)] exemplified disembodied technological progress "by the introduction of the turnip husbandry, or by the use of a more invigorating manure" and described its effect as raising the contributions of successive portions of capital:

> If, for example, the successive portions of capital yielded 100, 90, 80, 70, ... my rent would be 60 whilst the produce would be 340. If, instead of 100, 90, 80, 70, the produce should be increased to 125, 115, 105, 95, the rent would still be 60 whilst the produce would be increased to 440.

This is precisely the kind of technological progress nowadays called disembodied and represented by the growth of the multiplicative factor α in the production function (4) above. How does such progress affect total sustainable employment L? The elasticity of L with respect to α appears immediately from (14):

$$\frac{\partial L}{\partial \alpha} \frac{\alpha}{L} = \frac{1}{\gamma} \tag{15}$$

Since $0 < \gamma < 1$, this elasticity is positive: disembodied technological progress will raise sustainable employment. This agrees with Ricardo: such improvements "give a great stimulus to population."

3. *Sensitivity of Sustainable Employment to Embodied Technological*
    Progress

Ricardo [1821 (1951: 82)] then turns to a very different kind of technological progress:

> Such improvements do not increase the productive powers of the land; but they enable us to obtain its produce with less labour. They are rather directed to the formation of the capital applied to the land, than to the cultivation of the land itself. Improvements in agricultural implements, such as the plough and the thrashing machine, economy in the use of horses employed in husbandry, and a better knowledge of the veterinary art, are of this nature.

This is embodied technological progress, and it may take two alternative forms. First, it may reduce the labor a_1 absorbed in producing one physical unit of producers' good. Reducing a_1 can be seen as an example of process innovation within the producers' goods industry: the same quality of producers' goods may now be produced with less labor input per unit of output.

Second, embodied technological progress may reduce the labor a_2 absorbed in operating one physical unit of producers' good per unit of time. Reducing a_2 can be seen as an example of product innovation within the producers' goods industry: with the same labor input per unit of output, a higher—more automatic—quality of producers' goods may now be produced—requiring less labor to operate it.

Both improvements, whether reducing a_1 or a_2, represent reductions of m as defined by (10), and the elasticity of S with respect to m appears immediately from our solution (10) for desired capital stock:

$$\frac{\partial S}{\partial m} \frac{m}{S} = -\frac{1}{\gamma} \tag{16}$$

Since $0 < \gamma < 1$, this elasticity is negative: embodied technological progress, whether reducing a_1 or a_2, will raise physical desired capital stock. But what will it do to sustainable employment? Here, two forces are at work in opposite directions: while the number of physical units of producers' goods S is up, it now takes less labor to either build (a_1) or operate (a_2) each physical unit. Go back to our solution (14) for sustainable employment L containing the m defined in (10). Take the partial derivatives of L with respect to a_1 and a_2, using the chain rule

$$\frac{\partial[(1/m)^{1/\gamma}]}{\partial a_i} = \frac{\partial[(1/m)^{1/\gamma}]}{\partial(1/m)} \frac{\partial(1/m)}{\partial m} \frac{\partial m}{\partial a_i} = -\frac{1}{\gamma m}(1/m)^{1/\gamma} \frac{\partial m}{\partial a_i}$$

where $i = 1, 2$. Then use elasticities rather than partial derivatives of L, thus permitting things to cancel. In the numerators of those elasticities, use the assumption made in (4) that $\beta + \gamma = 1$ to write $\gamma = 1 - \beta$. Rearrange and find the two elasticities

$$\frac{\partial L}{\partial a_1} \frac{a_1}{L} = -\frac{(ru + e^{-ru} - 1)a_2/(1 - e^{-ru}) + \beta m}{(a_1/u + a_2)\gamma m} \frac{a_1}{u} \tag{17}$$

$$\frac{\partial L}{\partial a_2} \frac{a_2}{L} = -\frac{[(1 - e^{-ru})/(ru) - \gamma]a_1 r/(1 - e^{-ru}) + \beta a_2}{(a_1/u + a_2)\gamma m} a_2 \tag{18}$$

What are the signs of these two elasticities?

The first elasticity (17) is straightforward: a table of powers of e will show that $ru + e^{-ru} - 1$ is positive for any $ru > 0$, hence under the assumptions made, the elasticity (17) is unequivocally negative: embodied technological progress reducing the labor a_1 absorbed in producing one physical unit of producers' good will raise sustainable employment.

The second elasticity (18) is less straightforward. Could the bracket in its numerator be negative? Ultimately that question is an empirical one, so let us examine the sign of that bracket within empirically plausible ranges of the values of our parameters γ, r, and u. What are such ranges? As for r, Kuznets (1966: 421) found the rate of return on corporate assets to be 0.13 and 0.06 in underdeveloped and developed economies, respectively. These values are on the high side, because the return on non-corporate assets is lower than on corporate ones.

As for u, the U.S. Department of Commerce [(1966), (1969), and later] estimated useful lives of structures and equipment to be from 20 to 30 years in the United States. On underdeveloped economies Kuznets is silent.

For empirically plausible values of r and u table 3-1 shows the values of the function $(1 - e^{-ru})/(ru)$. For the bracket of (18) to be positive, γ will have to be less than the values shown of that function. Is it? In our production function (4) γ is the elasticity of output with respect to land. What is known about the land elasticity of output?

As we know, under profit maximization and pure competition the distributive shares would equal the exponents of an aggregate Cobb-Douglas function. If so, in developed economies γ must be far less than 1/4: Nordhaus and Tobin (1972: 61-64) summarized Denison's findings to the effect that in the United States, land's share declined from 9 to 3 percent from 1900 to 1950. They considered a land's share of 0.05 one of their stylized facts. A Ricardian economy was, of course, much more like today's underdeveloped economies. Here γ must still be somewhat less than 1/4. Kuznets (1966: 421) found the share of income from material assets defined as land *plus* reproducible assets to be around 1/4. Land may be the most important material asset but will still have a share less than 1/4.

As for direct estimates of γ as an exponent, Walters (1963: 32-33) gave us a survey of agricultural production functions for underdeveloped

TABLE 3-1. Mapping the Function $(1 - e^{-ru})/(ru)$

Rate of Interest r	Useful Life u	Function $(1 - e^{-ru})/(ru)$
0.04	20	0.69
0.04	40	0.50
0.08	20	0.50
0.08	40	0.30
0.16	20	0.30
0.16	40	0.16

and developed economies alike. He found few γ's higher than 1/2 and most around 1/4.

In summary, in the first five cases of table 3-1 γ is easily less than the function $(1 - e^{-ru})/(ru)$, so the bracket of (18) is easily positive. Only the sixth case, in which $r = 0.16$ and $u = 40$ requires a γ less than 1/4. But while in underdeveloped economies the rate of return to capital may well be as high as 0.16, useful life is unlikely to be as long as 40 years. Even if it were, there is, in the numerator of (18), still the term βa_2 to go. The possibility of a negative numerator of (18) is remote. We must expect the elasticity (18) to be negative. Embodied technological progress reducing the labor a_2 absorbed in operating one physical unit of producers' good per unit of time will raise sustainable employment.

4. *Sensitivity to Embodied Technological Progress: Ricardo's Own View*

Under embodied technological progress two forces were at work in opposite directions. While the number of physical units of producers' goods S is up, it now takes less labor to either build (a_1) or operate (a_2) each physical unit, we said. The "good" effect of the lower a_1 or a_2 is that the real cost of applying a portion of capital is lowered, consequently the margin of cultivation may be pushed farther out, and more consumers' goods can be produced. But can they also be sold? The "bad" effect of the lower a_1 or a_2 is that redundant labor may be laid off.

Ricardo saw both forces and was fully aware of the tug of war between them. In discussing them, he uses his terms "net produce" and "gross produce," which we must define. "Net produce" is the real profits bill; "gross produce" is the real profits bill *plus* the real wage bill—the rent bill plays no role in chapter 31. One may find three possibilities discussed by Ricardo.

First, the unhappy case that the number of physical units of producers' goods S is not raised enough to compensate for the less labor it now takes to either build (a_1) or operate (a_2) each physical unit. In that case [1821 (1951: 390 and 392)] "... there will necessarily be a diminution in the demand for labour, population will become redundant, and the situation of the labouring classes will be that of distress and poverty" and "... the opinion entertained by the labouring class, that the employment of machinery is frequently detrimental to their interests, is not founded on prejudice and error, but is conformable to the correct principles of political economy."

Second, the neutral case that the number of physical units of producers' goods S is raised exactly enough to compensate for the less labor it now takes to either build (a_1) or operate (a_2) each physical unit. In that case [1821 (1951: 390)]:

... it could not fail to follow from the reduction in the price of commodities consequent on the introduction of machinery, that with the same wants he would have increased means of saving,— increased facility of transferring revenue into capital. But with every increase of capital he would employ more labourers; and, therefore, a portion of the people thrown out of work in the first instance, would be subsequently employed; and if the increased production, in consequence of the employment of the machine, was so great as to afford, in the shape of net produce, as great a quantity of food and necessaries as existed before in the form of gross produce, there would be the same ability to employ the whole population, and, therefore, there would not necessarily be any redundancy of people.

Third, the happy case that the number of physical units of producers' goods S is raised more than enough to compensate for the less labor it now takes to either build (a_1) or operate (a_2) each physical unit. In that case [1821 (1951: 392)]:

... if the improved means of production, in consequence of the use of machinery, should increase the net produce of a country in a degree so great as not to diminish the gross produce, (I mean always quantity of commodities and not value,) then the situation of all classes will be improved. The landlord and capitalist will benefit, not by an increase of rent and profit, but by the advantages resulting from the expenditure of the same rent, and profit, on commodities, very considerably reduced in value, while the situation of the labouring classes will also be considerably improved; lst, from the increased demand for menial servants; 2dly, from the stimulus to savings from revenue, which such an abundant net produce will afford; and 3rdly, from the low price of all articles of consumption on which their wages will be expended.

Perhaps Ricardo's own balanced judgment appears most clearly from his concluding double negation [1821 (1951: 395)]: "The statements which I have made will not, I hope, lead to the inference that machinery should not be encouraged."

5. *History*

We have found no flaw in Ricardo's macroeconomic logic. We who have so much more and better data than he had do not think that the elasticity γ of output with respect to land is actually high enough to permit embodied technological progress to reduce sustainable employment; indeed we should expect embodied technological progress to increase sustainable employment—as it has done historically.

In 1821, the year Ricardo published his new chapter on machinery, the population of Great Britain was 15.5 million. By 1881, when the steam-engine technology of his day had run its course, the population of Great Britain had doubled. Britain was not as active as Germany and the United States in replacing steam-engine technology by the internal combustion engine and the chemical and electrical industries of the second industrial revolution. Even so, the population of Great Britain almost doubled once more between 1881 and 1981.

So much for Ricardo's macroeconomics.

IV. THE LABOR THEORY OF VALUE

1. *The Price Equation*

Ricardian microeconomics is less shiny but so closely linked to his macroeconomics that we already have the clue, i.e., our first-order condition (9).

Rearrange (9) and recall that if the derivative dX/dS of our production function (4) $X = f(S)$ is known, then its inverse $1/(dX/dS)$ is the derivative dS/dX of the inverse function $S = g(X)$ expressing physical capital stock required as a function of desired physical output. We may then write our first-order condition (9) as a beautifully simple price equation

$$P = mw \frac{dS}{dX} \tag{19}$$

where m was defined in (10). Now define

$$h \equiv \frac{a_1 r/a_2}{1 - e^{-ru}} \tag{20}$$

Into (19) insert the definition of m in (10), factor out a_2, insert (20), and write price as

$$P = (1 + h)a_2 w \frac{dS}{dX} \tag{21}$$

Here, multiplying direct labor a_2 by $(1 + h)$ will magnify it to the sum of all labor, indirect with compound interest as well as direct, per producers' good per unit of time. Multiplying by the money wage rate w will give us labor cost, indirect with compound interest as well as direct, per producers' good per unit of time. The derivative dS/dX is additional producers' goods required per additional physical unit of consumers' goods produced per unit of time. Multiplying by that derivative, then, will simply give us the marginal labor cost, indirect with compound interest as well as direct, of consumers' goods. With that, we may formulate the labor theory of value.

2. Relative Price of Two Consumers' Goods

In Ricardian microeconomics let there be two consumers' goods, called i and j, say deer and salmon, each being produced by its own type of producers' goods with their own durability. Write our price equation (21) for i and j, divide one by the other, let the money wage rate w cancel, and find relative price

$$\frac{P_i}{P_j} = \frac{(1 + h_i)a_{2i}dS_i/dX_i}{(1 + h_j)a_{2j}dS_j/dX_j} \tag{22}$$

Ricardo [1821 (1951: 26-27)] first offered a numerical example in which $h_i = h_j$:

Suppose that in the early stages of society, the bows and arrows of the hunter were of equal value, and of equal durability, with the canoe and implements of the fisherman, both being the produce of the same quantity of labour. Under such circumstances ... the comparative value of the fish and the game, would be entirely regulated by the quantity of labour realized in each.

What may have been true of deer and salmon in the early stages of society may not, however, be true of the industrial age unfolding before Ricardo's eyes. Here h_i may differ from h_j for two reasons.

First, h as defined by (20) contains the ratio a_1/a_2, and that ratio may differ between goods i and j or, in Ricardo's own words [1821 (1951: 32)]:

In one trade very little capital may be employed as circulating capital, that is to say, in the support of labour—it may be principally invested in machinery, implements, building, etc., capital of comparatively fixed and durable character. In another trade the same amount of capital may be used, but it may be chiefly employed in the support of labour, and very little may be invested in implements, machines, and buildings.

If, everything else being equal, $a_{1i}/a_{2i} > a_{1j}/a_{2j}$, then $h_i > h_j$, and according to (22), relative price will be higher than labor embodiments alone would lead us to believe.

Second, h as defined by (20) contains the denominator $1 - e^{-ru}$, and useful life u may differ between goods i and j or, in Ricardo's own words [1821 (1951: 32)]:

Again, two manufacturers may employ the same amount of fixed and the same amount of circulating capital; but the durability of their fixed capitals may be very unequal. One may have steam-engines of the value of £10,000, the other, ships of the same value.

If, everything else being equal, $u_i < u_j$, then $1 - e^{-ru_i} < 1 - e^{-ru_j}$, again $h_i > h_j$, and according to (22), relative price will be higher than labor embodiments alone would lead us to believe.

In a striking numerical example Ricardo [1821 (1951: 37)] summarized his modification of the labor theory of value:

> Suppose I employ twenty men at an expense of £1000 for a year in the production of a commodity, and at the end of the year I employ twenty men again for another year, at a further expense of £1000 in finishing or perfecting the same commodity, and that I bring it to market at the end of two years, if profits be 10 per cent., my commodity must sell for £2,310; for I have employed £1000 capital for one year, and £2,100 capital for one year more. Another man employs precisely the same quantity of labour, but he employs it all in the first year; he employs forty men at an expense of £2000, and at the end of the first year he sells it with 10 per cent. profit, or for £2,200. Here then are two commodities having precisely the same quantity of labour bestowed on them, one of which sells for £2,310—the other for £2,200.

Still, having thus looked his modification squarely in the face, Ricardo decided to ignore it [1821 (1951: 36)]:

> In the subsequent part of this work, though I shall occasionally refer to this cause of variation, I shall consider all the great variations which take place in the relative value of commodities to be produced by the greater or less quantity of labour which may be required from time to time to produce them.

3. *Conclusion on Ricardian Microeconomics*

Why do we consider Ricardo's microeconomics "less shiny"? Not merely because Ricardo saw but chose to ignore certain complications arising out of different proportions of circulating to fixed capital and out of different durabilities of fixed capital. Those complications merely made h_i differ from h_j in (22).

There is a more fundamental difficulty with (22) that Ricardo did not see. The two derivatives of (22), dS_i/dX_i and dS_j/dX_j are both derivatives of one variable with respect to another. Consequently, (22) merely expresses one variable ratio on its left-hand side in terms of another on the right-hand side. As a result, (22) is a property of the Ricardian system but not a solution to it. The two derivatives of (22) cannot be known until the margin of cultivation is known—not just the macroeconomic margin of cultivation determined by (10) but the microeconomic margins of cultivation, one for every crop. If tastes changed, microeconomic margins would change and, with them, the relative derivatives dS_i/dX_i to dS_j/dX_j and marginal costs. But in Ricardian microeconomics tastes found no room. They were still waiting for Walras. This is what Samuelson means when he says (1971: 404) that "the *new* embodied labor ratios have to be solved for by Walrasian conditions of the type Ricardo hoped to be able to ignore."

REFERENCES

H. Brems, "Ricardo's Long-run Equilibrium," *Hist. Polit. Econ.*, Fall 1970, *2*, 225-245.

S. Kuznets, *Modern Economic Growth, Rate, Structure, and Spread*, New Haven and London, 1966.

W. Nordhaus and J. Tobin, "Is Growth Obsolete?" *Fiftieth Anniversary Colloquium V by the National Bureau of Economic Research*, New York, 1972, 1-80.

L. L. Pasinetti, "A Mathematical Formulation of the Ricardian System." *Rev. Econ. Stud.*, Feb. 1960, *27*, 78-98.

D. Ricardo, *The Principles of Political Economy and Taxation*, third edition, London, 1821, reprinted in *The Works and Correspondence of David Ricardo*, P. Sraffa and M. H. Dobb (eds.), vol. I, New York, 1951.

P. A. Samuelson, "A Modern Treatment of the Ricardian Economy," *Quart. J. Econ.*, Feb.-May 1959, *73*, 1-35 and 217-231.

———, "Understanding the Marxian Notion of Exploitation: A Summary of the So-called Transformation Problem between Marxian Values and Competitive Prices," *J. Econ. Lit.*, June 1971, *9*, 399-431.

J. A. Schumpeter, *History of Economic Analysis*, New York, 1954.

U.S. Department of Commerce, Office of Business Economics, "New Estimates of Fixed Business Capital in the United States, 1925-65," *Surv. Curr. Bus.*, Dec. 1966, *46*, 34-40.

———, "Fixed Business Capital in the United States, 1925-68," *Surv. Curr. Bus.*, Feb. 1969, *49*, 20-27.

A. A. Walters, "Production and Cost Functions: An Econometric Survey," *Econometrica*, Jan.-Apr. 1963, *31*, 1-66.

W. Whewell, "Mathematical Exposition of Some of the Leading Doctrines in Mr. Ricardo's 'Principles of Political Economy and Taxation'," *Transactions of the Cambridge Philosophical Society*, 1833, *4*, 155-198.

CHAPTER 4   *Non Sequitur*

MARX (1818-1883)

Why don't people argue about the "meanings" of Wicksell the way they do about those of Ricardo and Marx?

Samuelson (1974: 64)

I. INTRODUCTION

1. *Marx's Problem*

Marx was more than an economic theorist: a philosopher, a historian, a journalist, an agitator, and a remote-control labor organizer. But for Marx economic theory came first, and as a theorist he is our man; we have known him for 119 years and shall not let philosophers, historians, or others tell us what to think of his economic theory. As an economic theorist Marx wanted to find the laws of motion of relative price, the rate of profit, and the real wage rate in a capitalist competitive economy.

2. *Marx's Method*

Like the Ricardian model, the Marxian model had two industries, a producers' goods and a consumers' goods industry. But in the Marxian model, it took producers' goods to produce producers' goods, land was ignored, and no diminishing returns were seen to anything. Marx used numerical examples but was neither a born nor a trained mathematician. Mathematical training might have saved him from his *non sequiturs*.

3. *Our Own Restatement*

Let us try to restate algebraically what parts of Marxian theory are well enough specified to permit such restatement. Samuelson (1957), (1971) has shown the way, and we shall follow him except on one point. We replace his (1957: 884), (1971: 413n) strong assumption of a one year useful life and simple interest by our weaker, more Marx-like, and more realistic assumption of a *u*-year useful life of producers' goods. In other words, we think of Marx's producers' goods as being as durable as the

Ricardian ones. If so, we should adopt the same compound interest with continuous compounding we used in our chapter 3 on Ricardo.

Let the notation of our restatement be as follows.

4. *Variables*

c $\equiv$ constant capital
H $\equiv$ revenue *minus* operating labor cost
J $\equiv$ present net worth of an investment project
k $\equiv$ present gross worth of an investment project
L $\equiv$ labor employed
P $\equiv$ price
r $\equiv$ rate of interest or profit
S $\equiv$ physical capital stock
s $\equiv$ surplus value
v $\equiv$ variable capital
W $\equiv$ wage bill
w $\equiv$ money wage rate
x_{ij} $\equiv$ physical units of ith industry's good demanded by jth industry
X_i $\equiv$ physical output of ith industry's good
Z $\equiv$ profits bill

5. *Parameters*

a $\equiv$ labor coefficient
b $\equiv$ capital coefficient
u $\equiv$ useful life of producers' goods

The symbol e is Euler's number, the base of natural logarithms. The symbol t is general time. The symbol τ is present time.

II. SIMULTANEOUS EQUALIZATION OF RATES OF SURPLUS VALUE AND PROFIT?

1. *Surplus Value*

Marx imagined a capitalist-entrepreneur producing commodities from labor hired and a physical capital stock of producers' goods owned.

The value in use of the labor hired was the value in exchange of the commodities produced. The value in exchange of the labor hired was called "variable" capital v and in Marx's words [1867 (1908: 190)] "is the value of the means of subsistence necessary for the maintenance of the labourer."

The value in use of the physical capital stock of producers' goods owned equaled their value in exchange. That, in turn, was called "constant" capital *c* and equaled the labor necessary to produce them.

"Surplus" value *s* was defined as the difference between the value in exchange of the commodities produced and the cost of all capital used, variable as well as constant. Notice that the source of surplus value was variable capital only, never constant capital.

2. Rates of Surplus Value versus Rates of Profit

Marx defined his rate of surplus value as *s/v* or surplus value divided by its source, variable capital. In volume I of *Capital* [1867 (1908)] he

FIGURE 4-1.
U.S. Capital Intensities
by Industry

Fortune, May 1974, 254.
Data: © 1974 Time, Inc.

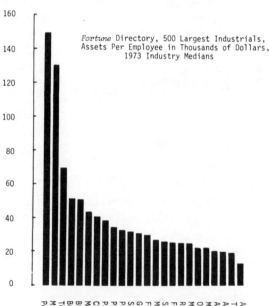

Fortune Directory, 500 Largest Industrials,
Assets Per Employee in Thousands of Dollars,
1973 Industry Medians

thought that competition would equalize rates of surplus value among industries or, in two industries, that

$$s_1/v_1 = s_2/v_2 \tag{1}$$

Marx defined his rate of profit as $s/(c + v)$ or surplus value divided by all capital, constant as well as variable. In volume III of *Capital* [1894 (1909)] Marx thought that competition would equalize rates of profit among industries:

$$s_1/(c_1 + v_1) = s_2/(c_2 + v_2) \tag{2}$$

In both (1) and (2) multiply across, subtract first result from second, and find

$$c_2 s_1 = c_1 s_2 \tag{3}$$

Multiplied across, (1) may be written

$$s_1 v_2 = s_2 v_1 \tag{4}$$

Divide (3) by (4) and find

$$c_1/v_1 = c_2/v_2 \tag{5}$$

from which we see that for simultaneous equalization of rates of surplus value (1) and of rates of profit (2) the ratio c/v between constant and variable capital must be the same in the two industries. Is it the same? In our own time it certainly isn't: figure 4-1 shows a wide variation of assets per employee among industries. In Marx's day the ratio probably wasn't the same either, and Marx struggled [1894 (1909: 183-186)] to "transform" the "values" of his volume I into the "prices" of his volume III. Let us examine his transformation problem.

III. THE TRANSFORMATION PROBLEM

1. *"Values" versus "Prices"*

Marx distinguished between "values" and "prices of production." The values of his volume I [1867 (1908)] resulted from equalization of rates of surplus value among industries. The prices of his volume III [1894 (1909)] resulted from equalization of rates of profit among industries. Does the difference matter? It does. Industry by industry, competitive prices will not normally reflect Marxian values. We must choose between values and prices. The choice is easy once we realize what perfect mobility of labor and capital does and does not do.

Assume perfect mobility of labor among industries. If one industry generated a higher rate of surplus value than another, would labor leave the low-rate industry and enter the high-rate industry? The answer is no, and the obvious reason is that a worker can tell what rate of surplus value he is creating only if the capitalist-entrepreneurs will open their books to him. What he can tell without the books is what money wage rate he is paid. If one industry offers a higher money wage rate than another, labor will leave the low-wage industry and enter the high-wage industry. That's all.

Next assume perfect mobility of capital among industries. If one industry generated a higher rate of surplus value than another, would capital leave the low-rate industry and enter the high-rate industry? Again the answer is no. From his books the capitalist-entrepreneur can tell what his surplus value s is, divide it by variable capital v, and find his rate of surplus value s/v. But why should he care? What matters to him is his rate of profit $s/(c + v)$ on all his capital, whether constant or variable. He will leave industries offering a low rate of profit and enter industries offering a high rate of profit. We can't say it better than Marx himself did in volume III [1894 (1909: 181)]:

> ... There is no doubt that, aside from unessential, accidental, and mutually compensating distinctions, a difference in the average rate of profit of the various lines of industry does not exist in reality, and could not exist without abolishing the entire system of capitalist production.

2. *Conclusion*

What perfect mobility of labor will equalize is the money wage rate, and what perfect mobility of capital will equalize is the rate of profit. Marx's equalization of rates of surplus value among industries was a *non sequitur*.

We can now take our stand on the transformation problem: we choose the prices of volume III rather than the values of volume I. We are in good company. Samuelson (1971: 413-414) has shown that Marx's own struggle with the transformation problem was inconsistent and (1971: 418-422) that Marx's treatment in volume I is redundant and may safely be replaced by his treatment in volume III. Joan Robinson [1942 (1966: 22)] agreed, and that is precisely what we shall do.

IV. RELATIVE PRICE

1. *Technology*

Let a Marxian model have two industries, a producers' good and a consumers' good industry, called $i = 1, 2$, respectively. In either industry let labor input and physical capital stock be in proportion to output:

$$L_i = a_i X_i \tag{6}$$

$$S_i = b_i X_i \tag{7}$$

Both industries use both inputs, so $a_i > 0$ and $b_i > 0$.

2. Zero Present Net Worth

Let a capitalist-entrepreneur in the ith industry consider acquiring a capital stock of S_i new physical units of producers' goods whose useful life is u. So he must be planning for u years. Let his annual physical output be X_i of the ith good to be sold at the price P_i. His revenue will then be $P_i X_i$. Since he is employing L_i men at the money wage rate w, his operating labor cost is $L_i w$. At time t, then, his revenue *minus* operating labor cost would be

$$H_i \equiv P_i X_i - L_i w \tag{8}$$

and per small fraction dt of a year located at time t in the future his revenue *minus* operating labor cost would be $H_i dt$.

Let there be a market in which money may be placed or borrowed at the stationary rate of interest r. Let that rate be applied when discounting future cash flows. As seen from the present time τ, then, his revenue *minus* operating labor cost would be $e^{-r(t-\tau)} H_i dt$. Define the present gross worth of the investment project as the present worth of the sum total of all future revenue *minus* operating labor cost over the entire useful life u of the new capital stock S_i or

$$k_i(\tau) \equiv \int_{\tau}^{\tau+u} e^{-r(t-\tau)} H_i dt \tag{9}$$

Here H_i as defined by (8) is not a function of t, hence may be taken outside the integral sign. The rate of interest r was said to be stationary, hence the coefficient of t is stationary. As a result, find the integral to be

$$k_i = \frac{1 - e^{-ru}}{r} H_i \tag{10}$$

P_1 is the price of a new physical unit of producers' goods. Assume the salvage value of the unit to be zero. The present net worth of the investment project is then defined as the present gross worth (10) *minus* the cost of acquisition of the new capital stock S_i or

$$J_i \equiv k_i - P_1 S_i \tag{11}$$

Insert (8) and (10) into (11) and write the present net worth of the investment project as

$$J_i = \frac{1 - e^{-ru}}{r} (P_i X_i - L_i w) - P_1 S_i \tag{12}$$

What can we do with our present net worth (12)? Ricardian present net worth had a maximum—which we found. Marxian present net worth has none. In Marx there is no diminishing return to anything—land, labor, or capital. Under a stationary technology (6) and (7), L_i and S_i are in direct proportion to X_i. For a given competitive price P_i, rate of interest r, useful life u, and money wage rate w, then, present net worth J_i of the investment project is in direct proportion to physical capital stock S_i and has no maximum. All is not lost however.

3. *Relative Price of Producers' and Consumers' Goods*

Pure competition, freedom of entry, and freedom of exit will make prices P_i adjust until—as in volume III but not volume I—rates of profits have been equalized among industries. We who have distinguished between interest and profits might now say that the equalized rate of profit in equilibrium must equal the rate of interest common to all borrowers. That equality is nothing but zero present net worth in all industries.

So good volume-III Marxists may drop our distinction between a rate of interest and a rate of profit, call both of them r, set present net worth (12) equal to zero, multiply it by $r/(1 - e^{-ru})$, divide it by physical output X_i, use (6) and (7), and write a Marxian price equation

$$P_i - a_i w - P_1 b_i r/(1 - e^{-ru}) = 0 \tag{13}$$

Now first write (13) for $i = 1$ and find the price of producers' goods

$$P_1 = \frac{a_1}{1 - b_1 r/(1 - e^{-ru})} w \tag{14}$$

Then write (13) for $i = 2$, insert (14), and write the price of consumers' goods

$$P_2 = \frac{1 + a_1(b_2/a_2 - b_1/a_1)r/(1 - e^{-ru})}{1 - b_1 r/(1 - e^{-ru})} a_2 w \tag{15}$$

Finally divide (14) by (15) and write the relative price of producers' and consumers' goods

$$\frac{P_1}{P_2} = \frac{1}{1 + a_1(b_2/a_2 - b_1/a_1)r/(1 - e^{-ru})} \frac{a_1}{a_2} \tag{16}$$

Does (16) have all that Marx called "socially necessary labor" in it, i.e., direct as well as indirect labor? It does. The production of the ith good absorbs direct labor according to the labor coefficient a_i and indirect labor according to the capital coefficient b_i.

But what is the rate of interest or profit r doing in (16)? Direct and indirect labor are both absorbed by the ith good but not at the same time.

The direct labor absorbed in the nth year of useful life of producers' goods is n years away from the indirect labor originally absorbed when the producers' goods were being built. Direct and indirect labor n years apart are not additive until synchronized. So one or both of them must be moved through time until they meet. But time is money, and the rate of interest or profit r is its price. That rate is inherent in synchronization, must appear in (16), and does so in the transcendental form $r/(1 - e^{-ru})$. A table of powers of e will show that the transcendental form is a rising function of r.

4. *A Labor Theory of Value?*

If relative price were expressed in nothing but relative labor embodiment, then the rate of interest or profit r should not appear in (16). Will it always appear?

The ratios b_i/a_i between capital and labor coefficients are capital-labor ratios or, as we could call them nowadays, capital intensities. Three possibilities immediately suggest themselves.

First, if the capital intensities of producers' and consumers' goods are the same, i.e.,

$$b_1/a_1 = b_2/a_2 \tag{17}$$

then the entire second term of the denominator of (16) will be zero, the rate of interest or profit r will disappear from (16), and the sensitivity $\partial(P_1/P_2)/\partial[r/(1 - e^{-ru})] = 0$.

Second, if producers' goods have a higher capital intensity than do consumers' goods, i.e.,

$$b_1/a_1 > b_2/a_2 \tag{18}$$

then the second term of the denominator of (16) will be negative, the sensitivity $\partial(P_1/P_2)/\partial[r/(1 - e^{-ru})] > 0$, and the relative price (16) will be the higher the higher the rate of interest or profit r.

Third, if producers' goods have a lower capital intensity than do consumers' goods, i.e.,

$$b_1/a_1 < b_2/a_2 \tag{19}$$

then the second term of the denominator of (16) will be positive, the sensitivity $\partial(P_1/P_2)/\partial[r/(1 - e^{-ru})] < 0$, and the relative price (16) will be the lower the higher the rate of interest or profit r.

Among our three possibilities the third one is the realistic one: Gordon (1961: 948) called attention to the fact that the capital goods sector is less capital intensive than the consumers' goods sector. In other words, (16) cannot be a labor theory of value.

V. THE REAL WAGE RATE

1. *The Factor-Price Frontier under Stationary Technology*

The real wage rate is just another relative price, i.e., the relative price of labor and consumers' goods, and is fully contained in our result (15). Rearrange the latter and write it as the real wage rate

$$\frac{w}{P_2} = \frac{1 - b_1 r/(1 - e^{-ru})}{[1 + a_1(b_2/a_2 - b_1/a_1)r/(1 - e^{-ru})]a_2} \tag{20}$$

Under stationary technology a_1, a_2, b_1, and b_2, how are the real wage rate w/P_2 and the rate of interest or profit r related? Let us first find how the real wage rate w/P_2 and the expression $r/(1 - e^{-ru})$ are related in (20), so take the derivative of the former with respect to the latter, let lots of things cancel, and find

$$\frac{\partial(w/P_2)}{\partial[r/(1 - e^{-ru})]}$$

$$= -\frac{a_1 b_2}{\{[1 + a_1(b_2/a_2 - b_1/a_1)r/(1 - e^{-ru})]a_2\}^2} \tag{21}$$

which is unequivocally negative. Now the expression $r/(1 - e^{-ru})$ is a rising function of r. Thus if according to (21) the real wage rate (20) and the expression $r/(1 - e^{-ru})$ are negatively related, so are the real wage rate (20) and the rate of interest or profit r. Under stationary technology, then, if the rate of interest or profit r is down the real wage rate w/P_2 is up.

2. *Technological Progress: Marx's Own View*

What interested Marx, however, was not stationary technology but the effect of technological progress upon the rate of profit and the real wage rate. Let us go back to his definition of the rate of profit $s/(c + v)$, divide numerator and denominator alike by v, and write it

$$\frac{s/v}{1 + c/v}$$

from which we see that if the rate of surplus value s/v stayed the same and technological progress raised the constant-to-variable capital ratio c/v, then the rate of profit would fall. But *would* the rate of surplus value s/v stay the same? In a labored numerical example in volume III [1894 (1909: 247)] Marx assumed that it did. In other volumes he differed. In volume I [1867 (1908: 422)] he said that "modern industry raises the productiveness of labour to an extraordinary degree." In volume II [1885 (1915: 267)] he offered examples:

Thus machinery shortens the building time of houses, bridges, etc.; a mowing and threshing machine, etc., shorten the working period required to transform the ripe grain into a finished product. Improved ship-building reduces by increased speed the time of turnover of capital invested in navigation.

Raised "productiveness of labour" must mean that either the same number of men produce more commodity value or fewer men are needed to produce the same commodity value. To be sure, constant capital c is up in the first place. Even so, nothing keeps the surplus value s, let alone the rate of surplus value s/v, from going up. But if both s/v and c/v are up, Marx cannot tell what would happen to his rate of profit. Yet, as Gottheil (1966: 99) reports, "in all the examples cited by Marx which deal with increasing organic compositions of capital the assigned increases in the productiveness of labor never suffice to maintain the rate of profit." We agree with Gottheil (1966: 100) that "this is convenience, not necessity." Marx's falling rate of profit was a *non sequitur*.

In conclusion, then, Marx's falling rate of profit was no necessity but certainly a possibility—one possibility out of three. We may as well begin our discussion of the three possibilities with the Marxian one.

3. *First Possibility: Falling Rate of Profit*

Suppose that the capitalist-entrepreneur feels somehow forced to adopt a new technology, although it offers him a lower rate of profit than he was earning before the new technology came along. Capitalist-entrepreneurs have been heard to lament such misfortune.

What *is* forcing him? Whatever his competitors are doing, a capitalist-entrepreneur may always remain in the old technology. If he fails to exercise that option the reason can only be that under the old technology his rate of profit would have been lower than it is under the new technology. Here, in our first possibility, the rate of profit r is down. Consequently, under the old technology the rate of profit would have been even lower—or our capitalist-entrepreneur would have exercised his option of remaining in the old technology! But if under the old technology the rate of profit were down, it follows from the negativity of (21) that the real wage rate must be up: the new technology adopted by all the competitors has depressed the price of consumers goods P_2 relative to the money wage rate w. We can certainly imagine a two-input production function in which technological progress will raise the real wage rate and reduce the rate of profit—although we know of no long periods or countries in which it has done so.

4. Second Possibility: Stationary Rate of Profit

Considered impossible by Marx, a stationary rate of profit r is a possibility to us—our second one. Here, under the new technology adopted by the competitors, the rate of profit is still the same as before. Consequently, under the old technology the rate of profit would have been down—or our capitalist-entrepreneur would have exercised his option of remaining in the old technology! But once more, if under the old technology the rate of profit were down, it follows from the negativity of (21) that the real wage rate must be up: the new technology adopted by all the competitors has depressed the price of consumers goods P_2 relative to the money wage rate w. We can certainly imagine a two-input production function in which technological progress will raise the real wage rate and leave the rate of profit unaffected, and we know of long periods in countries like the United States and Britain in which it has actually done so, cf. Phelps Brown (1973) and summary in Brems (1980: 38-42).

5. Third Possibility: Rising Rate of Profit

Considered equally impossible by Marx, a rising rate of profit r is a possibility to us—our third one. Here, under the new technology adopted by the competitors, the rate of profit is up. Consequently, under the old technology the rate of profit could have been down, the same, or up—but not as high as under the new technology. All three cases would keep our capitalist-entrepreneur from exercising his option of remaining in the old technology. From the negativity of (21) it follows that the real wage rate must be up, the same, or down, respectively: anything may happen to the real wage rate. Strange? Not at all. We can certainly imagine a two-input production function in which technological progress will raise, leave unaffected, or lower the real wage rate and raise the rate of profit— although we know of no long periods or countries in which it has done so.

6. A Fourth Possibility?

The one and only possibility that we cannot imagine is a two-input production function in which technological progress will reduce *both* the real wage rate and the rate of profit. The fruits of technological progress must accrue somewhere! Yet this possibility is the very one that Marx thought would prevail [1867 (1908: 708-709)]: "It follows therefore that in proportion as capital accumulates, the lot of the labourer, be his payment high or low, must grow worse." For documentation, Marx [1867 (1908: 739)] quotes Ducpétiaux, "inspector-general of Belgian prisons and charitable institutions, and member of the central commission of

Belgian statistics,'' who asked how such immiserization was possible and answered:

> ... by adopting expedients, the secret of which only the labourer knows; by reducing his daily rations; by substituting rye-bread for wheat; by eating less meat, or even none at all, and the same with butter and condiments; by contenting themselves with one or two rooms where the family is crammed together, where boys and girls sleep side by side, often on the same pallet; by economy of clothing, washing, decency; by giving up the Sunday diversions; by, in short, resigning themselves to the most painful privations.

What about a three-input production function like Ricardo's? Here technological progress could reduce both the real wage rate and the rate of profit but raise the real rent rate. Marx refused his teacher's help and had no land. His falling real wage rate was a *non sequitur.*

Enough about prices, wages, and profits. Let us finally turn to interindustry equilibrium.

VI. INTERINDUSTRY EQUILIBRIUM

1. *Quesnay-Marx*

Marx [1905-1910 (1923: 34)] called Quesnay's table ''the most ingenious invention of which political economy has until now been guilty.'' In his volume II Marx saw the interdependence of his two industries but dimmed in two respects. First, Marx never admitted preferences, consequently his consumers' goods industry never produced anything but a single consumers' good. That was a retreat from Quesnay's distinction between farm and city products. Second, written before volume III, volume II assumed [1885 (1915: 454)] ''that products are exchanged at their value.''

Define transactions x_{ij} as physical units of ith industry's good de-

TABLE 4-1. A Two-Sector Leontief Transactions Table

		Producers' Goods Industry (1)	Consumers' Goods Industry (2)	Row Total
Producers' Goods Industry	(1)	$P_1 x_{11}$	$P_1 x_{12}$	$P_1 X_1$
Consumers' Goods Industry	(2)	$P_2 x_{21}$	$P_2 x_{22}$	$P_2 X_2$

manded by jth industry and output X_i as physical output of ith industry's good. Multiplying x_{ij} and X_i by their price P_i will express them in terms of dollars, as shown in our Leontief transactions table in table 4-1.

Can we solve Marx's model of interindustry equilibrium for the physical outputs of its two industries? Let us write as many equations as Marx permits and begin with investment.

2. *Investment*

Marx's "simple reproduction" meant a stationary economy. Here there is no net investment. But just like a Ricardian stationary economy with a finite useful life u of producers' goods, a Marxian one must replace retired producers' goods. Let producers' goods have the same useful life whether used to produce producers' or consumers' goods. Let age distribution be even, then each year $1/u$ of the physical capital stock of the ith industry is retired and must be replaced. So investment demand by the ith industry is

$$x_{1i} = S_i/u \tag{22}$$

where $i = 1, 2$.

3. *Consumption*

As we saw in section IV,2 above, a capitalist-entrepreneur in the ith industry used a physical capital stock S_i to produce the physical output X_i sold at the price P_i. His revenue was then $P_i X_i$. Since he employed L_i men at the money wage rate w, his operating labor cost was $L_i w$, and his revenue *minus* operating labor cost was $H_i \equiv P_i X_i - L_i w$. That was his gross income before capital consumption allowances. Subtract his capital consumption allowances $P_1 x_{1i}$ and find his profits bill

$$Z_i \equiv P_i X_i - L_i w - P_1 x_{1i} \tag{23}$$

where $i = 1, 2$. In a stationary economy there is no accumulation, so let him consume his entire profits bill (23). Let labor employed in the ith industry consume its entire wage bill

$$W_i \equiv L_i w \tag{24}$$

Total consumption demand by the ith industry is then the sum of (23) and (24):

$$P_2 x_{2i} = W_i + Z_i = P_i X_i - P_1 x_{1i} \tag{25}$$

where $i = 1, 2$.

4. *Interindustry Equilibrium*

Recall two conditions for interindustry equilibrium in a Leontief transactions table. Here, a row will account for all demand satisfied by a sector's supply. Consequently, in equilibrium the row total must equal the sector's supply. In either industry, goods-market equilibrium will require the supply of goods to equal the demand for them:

$$X_i = \sum_{j=1}^{2} x_{ij} \qquad (26)$$

A column will account for all supplies satisfying a sector's demand. Consequently, the column total must equal the sector's demand. In equilibrium a sector must break even: its revenue must equal its expenditure. In other words, its row total must equal its column total.

Does a Marxian intersector equilibrium satisfy both equilibrium conditions? Multiply (26) by P_i and see that the first condition is satisfied. Insert (25) into the second row of our Leontief transactions table 4-1, find the column totals, and see that the second condition is satisfied. With both conditions satisfied, we may write the Leontief transactions table 4-1 as the Marx transactions table 4-2.

TABLE 4-2. Marx's Transactions in "Simple Reproduction"

		Producers' Goods Industry (1)	Consumers' Goods Industry (2)	Row Total
Producers' Goods Industry	(1)	$P_1 x_{11}$	$P_1 x_{12}$	$P_1 X_1$
Consumers' Goods Industry	(2)	$P_1 X_1 - P_1 x_{11}$	$P_2 X_2 - P_1 x_{12}$	$P_2 X_2$
Column Total		$P_1 X_1$	$P_2 X_2$	$P_1 X_1 + P_2 X_2$

5. *Solution for Physical Outputs?*

Define aggregate employment as the sum of labor employed in the two industries:

$$L \equiv \sum_{i=1}^{2} L_i \qquad (27)$$

Insert (6) into (27) and find

$$L = a_1 X_1 + a_2 X_2 \tag{28}$$

Insert (7) into (22) and the result into (26) and find

$$X_1 = b_1 X_1 / u + b_2 X_2 / u \tag{29}$$

Now if L were a parameter, (28) and (29) would be two linear equations in the two unknowns X_1 and X_2 and could easily be solved:

$$X_1 = \frac{b_2}{a_1 b_2 + a_2(u - b_1)} L \tag{30}$$

$$X_2 = \frac{u - b_1}{a_1 b_2 + a_2(u - b_1)} L \tag{31}$$

Was L a parameter to Marx? Marx was enough of an English classicist to think of labor as reproducible at a value in exchange equaling "the value of the means of subsistence necessary for the maintenance of the labourer," as we saw in the quote from Marx [1867 (1908: 190)]. But he was not enough of one to use this notion to determine sustainable employment, as Ricardo had done. To go that far, he would have needed a fixed quantity of land coupled with either Cantillon's fixed input-output coefficients or Ricardo's diminishing returns. Marx admired Ricardo but despised Malthus and overcame his dilemma by removing land from his model.

What are we to do with our labor employed L, then?

A simple possibility would be to get rid of it by dividing it away. Divide (30) by (31), let L and the denominators cancel, and find the relative size of the two sectors

$$X_1 / X_2 = b_2 / (u - b_1) \tag{32}$$

In English: the relative size X_1 / X_2 of the two sectors depends upon their capital coefficients b_1 and b_2 and the useful life of capital stock but not on total labor employed L.

VII. CONCLUSIONS

As a theorist measured by Cantillon, Ricardo, or Böhm-Bawerk standards, Marx is disappointing. Perhaps because of its sheer bulk, his system was inconsistent. Its first *non sequitur* was that rates of surplus value would be equalized among industries. Even if they were, the second *non sequitur* would still be that under technological progress the rate of profit would be falling. Even if it were, the third *non sequitur* would still be that the real wage rate would also be falling.

In economic history the three *non sequiturs* fared no better than they did in economic theory: none of them came true.

REFERENCES

H. Brems, *Inflation, Interest, and Growth—A Synthesis*, Lexington, Mass., 1980.
R. A. Gordon, "Differential Changes in the Prices of Consumers' and Capital Goods," *Amer. Econ. Rev.*, Dec. 1961, *51*, 937-957.
F. M. Gottheil, *Marx's Economic Predictions*, Evanston, Ill. 1966.
K. Marx, *Das Kapital: Kritik der politischen Oekonomie*, vol. I, *Der Produktionsprocess des Kapitals*, Hamburg, 1867; translated as *Capital: A Critique of Political Economy*, vol. I, *The Process of Capitalist Production* by Samuel Moore and Edward Aveling, edited by Friedrich Engels, revised and amplified according to the fourth German edition by Ernest Untermann, Chicago, 1908.
———, *Das Kapital: Kritik der politischen Oekonomie*, vol. II, *Der Circulationsprocess des Kapitals*, Hamburg, 1885; translated as *Capital: A Critique of Political Economy*, vol. II, *The Process of Circulation of Capital* by Ernest Untermann, edited by Friedrich Engels, Chicago, 1915.
———, *Das Kapital: Kritik der politischen Oekonomie*, vol. III, *Der Gesamtprocess der kapitalistischen Produktion*, Hamburg, 1894; translated as *Capital: A Critique of Political Economy*, vol. III, *The Process of Capitalist Production as a Whole* by Ernest Untermann, edited by Friedrich Engels, Chicago, 1909.
———, *Theorien über den Mehrwert*, K. Kautsky (ed.), Stuttgart, 1905-1910, Berlin 1923.
E. H. Phelps Brown, "Levels and Movements of Industrial Productivity and Real Wages Internationally Compared, 1860-1970," *Econ. J.*, Mar. 1973, *83*, 58-71.
J. Robinson, *An Essay on Marxian Economics*, London, 1942, 1966.
P. A. Samuelson, "Wages and Interest: A Modern Dissection of Marxian Economic Models," *Amer. Econ. Rev.*, Dec. 1957, *47*, 884-912.
———, "Understanding the Marxian Notion of Exploitation: A Summary of the So-Called Transformation Problem Between Marxian Values and Competitive Prices," *J. Econ. Lit.*, June 1971, *9*, 399-431.
———, "Insight and Detour in the Theory of Exploitation: A Reply to Baumol," *J. Econ. Lit.*, Mar. 1974, *12*, 62-70.

PART *IV*   1870-1930

Static and Dynamic General
Equilibrium

The Utility Function

Capital Theory

Partial Equilibrium

The Production Function

Capital and Money

Intertemporal Allocation
of Resources

I. THE SETTING

Our period covers the span from the second industrial revolution to the Great Depression. The foundation of the first industrial revolution had been the steam engine. The foundation of the second industrial revolution comprised three new industries, the electrical industry, the chemical industry, and the automotive industry. Their new technology was rooted in basic discoveries made half a century earlier.

1. *The Electrical Industry*

In 1819 Hans Christian Oersted had shown that electricity could produce magnetism, thus making the electric motor possible. In 1831 Michael Faraday had shown that, conversely, magnetism could produce electricity, thus making the electric generator possible. Neither became practical for another half-century. Having invented the incandescent lamp in 1879, Thomas Alva Edison built the first central electric power plant in 1881-1882. In 1881 Ernst Werner von Siemens put the electric motor on rails, thus making expansion of cities possible.

In communication, in 1876 Alexander Graham Bell used electromagnetism to transmit the sound of the human voice, and in 1895 Guglielmo Marconi used electromagnetic waves to demonstrate the wireless telegraph.

2. *The Chemical Industry*

Chemistry is concerned with the composition, structure, and reactivity of substances. Chemical engineering is concerned with finding ways of changing or synthesizing them on a large scale.

The first synthesis of an organic compound from inorganic material was Friedrich Wöhler's accidental synthesis of urea in 1828. His synthesis was unimportant industrially but radically changed the way chemists thought. In 1856 William Henry Perkin accidentally synthesized from coal tar a dye of a color unknown in nature. This was of industrial consequence: dyes, explosives, and drugs are synthesized largely from coal tar.

More difficult, but even more promising, was the synthesis of chemical compounds of high molecular weight, the polymers. In 1846 Christian Friedrich Schönbein accidentally converted one polymer, the molecule of cellulose, into another, the molecule of cellulose nitrate, unknown in nature, thus founding the collodion, cellophane, and celluloid industries. Until the end of the nineteenth century there was little inkling of the nature of atoms or the forces holding them together, and all three breakthroughs had been accidental. But in 1907 Leo Hendrik Baekeland successfully initiated in a laboratory nature's feat of polymerization, i.e., forming polymers from their component monomers. His new molecule was unknown in nature. He called it bakelite, and with it founded the synthetics industry which has produced a wide array of plastics, synthetic fibers, and synthetic rubber.

In our own century it has, in Haight's words (1964: 499-500), become "possible to think of desirable properties for materials to have, draw up chemical blueprints of the molecular structure of a material which will have these properties, then synthesize the material in the laboratory."

3. The Automotive Industry

In 1878 Nicolaus A. Otto and Eugen Langen built a four-stroke electric-ignition internal combustion engine burning coal gas. Theirs was not the first, but—like James Watt's steam engine—it sharply reduced fuel consumption and made the engine practical. The internal combustion engine converted much more of the energy received into work than the steam engine could do. In addition, it was smaller and lighter. In 1885 Karl Benz put it on (three) rubber wheels. In 1903 Wilbur and Orville Wright gave it wings and flew it 120 feet. In 1908 Henry Ford put the automobile into mass production.

In 1892 Rudolf Diesel patented, and in 1897 built, a four-stroke compression-ignition internal combustion engine burning coal dust. The Diesel engine was even more efficient than the Otto engine and would, after Diesel's mysterious death in 1913, power the world's ships and heavy-duty land transportation.

4. Markets and Market Structure

With sharply reduced costs of communication and transportation, the new industries would transcend local markets and be facing national or even international markets. Larger markets would intensify competition. At the same time the new technology came on a scale that only large firms could exploit. In the new industries the giant corporation emerged: Siemens in 1847, Allgemeine Elektrizitäts Gesellschaft 1883, Westinghouse 1886, Philips Gloeilampenfabrieken 1891, and General Electric 1892 in the electrical industry; E. I. Du Pont de Nemours in 1802—not a giant until it took up, at the turn of our own century, cellulose, lacquers, adhesives, finishes, and plastics[1]—Procter & Gamble in 1837, Badische Anilin- und Soda-Fabrik 1865, Monsanto 1901, and Union Carbide 1917 in the chemical industry; Ford Motor Company in 1903 and General Motors 1908 in the automobile industry; and Standard Oil of Ohio in 1870, U.S. Steel Corporation 1901, and S.K.F. 1907 in related industries. Where firm size grew even more rapidly than market size, pure competition might not be viable.

The giant corporation, innovation, and nonpure competition did not fit into the purely competitive static equilibrium theory that Schumpeter (1908) restated so well. Resolutely Schumpeter [1912 (1934)] discarded such theory in favor of a brilliant new departure in the form of a non-purely-competitive dynamic disequilibrium approach. But mainstream economic theory did not move until our next period.

5. *The Real Wage Rate*

The real wage rate may be seen as the outcome of a race between technology and population. If population is running away from technology, the real wage rate will be declining. Until the nineteenth century, population had by and large kept up with technology and kept the real wage rate roughly stationary. To Cantillon and Ricardo population was the equilibrating variable that would bring the real wage rate into accordance with a subsistence minimum. With the second industrial revolution came birth control, and it was no longer true that "Men multiply like Mice in a barn if they have unlimited Means of Subsistence."

In the late nineteenth century there was unmistakable evidence that in Western Europe and North America, for the first time in the history of mankind, technology was running away from population, and the real wage rate began climbing. Phelps Brown (1973) found the real wage rate and labor productivity to have been growing at the following annual rates:

	Real Wage Rate	Labor Productivity
United States 1890/99-1960	0.0208	0.0203
Germany 1890/99-1960	0.0161	0.0151
Sweden 1892/99-1960	0.0191	0.0223

[1]A thin thread connects the history of industry with the history of theory: the firm was founded by Eleuthère Irénée du Pont, son of the physiocrat Pierre Samuel du Pont (1739-1817), admiringly characterized by Schumpeter (1954: 226) as a "'go-getter' who never forgot honor and principle," and the able editor of *Ephémérides du citoyen*—where Turgot's work was first published. Father and son fled the French Revolution and settled in Wilmington, Delaware.

The rates of growth of the real wage rate and labor productivity show a correspondence equally good in the United States, where unionization came late and was weak, and Germany and Sweden, where unionization came early and was strong.

6. Government

By seventeenth-century and eighteenth-century standards the century between the Battle of Waterloo in 1815 and the First Battle of the Marne in 1914 was a peaceful one. Wars of unification in America in 1861-1865 and Germany in 1866 were won by the industrially superior North, and Yankees and Prussians became the leaders of the second industrial revolution.

Representative government spread to Central Europe. The franchise, the steadily climbing real wage rate, and social security—pioneered by Bismarck in 1883-1889—began to derevolutionize revolutionary socialism. Eduard Bernstein [1899 (1909), (1961)] urged the very political party Marx had helped founding to jettison Marx and found it increasingly ready to do so.

7. The Golden Decades after 1870

When after 1870 mainstream economics backed out of the dead-end street of the labor theory of value, a pent-up demand for and supply of fresh ideas were liberated. There was intellectual excitement as never before in economic theory. In the four decades following 1870 old problems such as relative price and the distributive shares found new and elegant solutions. New problems such as allocation of resources in a general equilibrium swiftly found equally elegant ones. When the four decades were over, came massive fratricide and after it what Samuelson (1947: 4) has called "the unmistakable signs of decadence which were clearly present in economic thought prior to 1930."

II. NOTATION

1. Variables

C ≡ consumption of all households
C_k ≡ consumption of kth household
c_j ≡ cost incurred by a firm in jth industry
E ≡ physical units of jth output exchanged per physical unit of $j + 1$st
g ≡ proportionate rate of growth
L ≡ labor employed

P_j ≡ price of jth output
p_i ≡ price of ith input
q ≡ weight of weighted sums
R_j ≡ money value of revenue of a firm in jth industry
r ≡ rate of interest
S ≡ physical capital stock
U_k ≡ one index of utility to the kth household
V_k ≡ another index of utility to the kth household
X_j ≡ jth physical output demanded by all households
X_{jk} ≡ jth physical output demanded by kth household
x_{ij} ≡ ith physical input demanded by jth industry
Y ≡ money value of income of all households
Y_k ≡ money value of income of kth household
y ≡ period of production
Z_j ≡ profits earned by a firm in jth industry

2. *Parameters*

A ≡ exponent of utility function
B ≡ exponent of utility function
a_{ij} ≡ ith physical input demanded per physical unit of output of jth industry
x_i ≡ ith physical input supplied by all households
x_{ki} ≡ ith physical input supplied by kth household

III. STATIC GENERAL EQUILIBRIUM: JEVONS, THE AUSTRIANS, WALRAS

1. *Allocation, Preferences, and Utility*

After 1870, the general problem of a market allocation of resources came into full view. A dramatic reallocation of resources manifested itself in the birth of new industries and the death of old ones and raised a question that the labor theory of value could never hope to answer. At best, and only in agony, the labor theory of value could explain relative prices. To come to grips with allocation of resources a theory must make room for preferences. That was what mainstream theory did after 1870.

While the inclusion of preferences is a necessary condition for the formulation of general equilibrium, it is not a sufficient condition. Cournot and Marshall (1890) used preferences very effectively to build partial-equilibrium models, but both recoiled from any attempt to build general-equilibrium ones.

Jevons, the Austrians, and Walras included preferences in a form that they must have thought of as tangible and tractable—so tangible and tractable that they expressed it in numbers and drew curves of it. The form was utility. If not yet practically measurable, utility was thought of as a measure. A measure of what? A measure of human sensation. The Austrians and Walras never mentioned sensations of pain. To Jevons, if positive, utility was a measure of pleasure, if negative, a measure of pain.

2. The Unwritten Utility Function

Had Jevons or the Austrians ever written a utility function, they would have written it the way Walras did, i.e., making utility a function of all goods consumed and yet making each of its partial derivatives a function of merely the quantity with respect to which the partial derivative was taken. For example, for the kth household consuming two goods they might have written the additive utility function

$$U_k = X_{1k}{}^A + X_{2k}{}^B$$

each of whose partial derivatives $\partial U_k/\partial X_{1k} = AX_{1k}{}^{A-1}$ and $\partial U_k/\partial X_{2k} = BX_{2k}{}^{B-1}$ would have been a funciton of merely the quantity with respect to which the partial derivative was taken.

By contrast, replace addition by multiplication and write

$$U_k = X_{1k}{}^A X_{2k}{}^B$$

each of whose partial derivatives $\partial U_k/\partial X_{1k} = AX_{1k}{}^{A-1}X_{2k}{}^B$ and $\partial U_k/\partial X_{2k} = X_{1k}{}^A BX_{2k}{}^{B-1}$ will be a function of the quantities X_{1k} and X_{2k} of *both* goods consumed.

An additive utility function could be called a partial-equilibrium utility function. In his restatement of Jevons, Edgeworth [1881 (1967: 104)] was the first to replace it by "utility . . . regarded as a function of the two variables, not the sum of two functions of each." Marshall, always in favor of partial equilibria, admitted [1890 (1920: 845)] that Edgeworth's revision had "great attractions to the mathematician; but it seems less adapted to express the every day facts of economic life than that of regarding, as Jevons did, the marginal utilities of apples as functions of [the quantity of apples] simply."

Next, let us consider the differences between Jevons, the Austrians, and Walras. The differences were twofold.

3. How General Were the Equilibria?

The first difference was the extent to which the equilibria were general ones. Jevons and Menger merely dealt with do-it-yourself households. Strictly speaking, such households can have no income and pay no prices. Wieser and Walras clearly separated industry from households. Once separated from households, industry demands inputs and supplies outputs; households demand outputs and supply inputs. It follows that Wieserian and Walrasian outputs supplied by industry were consumers' goods. Furthermore it follows that Wieserian and Walrasian inputs supplied by households were primary ones such as the various qualities of labor and the services of the various qualities of land. Outputs and inputs alike, then, were transacted in markets and had prices, and money incomes were earned and spent. A determination of such prices and incomes could now be attempted.

4. *Factor Supplies*

The second difference between Jevons, the Austrians, and Walras was their treatment of factor supplies. The Austrian treatment was the simplest. The endowment of households with inputs such as labor and land was a parameter. Austrian households never contemplated supplying more or less of their endowment: the entire endowment was supplied.

Jevons and Walras saw the part of endowment supplied as a variable, but their supply functions were quite different. To Jevons, labor was painful, and pain was a negative utility. Jevons's do-it-yourself households would supply labor until, on the margin, the utility of its output just balanced the disutility of its input. Walrasian households were not do-it-yourselfers but faced a market for their labor. Supplying more of it would deprive them of leisure, at first copious, later scarcer. Leisure yielded utility just as output consumed did. Walrasian households would supply labor until, on the margin, the added utility of a larger income just balanced the utility lost by the inroads it made on their leisure. No pain of labor was mentioned.

We shall devote chapters 5 and 6 to full treatments of Walras and the Austrians, respectively, and shall now report briefly on Jevons's exchange, labor, and capital equilibria.

5. *Jevons*

In his own words [1871 (1931: preface)], Jevons "attempted to treat Economy as a Calculus of Pleasure and Pain, and . . . sketched out, almost irrespective of previous opinions, the form which the science, as it seems to me, must ultimately take. I have long thought that as it deals throughout with quantities, it must be a mathematical science in matter if not in language." In the preface to the first edition all writers referred to except Garnier were English, their "weight of authority" was acknowledged, observing that, often in other sciences, "authority was on the wrong side."

The tone sharpened in the preface to the second edition [1879 (1931)]. English economics was characterized (xlii) as "insular narrowness" and (xlv) "a fool's paradise." The only hope (xliv) was "to fling aside, once and for ever, the mazy and preposterous assumptions of the Ricardian school." On the positive side (xxviii through xxxix) full tribute was paid to Cournot, Dupuit, and Gossen and, already in the first edition [1871 (1931: 159)], to Bernoulli.

6. Jevons On Exchange

In his chapter IV on pure exchange, Jevons visualized at first persons each of whom possessed one single kind of commodity. Later, Jevons [1871 (1931: 138)] supposed "that a person possesses one single kind of commodity, which we may consider to be money, or income." A general-equilibrium model in which inputs were supplied by households and demanded by industry would have explained how such income was earned, but Jevons never mentioned its source. Let us call such income Y_k and use it as a budget constraint.

Let the utility of the kth household be a function of the physical quantities of m commodities consumed:

$$U_k = U_k(X_{1k}, \ldots, X_{mk}) \tag{1}$$

Jevons never wrote an explicit utility function but did consider each of its partial derivatives as a function of merely the quantity with respect to which the partial derivative was taken. Assume $\partial U_k/\partial X_{jk} > 0$ and $\partial^2 U_k/\partial X_{jk}^2 < 0$.

Jevons's chapter on exchange referred not only to income Y_k but also to prices P_j of the m commodities. Define the money value of consumption in the kth household as the sum of the money values of the m commodities demanded by that household:

$$C_k \equiv \sum_{j=1}^{m} (P_j X_{jk}) \tag{2}$$

Let the kth household maximize its utility subject to the budget constraint

$$C_k = Y_k \tag{3}$$

Once income Y_k and price P_j have been referred to, we may as well follow the more articulate Walras: in the neighborhood of a utility maximum let the kth household change infinitesimally its X_{jk} by dX_{jk} and its $X_{(j+1)k}$ by $dX_{(j+1)k}$. Then two things may be said. First, the changes must not affect utility U_k, which is already at its maximum. Second, the changes must not violate the budget constraint (3): if the household wants to demand more of one commodity, it must demand less of another. Thus

$$dU_k \equiv \frac{\partial U_k}{\partial X_{jk}} \, dX_{jk} + \frac{\partial U_k}{\partial X_{(j+1)k}} \, dX_{(j+1)k} = 0$$

$$dC_k \equiv \frac{\partial C_k}{\partial X_{jk}} \, dX_{jk} + \frac{\partial C_k}{\partial X_{(j+1)k}} \, dX_{(j+1)k} = 0$$

The prices P_j are constants to the individual household. Treat them as such, use (1) and (2) to carry out the partial derivations, and find a Jevons-Walras household seeking the point at which the marginal rate of substitution equals *minus* the ratio between the marginal utilities as well as *minus* the price ratio or:

$$\frac{dX_{jk}}{dX_{(j+1)k}} = - \frac{\partial U_k / \partial X_{(j+1)k}}{\partial U_k / \partial X_{jk}} = - \frac{P_{j+1}}{P_j} \tag{4}$$

If the jth and the $j + 1$st commodities are priced at P_j and P_{j+1}, respectively, then P_{j+1}/P_j physical units of the jth commodity will exchange for one physical unit of the $j + 1$st. Call that ratio of exchange E, insert it into (4), and find Jevons's first property of his equilibrium ratio of exchange:

$$E \equiv \frac{P_{j+1}}{P_j} = \frac{\partial U_k / \partial X_{(j+1)k}}{\partial U_k / \partial X_{jk}} \tag{5}$$

or in his own words [1871 (1931: 139)]:

If for one pound of silk I can have three of cotton, then the degree of utility of cotton must be a third that of silk, otherwise I should gain by exchange. Thus the general result of the facility of exchange prevailing in a civilised country is, that a person procures such quantities of commodities that the final degrees of utility of any pair of commodities are inversely as the ratios of exchange of the commodities.

7. *Jevons on Labor*

Jevons's chapter on exchange referred to both income and prices—without revealing where such income was earned or by whom such prices were charged. Such references notwithstanding, we learn in chapter V on labor that his commodities were produced by do-it-yourself households from labor alone. To Jevons utility was a number measuring—if positive—a sensation of pleasure or—if negative—a sensation of pain. He proposed [1871 (1931: 178)] to "treat labour as simply one case of disutility or negative utility ..." Indeed, Jevons measured his "amount of labor'' not by hours worked but by the pain caused by them and, accordingly, measured labor's contribution to physical output by the derivative of it with respect to such pain. Let us use poetic licence, modernize Jevons, write labor performed by the kth household as its hours worked x_k, and write the utility of the kth household as a function of its physical quantities of m commodities consumed as well as of its hours worked:

$$U_k = U_k(X_{1k}, \ldots, X_{mk}, x_k) \tag{6}$$

Again, Jevons considered each of his partial derivatives as a function of merely the quantity with respect to which the partial derivative was taken. In accordance with Jevons's figure 9 [1871 (1931: 173)] assume $\partial U_k/\partial X_{jk} > 0$, $\partial^2 U_k/\partial X_{jk}^2 < 0$, $\partial U_k/\partial x_k < 0$, and $\partial^2 U_k/\partial x_k^2 < 0$.

In Jevons's production function—also not written explicitly—labor was the only input, but the do-it-yourself household would obviously have to produce several outputs. So let us write it with its only input on the left-hand side and all the outputs on the right-hand side:

$$x_k = x_k(X_{1k}, \ldots, X_{mk}) \tag{7}$$

where $\partial x_k/\partial X_{jk} > 0$ and equals the inverse $1/(\partial X_{jk}/\partial x_k)$ of the better known physical marginal productivity of labor $\partial X_{jk}/\partial x_k$. $\partial^2 x_k/\partial X_{jk}^2 > 0$.

Now assume the household to have succeeded in maximizing utility. In the immediate neighborhood of such a utility maximum let the kth household change infinitesimally its hours worked x_k by dx_k. It may then be said that the change must not affect utility U_k which is already at its maximum. Let us separate the positive from the negative effect upon utility. The positive effect is a chain rule multiplying marginal utility by physical marginal productivity: $(\partial U_k/\partial X_{jk})(\partial X_{jk}/\partial x_k)$, and the negative effect is the direct derivative $\partial U_k/\partial x_k$. Their sum must be zero for any output, say the jth and the $j + 1$st:

$$dU_k \equiv \frac{\partial U_k}{\partial X_{jk}} \frac{\partial X_{jk}}{\partial x_k} dx_k + \frac{\partial U_k}{\partial x_k} dx_k = 0$$

$$dU_k \equiv \frac{\partial U_k}{\partial X_{(j+1)k}} \frac{\partial X_{(j+1)k}}{\partial x_k} dx_k + \frac{\partial U_k}{\partial x_k} dx_k = 0$$

or, in Jevons's words [1871 (1931: 185)], "Labour will be carried on until the increment of utility from any of the employments just balances the increment of pain."

Divide dx_k away, rearrange, and find Jevons's second property of his equilibrium ratio of exchange:

$$\frac{\partial U_k/\partial X_{(j+1)k}}{\partial U_k/\partial X_{jk}} = \frac{\partial X_{jk}/\partial x_k}{\partial X_{(j+1)k}/\partial x_k} \tag{8}$$

How are Jevons's two properties (5) and (8) related? He [1871 (1931: 186)] was aware that if "the person is in a position to exchange with other persons," then his property (5) must apply to physical quantities *after production*, and his property (8) to physical quantities *after exchange*. In that case, the right-hand side of his (5) and the left-hand side of his (8) become equal and may be hooked up or, in Jevons's own words [1871 (1931: 192-193)]:

> The quantities of commodity given or received in exchange are directly proportional to the degrees or productiveness of labour applied to their production, and inversely proportional to the . . . prices of those commodities and to . . . their final degrees of utility.

8.   *Walras*

We shall devote our chapter 5 to the Walras version of general equilibrium. Smith had explained the price of outputs by cost of production: because 2 francs were paid out in rent, 2 francs in wages, and 1 franc in interest, a bottle of wine would sell for 5 francs. Austrians sometimes seemed to be offering the opposite explanation: because the bottle sells for 5 francs, 2 francs could be paid out in rent, 2 francs in wages, and 1 franc in interest. Offering such one-way causal relationships, Smith and the Austrians, like other good economists, did not always fully understand what they themselves were doing.

Walras understood. In an economy resting in competitive equilibrium, Walras asked, what are the physical quantities of outputs supplied by industry and demanded by households, what are the physical quantities of inputs supplied by households and demanded by industry, and what are the relative prices at which all such outputs and inputs are transacted? He understood that any determination of such a comprehensive equilibrium would have to be a *simultaneous* one—but did not understand that mere counting of equations and variables was not enough to establish such a determination.

9.   *The Austrians*

We shall devote our chapter 6 to the Austrian version of general equilibrium. Its unifying principle was that goods were valued because needed and that their value would depend on the need satisfied by the last unit available. That need would be the least important one. The unifying principle applied to households and firms alike. In households, goods were needed as outputs to maximize household utility. In firms, goods were needed as inputs to maximize firm profits. The unifying principle applied to reproducible and irreproducible goods alike. Applied to reproducible goods, the unifying principle applied both on the demand and the supply sides: costs of production would depend upon prices of inputs, and inputs were valued because needed.

10. *A Socialist General Equilibrium?*

The unifying principle would even transcend capitalism. Socialism would differ from capitalism merely by its absence of private property to capital and land: no household could earn interest, profits, or rent; only the government could do that and would distribute such incomes to the comrades according to set rules. Otherwise, a socialist economy would function much like a capitalist one. Specifically its households would be free to choose which job to take and which consumers' goods to buy.

On the functioning of socialism Marx and his followers had been silent. Personally without sympathy for socialism but a good Walrasian, Barone [1908 (1935)] did them the favor of writing the equations for prices and quantities of the primary inputs supplied by socialist households and the outputs demanded by them, counting equations and unknowns, and deciding that a socialist general equilibrium, too, was determinate and could be thought of as a simulation of purely competitive capitalism. The socialist managers would consider all prices parameters and hence act *as if* they were pure competitors. Those prices, in turn, would be fixed by the socialist ministry of production acting *as if* it were a Walrasian auctioneer engaged in *tâtonnement*. Thirty years later, Barone was to be followed by Lange and Lerner.

Walras [1874-1877 (1954: 268-269 and 289)] had determined the market price of durable producers' goods as a capitalization of their net income. But as von Mises [1920 (1935)] observed, under socialism no private individual could own such goods, earn a net income from them, demand them, or supply them. Consequently such goods could have no market price. Without market prices of durable producers' goods how could the ministry of production calculate the cost and hence the price of outputs? As we shall see in our next period, a Soviet mathematician (Kantorovich) was to offer an answer to von Mises's problem.

IV. THE UTILITY FUNCTION: JEVONS, EDGEWORTH, FISHER, PARETO, AND CASSEL

1. *Utility as a Measure of Sensation: The Pioneers and Edgeworth*

To Jevons, the Austrians, and Walras utility was a number measuring a sensation. So it was to Edgeworth who, in his first three lines [1881 (1967: l)], said that he wanted to apply mathematics to "the calculus of *Feeling*, of Pleasure and Pain ..."

An indifference map may be defined without abandoning such a meaning of utility—as Edgeworth [1881 (1967: 21)] did—or in the process of abandoning it—as Fisher [1892 (1925: 67-70)] did. Fisher used solid geometry to visualize a utility surface whose altitude above a horizontal consumption plane measures the sensation. Such a utility surface could intersect a horizontal plane above the horizontal consumption plane. The curve of intersection could be projected on the consumption plane and called an "indifference curve"—the term used by Fisher. A family of such indifference curves could be generated by moving the second horizontal plane from one position to another. Such a family of indifference curves would resemble the iso-altitude contour curves on a U.S. Geological Survey map, each carrying an altitude coordinate. Each Edgeworthian indifference curve would carry a coordinate measuring a sensation.

2. *Utility as an Index of Preference or Indifference: Fisher and Pareto*

Fisher [1892 (1925: 67-89)] and Pareto [1906 (1971: 105-133)] abandoned the meaning of utility as a measure of sensation.

Facing two events of consumption, all a household needs to decide before acting or not acting is whether the first event is preferred to the second, neither is preferred to the other, or the second is preferred to the first. If a utility index can unequivocally indicate such preference or indifference, it will have accomplished all that we need to accomplish. In Pareto's words, a utility index "must satisfy the following two conditions, and ... is arbitrary in other respects: (1) Two combinations between which the choice is indifferent must have the same index; (2) of two combinations, the one which is preferred to the other must have the larger index."

Several, indeed infinitely many, indices will serve equally well as long as they agree as to whether the first combination is preferred to the second, neither is preferred to the other, or the second is preferred to the first. Such agreement will occur as long as any index is a monotonic transformation of any other.

Let a first utility index be

$$V_k = V_k(X_{1k}, \ldots, X_{mk}) \tag{9}$$

Let a second one be

$$U_k = U_k(V_k) = U_k[V_k(X_{1k}, \ldots, X_{mk})] \tag{10}$$

such that any change of consumption pattern which changes V_k will change U_k in the same direction:

$$\frac{dU_k}{dV_k} > 0 \tag{11}$$

Now consider such a change in consumption pattern. Let the kth household change infinitesimally its X_{jk} by dX_{jk} and its $X_{(j+1)k}$ by $dX_{(j+1)k}$. The effect of such changes upon the V-index of utility is defined by the total differential

$$dV_k \equiv \frac{\partial V_k}{\partial X_{jk}} \, dX_{jk} + \frac{\partial V_k}{\partial X_{(j+1)k}} \, dX_{(j+1)k} \tag{12}$$

The effect upon the U-index of utility is defined by the total differential

$$dU_k \equiv \frac{dU_k}{dV_k} \frac{\partial V_k}{\partial X_{jk}} \, dX_{jk} + \frac{dU_k}{dV_k} \frac{\partial V_k}{\partial X_{(j+1)k}} \, dX_{(j+1)k} \tag{13}$$

In (13) factor out dU_k / dV_k, insert (12), and find

$$dU_k \equiv \frac{dU_k}{dV_k} \, dV_k$$

As long as (11) holds, if $dV_k \gtreqless 0$, then $dU_k \gtreqless 0$, respectively, and the U-scale and the V-scale will agree on preference or indifference, as Pareto required them to do. Let us take a closer look at indifference.

Using the V-scale, express indifference by setting (12) equal to zero, rearrange, and find the marginal rate of substitution

$$\frac{dX_{jk}}{dX_{(j+1)k}} = - \frac{\partial V_k / \partial X_{(j+1)k}}{\partial V_k / \partial X_{jk}} \tag{14}$$

Using the U-scale, express indifference by setting (13) equal to zero, rearrange, and find the marginal rate of substitution

$$\frac{dX_{jk}}{dX_{(j+1)k}} = - \frac{(dU_k / dV_k)[\partial V_k / \partial X_{(j+1)k}]}{(dU_k / dV_k)(\partial V_k / \partial X_{jk})} \tag{15}$$

According to (11), dU_k / dV_k cannot be zero, hence will cancel, and (15) will collapse into (14): the marginal rate of substitution is immune to our monotonic transformation. But the marginal rate of substitution is nothing but the slope of the indifference curve at the point whose coordinates indicate the initial consumption pattern. Repeating the argument for any consumption pattern, we find the entire indifference map to be immune to our monotonic transformation.

Having seen utility as an index of preference or indifference, we must relate it to demand. We shall then discover that the relation between utility and demand is a two-way street, and we shall move both ways.

3.   *From Utility to Demand: Differentiability of Utility Function*

First let us move from utility to demand and ask: given a differentiable utility function, can a demand function always be found by maximizing the utility function subject to a budget constraint? Walras took total differentials of his utility function and his budget constraint, set those differentials equal to zero, and found his household seeking the point at which the marginal rate of substitution equals *minus* the ratio between the marginal utilities as well as *minus* the price ratio or:

$$\frac{dX_{jk}}{dX_{(j+1)k}} = - \frac{\partial U_k/\partial X_{(j+1)k}}{\partial U_k/\partial X_{jk}} = - \frac{P_{j+1}}{P_j} \tag{16}$$

Mathematically speaking, we are trying to obtain the differential equation (16) associated with a given primitive, i.e., the given utility function. The calculus needed to do that is the differential calculus. Fortunately, if a function is differentiable in the first place, i.e., has neither gaps nor kinks in it, there is always a uniform, step-by step process of differentiation. No guesswork is necessary.

Will a pair X_{jk}, $X_{(j+1)k}$ satisfying (16) always represent a utility maximum? To see if it will, we must first do some definitional groundwork.[2]

4.   *Strict Quasi-concavity*

Let the kth household be facing two events of consumption, *a* and *b*. Each event represents a specific value of the pair X_{jk}, $X_{(j+1)k}$. Define arbitrary weights q and $1 - q$, where $0 < q < 1$. A weighted sum of the two events is then $qa + (1 - q)b$, and the utility of that weighted sum is $V_k[qa + (1 - q)b]$. Finally, let the utilities of the events *a* and *b* themselves be $V_k(a)$ and $V_k(b)$. Then if the utility of the weighted sum of events *a* and *b* is greater than at least one of the utilities of the events themselves, i.e., if either

$$V_k[qa + (1 - q)b] > V_k(a)$$

or

$$V_k[qa + (1 - q)b] > V_k(b) \tag{17}$$

then the utility function V_k is said to be strictly quasi-concave.

It follows immediately that if we replace our first utility index V_k defined by (9) by a second one U_k defined by (10), such that (11) holds, then either

---

[2]Our next two sections on strict quasi-concavity summarize Baumol (1977: 216-223), to whom the reader is referred.

$$U_k[qa + (1 - q)b] > U_k(a)$$

or

$$U_k[qa + (1 - q)b] > U_k(b) \qquad (18)$$

for, as Pareto said, any utility index must satisfy the condition that of two combinations, the one that is preferred to the other must have the larger index. In other words, if (17) is satisfied, then (18) will be, and the property of strict quasi-concavity will consequently be immune to our monotonic transformation of (9) into (10).

5. A Strictly Quasi-concave Utility Function Will Have Indifference Curves Convex to the Origin

In Figure IV-1 assume the events a and b to be located on an indifference curve. Consequently,

$$V_k(a) = V_k(b)$$

Define the event c as the weighted sum of the events a and b:

$$c \equiv qa + (1 - q)b$$

Could the event c be on the indifference curve? In a strictly quasi-concave utility function $V_k(c) > V_k(a) = V_k(b)$. Consequently, the event c cannot be on the indifference curve through a and b.

FIGURE IV-1.
A Strictly
Quasi-concave Utility
Function Will Have
Indifference Curves
Convex to the Origin

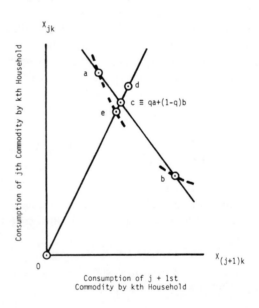

Draw a line from the origin through c. Consider an event d on that line beyond c. Could the event d be on the indifference curve? Since the event d has more of both commodities, it must also have more utility than the event c:

$$V_k(d) > V_k(c)$$

In a strictly quasi-concave utility function already $V_k(c) > V_k(a) = V_k(b)$. It follows *a fortiori* that $V_k(d) > V_k(a) = V_k(b)$. Consequently, the event d cannot be on the indifference curve through a and b either.

Finally consider an event e on the same line but inside c. Could the event e be on the indifference curve? Since the event e has less of both commodities, it must also have less utility than the event c:

$$V_k(e) < V_k(c)$$

In a strictly quasi-concave utility function $V_k(c) > V_k(a) = V_k(b)$. Consequently, nothing in (17) prevents $V_k(e) = V_k(a) = V_k(b)$. Consequently, the event e could be on the broken indifference curve through a and b, and the latter must then be convex to the origin. If so, a pair X_{jk}, $X_{(j+1)k}$ satisfying (16) will indeed represent a utility maximum.

6. Income and Substitution Effects: Slutsky

Basically, Slutsky [1915 (1952)] had taken us this far. He then wished to decompose the effect of a price change dP_j into a substitution effect and an income effect.[3] His substitution effect was very similar to the later and more familiar Hicks-Allen (1934) one. The difference between them, which will vanish when the price change dP_j approaches zero, was this.

The Slutsky substitution effect was a movement from the original consumption point along a *budget* line sloped according to the new price ratio to a position of tangency with an indifference curve. The income effect was the jump from the latter tangency point to the new consumption point. The Hicks-Allen substitution effect was a movement from the original consumption point along an *indifference* curve to a position of tangency with a budget line sloped according to the new price ratio. The income effect was the jump from the latter tangency point to the new consumption point.

7. From Demand to Utility: Integrability of Utility Function

Let us now move the opposite way on our two-way street, i.e., from demand to utility and ask: given an observed demand function, can a util-

---

[3]Slutsky's article does not read easily. Readers needing help will find it in Baumol (1977: 209-212; 336-339) and Katzner (1970: 54-59).

ity function always be found whose maximization subject to a budget constraint will deliver the given demand function?

Equation (16) is still a first-order condition for a utility maximum subject to a budget constraint and had better be satisfied by the utility function we are looking for.

Mathematically speaking, we are now trying to recover the primitive that gave rise to the differential equation (16). The calculus needed to do that is the integral calculus. Unfortunately, there is no uniform, step-by-step process of integration as there was for differentiation. Guesswork is necessary: "thinking backwards," one must try to think of something whose derivative equals what is under the integral sign. Consequently, the utility function we are looking for cannot always be found.

Giovanni Battista Antonelli [1886 (1968)]—not to be confused with Étienne Antonelli—and Fisher [1892 (1925: 86-89)] were the first to see the two-way street and with it the integrability problem.[4]

8. *The Ultimate Purge: Cassel's Revealed Preference*

So when maximized subject to a budget constraint, a strictly quasi-concave utility index will tell us everything we wish to know about demand—it has no other purpose and is a sufficient condition for serving that purpose. But while demand is observable, a strictly quasi-concave utility index corresponding to it may not always be found. Could we do without it? If, as Schumpeter (1954: 1067) put it, "everything else is idle decoration," why not purge economic theory of its nonobservable utility indices and start with the observable demand functions themselves? Cassel (1899), [1918 (1932)] was the first to do so consistently.

V. CAPITAL THEORY: JEVONS AND BÖHM-BAWERK

1. *The Time Structure of Production*

After 1870, the general problem of the time structure of production came into full view. New technology came embodied in what Ricardo had called "machinery" and what the Austrians called "roundabout methods of production." Ricardo's labor-capital substitution problem would have to be looked into once again.

2. *Jevons and Böhm-Bawerk*

In a partial equilibrium Jevons saw much of what Böhm-Bawerk was to see: what took time in a capitalist process of production was the matur-

---

[4]The reader will find a modern treatment of integrability in Katzner (1970: 65-74).

ing of output in slow organic growth in agriculture, cattle raising, forestry, and winery or in time-consuming construction jobs. Physical capital stock in such processes of production could be seen as the stock of intermediate goods building up during the period of production such as the maturing wine, the growing mass of timber, etc. Jevons went Böhm-Bawerk one better and applied compound interest with annual compounding to such cases [1871 (1931: 239)]:

> Every pound invested at the commencement of a business becomes 1.63 pounds at the end of ten years, 11.47 pounds at the end of fifty years, and no less than 131.50 pounds at the end of a century, the rate of interest being taken at five per cent. Thus it cannot be profitable to store wine for fifty years, unless it become about twelve times as valuable as it was when new. It cannot pay to plant an oak and let it live a century, unless the timber then repays the cost of planting 132 times.

Jevons [1871 (1931: 245)] defined his period of production as "the time elapsing between the expenditure of the labour and the enjoyment of the result" and made "produce for the same amount of labour" a rising function of it or, in our own notation, $S = S(y)$ where $dS/dy > 0$. He then took what he called [1871 (1931: 246)] "the rate of increase of the produce divided by the whole produce" and found "the rate of interest to be represented by [it]":

$$g_S \equiv \frac{dS}{dy} \frac{1}{S} = r$$

In simple English, then, the wine will be stored, or the timber left standing, up to the point where the rate of growth of its value or its quantity, respectively, with respect to the period of production will equal the rate of interest. At five percent interest, the last extension of the period of production must yield a five percent growth of the value of the wine or the quantity of the timber. Or, as Wicksell would have put it, the "natural" rate of interest must equal the money rate.

Thus far Jevons anticipated Böhm-Bawerk. But no farther. As we shall see in chapter 7, in a general-equilibrium model Böhm-Bawerk established the relations between the period of production, the rate of interest, and the real wage rate. Jevons did no such thing but made the odd statement [1871 (1931: 255)] that "I conceive that the returns to capital and labour are independent of each other." Equally strangely, Jevons [1871 (1931: 222)] saw "no close or necessary connection between the employment of capital and the processes of exchange."

VI. SYNTHESIS OF PARTIAL EQUILIBRIUM: MARSHALL

1. *The Elements of the Synthesis*

With loving care and superior expository skill, Marshall [1890 (1920)] integrated into one massive volume the marginal utility of Jevons, the Austrians, and Walras; Cournot's and Dupuit's demand curves; Cournot's monopoly; Dupuit's consumers' surplus; and von Thünen's marginal productivity. Of such predecessors only von Thünen received adequate tribute—in striking contrast to the overstated tribute paid to Ricardo and John Stuart Mill.

2. *Small Is Beautiful*

Unlike Gossen and Menger but like Walras and Wieser, Marshall clearly separated industry from households. Once separated from households, industry demands inputs and supplies outputs; households demand outputs and supply inputs. Marshall's equilibria were partial ones. He made them two-dimensional, simple, and neat by keeping everything small. First, Marshall kept the fraction of a household's budget spent on any single output small enough to enable him to ignore the effects of such expenditure upon the demand for other outputs. Second, Marshall kept his "representative firm" small enough to enable him to ignore the effects of its output upon market price. A Marshallian industry was a collection of such firms, all producing the same product. Third, Marshall kept such an industry itself small enough to enable him to ignore the effects of its input or output upon other industries.

As a result, the supply and demand curves of such a purely competitive industry could be considered independent of the rest of the economy, hence of each other, and would intersect in a point constituting a purely competitive partial equilibrium.

A system of such purely competitive partial equilibria faced three challenges.

3. *Increasing Returns to Scale*

Marshall, a good observer, observed the increasing returns to scale inherent in the second industrial revolution. They posed the first challenge to his purely competitive partial equilibria. Marshall did not wish to surrender his assumption of pure competition and went to great lengths to demonstrate the existence of decreasing returns to scale within the firm. First, there was what we might call the Buddenbrooks[5] syndrome. Think-

[5]Thomas Mann [1901 (1924)].

ing of proprietorships or family corporations, Marshall explained that whatever bounds to firm size existed, growth towards them would always be slow, and alas, after three generations the entrepreneurial spirit would have spent itself: the founder's grandson would turn his attention to the fine arts. Second, Marshall explained that whatever increasing returns to scale existed were external to the firm, hence resulted from industry size but not firm size.

Marshall's sole concession was his monopoly model offered in book v, chapter 14. Instead of using marginal conditions as Cournot had done, Marshall used total ones. Perhaps for that reason, Cournot's marginal-revenue concept was forgotten and had to be rediscovered in the 1930s, as we shall see in our next period.

4. *Interindustry Complementarity or Substitutability*

The second challenge faced by Marshall's purely competitive partial equilibria was interindustry complementarity or substitutability. A full treatment would require a microeconomic general equilibrium like that of Walras. Marshall did not wish to go that far. His sole concession was his rudimentary note xxi of the mathematical appendix.

5. *The Distributive Shares*

Being by their very nature economywide, factor markets posed the third challenge faced by Marshall's purely competitive partial equilibria. A full treatment of them would require an aggregative general equilibrium like that of Böhm-Bawerk. Marshall did not wish to go that far but tried to keep even his labor market small, e.g., his market for plasterers. As a result, his treatment of the distributive shares in book vi was his weakest performance.

6. *Marshall and Mathematics*

Himself a trained mathematician, Marshall in 1906 gave Bowley the strange advice to "use mathematics as a shorthand language, rather than as an engine of inquiry." Had Marshall followed his own advice, he could not have written his mathematical appendix and probably not the rest of his *Principles* either. In this sense, he "hid the tool that had done the work," as Schumpeter (1951: 97) put it.

VII. THE PRODUCTION FUNCTION: WICKSTEED, CLARK, AND WICKSELL

1. *The Large Firm*

Marshall notwithstanding, the technology of the second industrial revolution came on a scale that only large firms could exploit. In the new industries the giant corporation emerged, but economic theory came to grips with it rather slowly. With Schumpeter (1954: 1048), we may well ask "why results were established in and after 1930 that might easily have been established by 1890." Let us summarize what *was* established before 1930.

2. *Production, Cost, Revenue, and Profits*

Let all firms in the jth industry, established as well as potential ones, be alike and have the differentiable production function

$$X_j = X_j(x_{1j}, \ldots, x_{nj}) \tag{19}$$

where $\partial X_j/\partial x_{ij} > 0$, $\partial^2 X_j/\partial x_{ij}^2 < 0$, and $\partial^2 X_j/[\partial x_{(i+1)j}\partial x_{ij}] > 0$.

Define the money value of the cost incurred by such a firm as the sum of the money values of the inputs demanded by that firm:

$$c_j \equiv \sum_{i=1}^{n} (p_i x_{ij}) \tag{20}$$

Relative to the markets for the inputs demanded by it, let the firm be small enough to have no influence on the prices p_i of such inputs. Relative to the market for the output supplied by it, let the firm be possibly large enough to have an influence on the price P_j of such output and to be facing the differentiable demand function

$$P_j = P_j(X_j) \tag{21}$$

where $dP_j/dX_j \leq 0$. Given such a demand function, define the money value of the revenue of the firm as the money value of the output supplied:

$$R_j \equiv P_j X_j \tag{22}$$

Finally, define the profits earned by the firm as the difference between revenue and cost:

$$Z_j \equiv R_j - c_j \tag{23}$$

and let them be maximized.

3. *Profit Maximization*

Insert (19) through (22) into (23), recall the chain rule $\partial P_j/\partial x_{ij} \equiv (dP_j/dX_j)(\partial X_j/\partial x_{ij})$, vary the *i*th input, and take the partial derivative of profits with respect to it. A first-order condition for a profit maximum is that all such partial derivatives be zero:

$$\frac{\partial Z_j}{\partial x_{ij}} = \left(P_j + \frac{dP_j}{dX_j}\,X_j\right)\frac{\partial X_j}{\partial x_{ij}} - p_i = 0$$

or rearranging:

$$p_i = \left(P_j + \frac{dP_j}{dX_j}\,X_j\right)\frac{\partial X_j}{\partial x_{ij}} \tag{24}$$

The parenthesis of (24) is marginal revenue, defined by Cournot, seen as a modification of von Thünen by Berry [1891 (1968: 314)], clearly related to price elasticity by Johnson and Sanger [1894 (1968: 45-46)], but not baptized until 1933. What (24) says is that any input should be hired up to the point where its price equals its marginal revenue productivity.

4. *Returns to Scale*

In the production function (19), let the firm change infinitesimally all its inputs x_{ij} by the independent increments dx_{ij}. Incremental output will then be defined as the total differential

$$dX_j \equiv \frac{\partial X_j}{\partial x_{1j}}\,dx_{1j} + \cdots + \frac{\partial X_j}{\partial x_{nj}}\,dx_{nj} \tag{25}$$

Since the increments were assumed to be independent, we are free to make them proportional:

$$dx_{ij} = \lambda x_{ij}$$

where λ is a small positive constant common to all inputs. Insert into (25) and write

$$\lambda X_j \lessgtr dX_j = \lambda\left(\frac{\partial X_j}{\partial x_{1j}}\,x_{1j} + \cdots + \frac{\partial X_j}{\partial x_{nj}}\,x_{nj}\right) \tag{26}$$

If $\lambda X_j < dX_j$, an increase of all inputs in the proportion λ will increase output in more than that proportion, and returns to scale are said to be increasing. If $\lambda X_j = dX_j$ an increase of all inputs in the proportion λ will increase output in that proportion, and returns to scale are said to be constant. If $\lambda X_j > dX_j$, an increase of all inputs in the proportion λ will increase output in less than that proportion, and returns to scale are said to be decreasing.

In (26) ignore dX_j, divide on both sides by λ, and write it as

$$X_j \gtreqless \frac{\partial X_j}{\partial x_{1j}} x_{1j} + \cdots + \frac{\partial X_j}{\partial x_{nj}} x_{nj} \tag{27}$$

Into (27) insert (24), multiply on both sides by marginal revenue, and find three possibilities:

$$\left(P_j + \frac{dP_j}{dX_j} X_j \right) X_j \gtreqless p_1 x_{1j} + \cdots + p_n x_{nj} \tag{28}$$

Since all firms within an industry, established as well as potential ones, have been assumed to be alike, (28) holds for any of them.

5. Will the Slices Add Up to the Pie?

The question is whether the distributive claims on the firm will add up to the pie to be distributed. The sum of the distributive claims is the right-hand side of (28). The pie to be distributed by the firm is its revenue—which doesn't appear isolated on the left-hand side of (28). What does appear is the product of marginal revenue and output. Depending on the nature of the market, that product is less than or equal to revenue. Furthermore, depending on the nature of the production function, the left-hand side of (28) will be less than, equal to, or greater than the right-hand side. In general, then, the slices will not add up to the pie.

In a special case, however, they will. Under pure competition the firm is so small relative to its output market that it cannot influence the price of its output. In that case $dP_j / dX_j = 0$, marginal revenue in (24) and (28) collapses into price P_j of output, and the first-order condition (24) for a profit maximum collapses into the condition that any input should be hired up to the point where its price equals its marginal *value* productivity. Furthermore, under constant returns to scale the equality sign of (28) holds. So in the special combination of profit maximization with pure competition and constant returns to scale, each input will be paid its marginal value productivity, and the distributive shares thus determined will indeed add up to the pie to be distributed. Such adding up will be true not only for the firm but for the industry and the economy as well. For the industry because all firms are alike. For the economy because all its industries are in equilibrium in the sense just defined.

6. Rigorous Product Exhaustion: Wicksteed

Philip Henry Wicksteed, unitarian minister, medievalist, and University of London Extension lecturer, wrote about Dante and Ibsen and was the first to write a linearly homogeneous production function and to show that under pure competition its linear homogeneity would guarantee product exhaustion. "Without any claim to originality," as Wicksteed misleadingly said in his preface, he accomplished three important things.

First, as we saw, the period 1770-1870 had come close to a generalization of the marginal-productivity concept. But the partial derivative of physical output with respect to land itself still remained to be taken. Wicksteed's first accomplishment was to take it. He [1894 (1932: 21)] began by drawing two alternative diagrams.

In the first diagram he plotted variable Ricardian "portions of capital" on the horizontal axis and their marginal productivity on the vertical axis, keeping land constant. Thus he determined wages and profits directly and rent residually. In the second diagram he plotted variable "doses of land" on the horizontal axis and *their* marginal productivity on the vertical axis, keeping his Ricardian portion constant. Thus he determined rent directly and wages and profits residually.

He then showed that if the production function was linearly homogeneous, then the marginal productivity of a dose of land *times* number of doses applied *plus* the marginal productivity of a portion of capital *times* number of portions applied would equal the product. Thus the marginal-productivity concept had finally been fully generalized, and land could finally be treated as any other input, or in Wicksteed's words [1894 (1932: 47)]:

'Rent is not the cause but the effect of the exchange value of the product' we read in our books. Precisely so, and since the law of rent is also the law of wages and the law of interest, it is equally true that 'wages are not the cause but the effect of the exchange value of the product.' And so too with interest.

Wicksteed's second accomplishment [1894 (1932: 33)] was to abandon classical "factors of production" and generalize further:

We must regard every kind and quality of labour that can be distinguished from other kinds and qualities as a separate factor; and in the same way every kind of land will be taken as a separate factor. Still more important is it to insist that instead of speaking of so many [pounds sterling] worth of capital we shall speak of so many ploughs, so many tons of manure, and so many horses, or foot-pounds of "power." Each of these may be scheduled in its own unit, and when this has been done the enumeration of the factors of production may be regarded as complete.

Wicksteed concluded: "On this understanding it is of course obvious that a proportional increase of all the factors of production will secure a proportional increase of the product." The sentence shows that with Wicksteed's discovery of linear homogeneity went his belief that such linear homogeneity was "of course obvious." If you are careful enough to include and vary *all* inputs in your production function, leaving out no "scarce" or "constant" input, your function *must* be linearly homogeneous! As Samuelson (1947: 84) has observed, such a statement could never be refuted by experiment: if someone performs an experiment in which doubling all inputs does not double output, he may always be accused of having forgotten some "constant" input.

If linear homogeneity were "of course obvious," Wicksteed could not be expected to refer to nonlinear homogeneity—and in his *Co-ordination* never did. Consequently, what he did write [1894 (1932: 37)] was the exact replica of our (27) purged of its inequality signs. Later, in his nonmathematical work [1910 (1950: I, 373, and II, 529-530)], Wicksteed formally withdrew his passages on linear homogeneity and replaced them with passages so vague as to be of little help. Our (27) purged of its inequality signs is, of course, Euler's theorem for the special case of linear homogeneity. By name, Euler's theorem was never mentioned by Wicksteed but was first brought into economic theory by Flux (1894) in his review of Wicksteed.

Wicksteed's third accomplishment was to see nonpure competition. Once a "proportional increase of all the factors of production" had secured an "of course obvious" proportional increase of the product, could consumers be found to consume it? Wicksteed [1894 (1932: 35-36)] did consider "actual or virtual monopoly" and faced squarely the possibility that demand "is not indefinitely elastic." If not, the product will have to be "pushed," and "if each unit of physical product is backed by the same amount of pushing . . ., the response will be slower as the amount increases." Here, Wicksteed surrendered the assumption of pure competition, anticipated Chamberlin's distinction between production cost and selling cost, and concluded [1894 (1932: 38)] "that we have not raised any commanding presumption that industries concentrated in a few hands come under this law [of product exhaustion]."

7. Intuitive Product Exhaustion: Clark

As Wicksteed had drawn diagrams for land and portions of capital, Clark [1899 (1931: 198-204)] drew such diagrams for capital and labor.

In the first diagram he plotted variable labor on the horizontal axis and its marginal productivity on the vertical axis, keeping capital constant. Thus he determined wages directly and interest residually. In the second diagram he plotted variable capital on the horizontal axis and its marginal productivity on the vertical axis, keeping labor constant. Thus he determined interest directly and wages residually. Clark concluded: "static conditions ... exclude ... a profit by making these two areas equal." Whether determined directly or residually, then, the two areas would be equal. Clark did not mention the production function or its properties.

8.   Nonconstant Returns to Scale: Wicksell

Wicksell [1901 (1934: 128-129)] examined the stability of a product-exhaustion equilibrium by asking what would happen if, still assuming pure competition, returns to scale were not constant. Under pure competition the left-hand side of (28) is revenue $P_j X_j$. Wicksell added exit and entry to the picture and thought of the scale of our production function (19) as passing gradually through three domains.

The first domain consisted of relatively low scales on which the returns to scale would be increasing. Here the less-than signs of (26) and (28) would apply. Consequently, if every input were paid its marginal value productivity, the entrepreneur would find himself going broke. The slices would be adding up to more than the pie! With such negative profits, there would be exit from the industry, and the number of firms in it would be declining. With fewer firms, each firm would be growing in scale, hence passing out of the first domain and into the second.

The second domain consisted of relatively medium scales on which the returns to scale would be constant. Here the equality signs of (26) and (28) would apply. Consequently, if every input were paid its marginal value productivity, the entrepreneur would find himself just breaking even. The slices would be adding up to just the pie! With such zero profits, there would be neither exit from nor entry into the industry, and the number of firms in it would remain stationary. With a stationary number of firms, each firm would remain stationary in scale and remain in the second domain.

Wicksell's third domain consisted of relatively high scales on which the returns to scale would be decreasing. Here the greater-than signs of (26) and (28) would apply. Consequently, if every input were paid its marginal value productivity, the entrepreneur would find himself with something left—a distributive share not explained by the marginal-productivity principle. The slices would be adding up to less than the pie! With such positive profits, there would be entry into the industry, and the number of firms in it would be growing. With more firms, each firm would be declining in scale, hence passing out of the third domain and back into the second.

9. *Nonpure Competition: Wicksell*

Unlike Marshall, Wicksell was willing to surrender the assumption of pure competition. In [1901 (1934: 129)] he defined his "optimum scale" as lying "at the point of transition from 'increasing' to 'diminishing returns' (relative to the scale of production). The firm will here conform to the law of constant returns." At such an optimum scale firms might still be [1901 (1934: 130)] "numerous enough for perfect competition to be maintained," or they might not: "If the optimum scale of the enterprise is so high, and the number of enterprises consequently so small, that the owners can easily combine in a *ring, trust, or cartel*; then there no longer exists any equilibrium of the kind we are here considering."

VIII. CAPITAL AND MONEY: FISHER AND WICKSELL

1. *Financing the Capitalist Process of Production*

New technology came with a time structure that made it very capital-intensive. The general problem of industrial finance came into full view. With the need for them, new financial instruments came into existence. One was the large corporation offering equity in liquid form and at limited liability. Another was the large commercial bank creating a new kind of money, i.e., drawing rights upon itself disposed of by checks.

2. *An Old Issue Reopened*

To Petty and Yarranton, the rate of interest was determined by the supply of and the demand for money. To Hume, Turgot, Smith, Böhm-Bawerk, and Fisher, the rate of interest was "determined by impatience to spend income and opportunity to invest it," as Fisher (1930: title page) put it.

The Petty-Hume problem of what determined the rate of interest would have to be looked into once again.

3. *Fisher*

Any model admitting inflation as an equilibrating variable will immediately have two additional ones, i.e., the nominal and the real rate of interest. As we saw, a glimpse of that distinction was, perhaps, caught by Turgot. But Fisher was the first to articulate it.

Just as we ran the government budget constraint in reverse and applied it to the case of a fiscal *surplus* in order to understand Lauderdale, we shall have to run the distinction between a nominal and a real rate of interest in reverse and apply it to the case of *deflation* in order to understand Fisher. Writing in the closing years of the late-nineteenth-century price decline, Fisher (1896: 8-9) distinguished between a rate of interest in gold (the nominal rate of interest), called *i*, and a rate of interest in wheat (the real rate of interest), called *j*. Calling the rate of appreciation of gold in terms of wheat *a*, he wrote

$$1 + j = (1 + a)(1 + i) \tag{29}$$

In other words, in the case of deflation the real rate of interest *j* would be greater than the nominal one *i*.

Fisher may be summarized by saying that monetary policy may affect the nominal rate of interest but never the real one.

4.   *Wicksell*

Having restated Böhm-Bawerk, Wicksell [1893 (1954)] began to wonder how a "natural" rate of interest thus determined was related to the rate of interest observed in markets where the supply of money met the demand for it. If commercial banks could create money in the form of drawing rights upon themselves, disposed of by checks, such a supply of money would be quite flexible. Would the "money" rate of interest determined by such supply coincide with the "natural" rate? If it didn't, would some equilibrating variable be set in motion and keep moving until the two rates coincided?

We shall devote our chapter 8 to Wicksell's [1898 (1936)] answer, made possible by a method fundamentally new in three respects. First, Wicksell's method was explicitly macroeconomic, second, it was explicitly dynamic and, third, it was an explicit disequilibrium method based upon adaptive expectations whose disappointment constituted the motive force of the system.

Wicksell may be summarized by saying that monetary policy may affect the money rate of interest but never the natural one. Wicksell's distinction was not the same as Fisher's. Wicksell [1898 (1936: 165-166)] knew Fisher's work and reversed it from the case of deflation to the case of inflation: "entrepreneurs incur their 'expense' (wages, rents, etc.) when things are cheap, and dispose of their product after prices have gone up." Strangely enough, Wicksell was unimpressed: "Such a rise in prices ... does not provide [the entrepreneurs] with the means of paying a higher rate of interest." Wicksell identified himself with his entrepreneurs, who would never anticipate such a rise in prices, because they always expected current prices to prevail in the future. Rational expectations had not yet arrived!

IX. DYNAMIC GENERAL EQUILIBRIUM: CASSEL

1. *Walras–Cassel–von Neumann*

A writer less generous than Cassel would be hard to find. Marx at least paid tribute to Quesnay and Ricardo. Cassel paid tribute to nobody. Walras had written the first system of simultaneous equations of general equilibrium. Pareto had purged it of any measure of sensations. Cassel followed both but mentioned neither.

We must not treat Cassel the way he treated others. We must respect him as a pioneer. He [1918 (1932: 32-41 and 152-155)] was the first to dynamize general equilibrium into his "uniformly progressing state," thus inspiring John von Neumann who, as Weintraub (1983: 4-5) has pointed out, knew the Walras system only in its Cassel version. In a dynamic system, each variable should carry a time coordinate. We use t for time.

2. *Output and Input; Consumption and Income*

Let there be m outputs X_j supplied by industry, demanded by s households, and priced P_j, on the one hand, and n primary inputs x_i supplied by the s households, demanded by industry, and priced p_i, on the other. Using this distinction, define the money value of consumption in the kth household as the sum of the money values of the outputs demanded by that household:

$$C_k(t) \equiv \sum_{j=1}^{m} [P_j(t)X_{jk}(t)] \qquad (30)$$

Define the money value of consumption of all households as the sum of the money values of the individual consumption:

$$C(t) \equiv \sum_{k=1}^{s} C_k(t) \qquad (31)$$

Define the number of physical units of the jth output demanded by all households as the sum of the physical units of that output demanded by each household:

$$X_j(t) \equiv \sum_{k=1}^{s} X_{jk}(t) \qquad (32)$$

Define the money value of the income of the kth household as the sum of the money values of the primary inputs supplied by that household:

$$Y_k(t) \equiv \sum_{i=1}^{n} [p_i(t)x_{ki}(t)] \qquad (33)$$

Define the money value of the incomes of all households as the sum of the money values of the individual income:

$$Y(t) \equiv \sum_{k=1}^{s} Y_k(t) \tag{34}$$

Define the number of physical units of the ith primary input supplied by all households as the sum of the physical units of that input supplied by each household:

$$x_i(t) \equiv \sum_{k=1}^{s} x_{ki}(t) \tag{35}$$

As the Austrians had done, Cassel assumed the primary input x_{ki} supplied by the kth household to be its entire endowment; consequently x_i is the endowment of the entire economy with the ith primary input, a parameter.

3. *Growth, Interest, and Saving*

Let the proportionate rate of growth $g_j(t)$ of the jth physical output be defined

$$X_j(t + 1) \equiv [1 + g_j(t)]X_j(t) \tag{36}$$

Wicksell [1919 (1934: 225-226)] criticized Cassel's failure to incorporate his treatment of capital and interest into his algebra. Let us incorporate it in the simplest possible way, i.e., in the form of a von Neumann assumption of a universal period of production of one time unit: at time $t + 1$ let the jth physical output be $X_j(t + 1)$ and the ith physical input absorbed one time unit earlier be

$$x_{ij}(t) = a_{ij}X_j(t + 1) \tag{37}$$

All inputs, then, will have to be purchased one time unit before output can be sold, hence will need financing. Let capitalists finance them at the rate of interest $r(t)$.

In a growing economy somebody must be saving. Who? Assume that income from primary inputs is never saved and income from interest never consumed, then

$$C(t) = Y(t) \tag{38}$$

4. *Industry Demand for Input*

We use Cassel's growth rate $g_j(t)$ to express industry demand for input. Insert (36) into (37) and find

$$x_{ij}(t) = a_{ij}[1 + g_j(t)]X_j(t) \tag{39}$$

To Cassel [1918 (1932: 153)], then, the current physical input required per physical unit of current output was a new coefficient that would "contain, in addition to the elements of the old 'technical coefficients,' only the rate of progress ..."

5. Industry Supply of Output

We use Cassel's interest rate $r(t)$ to express the price at which industry will supply its output. Under pure competition and freedom of entry and exit, profits must be zero. Consequently, for the jth output the sum of all cost per unit at time t with interest added at the rate r must be equal to the price of the jth output at time $t + 1$:

$$P_j(t + 1) = [1 + r(t)] \sum_{i=1}^{n} [a_{ij}p_i(t)] \tag{40}$$

6. Household Demand for Output

Having no use for utility and its maximization, Cassel went straight to household demand and expressed it as a function of, first, prices of all outputs and, second, household income:

$$X_{jk}(t) = X_{jk}(t)[P_1(t), \ldots, P_m(t), Y_k(t)] \tag{41}$$

7. Balanced, Steady-State Growth of Outputs and Inputs

Cassel's growth of physical outputs and inputs was balanced and steady-state. Balanced growth means that the proportionate rates of growth of all physical outputs are equal:

$$g_1(t) = \cdots = g_m(t) \tag{42}$$

Steady-state growth means that the proportionate rates of growth of all physical outputs are stationary:

$$g_j(t + 1) = g_j(t); \qquad j = 1, \ldots, m \tag{43}$$

Cassel's "uniformly progressing state" was progressing only in its physical outputs and inputs. All its prices and its rate of interest were assumed to be stationary:

$$P_j(t + 1) = P_j(t); \qquad j = 1, \ldots, m \tag{44}$$

$$p_i(t + 1) = p_i(t); \qquad i = 1, \ldots, n \tag{45}$$

$$r(t + 1) = r(t) \tag{46}$$

8. Equilibrium

Finally, Cassel imposed his equilibrium conditions that the number of units of jth physical output supplied by industry must equal the sum of all physical units demanded by households and that the number of units of ith physical input demanded by industry must equal the sum of all physical units supplied by households.

9. The Existence of a Solution?

Like Walras, Cassel failed to prove the existence of a solution. Cassel's proof was intuitive and may be summarized as follows. Input prices will equalize the given supply of any input with the demand for it. Once such prices are known, all incomes are known. Multiply each price by the technical coefficient for an industry, add such products for that industry, add interest in accordance with (40), and find the price of the output of that industry. Once all incomes and such prices are known, consumer demand (41) follows. Output prices will equalize the supply of any output with the demand for it. Once such industry supplies are known, multiply each of them by the technical coefficient for an input, add growth in accordance with (39), add such products for that input, and find the aggregate demand for it. Input prices will equalize the given supply of any input with such demand for it. Thus we are back at our point of departure. Unlike Walras, Cassel was a mathematician before he turned to economics. But like Walras, he counted equations and unknowns and merely said [1918 (1932: 137)] that equal numbers of them would "generally" suffice to determine the unknowns—with one reservation.

Like the Walras system, the Cassel system was homogeneous of degree zero in its prices, money expenditures, and money incomes. In this sense the system was indeterminate. The job of determining absolute prices, money expenditure, or money incomes would be left, Cassel [1918 (1932: 151-152)] said, to monetary policy. Here we see Cassel anticipating Friedman's dichotomy between nominal and real variables: monetary policy can affect nominal variables but never real ones.

10. Cassel and von Neumann

To see how close Cassel came to anticipating von Neumann, let us now do two things Cassel himself never did, i.e., first multiplying (39) by p_i and, second, multiplying (40) by $X_j(t)$.

Sum (39) over outputs and use (42) to strip $g_j(t)$ of its subscript and (43) to strip it of its time coordinate. Then multiply both sides by p_i, sum over input, factor out $(1 + g)$, and write

$$\sum_{i=1}^{n} [p_i x_i(t)] = (1 + g) \sum_{i=1}^{n} \sum_{j=1}^{m} [a_{ij} p_i X_j(t)] \tag{47}$$

Use (33), (34), and (35) to see that the left-hand side of (47) is nothing but the money value of the incomes of all households at time t.

On the right-hand side, write (37) for $t - 1$, then use (33), (34), and (35) to see that the double summation is nothing but the money value of the incomes of all households at time $t - 1$.

Consequently, we may write (47) as

$$Y(t) = (1 + g) Y(t - 1) \tag{48}$$

In (40) use (44), (45), and (46) to strip $P_j(t + 1)$, $p_i(t)$, and $r(t)$, respectively, of their time coordinates. Then multiply both sides by $X_j(t)$, sum over outputs, factor out $(1 + r)$, and write

$$\sum_{j=1}^{m} [P_j X_j(t)] = (1 + r) \sum_{j=1}^{m} \sum_{i=1}^{n} [a_{ij} p_i X_j(t)] \tag{49}$$

Use (30), (31), and (32) to see that the left-hand side of (49) is nothing but the money value of the consumption of all households at time t. The double summation on the right-hand side of (49) is the same as that of (47), i.e., nothing but the money value of the incomes of all households at time $t - 1$. Consequently, we may write (49) as

$$C(t) = (1 + r) Y(t - 1) \tag{50}$$

11. *Rate of Growth Equals Rate of Interest*

Capitalists charge interest at the rate r, so at time t the sum of money owed to them is $(1 + r) Y(t - 1)$. Can the entrepreneurs pay such a debt? They can if they can sell their output at the value $C(t)$, thus satisfying (50). Can such a sale be financed? It can if at time t capitalists save their entire interest earnings and lend the entrepreneurs the sum $Y(t)$ financing new purchases of primary inputs, whose owners, in turn, will consume it:

$$Y(t) = C(t) \tag{38}$$

But then the left-hand sides of (48) and (50) will be equal, consequently, their right-hand sides must be equal, and the rate of growth must be equal to the rate of interest:

$$g = r$$

Did Cassel himself see such an equality? Cassel [1918 (1932: 63)] did estimate a Swedish long-run equilibrium rate of growth of three percent per annum and [1918 (1932: 247-248)] a long-run equilibrium rate of interest of three to four percent per annum. But he never related the two rates to each other and never explicitly endorsed our extreme von Neumann assumptions on saving, i.e., that income from primary inputs is never saved and income from interest never consumed.

In both rigor and substance von Neumann was to go far beyond Cassel. Like Walras, Cassel allowed for substitution in consumption but failed to allow for it in production: Walras's "coefficients de fabrication" became Cassel's "technical coefficients." Like Walras, Cassel failed to treat the distinction between free and economic goods as endogeneous, yet ironically offered [1918 (1932: 145-146)] an excellent example of a good that would be free under one technology but economic under another: when used merely to generate mechanical power, the waterfalls of Scandinavia were abundant and their power "very cheap ... if not valueless." Used to generate electric power, they became scarce, which "raised the price of natural waterpower."

X. INTERTEMPORAL ALLOCATION OF RESOURCES: RAMSEY

1. *Walras-Cassel-Ramsey*

Walras asked how a competitive economy would allocate inputs among outputs and outputs among households. His question was new, but his general equilibrium was a static one never involving intertemporal allocation: no household ever saved.

Considering intertemporal allocation of resources, Cassel showed that in a growing economy the current physical input required per physical unit of current output was a new coefficient $a_{ij}[1 + g_j(t)]$ which would contain, in addition to the old technical coefficient a_{ij}, the rate of growth $g_j(t)$. But Cassel's dynamic general equilibrium was positive, not normative, economic theory never asking what the *optimal* saving would be.

The first to formulate the problem of optimal saving was a brilliant 25-year-old mathematician and philosopher, who was to die within two years.

2. *The Ramsey Model*

Ramsey [1928 (1968: 129-143)] considered a one-good macroeconomic model in which a production function expressed current physical output as a function of current labor employed and current physical capital stock:

$$X = X(L, S) \tag{51}$$

In the general Ramsey model, let us assume that $\partial X/\partial L > 0$, $\partial X/\partial S > 0$, $\partial^2 X/\partial L^2 < 0$, and $\partial^2 X/\partial S^2 < 0$. Let part of current physical output be consumed and the rest be added to physical capital stock:

$$X = C + \frac{dS}{dt} \tag{52}$$

Let a community utility function express current utility as a sum of the utilities of current physical consumption and current labor employed:

$$U = U_C(C) + U_L(L) \tag{53}$$

called "net enjoyment" by Ramsey, where $dU_C/dC > 0$ and $dU_L/dL < 0$. Let us go beyond him and add that $d^2U_C/dC^2 < 0$ and $d^2U_L/dL^2 < 0$.

Via equations (51) and (52) equation (53) will express current utility U as a function of current labor employed L, current physical capital stock S, and current physical investment dS/dt. Ramsey's problem was to determine which time paths of those variables would maximize an integral of current utility U with respect to time. Which integral?

Should future utilities be discounted? Ramsey [1928 (1968: 129)] cavalierly dismissed such discounting as "a practice which is ethically indefensible and arises merely from the weakness of the imagination" but, in the last third of his paper, did consider it as a special case.

In Ramsey's general case let the community maximize $\int_0^\infty U dt$, i.e., the sum of all future undiscounted utilities (53) from time zero to infinity. As it happened, Ramsey's general case was a case of common occurrence in the calculus of variations[6] which teaches us that if current utility U were a function of L, dL/dt, S, and dS/dt, then the two Euler equations

$$\frac{\partial U}{\partial L} - \frac{d}{dt}\left[\frac{\partial U}{\partial(dL/dt)}\right] = 0 \tag{54}$$

$$\frac{\partial U}{\partial S} - \frac{d}{dt}\left[\frac{\partial U}{\partial(dS/dt)}\right] = 0 \tag{55}$$

would be the first-order conditions for such a maximum. Since in our particular case current utility U is not a function of dL/dt but merely of L, S, and dS/dt, the square bracket of (54) equals zero, and (54) collapses into $\partial U/\partial L = 0$.

---

[6]The reader needing help on the calculus of variations will find it in Allen (1938: 521-541), who uses the Ramsey model as one of his examples, and in Lancaster (1968: 376-384).

3.   *First Euler Equation*

Write (52) as

$$C = X - \frac{dS}{dt} \tag{56}$$

insert (51) into it, insert the result into (53), take the partial derivative of (53) with respect to labor employed L, and use the chain rule to find

$$\frac{\partial U}{\partial L} = \frac{dU_C}{dC} \frac{\partial C}{\partial X} \frac{\partial X}{\partial L} + \frac{dU_L}{dL} \tag{57}$$

Here, since we are taking our partial derivative with respect to L, our S in (51) and our dS/dt in (56) should be treated as constants, consequently, according to (56), $\partial C/\partial X = 1$. Insert that into (57), recall that in our particular case $\partial U/\partial L = 0$, rearrange, and find the first Euler equation (54) saying that

$$\frac{\partial X}{\partial L} = - \frac{dU_L/dL}{dU_C/dC} \tag{58}$$

or, in English, that the physical marginal productivity of labor should equal *minus* the ratio between the, negative, marginal utility of labor and the, positive, marginal utility of consumption.

4.   *Second Euler Equation*

Let us first find $\partial U/\partial S$. Again write (52) as (56), insert (51) into it, insert the result into (53), take the partial derivative of (53) with respect to physical capital stock S, and use the chain rule to find

$$\frac{\partial U}{\partial S} = \frac{dU_C}{dC} \frac{\partial C}{\partial X} \frac{\partial X}{\partial S} \tag{59}$$

Here, since we are taking our partial derivative with respect to S, our L in (51) and our dS/dt in (56) should be treated as constants, consequently, according to (56), $\partial C/\partial X = 1$. Insert that into (59) and find the first term of the second Euler equation (55) to be

$$\frac{\partial U}{\partial S} = \frac{dU_C}{dC} \frac{\partial X}{\partial S} \tag{60}$$

Next let us find the second term of the second Euler equation (55). Once again write (52) as (56), insert (51) into it, insert the result into (53), take the partial derivative of (53) with respect to investment dS/dt, and use the chain rule to find

$$\frac{\partial U}{\partial(dS/dt)} = \frac{dU_C}{dC}\frac{\partial C}{\partial(dS/dt)} \tag{61}$$

Here, since we are taking our partial derivative with respect to dS/dt, our L and S in (51) and hence X in (56) should be treated as constants, consequently, according to (56), $\partial C/\partial(dS/dt) = -1$. Insert that into (61) and find the entire second Euler equation (55) saying that

$$\frac{\partial X}{\partial S} = -\frac{d(dU_C/dC)/dt}{dU_C/dC} \equiv -g_{dU_C/dC} \tag{62}$$

or, in English, that the physical marginal productivity of capital stock should equal *minus* the, negative, growth rate of the marginal utility of consumption.

Ramsey's two Euler equations (54) and (55) were differential equations that happened to have the neat economic interpretations (58) and (62). But could Ramsey recover the primitive that gave rise to his differential equations? As we saw, current utility U was a function of current labor employed L, current physical capital stock S, and current physical investment dS/dt but not of time itself explicitly. In that case, which Lancaster (1968: 379) calls a "case of common occurrence," Ramsey could recover his primitive, and let us see how.

5. Recovering the Primitive Giving Rise to the Euler Equations

Multiply physical output X by the marginal utility of consumption dU_C/dC and use the production function (51) to take the derivative of that product with respect to time

$$\frac{d}{dt}\left(X\frac{dU_C}{dC}\right) = X\frac{d}{dt}\left(\frac{dU_C}{dC}\right) + \frac{dU_C}{dC}\left(\frac{\partial X}{\partial L}\frac{dL}{dt} + \frac{\partial X}{\partial S}\frac{dS}{dt}\right)$$

Insert the Euler results (58) and (62), let dU_C/dC cancel, factor out $d(dU_C/dC)/dt$, use (52) to write $X - dS/dt = C$, and find

$$\frac{d}{dt}\left(X\frac{dU_C}{dC}\right) = C\frac{d}{dt}\left(\frac{dU_C}{dC}\right) - \frac{dU_L}{dL}\frac{dL}{dt} \tag{63}$$

To recover our primitive we must make (63) integrable. We take three steps. First, prepare for integration by parts by taking the derivative of the product $C(dU_C/dC)$ with respect to time:

$$\frac{d}{dt}\left(C\frac{dU_C}{dC}\right) = C\frac{d}{dt}\left(\frac{dU_C}{dC}\right) + \frac{dU_C}{dC}\frac{dC}{dt} \tag{64}$$

Second and third, remember the chain rule

$$\frac{dU_C}{dC}\frac{dC}{dt} = \frac{dU_C}{dt} \tag{65}$$

$$\frac{dU_L}{dL}\frac{dL}{dt} = \frac{dU_L}{dt} \tag{66}$$

Insert (65) into (64), (64) and (66) into (63), rearrange the latter, and write it

$$\frac{d}{dt}\left(X\frac{dU_C}{dC}\right) - \frac{d}{dt}\left(C\frac{dU_C}{dC}\right) = -\left(\frac{dU_C}{dt} + \frac{dU_L}{dt}\right) \tag{67}$$

All terms of (67) are now derivatives with respect to time, hence may be considered integrands of an integration with respect to time. Take the indefinite integral of (67) with respect to time, use (52) to write $X - C = dS/dt$, and recover the primitive

$$\frac{dS}{dt}\frac{dU_C}{dC} = K - (U_C + U_L) \tag{68}$$

where K is the arbitrary constant of an indefinite integral.

We can assign an economic meaning to our arbitrary constant K, as well as make the maximum of $\int_0^\infty U dt$ a finite one, by letting either our marginal productivity of capital or our marginal utility of consumption vanish, as we shall now see.

6. Satiation in Production or Consumption

First, imagine our production function (51) to have the property that

$$\lim_{S\to\infty}\frac{\partial X}{\partial S} = 0 \tag{69}$$

and call that limit a satiation in production. At that limit further saving and investment would be pointless, consequently,

$$\lim_{t\to\infty}\frac{dS}{dt} = 0 \tag{70}$$

Second, imagine our utility function (53) to have the property that

$$\lim_{C\to\infty}\frac{dU_C}{dC} = 0 \tag{71}$$

and call that limit a satiation in consumption.

Now assume at least one of (70) and (71) to hold. Then at least one of the factors of the product $(dS/dt)(dU_C/dC)$ on the left-hand side of (68), and hence that product itself, will be approaching zero. Consequently, the right-hand side of (68) must also be approaching zero, which it can do if and only if our arbitrary constant K is no greater than the highest obtainable net enjoyment $U_C + U_L$, i.e., ultimate bliss.

Next consider a finite time. Here, physical capital stock S will be finite and its physical marginal productivity $\partial X/\partial S$ and time derivative dS/dt positive. Furthermore physical consumption C will be finite and its marginal utility dU_C/dC positive. As a result, both factors of the product $(dS/dt)(dU_C/dC)$ on the left-hand side of (68), and hence that product itself, will be positive. Consequently, the right-hand side of (68) must also be positive, which it can be if and only if our arbitrary constant K is no less than the highest obtainable net enjoyment $U_C + U_L$, i.e., ultimate bliss.

Thus we have trapped our arbitrary constant K: if it can be neither greater nor less than ultimate bliss, it must be equal to it, and we may then use Ramsey's [1928 (1968: 133)] own words to express his primitive (68) in English, i.e., the "rate of saving multiplied by marginal utility of consumption should always equal bliss minus actual rate of utility enjoyed."

7. Conclusion

Ramsey may be criticized for his use of additive, undiscounted, community utility. But he did open a road that has been carrying heavy traffic ever since and has led us all the way to such things as the turnpike theorems of Dorfman-Samuelson-Solow and Morishima and optimal control theory.

REFERENCES

R. G. D. Allen, *Mathematical Analysis for Economists*, London, 1938.
G. B. Antonelli, *Sulla teoria matematica della economia politica*, Pisa, 1886, translated as "On the Mathematical Theory of Political Economy" by J. S. Chipman in W. J. Baumol and S. M. Goldfeld (eds.), *Precursors in Mathematical Economics: An Anthology*, London, 1968, 33-39.
E. Barone, "Il ministero della produzione nello stato collettivista," *Giornale degli economisti*, Sep.-Oct. 1908, *37*, 267-293, 391-414, translated as "The Ministry of Production in the Collectivist State," in F. A. Hayek (ed.), *Collectivist Economic Planning*, London, 1935.
W. J. Baumol, *Economic Theory and Operations Analysis*, Englewood Cliffs, N.J., fourth edition, 1977.
E. Bernstein, *Die Voraussetzungen des Sozialismus und die Aufgaben der Sozialdemokratie*, Stuttgart, 1899, translated as *Evolutionary Socialism* by E. C. Harvey, London, 1909, New York, 1961.
A. Berry, "The Pure Theory of Distribution," *Report of the Sixtieth Meeting of the British Association for the Advancement of Science*, 1891, reprinted in

W. J. Baumol and S. M. Goldfeld (eds.), *Precursors in Mathematical Economics: An Anthology*, London, 1968, 314-315.

E. von Böhm-Bawerk, *Positive Theorie des Kapitales*, Innsbruck, 1888, translated as *Positive Theory of Capital* by W. Smart, New York, 1891, reprinted 1923.

G. Cassel, "Grundriss einer elementaren Preislehre," *Zeitschrift für die gesamte Staatswissenschaft*, 1899, *55*, 395-458.

————, *Theoretische Sozialökonomie*, Leipzig, 1918, translated as *The Theory of Social Economy* by S. L. Barron, New York, 1932.

J. B. Clark, *The Distribution of Wealth: A Theory of Wages, Interest, and Profits*, New York, 1899, 1931.

F. Y. Edgeworth, *Mathematical Psychics: An Essay on the Application of Mathematics to the Moral Sciences*, London, 1881, New York, 1967.

I. Fisher, *Mathematical Investigations in the Theory of Value and Prices*, New Haven, 1892, reprinted 1925.

————, "Appreciation and Interest," *Publications of the American Economic Association*, Aug. 1896, *11*, 331-442.

————, *The Theory of Interest*, New York, 1930.

A. W. Flux, review of Wicksteed's *Co-ordination*, *Econ. J.*, June 1894, *4*, 308-313, reprinted in W. J. Baumol and S. M. Goldfeld (eds.), *Precursors in Mathematical Economics: An Anthology*, London, 1968, 326-331.

G. P. Haight, Jr., *An Introduction to Physical Science*, New York and London, 1964.

J. R. Hicks and R. G. D. Allen, "A Reconsideration of the Theory of Value," *Economica*, 1934, *1*, 52-76 and 196-219.

W. S. Jevons, *The Theory of Political Economy*, London, 1871, second edition, London 1879, edited with notes and an extension of the bibliography by H. S. Jevons, London, 1931.

W. E. Johnson and C. P. Sanger, "On Certain Questions Connected with Demand," *Cambridge Economic Club*, Easter Term, 1894, reprinted in W. J. Baumol and S. M. Goldfeld (eds.), *Precursors in Mathematical Economics: An Anthology*, London, 1968, 42-48.

D. W. Katzner, *Static Demand Theory*, New York and London, 1970.

K. Lancaster, *Mathematical Economics*, New York and London, 1968.

T. Mann, *Buddenbrooks: Verfall einer Familie*, Berlin, 1901, translated as *Buddenbrooks* by H. T. Lowe-Porter, New York, 1924.

A. Marshall, *Principles of Economics*, London, 1890, eighth edition, London, 1920.

C. Menger, *Grundsätze der Volkswirthschaftslehre*, Vienna, 1871, reprinted by the London School of Economics and Political Science, 1934, translated as *Principles of Economics* by and edited by J. Dingwall and B. F. Hoselitz with an introduction by F. H. Knight, Glencoe, Ill., 1950.

L. von Mises, "Die Wirtschaftsrechnung im sozialistischen Gemeinwesen," *Archiv für Sozialwissenschaft und Sozialpolitik*, Apr. 1920, *47*, 86-121, translated as "Economic Calculation in the Socialist Commonwealth," in F. A. Hayek (ed.), *Collectivist Economic Planning*, London, 1935.

V. Pareto, *Manuale di economia politica con una introduzione alla scienza so-*

ciale, Milan, 1906, revised as *Manuel d'economie politique*, Paris, 1909, translated as *Manual of Political Economy* by Ann S. Schwier from the French edition, New York, 1971. On the translation see W. Jaffé, "Pareto Translated: A Review Article," *J. Econ. Lit.*, Dec. 1972, *10*, 1190-1201 with subsequent colloquium by J. F. and A. S. Schwier, W. Jaffé, and V. J. Tarascio in *J. Econ. Lit.*, Mar. 1974, *12*, 78-96.

E. H. Phelps Brown, "Levels and Movements of Industrial Productivity and Real Wages Internationally Compared, 1860-1970," *Econ. J.*, Mar. 1973, *83*, 58-71.

F. P. Ramsey, "A Mathematical Theory of Saving," *Econ. J.*, Dec. 1928, *38*, 543-559, reprinted in W. J. Baumol and S. M. Goldfeld (eds.), *Precursors in Mathematical Economics: An Anthology*, London, 1968, 129-143.

P. A. Samuelson, *Foundations of Economic Analysis*, Cambridge, Mass., 1947.

J. A. Schumpeter, *Das Wesen und der Hauptinhalt der theoretischen Nationalökonomie*, Leipzig, 1908.

——, *Theorie der wirtschaftlichen Entwicklung*, Leipzig, 1912, translated as *The Theory of Economic Development* by R. Opie, Cambridge, Mass., 1934.

——, *History of Economic Analysis*, New York, 1954.

E. E. Slutsky, "Sulla teoria del bilancio del consumatore," *Giornale degli economisti*, 1915, *51*, 1-26, translated as "On the Theory of the Budget of the Consumer" by Olga Ragusa in G. J. Stigler and K. E. Boulding (eds.), *Readings in Price Theory*, Chicago and Homewood, Ill., 1952, 27-56.

L. Walras, *Eléments d'économie politique pure*, Lausanne, Paris, and Basle, 1874-1877, translated as *Elements of Pure Economics or the Theory of Social Wealth* by W. Jaffé, Homewood, Ill., 1954.

E. R. Weintraub, "On the Existence of a Competitive Equilibrium: 1930-1954," *J. Econ. Lit.*, Mar. 1983, *21*, 1-39.

K. Wicksell, *Ueber Wert, Kapital und Rente*, Jena, 1893, translated as *Value, Capital and Rent* by S. H. Frohwein, London, 1954.

——, *Geldzins und Güterpreise*, Jena, 1898, translated as *Interest and Prices* by R. F. Kahn with an introduction by Bertil Ohlin, published on behalf of the Royal Economic Society, London, 1936.

——, *Föreläsningar i nationalekonomi*, I, Lund, 1901, translated as *Lectures on Political Economy*, I by E. Classen and edited by Lionel Robbins, London, 1934.

——, "Professor Cassels nationalekonomiska system," *Ekonomisk Tidskrift*, 1919, *21*, 195-226, translated as "Professor Cassels nationalökonomisches System," *Schmollers Jahrbuch*, 1928, *52*, 771-808, and as "Professor Cassel's System of Economics," in K. Wicksell, *Lectures on Political Economy*, I, London, 1934, 219-257.

P. H. Wicksteed, *The Co-ordination of the Laws of Distribution*, London, 1894, reprinted by the London School of Economics in 1932 with 14 misprints corrected but not the dP/dC on mid-page 32, which should have been dP/dL.

——, *The Common Sense of Political Economy*, London, 1910, edited with an introduction by Lionel Robbins, New York, 1950, I-II.

F. von Wieser, *Der natürliche Werth*, Vienna 1889, translated as *Natural Value* by C. A. Malloch and edited with a preface and analysis by W. Smart, Glasgow, 1893, reprinted New York, 1930.

CHAPTER 5   Static General Equilibrium

WALRAS (1834-1910)

> A Léon Walras, né à Evreux en 1834, professeur à
> l'Académie et à l'université de Lausanne qui, le
> premier, a établi les conditions générales de l'équilibre
> économique fondant ainsi "l'École de Lausanne."[1]
> Pour honorer cinquante ans de travail désinteressé.[1]

> ... so far as pure theory is concerned, Walras is in my
> opinion the greatest of all economists.
>
> Schumpeter (1954: 827)

I. INTRODUCTION

1. Walras's Problem

Walras asked a question more comprehensive than any asked before:
In an economy resting in competitive equilibrium, what are the physical
quantities of outputs supplied by industry and demanded by households,
what are the physical quantities of inputs supplied by households and demanded by industry, and what are the relative prices at which all such
outputs and inputs are transacted?

The part of Walras's question never asked before was the allocation
part: How do households allocate their endowments of labor and land
between withholding from the market and supplying to the market? How
are the inputs supplied to the market allocated among outputs produced?
How are outputs produced allocated among households? The full allocation question had never been asked before. An answer would have required the admission of preferences to economic theory, but the value
paradox had barred preferences from admission.

The part of Walras's question often asked before was the question of

---

[1]"To Léon Walras, born in Evreux in 1834, Professor at the Academy and at the
University of Lausanne, who as the first established the general conditions of economic equilibrium, thus founding the Lausanne School. In honor of fifty years of self-
less work" (my translation). Such was the text of a bronze plaque on the wall of the
Academy of Lausanne, unveiled in 1910 and commemorating the fiftieth anniversary
of the publication of Walras's first professional book, *L'économie politique et la justice*—which, incidentally, gave no hint of what was to come in 1874-1877.

relative prices. Adam Smith had offered the answer that price of output would equal cost of production: because 2 francs were paid out in rent, 2 francs in wages, and 1 franc in interest, a bottle of wine would sell for 5 francs. Austrians had offered the opposite answer that prices of inputs were determined by the price of output via imputation: because the bottle sells for 5 francs, 2 francs could be paid out in rent, 2 francs in wages, and 1 franc in interest. So in Walras's own words [1874-1877 (1954: 211)]:

> It still remains to be seen whether it was because 2 francs were paid out in rent, 2 francs in wages and 1 franc in interest that this bottle of wine sells for 5 francs, or whether it is because the bottle sells for 5 francs that 2 francs were paid out in rent, 2 francs in wages and 1 franc in interest.

2. *Walras's Method*

Walras's method was to write as many equations as he had unknowns. Mathematics had long since been applied to science and engineering. It was Walras's accomplishment to apply it to economics. What inspired him? Jaffé [1964 (1968: 450)] found the answer. As a 19-year old, Walras had read a once famous text in mechanics, Louis Poinsot's *Eléments de statique* (1803), and he kept it as a companion book throughout his life. The book, in Jaffé's words, "bristles with systems of simultaneous equations, ... and contains the postulate that these systems have determinate solutions if they consist in as many independent equations as unknowns."

This was not the first time that other fields had inspired economics. Names like Bernoulli and Quesnay come to mind. It was not the last time either, as we shall exemplify by the name von Neumann. Such inspiration does not detract from the accomplishment of the writer thus inspired: why was nobody before him receptive enough for such inspiration?

3. *Our Own Restatement*

In this chapter, let us restate[2] as succinctly as possible the Walras vision: consider *m* outputs, *n* inputs, and *s* households. Industry demands inputs and supplies outputs; households demand outputs and supply inputs. Express equilibrium demand, supply, and relative price in all resulting, purely competitive, markets as a system of equations involving nothing more advanced than Walras's own total differentials. Let the notation of such a system be as follows.

---

[2]For a careful critique of an earlier draft of our restatement I am grateful to the late William Jaffé.

4. *Variables*

C_k ≡ money value of consumption in kth household
P_j ≡ price of jth output
p_i ≡ price of ith input
U_k ≡ utility to the kth household
X_j ≡ jth physical output supplied by industry
X_{jk} ≡ jth physical output demanded by kth household
x_i ≡ ith physical input demanded by industry
x_{ki} ≡ ith physical input supplied by kth household
Y_k ≡ money value of income of kth household

5. *Parameters*

a_{ij} ≡ ith physical input demanded by industry per physical unit of jth output ("coefficient de fabrication")
q_{ki} ≡ endowment of kth household with ith physical input

II. THE MODEL

1. *Household Consumption and Income*

Define the money value of consumption in the kth household as the sum of the money values of the outputs demanded by that household:

$$C_k \equiv \sum_{j=1}^{m} (P_j X_{jk}) \tag{1}$$

Of such equations we have s, one for each household.
Define the money value of the income of the kth household as the sum of the money values of the inputs supplied by that household:

$$Y_k \equiv \sum_{i=1}^{n} (p_i x_{ki}) \tag{2}$$

Of such equations we have s, one for each household.
The economy is a stationary one, hence there is no saving, indeed no household saves. We may then write Walras's [1874-1877 (1954: 238)] budget constraint as

$$C_k = Y_k \tag{3}$$

Not until the entire Walras system lies unfolded before us will we be able to see that of equations (3) we have merely $s - 1$, to be demonstrated in section II,10.

2. *Household Endowments and Utility*

Walras [1874-1877 (1954: 237)] thought of his inputs as "... a certain quantity of land-service per day from a hectare of such and such a piece of land; a certain quantity of labour per day from such and such a person; a certain quantity of capital-service per day from such and such a capital good. Let the kinds of these services be *n* in number."

Let the *k*th household possess certain initial endowments of potential inputs $q_{k1}, \ldots, q_{kn}$. Such a household had a choice: "... anyone, at will, [might] either hire out or keep for himself all or part of the services of his own land, personal faculties and capital ..." Some of the potential inputs, then, would become actual inputs $x_{k1}, \ldots, x_{kn}$, and some, i.e., $q_{k1} - x_{k1}, \ldots, q_{kn} - x_{kn}$, would be withheld from the market for the household itself to enjoy, yielding utility just as the outputs consumed did:

$$U_k = U_k(X_{1k}, \ldots, X_{mk}, q_{k1} - x_{k1}, \ldots, q_{kn} - x_{kn}) \qquad (4)$$

Walras's [1874-1878 (1954: 120 and 126-127)] utility ("effective utility") function was always an additive one. As a result, each of its partial derivatives ("rareté") was a function of merely the quantity with respect to which the partial derivative was taken. In our (4), q_{ki} are parameters, $\partial U_k/\partial X_{jk} > 0$, $\partial U_k/\partial(q_{ki} - x_{ki}) > 0$, $\partial^2 U_k/\partial X_{jk}^2 < 0$, and $\partial^2 U_k/\partial(q_{ki} - x_{ki})^2 < 0$. Consequently, $\partial U_k/\partial x_{ki} < 0$ and $\partial^2 U_k/\partial x_{ki}^2 < 0$. Thus the signs of the first and second derivatives of a Walrasian labor supply function are the same as those of a Jevonian one, but for a different reason: to Walras longer working hours deprived the household of leisure, at first copious, later scarce. To Jevons longer working hours caused outright pain!

Walras's utility maximization is best set out in three distinct phases, first, substitution between outputs demanded, second, substitution between inputs supplied and, third, substitution between outputs and inputs.

3. *Utility Maximization: Substitution between Outputs Demanded*

Let the household have succeeded in maximizing its utility. Then, in the immediate neighborhood of such a utility maximum, consider first, as Walras [1874-1877 (1954: 124-127, 164)] did, the substitution between two outputs demanded. Let the *k*th household change infinitesimally its X_{jk} by dX_{jk} and its $X_{(j+1)k}$ by $dX_{(j+1)k}$. Then two things may be said. First, the changes must not affect utility U_k, which is already at its maximum. Second, the changes must not violate the budget constraint (3): if the household wants to demand more of one output, it must demand less of another. Thus

$$dU_k \equiv \frac{\partial U_k}{\partial X_{jk}} \, dX_{jk} + \frac{\partial U_k}{\partial X_{(j+1)k}} \, dX_{(j+1)k} = 0$$

$$dC_k \equiv \frac{\partial C_k}{\partial X_{jk}} \, dX_{jk} + \frac{\partial C_k}{\partial X_{(j+1)k}} \, dX_{(j+1)k} = 0$$

Relative to the markets for the outputs demanded by it, let the household be small enough to have no influence on the prices P_j of outputs. Treating prices P_j as constants, use (1) and (4) to carry out the partial derivations and find

$$\frac{dX_{jk}}{dX_{(j+1)k}} = - \frac{\partial U_k/\partial X_{(j+1)k}}{\partial U_k/\partial X_{jk}} = - \frac{P_{j+1}}{P_j} \tag{5}$$

or in Walras's [1874-1877 (1954: 164)] words: "... the condition of maximum satisfaction of wants ... always consists in the attainment of equality between the ratio of the *raretés* of any two commodities and the price of one in terms of the other ..." In other words, a household maximizes its utility subject to a budget constraint by seeking the point at which the marginal rate of substitution equals *minus* the ratio between the marginal utilities as well as *minus* the price ratio.

4. *Utility Maximization: Substitution between Inputs Supplied*

Let the household have succeeded in maximizing its utility. Then, in the immediate neighborhood of such a utility maximum, consider second, as Walras [1874-1877 (1954: 238 referring to 125 and 257-258)] did indirectly, the substitution between two inputs supplied. Let the kth household change infinitesimally its x_{ki} by dx_{ki} and its $x_{k(i+1)}$ by $dx_{k(i+1)}$. Then two things may be said. First, the changes must not affect utility U_k which is already at its maximum. Second, the changes must not violate the budget constraint (3): if the household wants to supply less of one input, it must supply more of another. Thus

$$dU_k \equiv \frac{\partial U_k}{\partial x_{ki}} \, dx_{ki} + \frac{\partial U_k}{\partial x_{k(i+1)}} \, dx_{k(i+1)} = 0$$

$$dY_k \equiv \frac{\partial Y_k}{\partial x_{ki}} \, dx_{ki} + \frac{\partial Y_k}{\partial x_{k(i+1)}} \, dx_{k(i+1)} = 0$$

Relative to the markets for the inputs supplied by it, let the household be small enough to have no influence on the prices p_i of inputs. Treating prices p_i as constants, use (2) and (4) to carry out the partial derivations and find

$$\frac{dx_{ki}}{dx_{k(i+1)}} = - \frac{\partial U_k/\partial x_{k(i+1)}}{\partial U_k/\partial x_{ki}} = - \frac{p_{i+1}}{p_i} \tag{6}$$

5. *Utility Maximization: Substitution between Outputs and Inputs*

Let the household have succeeded in maximizing its utility. Then, in the immediate neighborhood of such a utility maximum, consider third, as Walras [1874-1877 (1954: 238 and 257-258] did by direct analogy, the substitution between an output demanded and an input supplied. Let the kth household change infinitesimally its X_{jk} by dX_{jk} and its x_{ki} by dx_{ki}. Then two things may be said. First, the changes must not affect utility U_k which is already at its maximum. Second, the changes must not violate the budget constraint (3): if the household wants to demand more of one output, it must supply more of some input. Thus

$$dU_k \equiv \frac{\partial U_k}{\partial X_{jk}} \, dX_{jk} + \frac{\partial U_k}{\partial x_{ki}} \, dx_{ki} = 0$$

$$dC_k - dY_k \equiv \frac{\partial C_k}{\partial X_{jk}} \, dX_{jk} - \frac{\partial Y_k}{\partial x_{ki}} \, dx_{ki} = 0$$

Assume prices of outputs and inputs to be beyond the household's control, use (1), (2), and (4) to carry out the partial derivations, and find

$$\frac{dX_{jk}}{dx_{ki}} = - \frac{\partial U_k/\partial x_{ki}}{\partial U_k/\partial X_{jk}} = \frac{p_i}{P_j} \tag{7}$$

For each household the system (5) through (7) contains $m + n - 1$ equations, hence there are $(m + n - 1)s$ such equations for the economy. The system (5) through (7) determines the kth household's demand for outputs and supply of inputs by requiring equality between the marginal-utility ratio and the price ratio for any pair of outputs demanded and inputs supplied. Walras [1874-1877 (1954: 44)] held this principle to be the very foundation of the whole edifice of economics:

> Everyone competent in the field knows that the theory of exchange based on the proportionality of prices to intensities of the last wants satisfied (i.e. to Final Degrees of Utility or Grenznutzen), which was evolved almost simultaneously by Jevons, Menger and myself, and which constitutes the very foundation of the whole edifice of economics, has become an integral part of the science in England, Austria, the United States, and wherever pure economics is developed and taught.

6. *Industry Supply of Output*

Under pure competition and freedom of entry and exit, the *j*th industry will supply its output at a price equaling unit cost:

$$P_j = \sum_{i=1}^{n} (a_{ij}p_i) \tag{8}$$

where a_{ij} is the ith input demanded by industry per physical unit of jth output, a technologically given parameter called by Walras [1874-1877 (1954: 239)] "coefficient de fabrication." Of such equations we have m, one for each output.

7. Equilibrium in Output Markets

The number of physical units supplied by the jth industry must equal the sum of all physical units of its output demanded by households:

$$X_j = \sum_{k=1}^{s} X_{jk} \tag{9}$$

Of such equations we have m, one for each output.

8. Industry Demand for Input

By definition of a_{ij} the number of physical units of the ith input demanded by industry must equal the sum of all the m outputs, each multiplied by its input-output coefficient with respect to the ith input:

$$x_i \equiv \sum_{j=1}^{m} (a_{ij}X_j) \tag{10}$$

Of such equations, we have n, one for each input.

9. Equilibrium in Input Markets

The number of physical units of the ith input demanded by industry must equal the sum of all physical units of that input supplied by households:

$$x_i = \sum_{k=1}^{s} x_{ki} \tag{11}$$

Of such equations we have n, one for each input.

10. Walras's Law

We can now see why we have merely $s - 1$ equations of the type (3). Sum equation (1) over all the s households. Upon the summation use (9), (8), and (10) in that order to find

$$\sum_{k=1}^{s} C_k = \sum_{i=1}^{n} (p_i x_i)$$

Upon this use (11) and (2) in that order to find

$$\sum_{k=1}^{s} C_k = \sum_{k=1}^{s} Y_k \tag{12}$$

Without using (3), then, we have found that the aggregate money value of consumption equals the aggregate money value of income. Now let (3) be satisfied by each of the first $s - 1$ households, sum over those households, and find

$$\sum_{k=1}^{s-1} C_k = \sum_{k=1}^{s-1} Y_k \tag{13}$$

Subtract (13) from (12) and find

$$C_s = Y_s \tag{14}$$

Consequently, if (3) is satisfied by each of the first $s - 1$ households, it is also satisfied by the sth household. Eq. (14), then, may be derived from the entire system and is not an independent equation. Of independent equations of type (3) we have only $s - 1$. This carries us to the counting of equations and variables.

III. SOLUTIONS?

1. *Counting Equations and Variables*

Of equations we have

Type	Number	Type	Number
(1)	s	(8)	m
(2)	s	(9)	m
(3)	$s - 1$	(10)	n
(4)	s	(11)	n
(5) through (7)	$(m + n - 1)s$		

or a total of $(m + n)(s + 2) + 3s - 1$. Of variables we have

Variable	Number	Variable	Number
C_k	s	x_{ki}	ns
p_i	n	X_j	m
P_j	m	X_{jk}	ms
U_k	s	Y_k	s
x_i	n		

or a total of $(m + n)(s + 2) + 3s$. So the number of variables exceeds the number of equations by one, and the system is in some sense indeterminate. In which sense? Suppose the system to be satisfied by a set of prices p_i and P_j, money expenditures C_k, and money incomes Y_k. Now if in this set every variable were multiplied by the same arbitrary positive constant λ, equations (1) through (3) and (5) through (8) would still hold—and no other equations contain p_i, P_j, C_k or Y_k. Consequently, if the system were satisfied by one set of prices, money expenditures, and money incomes, it would be satisfied by infinitely many. In this sense the system is indeterminate: it cannot determine absolute prices, money expenditures, or money incomes. That job would be left to monetary theory.

But if in all equations containing prices p_i and P_j, money expenditures C_k, and money incomes Y_k we divide every p_i, P_j, C_k, and Y_k by the price of an arbitrary good, the *numéraire*, those equations will still hold, and we will eliminate the price of our *numéraire* as a variable and have the same number of equations and variables, $(m + n)(s + 2) + 3s - 1$. This led Walras to believe that his system determined relative prices, money expenditures, and money incomes, or in his own words [1874-1877 (1954: 43-44)]: "The aforementioned problems of exchange, production . . . are determinate problems, in the sense that the number of equations entailed is equal to the number of the unknowns."

In his lesson 7, Walras did discuss special cases, illustrated graphically, in which the same number of equations and variables failed to produce unique solutions. But in his remaining 35 lessons those examples never bothered him again.

2.   *Beyond Our Restatement*

There was more to Walras than the core restated. As for scope, there were insights into the nature of capital, interest, and money. Indeed, the fourth edition of *Éléments* (1900) contained a Keynes-like rate of interest equilibrating the demand for cash balances with the available quantity of money. Without incorporating it into his general equilibrium, Walras [1874-1877 (1954: 431-446)] was aware of monopoly and reproduced what was known about it since Cournot and Dupuit. As for input-output coefficients, Walras's first edition used fixed ones. But once Barone[3] had

---

[3]For a full account of the part played by Barone, see Jaffé [1964 (1968)]. Before Barone, Walras's engineering colleague, Hermann Amstein (1840-1922), had tried to teach him the minimization of unit cost subject to a production function with variable coefficients of fabrication—with and without the use of a Lagrange multiplier. But even without the Lagrange multiplier, Amstein's rigor was, in Jaffé's words, "far beyond Walras's ken" in 1877.

helped him understand marginal productivity, Walras became pleased with its symmetry and beauty and incorporated it into his fourth edition—in his own words [1874-1877 (1954: 385)]:

> ... the theory of marginal productivity ... shows the underlying motive of the demand for services and the offer of products by entrepreneurs, just as the theory of final utility shows the underlying motive of the demand for products and offer of services by landowners, workers and capitalists.

IV. CONCLUSION

To Georges Renard Walras wrote: "If one wants to harvest quickly, one must plant carrots and salads; if one has the ambition to plant oaks, one must have the sense to tell oneself: my grandchildren will owe me this shade," [Étienne Antonelli (1939: 8)]. Six Walrasian grandchildren have won the Nobel Memorial Prize for their work in general equilibrium but, as grandchildren, belong in our next period, 1930-1980.

REFERENCES

E. Antonelli, *L'économie pure du capitalisme*, Paris, 1939.
W. Jaffé, "New Light on an Old Quarrel," *Cahiers Vilfredo Pareto*, 1964, *3*, 63-102. The part dealing with Amstein's early help is reprinted in W. J. Baumol and S. M. Goldfeld (eds.), *Precursors in Mathematical Economics: An Anthology*, London, 1968.
——, "Walras, Léon," *International Encyclopedia of the Social Sciences*, New York, 1968, *16*, 447-453.
J. A. Schumpeter, *History of Economic Analysis*, New York, 1954.
L. Walras, *Eléments d'économie politique pure*, Lausanne, Paris, and Basle, 1874-1877, translated as *Elements of Pure Economics or the Theory of Social Wealth* by W. Jaffé, Homewood Ill., 1954.

CHAPTER 6 Imputation and Static General Equilibrium

MENGER (1840-1921)
WIESER (1851-1926)

> *Menger reformed a science in which rigidly exact*
> *thought was much more recent and imperfect than in*
> *the science which Copernicus placed on new*
> *foundations.*
>
> Schumpeter (1951: 85)

I. INTRODUCTION

1. A New Foundation

Three-quarters of a century after Newton's unpublished discovery of the derivative—and a half-century after Leibnitz's published discovery of it—the derivative of utility with respect to amount possessed was taken by Bernoulli.

Menger never referred to Bernoulli. In 1871 he had not learned calculus—later in life he tried to teach it to himself and struggled manfully with it, as we know from his son, Karl Menger (1971: 44). What he did know was that goods were valued because needed and that their value would depend on the need satisfied by the last unit available. That need would be the least important need: take the last unit away, and the consumer would still satisfy his higher-priority needs and merely go without the satisfaction of his least important one. That was all, but with that Menger had put economic theory on a new foundation.

At first sight, that foundation might seem narrow. On the face of it, it could apply only to consumers' goods. But while consumers' goods satisfied needs directly, producers' goods satisfied them indirectly. Producers' goods, too, were valued because needed. But how needed they were would depend upon two things: first, how productive they were in producing consumers' goods and, second, how needed those consumers' goods were. That brings us to the principle of imputation. Both Menger [1871 (1950: 152 *et passim*)] and Wieser [1889 (1930: books III through V)] used the principle of imputation. But Menger used it more narrowly, confining himself to do-it-yourself households.

2. *Menger's Imputation: Do-It-Yourself Households*

Did Menger know physical marginal productivity? He had little patience with any purely physical input-output relationships. He always hurried on from physical marginal productivity $\partial X/\partial x_i$ of the *i*th input to the chain rule $\partial U/\partial x_i \equiv (\partial U/\partial X)(\partial X/\partial x_i)$ measuring, in his own words [1871 (1950: 164)], "... the importance of the satisfactions provided for by the portion of the product that would remain unproduced if we were not in a position to command the given quantity of the good of higher order."

In other words, Menger was measuring marginal *utility*[1] productivity. Such a measure made sense if and only if he were thinking of do-it-yourself households, and so he was. His do-it-yourself households would exchange the goods that they had produced, and the core of Menger's book was devoted to an analysis of such exchange.

3. *Wieser's Imputation: Industry Separated from Households*

For a separation of industry from households we must turn to Wieser. Once separated from households, industry demands inputs and supplies outputs; households demand outputs and supply inputs. Both inputs and outputs, then, are transacted in markets and have prices. The Austrian unifying principle applied to households and firms alike. In households, goods were needed as outputs to maximize household utility. In firms, goods were needed as inputs to maximize firm profits, or in Wieser's own words [1889 (1930: 55)]:

> In every self-contained private economy utility is the highest
> principle; but, in the business world, wherever the providing of
> society with goods is in the hands of undertakers who desire to
> make a gain out of it, and to obtain a remuneration for their
> services, exchange value takes its place.

4. *Wieser's Primitive Form*

Wieser's form was not up to his vision. He wrote [1889 (1930: 88)] no more than a minuscule part of the equations of his system, i.e., a product-exhaustion theorem consisting of three equations (one for each output) and three unknowns (the input prices called x, y, and z). This was misleading—certainly to his readers and perhaps to himself—in two respects.

First, Wieser's counting of equations and unknowns was misleading.

---

[1]Menger himself never used the term "Grenznutzen" (marginal utility). It was coined by Wieser (1884).

An *m*-output, *n*-input system would have *m* product-exhaustion equations in *n* input prices and thus would not have the same number of equations and unknowns. But the system would, of course, need equations for other variables, among them variables for which Wieser used numbers. Such other equations Wieser never mentioned, let alone wrote.

Second, had Wieser known the calculus, he would have known what a differentiable function is. At a point of a production function the physical marginal productivity of an input is the partial derivative of the function with respect to that input at that point. A derivative is a limit. If that limit is the same whether the point is approached from the left or from the right, the function is said to be differentiable at that point. Wieser fussed about the difference between approaching the point from the left or from the right and considered it "the error in Menger's theory" [1889 (1930: 85)] to have approached the point from the left. Had Wieser known the calculus he would also have known Euler's theorem and seen his product exhaustion as an application of it to the case of constant returns to scale. Wieser [1889 (1930: 83)] fussed about "the best combination now broken up" but never seriously discussed scale or the returns to it. All the fuss was, as Schumpeter (1954: 914n) put it, due to "lack of experience in handling the relevant concepts."

5.   *Our Own Restatement*

We shall set out Wieser's principle of imputation as he might have done himself, had his form been up to his substance. There is more to his principle than just price theory.

Inherent in it is, first, a theory of allocation. The first-order condition for a profit maximum is that any input be hired up to the point where its price equals its marginal value productivity. That condition tells the firm how much of each input to hire. In a market within which an input is perfectly mobile, its price must be uniform throughout the market. It follows that so must its marginal value productivity. That condition determines the allocation of inputs among outputs.

Inherent in the principle of imputation is, second, a theory of cost. Quantity of input hired *times* its price is the cost of the input. Summing over all inputs hired by the firm will give us the cost of production of the output produced by the firm.

Inherent in the principle of imputation is, third, a theory of income. Quantity of input hired *times* its price is also the income of the household whose input is being hired. As Say had already realized, cost and income are the same thing seen from two different angles. Summing over all firms hiring the same input will give us the income of all households supplying it.

A Wieser theory of imputation, then, is in one sweep a theory of price, allocation, cost, and income. We shall set it out with specified functional forms and explicit solutions for the simplest imaginable case of two outputs, two inputs, and two households. How many firms? Let all firms within an industry, established as well as potential ones, be alike. Let production functions be linearly homogeneous, and let competition be pure. Then all firms have zero profits, and their number does not matter.

Let the notation of our restatement be as follows.

6. Variables

C_k ≡ money value of consumption in kth household
c_j ≡ money value of cost incurred by firm in jth industry
P_j ≡ price of jth output
p_i ≡ price of ith input
R_j ≡ money value of revenue of firm in jth industry
U_k ≡ utility to the kth household
X_j ≡ jth physical output supplied by industry
X_{jk} ≡ jth physical output demanded by kth household
x_{ij} ≡ ith physical input demanded by jth industry
Y_k ≡ money value of income of kth household
Z_j ≡ profits earned by firm in jth industry

7. Parameters

A ≡ elasticity of utility with respect to first output
a_j ≡ multiplicative factor of production function for jth output
α_j ≡ elasticity of jth output with respect to first input
B ≡ elasticity of utility with respect to second output
β_j ≡ elasticity of jth output with respect to second input
q_{ki} ≡ endowment of kth household with ith physical input

II. A NEOCLASSICAL THEORY OF THE HOUSEHOLD

1. Utility, Consumption, and Income

Households demand outputs and supply inputs. Let the kth household have the differentiable utility function

$$U_k = U_k(X_{1k}, \ldots, X_{mk}) \tag{1}$$

Define the money value of consumption in the kth household as the sum of the money values of the outputs demanded by that household:

$$C_k \equiv \sum_{j=1}^{m} (P_j X_{jk}) \tag{2}$$

Relative to the markets for the outputs demanded by it, let the household be small enough to have no influence on the prices P_j of such outputs.

The endowment q_{ki} of the kth household with the ith physical input is a parameter. Unlike Walrasian or Marshallian households, Austrian ones never contemplate supplying more or less of their endowment: the entire endowment is supplied. Define the money value of the income of the kth household as the sum of the money values of the inputs supplied by that household:

$$Y_k \equiv \sum_{i=1}^{n} (p_i q_{ki}) \tag{3}$$

Relative to the markets for the inputs supplied by it, let the household be small enough to have no influence on the prices p_i of such inputs.

A Menger-Wieser economy is a stationary one, hence there is no saving. Indeed, let no household save:

$$C_k = Y_k \tag{4}$$

With endowment q_{ki} a parameter and price p_i perceived of as given to it, the household will perceive of its income (3) as given to it. Consequently, the household will conceive of (4) as a budget constraint subject to which utility is maximized. We may maximize it the way Walras did, by using total differentials.

2. Utility Maximization

Like a Walras household, a Menger-Wieser household will then be seeking the point at which the marginal rate of substitution equals *minus* the ratio between the marginal utilities as well as *minus* the price ratio:

$$\frac{dX_{jk}}{dX_{(j+1)k}} = - \frac{\partial U_k/\partial X_{(j+1)k}}{\partial U_k/\partial X_{jk}} = - \frac{P_{j+1}}{P_j} \tag{5}$$

Having said as much as can be said without specifying our utility function (1), let us specify it.

3. A Cobb-Douglas Form of the Utility Function

In a miniature Menger-Wieser economy of two outputs, two inputs, and two households let the utility function be of Cobb-Douglas form:

$$U_1 = X_{11}{}^A X_{21}{}^B \tag{6}$$

$$U_2 = X_{12}{}^A X_{22}{}^B \tag{7}$$

where A and B are parameters lying between zero and one. It is unnecessary—but possible—to assume that A and B differ between the two persons. It is unnecessary to assume that $A + B = 1$.

Given the utility functions (6) and (7), the derivatives $\partial U_k / \partial X_{jk}$ may now be taken

$$\frac{\partial U_1}{\partial X_{11}} = \frac{A U_1}{X_{11}}$$

$$\frac{\partial U_2}{\partial X_{12}} = \frac{A U_2}{X_{12}}$$

$$\frac{\partial U_1}{\partial X_{21}} = \frac{B U_1}{X_{21}}$$

$$\frac{\partial U_2}{\partial X_{22}} = \frac{B U_2}{X_{22}}$$

and our system (5) will collapse into

$$P_1 X_{11}/A = P_2 X_{21}/B \tag{8}$$

$$P_1 X_{12}/A = P_2 X_{22}/B \tag{9}$$

Furthermore, equations (2) and (4) will collapse into the two budget constraints

$$Y_1 = P_1 X_{11} + P_2 X_{21} \tag{10}$$

$$Y_2 = P_1 X_{12} + P_2 X_{22} \tag{11}$$

which together with (8) and (9) constitute four equations in four unknowns X_{jk} and permit us to find the four demand equations

$$X_{11} = \frac{A}{A + B} \frac{Y_1}{P_1} \tag{12}$$

$$X_{12} = \frac{A}{A + B} \frac{Y_2}{P_1} \tag{13}$$

$$X_{21} = \frac{B}{A + B} \frac{Y_1}{P_2} \tag{14}$$

$$X_{22} = \frac{B}{A + B} \frac{Y_2}{P_2} \tag{15}$$

All four demand functions have income elasticities of *plus* one, direct price elasticities of *minus* one, and cross elasticities of zero. Such simple results followed from the Cobb-Douglas form of the utility functions (6) and (7).

4. Household Income

In our miniature Menger-Wieser economy, functional and personal income distribution will become identical if the first household is assumed to own the first input and the second household to own the second: the four endowments q_{ki} will then be

$$q_{11} > 0 \tag{16}$$

$$q_{12} = 0 \tag{17}$$

$$q_{21} = 0 \tag{18}$$

$$q_{22} > 0 \tag{19}$$

and the incomes of the two households will be

$$Y_1 = p_1 q_{11} \tag{20}$$

$$Y_2 = p_2 q_{22} \tag{21}$$

III. A NEOCLASSICAL THEORY OF INDUSTRY

1. *Production, Cost, Revenue, and Profits*

In section VII of our introduction to the period 1870-1930 we summarized a neoclassical theory of the industry as follows. All firms in the jth industry, established as well as potential ones, were assumed to be alike and have the differentiable production function

$$X_j = X_j(x_{1j}, \ldots, x_{nj}) \tag{22}$$

The money value of the cost incurred by such a firm was defined as the sum of the money values of the inputs demanded by that firm:

$$c_j \equiv \sum_{i=1}^{n} (p_i x_{ij}) \tag{23}$$

The firm was assumed to be facing the differentiable demand function

$$P_j = P_j(X_j) \tag{24}$$

Given such a demand function, the money value of the revenue of the firm was defined as the money value of the output supplied:

$$R_j \equiv P_j X_j \tag{25}$$

Finally, the profit earned by the firm was defined as the difference between revenue and cost:

$$Z_j \equiv R_j - c_j \tag{26}$$

and was then maximized. A first-order condition for a profit maximum was found to be that any input should be hired up to the point where its price equals its marginal revenue productivity:

$$p_i = \left(P_j + \frac{dP_j}{dX_j} X_j \right) \frac{\partial X_j}{\partial x_{ij}} \tag{27}$$

2. Pure Competition and Constant Returns to Scale

Both Menger [1871 (1950: 197-216)] and Wieser [1889 (1930: 105-110)] briefly discussed monopoly, but their main concern was pure competition. Here, the firm was so small relative to its output market that it could not influence the price of its output. In that case, $dP_j/dX_j = 0$, marginal revenue collapsed into price P_j of output, and the first-order condition (27) for a profit maximum collapsed into the condition that any input should be hired up to the point where its price equaled its marginal *value* productivity:

$$p_i = P_j \frac{\partial X_j}{\partial x_{ij}} \tag{28}$$

In the special case of pure competition and constant returns to scale we showed that the product-exhaustion theorem would hold:

$$P_j X_j = p_1 x_{1j} + \ldots + p_n x_{nj} \tag{29}$$

holding not only for the firm but for the industry and the economy as well. Written for his three-output, three-input system, our product-exhaustion theorem (29) was, as we observed above, the only mathematics Wieser ever wrote.

Having said as much as can be said without specifying our production function (22), let us specify it.

3. A Cobb-Douglas Form of the Production Function

In a miniature Menger-Wieser economy of two outputs, two inputs, and two households let the production function be of Cobb-Douglas form:

$$X_1 = a_1 x_{11}^{\alpha_1} x_{21}^{\beta_1} \tag{30}$$

$$X_2 = a_2 x_{12}^{\alpha_2} x_{22}^{\beta_2} \tag{31}$$

where $0 < \alpha_j < 1$, $0 < \beta_j < 1$, $a_j > 0$, and $\alpha_j + \beta_j = 1$.

Given the production functions (30) and (31), the derivatives $\partial X_j/$ ∂x_{ij} may now be taken, and our system (28) will collapse into

$$p_1 = \alpha_1 P_1 X_1 / x_{11} \tag{32}$$

$$p_1 = \alpha_2 P_2 X_2 / x_{12} \tag{33}$$

$$p_2 = \beta_1 P_1 X_1 / x_{21} \tag{34}$$

$$p_2 = \beta_2 P_2 X_2 / x_{22} \tag{35}$$

Multiply (32) and (34) by x_{11} and x_{21}, respectively, and add them, multiply (33) and (35) by x_{12} and x_{22}, respectively, and add them, and find our product-exhaustion theorem (29) collapsing into

$$P_1 X_1 = p_1 x_{11} + p_2 x_{21} \tag{36}$$

$$P_2 X_2 = p_1 x_{12} + p_2 x_{22} \tag{37}$$

We are done with households and industries. All that remains is to impose equilibrium conditions upon the system.

IV. EQUILIBRIUM CONDITIONS: ALL MARKETS CLEAR

1. *Input-Market Equilibrium*

Input-market equilibrium requires the supply of inputs to equal the demand for them:

$$q_{11} = x_{11} + x_{12} \tag{38}$$

$$q_{22} = x_{21} + x_{22} \tag{39}$$

2. *Output-Market Equilibrium*

Equilibrium in the market for the first output requires the supply of it to equal the demand for it:

$$X_1 = X_{11} + X_{12} \tag{40}$$

Must the same not be true of the market for the second output? Indeed it must, but not as a new and independent condition. Add the product-exhaustion theorem (36) and (37), use first (38) and (39), then (20) and (21), and find

$$P_1 X_1 + P_2 X_2 = Y_1 + Y_2$$

Multiply the demand equations (12) through (15) by their respective prices P_j, add all four of them together, use (40), and find

$$P_1 X_1 + P_2 (X_{21} + X_{22}) = Y_1 + Y_2$$

Thus it follows from equations already written that for the second output as well, supply equals demand:

$$X_2 = X_{21} + X_{22} \tag{41}$$

So we have encountered Walras's Law: if in an economy with four markets three of them are in equilibrium, the fourth must also be.

Our variables are the following prices, quantities, and money incomes:

$$P_1, P_2 \qquad X_{11}, X_{12}, X_{21}, X_{22}$$

$$p_1, p_2 \qquad x_{11}, x_{12}, x_{21}, x_{22}$$

$$X_1, X_2 \qquad Y_1, Y_2$$

Can we find unique solutions for all variables? Not for all of them. Like the Walras system, our system is homogeneous of degree zero in its prices, money expenditures, and money incomes. Like Walras, we must choose a *numéraire* and divide all equations containing prices, money expenditures, and money incomes by it. That will eliminate the price of the *numéraire* itself as a variable and leave us with physical quantities and the relative prices, money expenditures, and money incomes as variables. Can we solve our Menger-Wieser system for those variables? Let us try.

V. SOLUTIONS

1. *Allocation of Inputs Among Outputs*

Let us begin with the allocation of inputs among outputs x_{ij}. Multiply the demand equations (12) through (15) by their respective prices P_j, add (13) to (12) and (15) to (14), insert the output-equilibrium conditions (40) and (41) and the product-exhaustion theorems (36) and (37), and find $A(p_1 x_{21} + p_2 x_{22}) = B(p_1 x_{11} + p_2 x_{21})$. Then divide (32) by (34) and (33) by (35) and find $p_1/p_2 = \alpha_1 x_{21}/(\beta_1 x_{11}) = \alpha_2 x_{22}/(\beta_2 x_{12})$, insert that, apply to the input-equilibrium conditions (38) and (39), and find the solutions for the allocation of inputs among outputs:

$$x_{11} = \frac{\alpha_1 A}{\alpha_1 A + \alpha_2 B} \, q_{11} \tag{42}$$

$$x_{12} = \frac{\alpha_2 B}{\alpha_1 A + \alpha_2 B} \, q_{11} \tag{43}$$

$$x_{21} = \frac{\beta_1 A}{\beta_1 A + \beta_2 B} \, q_{22} \tag{44}$$

$$x_{22} = \frac{\beta_2 B}{\beta_1 A + \beta_2 B} \, q_{22} \qquad (45)$$

2. Relative Prices

The relative price of inputs p_2/p_1 may be found in two ways. Either we may divide (34) by (32) and insert (42) and (44). Or we may divide (35) by (33) and insert (43) and (45). The results are the same:

$$\frac{p_2}{p_1} = \frac{\beta_1 A + \beta_2 B}{\alpha_1 A + \alpha_2 B} \frac{q_{11}}{q_{22}} \qquad (46)$$

To find output prices relative to the *numéraire* p_1, we may first divide (32) by P_1, insert (30) divided by x_{11}, rearrange, insert (42) and (44), and find P_1/p_1. We may then divide (33) by P_2, insert (31) divided by x_{12}, rearrange, insert (43) and (45), and find P_2/p_1. The results are

$$\frac{P_1}{p_1} = \frac{1}{a_1 \alpha_1{}^{\alpha_1} \beta_1{}^{\beta_1}} \left(\frac{\beta_1 A + \beta_2 B}{\alpha_1 A + \alpha_2 B} \frac{q_{11}}{q_{22}} \right)^{\beta_1} \qquad (47)$$

$$\frac{P_2}{p_1} = \frac{1}{a_2 \alpha_2{}^{\alpha_2} \beta_2{}^{\beta_2}} \left(\frac{\beta_1 A + \beta_2 B}{\alpha_1 A + \alpha_2 B} \frac{q_{11}}{q_{22}} \right)^{\beta_2} \qquad (48)$$

3. Outputs

Simply insert the solutions (42) through (45) for the allocation of inputs among outputs into the production functions (30) and (31) and find the solutions for outputs:

$$X_1 = a_1 \left(\frac{\alpha_1 A q_{11}}{\alpha_1 A + \alpha_2 B} \right)^{\alpha_1} \left(\frac{\beta_1 A q_{22}}{\beta_1 A + \beta_2 B} \right)^{\beta_1} \qquad (49)$$

$$X_2 = a_2 \left(\frac{\alpha_2 B q_{11}}{\alpha_1 A + \alpha_2 B} \right)^{\alpha_2} \left(\frac{\beta_2 B q_{22}}{\beta_1 A + \beta_2 B} \right)^{\beta_2} \qquad (50)$$

4. Allocation of Outputs Among Households

Insert (20) and (47) into (12) and find X_{11}. Insert (21), (46), and (47) into (13) and find X_{12}. Insert (20) and (48) into (14) and find X_{21}. Insert (21), (46), and (48) into (15) and find X_{22}. Then the allocation of output among households is

$$X_{11} = \frac{A}{A + B} \, a_1 \alpha_1{}^{\alpha_1} \beta_1{}^{\beta_1} \left(\frac{\alpha_1 A + \alpha_2 B}{\beta_1 A + \beta_2 B} \frac{q_{22}}{q_{11}} \right)^{\beta_1} q_{11} \qquad (51)$$

$$X_{12} = \frac{A}{A + B} \, a_1 \alpha_1{}^{\alpha_1} \beta_1{}^{\beta_1} \left(\frac{\beta_1 A + \beta_2 B}{\alpha_1 A + \alpha_2 B} \, \frac{q_{11}}{q_{22}} \right)^{\alpha_1} q_{22} \tag{52}$$

$$X_{21} = \frac{B}{A + B} \, a_2 \alpha_2{}^{\alpha_2} \beta_2{}^{\beta_2} \left(\frac{\alpha_1 A + \alpha_2 B}{\beta_1 A + \beta_2 B} \, \frac{q_{22}}{q_{11}} \right)^{\beta_2} q_{11} \tag{53}$$

$$X_{22} = \frac{B}{A + B} \, a_2 \alpha_2{}^{\alpha_2} \beta_2{}^{\beta_2} \left(\frac{\beta_1 A + \beta_2 B}{\alpha_1 A + \alpha_2 B} \, \frac{q_{11}}{q_{22}} \right)^{\alpha_2} q_{22} \tag{54}$$

5. Income Distribution

Divide (20) by p_1. Divide (21) by p_1 and insert (46). Then money incomes relative to the *numéraire* p_1 are

$$\frac{Y_1}{p_1} = q_{11} \tag{55}$$

$$\frac{Y_2}{p_1} = \frac{\beta_1 A + \beta_2 B}{\alpha_1 A + \alpha_2 B} \, q_{11} \tag{56}$$

The distributive shares are then

$$\frac{Y_1}{Y_1 + Y_2} = \frac{\alpha_1 A + \alpha_2 B}{A + B} \tag{57}$$

$$\frac{Y_2}{Y_1 + Y_2} = \frac{\beta_1 A + \beta_2 B}{A + B} \tag{58}$$

VI. CONCLUSION

If a theory of price, allocation, cost, and income is inherent in Wieser's principle of imputation, then our mathematical formalization has not gone beyond his principle. We have merely found explicit solutions for the allocation of input among outputs, for relative prices, for outputs, for the allocation of outputs among households, and for income distribution. Under the assumptions made about the form of utility and production functions used and the values of parameters involved, all solutions exist, are positive, and are unique. As for quantities, then, both outputs will be produced, each output will absorb both inputs, and each household will consume both outputs. As for prices, then, both inputs and both outputs will have positive prices, hence be economic goods.

According to our explicit solutions (42) through (58), ultimately every variable is determined by four categories of parameters. First, engineering delivers the technology parameters α_j and β_j. Second, physiology and psychology deliver the want parameters A and B. Third, nature delivers the resource parameters q_{ki}. Fourth, legal institutions establish private ownership to those resources, making it possible for private persons to earn an income from them. None of the four taken alone would suffice to determine the system—as the classical school, the marginal utility school, or the institutionalist school may have believed that one or the other of them would. Economics is nothing less than the full interaction of prices and quantities against the background of given technology, wants, resources, and legal institutions.

REFERENCES

C. Menger, *Grundsätze der Volkswirthschaftslehre*, Vienna, 1871, reprinted by the London School of Economics and Political Science, 1934, translated as *Principles of Economics* by and edited by J. Dingwall and B. F. Hoselitz with an introduction by F. H. Knight, Glencoe, Ill., 1950.

K. Menger, "Austrian Marginalism and Mathematical Economics," in J. R. Hicks and W. Weber (eds.), *Carl Menger and the Austrian School of Economics*, Vienna, 1971, 38-60.

J. A. Schumpeter, "Carl Menger 1840-1921," *Ten Great Economists from Marx to Keynes*, New York, 1951.

———, *History of Economic Analysis*, New York, 1954.

F. von Wieser, *Ursprung und Hauptgesetze des wirtschaftlichen Werthes*, Vienna, 1884.

———, *Der natürliche Werth*, Vienna, 1889, translated as *Natural Value* by C. A. Malloch and edited with a preface and analysis by W. Smart, Glasgow, 1893, reprinted New York, 1930.

CHAPTER 7 Static General Equilibrium of Labor and Capital

BÖHM-BAWERK (1851-1914)

The roundabout ways of capital are fruitful but long;
they procure us more or better consumption goods,
but only at a later period of time.
Böhm-Bawerk [1888 (1923: 82)]

I. INTRODUCTION

1. Böhm-Bawerk's Problem

Capital is necessary in production, and its necessity has something to do with time. In the capitalist production process, what precisely is it that takes time? Two different types of capital have been distinguished by economists: circulating and fixed. In the case of fixed capital, what takes time is the utilization of durable plant and equipment. Böhm-Bawerk said nothing about fixed capital. His problem was circulating capital. Here, what takes time is the maturing of output in slow organic growth in agriculture, cattle raising, forestry, and winery or in time-consuming construction jobs. Böhm-Bawerk assumed a continuous succession of labor inputs throughout the period of production. What capital does is to advance the wages of such a continuous succession of labor inputs.

Böhm-Bawerk assumed pure competition and freedom of entry and exit in a stationary economy with given factor supplies, i.e., available real capital stock and labor force. To establish equilibrium in his factor and goods markets, Böhm-Bawerk saw three equilibrating variables, the length of the period of production, the rate of interest, and the real wage rate. His problem was to determine their level.

2. Böhm-Bawerk's Method

Like Cantillon and Ricardo, Böhm-Bawerk had a mathematical mind but no mathemathical training. Like Ricardo's, his method was the numerical example. As for interest, his interest on debt incurred was simple interest. Compounding, let alone continuous compounding, was never used. The door to the room of the natural exponential function remained locked to Böhm-Bawerk.

3. *Our Own Restatement*

The key to the door was Euler's number e, discovered in 1748, of which it was true that $d(e^u)/dx = e^u du/dx$. We wish to show that Böhm-Bawerk's results depended on neither his simple interest nor his choice of numerical examples. To show that, we apply continuous compounding, use Euler's number, and make ourselves comfortable in the room of the natural exponential function. Here, a simple and elegant form of Böhm-Bawerk's results may be found with a minimum of effort.

Let the notation of our restatement be as follows.

4. *Variables*

D ≡ desired money capital stock
J ≡ present net worth of an endless succession of future production runs
L ≡ labor employed in a production run
r ≡ rate of interest per annum with continuous compounding
W ≡ money wage bill per annum in a production run
w ≡ money wage rate per annum
X ≡ physical output maturing at the end of a period of production
y ≡ period of production

5. *Parameters*

a ≡ multiplicative factor in production function
α ≡ elasticity of physical output per annum per man with respect to period of production
F ≡ available labor force
P ≡ price of output
S ≡ available real capital stock

The symbol e is Euler's number, the base of natural logarithms. The symbol t is general time. The symbol τ is present time. The symbol v is vintage.

Interest and money wage rates are treated as constants in firm equilibrium but as equilibrating variables in general equilibrium.

II. FIRM EQUILIBRIUM: ONE VINTAGE AT A TIME

1. *Optimizing the Period of Production*

Call a production run started at time v a production run of vintage v. Let y be the length of the period of production. Not until a production run of vintage v is completed will another vintage $v + y$ be started. The physical output X will then mature at times $v + y$, $v + 2y$, ... in endless succession. The value of the physical output maturing is PX.

The optimal period of production is one that maximizes the present net worth as seen from time v of such an endless succession of future vintages. Let a stationary rate of interest r be applied when discounting future cash flows. The present gross worth of the succession is the present worth as seen from time v of all future values PX maturing every yth year and discounted at the rate of interest r, or

$$PX(e^{-ry} + e^{-2ry} + e^{-3ry} + \cdots) \tag{1}$$

Inside the parenthesis is an infinite geometrical progression with the first term and the common ratio both being e^{-ry}. Its sum is

$$\frac{e^{-ry}}{1 - e^{-ry}} = \frac{1}{e^{ry} - 1} \tag{2}$$

But why should roundabout methods be considered in the first place? Because, Böhm-Bawerk said, the longer the period of production the larger is physical output per annum per man.

The average physical output per annum of a production run producing the physical output X every yth year is X/y. Let a production run of vintage v employ L men continuously. Then average physical output per annum per man is $X/(Ly)$. Let α be the elasticity of average physical output per annum per man $X/(Ly)$ with respect to the period of production y, and let the production function be of constant-elasticity form:

$$X/(Ly) = ay^{\alpha} \tag{3}$$

where $0 < \alpha < 1$ and $a > 0$. Both are stationary: there is no technological progress. Use (2) and (3) to write (1) as

$$\frac{aLPy^{\alpha+1}}{e^{ry} - 1} \tag{4}$$

So much for gross worth. What does it cost to operate the endless succession of future vintages? We said that a production run of vintage v employs L men continuously and pays each man the money wage rate w per annum. Consequently, its money wage bill per annum is

$$W \equiv Lw \tag{5}$$

The future wage bill paid out during a small fraction dt of a year located at time t is then $Lwdt$. As seen from time v, the present worth of that future wage bill is $e^{-r(t-v)}Lwdt$, and the present worth of all such future wage bills is

$$\int_v^{\infty} e^{-r(t-v)}Lwdt$$

Here L and w are both stationary and may move outside the integral sign. Then the integral is easily found to be

$$Lw/r \qquad (6)$$

Define present net worth J as seen from time v of the endless succession of future vintages as their present gross worth (4) *minus* the present worth of all their future wage bills (6), or

$$J \equiv \left(\frac{aPy^{\alpha+1}}{e^{ry} - 1} - \frac{w}{r} \right) L \qquad (7)$$

Maximize (7) by manipulating the period of production y. The firm was said to be purely competitive; consequently, price P of output and prices r and w of inputs are given to it and may be treated as constants. Keeping labor employed L constant, differentiate (7) partially with respect to y and find the first-order condition for a maximum

$$\frac{\partial J}{\partial y} = \frac{e^{ry}(\alpha + 1 - ry) - (\alpha + 1)}{(e^{ry} - 1)^2} aLPy^{\alpha} = 0 \qquad (8)$$

As long as the price of output is positive and any labor is to be hired at all, aLP cannot be zero. Eq. (8) will be satisfied by $y = 0$, but then according to (3), output per man would be zero too. More interestingly, (8) will be satisfied by

$$j \equiv e^{ry}(\alpha + 1 - ry) - (\alpha + 1) = 0 \qquad (9)$$

To see if the second-order condition for a maximum is satisfied, differentiate (8) partially once more and find the second partial derivative of present net worth (7) to be

$$\frac{\partial^2 J}{\partial y^2} = \frac{(e^{ry} - 1)^2 dj/dy - jd[(e^{ry} - 1)^2]/dy}{(e^{ry} - 1)^4} aLPy^{\alpha}$$

$$+ \frac{j}{(e^{ry} - 1)^2} \alpha aLPy^{\alpha-1}$$

But according to the first-order condition (9) $j = 0$, so the second derivative collapses into

$$\frac{\partial^2 J}{\partial y^2} = \frac{(\alpha - ry)e^{ry}r}{(e^{ry} - 1)^2} aLPy^{\alpha} \qquad (10)$$

Is this second derivative negative?

Eq. (9) is a transcendental equation in y permitting no explicit solution. A graphical solution, however, is easy. On the vertical axis of a diagram, plot the two terms of (9) as functions of y plotted on the horizontal axis. Figure 7-1 shows the first term of (9) as a curve starting at the value α

FIGURE 7-1. Mapping the Two Terms of First-Order Condition (9) for α = 1/2, $r = 0.04$

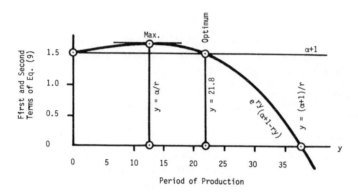

+ 1 for $y = 0$, rising to a maxiumum for $y = α/r$, then falling to the value zero for $y = (α + 1)/r$, and being negative thereafter.

The second term of (9), $α + 1$, is not a function of y, hence appears as a horizontal line at the height $α + 1$. Eq. (9) is satisfied where curve and line intersect. They do so twice. They intersect first at $y = 0$, but then according to (3), output per man would be zero. They intersect second, and more interestingly, at a value y such that

$$α/r < y < (α + 1)/r \qquad (11)$$

According to (11), $α < ry$; consequently, the second derivative (10) is negative, and the second-order condition for a maximum net worth is satisfied.

2.   Sensitivity of Optimized Period of Production to Rate of Interest

As observed above, (9) is a transcendental equation in y permitting no explicit solution. Otherwise it is simple: other than the variable y, it contains only the rate of interest r and the elasticity $α$ and has a remarkably simple sensitivity to the rate of interest r, found by differentiating it with respect to r. So r is now the variable with respect to which we are differentiating, and y is a function of r; consequently

$$\frac{de^{ry}}{dr} = e^{ry}\frac{d(ry)}{dr} = e^{ry}\left(r\frac{dy}{dr} + y\right) \qquad (12)$$

Using (12), differentiate (9) implicitly with respect to r and find

$$\frac{d[e^{ry}(α + 1 - ry)]}{dr} = e^{ry}(α - ry)\left(r\frac{dy}{dr} + y\right) = 0$$

For a finite value of the product ry, e^{ry} can never be zero. According to (11), $\alpha < ry$; consequently, $\alpha - ry$ cannot be zero either. So the last factor must be:

$$r \frac{dy}{dr} + y = 0$$

or

$$\frac{dy}{dr} \frac{r}{y} = -1 \tag{13}$$

which says that the elasticity of the optimal period of production y with respect to the rate of interest r is *minus* one. That is another way of saying that r and y are in inverse proportion and that their product is some constant. Our result (13) will facilitate the interpretation of our later results.

3. Desired Capital Stock in Vintage v at Time τ

What capital does is to finance the wages paid by the firm. The wage bill per small fraction dt of a year located at time t is $W dt$. As seen from time τ, the present worth of it is $We^{r(\tau - t)} dt$. As seen from time τ, the present worth of sums borrowed between time v and time τ to finance all wages paid in the production run of vintage v is the integral

$$D_v(\tau) \equiv \int_v^\tau We^{r(\tau - t)} dt$$

The wage bill W is no function of time t, hence may be taken outside the integral sign. Our rate of interest r was said to be stationary, hence the coefficient r of t is stationary too. As a result find the integral to be

$$D_v(\tau) = \frac{e^{r(\tau - v)} - 1}{r} W \tag{14}$$

4. Competitive Equilibrium in Vintage v at the End of the Production Run

In (14) replace τ by $v + y$ and find the value, as seen at the end of the production run, of the sums borrowed with compound interest to finance all wages paid over the entire production run of vintage v

$$D_v(v + y) = \frac{e^{ry} - 1}{r} W \tag{15}$$

To pay off that accumulated debt, a physical output X, valued PX, is maturing at time $v + y$. Under pure competition and freedom of entry and exit, profits over and above all wages paid with compound interest (15) will be washed away, and the firm will break even:

$$PX = \frac{e^{ry} - 1}{r} W \tag{16}$$

Eq. (16) is the clue to, first, labor's share, and second, the real wage rate.

5. Competitive Equilibrium: Labor's Share in Vintage v

Divide both sides of (16) by y, rearrange, and write it

$$\frac{W}{PX/y} = \frac{ry}{e^{ry} - 1} \tag{16}$$

In (16) the left-hand side is money wage bill per annum divided by the money value of average physical output per annum or labor's share.

6. Competitive Equilibrium: Real Wage Rate in Vintage v

Insert (3) and (5) into (16) and express the real wage rate as

$$\frac{w}{P} = \frac{ry}{e^{ry} - 1} ay^{\alpha} \tag{17}$$

Our result (13) facilitates the interpretation of our results (16) and (17). If the elasticity of the optimal period of production y with respect to rate of interest r is *minus* one, then r and y are in inverse proportion, and their product ry is some constant. As a result, according to (16), labor's share is a constant, and according to (17), the real wage rate w/P is a constant *times* the period of production y raised to the power α. In other words, the elasticity of the real wage rate w/P with respect to the period of production y is α.

III. FIRM EQUILIBRIUM: NEW VINTAGES STARTED CONTINUOUSLY

Until now, an old vintage was assumed to be completed before a new one was started. But let us now assume that new vintages are started continuously. Let all of them be exactly like vintage v except for their timing. Then all results arrived at for vintage v will hold for all of them, and vintages will be perfectly staggered in the sense that at any moment y vintages will be in operation, each employing L men, and that aggregate employment will be Ly.

Find the present worth as seen from time τ of sums borrowed between time $\tau - y$ and time τ to finance all wages paid in production runs of *all* vintages in operation at time τ. To find such present worth we must integrate (14) once more. Eq. (14) was the result of integrating with respect to time t. Now we must integrate it with respect to vintage v. Our double integral is

$$D(\tau) \equiv \int_{\tau-y}^{\tau} D_v(\tau)\,dv = \int_{\tau-y}^{\tau} \frac{e^{r(\tau-v)} - 1}{r}\,W\,dv$$

The wage bill W is a function of neither time t nor vintage v, hence once again may be taken outside the integral sign, and so may our stationary rate of interest r. As a result, find the integral to be

$$D(\tau) = \frac{e^{ry} - 1 - ry}{r}\,\frac{W}{r}$$

Insert (5), multiply and divide by y, divide by the price P of output, and express desired real capital stock in all vintages as

$$D/P = HLwy/(Pr) \tag{18}$$

where

$$H \equiv \frac{e^{ry} - 1 - ry}{ry}$$

Insert the real wage rate (17) into (18), rearrange, and express the period of production as

$$y = \left[\frac{(e^{ry} - 1)D/P}{aHLy} \right]^{1/(a+1)} \tag{19}$$

IV. EQUILIBRIUM SOLUTIONS AND THEIR SENSITIVITIES TO FACTOR SUPPLIES

1. *Capital-Market and Labor-Market Equilibrium Conditions*

Böhm-Bawerk's economy was a stationary one. Typically Austrian, it had given factor supplies, i.e., given available real capital stock and labor force. Capital-market equilibrium requires available real capital stock to equal the desired one:

$$S = D/P \tag{20}$$

As we have observed, at any moment y vintages are in operation, each employing L men. Aggregate employment, then, is Ly. Labor-market equilibrium requires available labor force to equal aggregate employment:

$$F = Ly \tag{21}$$

2.   Equilibrium Solution for the Period of Production

In equilibrium the period of production must be long enough to absorb the entire available real capital stock and employ the entire available labor force or, in Böhm-Bawerk's own words [1888 (1923: 386)]:

> We must, in any case, assume such a period of production that, during its continuance, the entire disposable fund of subsistence is required for, and is sufficient to pay for, the entire quantity of labour offering itself. If the period were to be shorter than this, some capital would remain unemployed; if longer, all the workers could not be provided for over the whole period; the result would always be a supply of unemployed economic elements urgently offering their services.

To find the period of production equilibrating both factor markets, insert (20) and (21) into (19) and find the equilibrium solution for the period of production

$$y = \left[\frac{(e^{ry} - 1)S}{aFH} \right]^{1/(\alpha+1)} \tag{22}$$

Our result (22) is a transcendental equation but is as good as an explicit solution: if the elasticity of optimal period of production y with respect to rate of interest r is *minus* one, r and y are in inverse proportion, and their product is some constant. As a result, we have nothing but constants and parameters on the right-hand side of (22).

The elasticity of the equilibrium solution (22) with respect to available real capital stock S is $1/(\alpha + 1)$, a positive proper fraction: the period of production is up if available real capital stock S is up. But y is up in less than proportion to S.

The elasticity of the equilibrium solution (22) with respect to available labor force F is $-1/(\alpha + 1)$, a negative proper fraction: the period of production is down if available labor force F is up. But y is down in less than proportion to F.

3.   Equilibrium Solution for the Rate of Interest

According to the elasticity (13) the rate of interest r is in inverse proportion to the period of production y and hence may be written as some constant *divided by* the equilibrium solution (22). Written as such a division, the rate of interest r is seen to be determined ultimately by three parameters: available real capital stock S, available labor force F, and the elasticity α of physical output per annum per man with respect to the period of production or, in Böhm-Bawerk's own words [1888 (1923: 401)]:

We have, then, over the sphere of our investigation so far, to record three elements or factors which act as decisive determinants of the rate of interest: the Amount of the national subsistence fund, the Number of workers provided for by it, and the Degree of productivity in extending production periods.

How sensitive is this solution to the factor supplies? The elasticity of the rate of interest with respect to available real capital stock S is seen to be $-1/(\alpha + 1)$, a negative proper fraction: the rate of interest r is down if available real capital stock S is up. But r is down in less than proportion to S. Also, the elasticity of the rate of interest with respect to available labor force F is seen to be $1/(\alpha + 1)$, a positive proper fraction: the rate of interest r is up if available labor force is up. But r is up in less than proportion to F, or, in Böhm-Bawerk's own words [1888 (1923: 401)]:

And the way in which these three factors affect the rate may be put as follows:—

In a community interest will be high in proportion as the national subsistence fund is low, as the number of labourers employed by the same is great, and as the surplus returns connected with any further extension of the production period continue high.

This is the way in which the interest rate should be formed, and the way in which it should alter, if our theory is correct.

4. *Equilibrium Solution for the Real Wage Rate*

According to (17) the real wage rate w/P is a constant *times* the period of production y raised to the power α and hence may be written as that constant *times* the equilibrium solution (22) raised to the power α. In other words, the elasticity of the real wage rate w/P with respect to available real capital stock S is $\alpha/(\alpha + 1)$, a positive proper fraction: the real wage rate w/P is up if available real capital stock S is up. But w/P is up in less than proportion to S. Also, the elasticity of the real wage rate w/P with respect to available labor force F is $-\alpha/(\alpha + 1)$, a negative proper fraction: the real wage rate w/P is down if available labor force F is up. But w/P is down in less than proportion to F.

Böhm-Bawerk saw his theory as a theory of interest and did not [1888 (1923: 420)] "pretend, in the somewhat sketchy suggestions which this chapter contains on the subject of wage, to have given a perfect theory of that matter." But he did, at least, give us the Wicksell Effect. Comparing his own theory to the classical English wage-fund doctrine, he [1888 (1923: 420)] emphasized that "the increase of the subsistence fund is, ... principally, used up in lengthening the production period, ...; the rise [in the wages of labour] . . . being in a much weaker ratio than the increase in the subsistence fund''—as we just found: the elasticity of the real wage rate w/P with respect to available real capital stock S was the positive proper fraction $\alpha/(\alpha + 1)$. Böhm-Bawerk concluded that "the English Wage Fund theory has thus a core of truth, but it is wrapped up in a quite overpowering mass of error."

Still using simple interest, Wicksell [1893 (1954: 138-139)] restated Böhm-Bawerk mathematically and summarized his main result in one sentence—the Wicksell Effect: "In the case of a relative increase of the national capital the wage [rate] increases and the level of interest decreases." Using continous compounding, we agree.

5. *Stability of General Equilibrium*

Such was the nature of the delicate interaction among the three equilibrating variables of Böhm-Bawerk's general equilibrium, i.e., the period of production y, the rate of interest r, and the real wage rate w/P. Let us finally show that his equilibrium was stable.

Let the rate of interest r be higher than its equilibrium value. According to our elasticity (13), a shorter period of production will then be optimal. For three reasons, desired real capital stock in all vintages (18) will then be lower.

First, with a shorter period of production goes lower productivity of labor, so according to (17), firms offer a lower real wage rate w/P, a factor of (18). Second, a vintage may still employ L men, but with a shorter period of production y, fewer vintages will now be in operation, and aggregate labor employed Ly, another factor of (18), is lower. The excess supply in the labor market will reinforce the downward pressure on the real wage rate. Third, it all began with the rate of interest r, a denominator of (18), being higher. With (18) down, there is excess supply in the capital market, and competition among lenders will put a downward pressure on the rate of interest, tending to move it back to its equilibrium value. Vice versa if the rate of interest were lower than its equilibrium value.

REFERENCES

E. von Böhm-Bawerk, *Positive Theorie des Kapitales*, Innsbruck, 1888, translated as *Positive Theory of Capital* by W. Smart, New York, 1891, reprinted 1923.
K. Wicksell, *Ueber Wert, Kapital und Rente*, Jena, 1893, translated as *Value, Capital and Rent* by S. H. Frohwein, London, 1954.

CHAPTER 8 Capital Theory Meets Monetary Theory

WICKSELL (1851-1926)

> *Must not the "natural" rate of interest, governed by the marginal productivity of capital, i.e., of the roundabout methods of production which would exist if money were not used, have some connection with the rate of interest as it actually appears on the capital market? There was only one possible answer. But what was this connection?*
>
> Ohlin (1936: viii)

I. INTRODUCTION

1. Wicksell's Problem

Having restated Böhm-Bawerk so lucidly and succinctly, Wicksell [1893 (1954)] began to wonder how the highly abstract "natural" rate of interest thus determined was related to the rate of interest observed in everyday practice in markets where the supply of money met the demand for it. If commercial banks could create money in the form of drawing rights upon themselves, disposed of by checks, such a supply of money would be quite flexible. Would the rate of interest determined by such a supply coincide with the Böhm-Bawerk "natural" rate? Why should it? And if it didn't, would some equilibrating variable be set in motion and keep moving until the two rates coincided? What would such an equilibrating variable be?

A correct answer would settle an issue as old as economic theory itself. To Petty, Yarranton, and Keynes, the rate of interest was determined by the supply of and the demand for money. To Turgot, Smith, Böhm-Bawerk, and Fisher, the rate of interest was "determined by impatience to spend income and opportunity to invest it," as Fisher (1930: title page) put it.

2. Wicksell's Method

In Wicksell's answer, capital theory met monetary theory, and the barrier between them was broken for good. That in itself was a historic accomplishment. What made it possible was Wicksell's deployment of a method fundamentally new in three respects. First, it was explicitly macroeconomic—confronting aggregate supply and aggregate demand. Second, it was explicitly dynamic—carefully emphasizing the timing of events. Third, Wicksell's method was an explicit disequilibrium method—expectations generally were not fulfilled, and their disappointment constituted the very motive force of the system.

Wicksell's point of departure was a Böhm-Bawerk model of circulating capital. What capital does here is to advance the wages of labor. But Wicksell [1898 (1936: 136)] simplified Böhm-Bawerk by freezing the period of production at one year, "as would be the case if technical conditions firmly prevented any extension or contraction." With that, Wicksell was back at the "prematurely discarded" [1898 (1936: 130)] classical wage-fund doctrine.

Within such a framework, Wicksell put a commercial bank between his entrepreneurs and his capitalists. Ahead of his own time, Wicksell assumed that "all payments are affected by means of cheques, which are normally subject to far more lenient legal restrictions than are notes." From such a bank entrepreneurs would borrow. In such a bank capitalists would make deposits. For simplicity's sake, Wicksell assumed [1898 (1936: 140)] that entrepreneurs would be paying and capitalists would be earning the same rate of interest, called the "money" rate of interest.

3. *Our Own Restatement*

Wicksell's dynamic disequilibrium model is like a good play unfolding slowly. Nobody knows what the ending will be. There are no redundant actors, but the order in which actors appear on the stage is crucial. The Wicksellian play has only four actors: entrepreneurs, the bank, labor, and the capitalists. The capitalists have an instant part-time job as retailers: at the end of each year they buy that year's output from the entrepreneurs and retain part of it for their own consumption. At the beginning of the following year they sell the rest to labor.

Wicksell's play used nothing but succinct lucid German surrounding a numerical example. The temptation to restate it in terms of first-order difference equations is irresistible, and we shall not resist it.

Let the notation of our restatement be as follows.

4. *Variables*

g_v ≡ rate of growth of variable v
κ ≡ natural rate of interest
L ≡ labor employed in a production run

P ≡ retail price at which capitalist-retailers sell to labor
p ≡ wholesale price at which entrepreneurs sell to capitalist-retailers
R ≡ money interest bill
r ≡ money rate of interest
W ≡ money wage bill
w ≡ money wage rate
X ≡ physical output
Z ≡ money profits bill

5. *Parameters*

a ≡ labor productivity in a one-year period of production
F ≡ available labor force
S ≡ available real capital stock

The time coordinate is t. The unit of time is the year. Let year t be the year beginning at time t.

In Wicksell's disequilibrium the distinction between expected and actual price is vital. So let an asterisk indicate an expected price: $*P(t + 1)$ is price expected at time t to prevail at time $t + 1$.

II. A MONEY RATE OF INTEREST

1. *The Wicksellian Sequence*

Let us now spell out Wicksell's sequence as carefully as he did in words but, unlike him, let us write his underlying first-order difference equations. Once we have written those difference equations, holding for any t, we may bring in his "natural" rate of interest, confront it with his money rate of interest, and produce Wicksell's conclusion.

2. *Labor Market at Time t*

At time t let the entrepreneurs start a one-year production run. At the money rate of interest $r(t)$ they borrow the wage bill $W(t)$ in the bank and spend it at once hiring labor $L(t)$ at the money wage rate $w(t)$. They are willing to pay—and competition with other entrepreneurs will force them to pay—a wage bill $W(t)$ at which they expect no profits in excess of interest:

$$[1 + r(t)] W(t) = *p(t + 1)X(t + 1) \qquad (1)$$

Here, $*p(t + 1)$ is the wholesale price at which entrepreneurs expect to sell their physical output $X(t + 1)$ maturing a year hence. Entrepreneurs always expect the current price to prevail in the future:

$$*p(t + 1) = p(t) \qquad (2)$$

3. *Retail Goods Market at Time t*

Having been paid its wage bill $W(t)$, labor immediately spends it. At the retail price $P(t)$ labor buys consumers' goods from the capitalist-retailers who, in turn, deposit the proceeds $W(t)$ in the bank at the rate of interest $r(t)$.

4. *Wholesale Goods Market at Time t + 1*

A year passes, the production run is completed, and output matures as expected and is sold to the capitalist-retailers at the actual wholesale price $p(t + 1)$. We just saw in (1) that entrepreneurs were bidding up the wage bill $W(t)$ so as to expect no profits in excess of interest. In the special case where price happens to fulfill entrepreneurial expectations, $p(t + 1) = *p(t + 1)$, there will indeed be no such profits. But price may or may not fulfill entrepreneurial expectations, and profits in excess of interest are defined

$$Z(t + 1) \equiv [p(t + 1) - *p(t + 1)]X(t + 1) \tag{3}$$

How did the capitalist-retailers decide on the actual wholesale price $p(t + 1)$? The wholesale price $p(t + 1)$ offered by them equals the retail price at which they now expect to sell:

$$p(t + 1) = *P(t + 1) \tag{4}$$

Capitalist-retailers, too, always expect the current price to prevail in the future:

$$*P(t + 1) = P(t) \tag{5}$$

How do capitalist-retailers finance their purchase at the wholesale price $p(t + 1)$?

At time t they deposited the proceeds $W(t)$ in the bank at the rate of interest $r(t)$. With accumulated interest, then, their account is now $[1 + r(t)]W(t)$. According to (1), if $p(t + 1) = *p(t + 1)$, then depleting the account would finance the entire purchase. But at a wholesale price $p(t + 1)$ higher than $*p(t + 1)$, depleting the account would not suffice. In that case capitalist-retailers would borrow—but only for an instant—the amount (3) in the bank, thus financing the entire purchase. From their proceeds the entrepreneurs, on their side, would first pay back their debt (1) to the bank and then consume the remainder (3) by purchasing consumers' goods from the capitalist-retailers. That would enable the capitalist-retailers, on their side, to pay back, still at time $t + 1$, *their* debt (3) to the bank. Since the debt existed only for an instant, there is no interest on it, and the capitalist-retailers may now consume their own interest bill

$$R(t + 1) \equiv r(t)W(t) \tag{6}$$

So entrepreneurs have consumed their profits bill (3) and capitalist-retailers their interest bill (6). Now insert (l) into (6), add (3) and (6), let the terms $*p(t + 1)X(t + 1)$ cancel, and write the sum of the profits and interest bills consumed as

$$Z(t + 1) + R(t + 1) = p(t + 1)X(t + 1) - W(t) \tag{7}$$

Divide that sum by the wholesale price $p(t + 1)$ to find the physical quantity of output consumed by entrepreneurs and capitalist-retailers. Subtract that physical quantity from total physical output to find the physical quantity of output left for labor to consume

$$X(t + 1) - [Z(t + 1) + R(t + 1)]/p(t + 1) = W(t)/p(t + 1) \tag{8}$$

But according to (4) and (5) taken together, $p(t + 1) = P(t)$. So what the capitalist-retailers are now, at time $t + 1$, offering for sale in the retail market is the physical quantity $W(t)/P(t)$—exactly the same they offered a year ago! Can labor buy that quantity?

5. Labor Market at Time $t + 1$

We are still at time $t + 1$. Having sold their physical output $X(t + 1)$ at the wholesale price $p(t + 1)$, having paid back their debt (1) to the bank and consumed their profits bill (3) financed, if positive, by the capitalist-retailers, the entrepreneurs are now ready to embark upon another one-year production run. At the money rate of interest $r(t + 1)$ they borrow the wage bill $W(t + 1)$ in the bank and spend it at once hiring labor $L(t + 1)$ at the money wage $w(t + 1)$. Once again they are willing to pay and will be forced to pay a wage bill at which they expect no profits in excess of interest:

$$[1 + r(t + 1)]W(t + 1) = *p(t + 2)X(t + 2) \tag{1}$$

where $*p(t + 2)$ is the wholesale price at which entrepreneurs expect to sell their physical output $X(t + 2)$ maturing a year hence. Entrepreneurs always expect the current price to prevail in the future:

$$*p(t + 2) = p(t + 1) \tag{2}$$

6. Retail Goods Market at Time $t + 1$

Entrepreneurs have already consumed their profits bill (3) and the capitalist-retailers their interest bill (6). That leaves labor to consume its new wage bill. When the entrepreneurs embarked upon their new production run, they paid out the new wage bill $W(t + 1)$. So at a market-clearing retail price $P(t + 1)$ the physical quantity $W(t)/P(t)$ will now meet the new demand $W(t + 1)$:

$$P(t + 1)W(t)/P(t) = W(t + 1) \qquad (9)$$

The capitalist-retailers, still at time $t + 1$, will deposit the proceeds $W(t + 1)$ from their retail sales to labor. We have come full circle and have determined our sequence: all difference equations implied by Wicksell and written as (1) through (9) turned out to be of the first order. They hold for any t. Can we now find the rate of inflation?

7. Inflation, If Any, Will Be Steady-State

Define the actual rate of inflation apparent at time $t + 1$:

$$p(t + 1) \equiv [1 + g_p(t + 1)]p(t) \qquad (10)$$

Rearrange (9), write (4), (5), and (10) for $t + 2$, and find

$$\frac{W(t + 1)}{W(t)} = \frac{P(t + 1)}{P(t)} = \frac{p(t + 2)}{p(t + 1)} \equiv 1 + g_p(t + 2) \qquad (11)$$

Under a consistent interest policy

$$r(t + 1) = r(t) \qquad (12)$$

Under full employment in a one-year period of production, physical output is always the same:

$$X(t + 2) = X(t + 1) \qquad (13)$$

Divide (1) written for $t + 1$ by (1) written for t, insert (2), (12), (13), and (10), and find

$$\frac{W(t + 1)}{W(t)} = \frac{{}^*p(t + 2)}{{}^*p(t + 1)} = \frac{p(t + 1)}{p(t)} \equiv 1 + g_p(t + 1) \qquad (14)$$

Comparing (11) and (14), we find the far left-hand sides the same; consequently,

$$g_p(t + 2) = g_p(t + 1) \qquad (15)$$

Under a consistent interest policy, then, inflation—if any—will be steady-state inflation. But *will* there be inflation? And if so, at what rate? To answer that question, we must bring in Wicksell's "natural" rate of interest.

III. THE NATURAL RATE OF INTEREST

Our full-scale Böhm-Bawerk model in chapter 7 used a production function (3) of constant-elasticity form. In this production function let us set the period of production $y = 1$. Consequently, a Wicksellian entrepreneur hiring labor $L(t)$ at time t will see his physical output $X(t + 1)$ maturing at time $t + 1$ at the physical labor productivity

$$X(t + 1)/L(t) = a \tag{16}$$

Labor was hired at the money wage rate $w(t)$, so his money wage bill was

$$W(t) \equiv L(t)w(t) \tag{17}$$

Physical output was sold at the price $p(t + 1)$, so his revenue was $p(t + 1)X(t + 1)$. The "natural" rate of interest κ was then the internal rate of return of such a one-year investment and was defined

$$(1 + \kappa)W(t) \equiv p(t + 1)X(t + 1) \tag{18}$$

In an aggregative Böhm-Bawerk model collapsed into a classical wage-fund doctrine, physical capital stock S consisted of a single good, priced $p(t + 1)$, and fed labor $L(t)$ for one year at a real wage rate $w(t)/p(t + 1)$:

$$S = L(t)w(t)/p(t + 1) \tag{19}$$

If the available physical capital stock could employ more man-years than were available, $L(t) > F$, there would be positive excess demand in the labor market, and eager entrepreneurs would bid up the real wage rate until $L(t) = F$. Vice versa, if the available physical capital stock could not employ all available man-years, $L(t) < F$, there would be negative excess demand in the labor market, and eager wage earners would be willing to work at a lower real wage rate until

$$L(t) = F \tag{20}$$

Finally, solve for the natural rate of interest by inserting (16), (17), (19), and (20) into (18) and find

$$1 + \kappa = aF/S \tag{21}$$

Here is one *plus* the natural rate of interest expressed in terms of the parameters of the collapsed Böhm-Bawerk model. How does it depend upon those parameters? It will be, first, in direct proportion to the labor productivity a of a one-year period of production, second, in direct proportion to available labor force F and, third, in inverse proportion to available physical capital stock S.

Let us now confront Wicksell's money rate of interest with his natural rate thus determined.

IV. CONFRONTATION OF MONEY WITH NATURAL RATE OF INTEREST

Divide (18) by (1), insert (2) and (10), rearrange, and express the rate of inflation as a function of the natural and the money rate of interest. We are home:

$$g_p(t + 1) = \frac{\kappa - r(t)}{1 + r(t)} \tag{22}$$

shown in figure 8-1. The function has the intercept κ with both the vertical and the horizontal axis.

Our solution (22) yields impeccable Wicksellian results: if the natural rate is higher than the money rate, i.e., if $\kappa > r(t)$, then $g_p > 0$, and there will be inflation. If the natural rate is equal to the money rate, i.e., if $\kappa = r(t)$, then $g_p = 0$, and there will be stationary prices. If the natural rate is less than the money rate, i.e., if $\kappa < r(t)$, then $g_p < 0$, and there will be deflation.

FIGURE 8-1. Mapping the Function (22) for a Natural Rate of Interest $\kappa = 0.04$

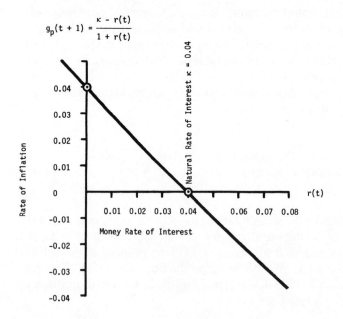

V. CONCLUSION

1. *Price as the Equilibrating Variable*

Wicksell put money and banking into a simplified Böhm-Bawerk model. His money included bank deposits disposed of by writing generally accepted checks. Such a money supply was quite flexible, and large commercial banks would have some control over the money rate of interest. What were the economic effects of such flexibility?

The money rate of interest would not have to coincide with a Böhm-Bawerk "natural" rate of interest at all times. If it did not, Böhm-Bawerk physical output and real wage rate would still prevail—determined as they were by available labor force and available real capital stock. But nominal values would be changing. If the natural rate of interest were higher than the money rate of interest, entrepreneurs would be induced—and the money supply correspondingly expanded—to pay a higher money wage rate. Physically speaking, nothing would come of this, for when labor spent the higher money wage rate, prices would rise correspondingly and unexpectedly leave the real wage rate unchanged. There would be a cumulative process of inflation expected by nobody. Eventually, such inflation would drain the banks for cash, so the money rate of interest would have to be raised to equality with the natural rate—thus stopping the expansion of credit.

If the natural rate of interest were lower than the money rate of interest, entrepreneurs would be induced—and the money supply correspondingly contracted—to pay a lower money wage rate. Again, physically speaking, nothing would come of this, for when labor spent the lower money wage rate, prices would fall correspondingly and unexpectedly leave the real wage rate unchanged. There would be a cumulative process of deflation expected by nobody. Eventually, such deflation would leave the banks with so much cash that the money rate of interest would have to be lowered to equality with the natural rate—thus stopping the contraction of credit.

So in the Wicksellian model, price is the equilibrating variable. A beautiful mechanical analogy was used to illustrate its working [1898 (1936: 135-136)]:

> The two rates of interest still reach ultimate equality, but only after, and as a result of, a previous movement of prices. Prices constitute, so to speak, a spiral spring which serves to transmit the power between the natural and the money rates of interest; but the spring must first be sufficiently stretched or compressed. In a pure cash economy, the spring is short and rigid; it becomes longer and more elastic in accordance with the stage of development of the system of credit and banking.

2. Wicksell, Keynes, and Phillips

As we said, Wicksell's method was fundamentally new in three respects. It was a macroeconomic, dynamic, disequilibrium method. The first respect survived the Keynesian revolution, indeed was the hallmark of the Keynesian revolution. The last two respects were lost in it.

But there was no unemployment in the Wicksellian model; the labor market always cleared at full employment. And there was no liquidity preference either. Nobody held money in liquid form. Money came into existence as a loan to entrepreneurs, who immediately spent it hiring labor. Labor immediately spent it buying consumers' goods. Capitalist-retailers held their assets in interest-bearing form.

Wicksellian inflation was always of the pure demand-pull variety. Theorists had to wait for another sixty years for cost-push inflation in the form of the Phillips (1958) curve: within their province but tempered by unemployment, labor unions will seek a relative gain by raising the money wage rate. Theorists had to wait even longer before labor's inflationary expectations were incorporated into the Phillips curve: instead of always expecting current prices to prevail in the future, labor learns from experience. By expecting inflation, labor is compelled to contribute to it.

3. Wicksell and Monetarists

Fisher's "nominal" rate of interest is *not* Wicksell's "money" rate of interest. Fisher's nominal rate includes inflationary expectations. Neither Wicksellian borrowers nor Wicksellian lenders ever expect inflation; consequently, the money rate agreed on will never include such inflationary expectations. Wicksell [1898 (1936: 165-166)] knew Fisher's work (1896) but like Keynes (1936: 142-143) rejected it. The day of rational expectations had not dawned yet!

The Wicksellian notion of a clearing labor market is, however, a forerunner of a monetarist "natural" rate of unemployment.

REFERENCES

E. v. Böhm-Bawerk, *Positive Theorie des Kapitales*, Innsbruck, 1888, translated as *Positive Theory of Capital* by W. Smart, New York, 1891, reprinted 1923.
I. Fisher, "Appreciation and Interest," *Publications of the American Economic Association*, Aug. 1896, *11*, 331-442.
——, *The Theory of Interest*, New York, 1930.
J. M. Keynes, *The General Theory of Employment, Interest, and Money*, London, 1936.
B. Ohlin, "Introduction" to Wicksell (1936).

A. W. Phillips, "The Relation between Unemployment and the Rate of Change of Money Wage Rates in the United Kingdom, 1861-1957," *Economica*, Nov. 1958, *25*, 283-299.

K. Wicksell, *Ueber Wert, Kapital und Rente*, Jena, 1893, translated as *Value, Capital and Rent* by S. H. Frohwein, London, 1954.

———, *Geldzins und Güterpreise*, Jena, 1898, translated as *Interest and Prices* by R. F. Kahn with an introduction by Bertil Ohlin, published on behalf of the Royal Economic Society, London, 1936.

I. THE SETTING

Our period opens with the Great Depression and closes with the Great Inflation. Between them lie the Second World War and the third industrial revolution. The foundation of the first industrial revolution had been the steam engine. The foundation of the second industrial revolution had been three new industries, the electrical industry, the chemical industry, and the automotive industry. The foundation of the third industrial revolution is the mid-twentieth century twin breakthrough of nuclear energy and high-speed electronic computation.

1. *The Nuclear Age*

Both world wars accelerated technological progress. On the eve of the second, in 1939, nuclear fission was interpreted by Otto Robert Frisch and Lise Meitner. Its military application ended the war six years later. Its commercial application generated electricity first sold to the public in 1957 and powered the first merchant vessel in 1959. The energy that uranium holds is very great: one pound of enriched uranium contains nearly three million times the energy in one pound of coal. Of such available energy a light-water reactor can extract 1 percent; an advanced converter reactor, 3 percent; and a breeder reactor, 70 percent [Weaver et al. (1981: 66-67)].

At the close of our period 72 nuclear power plants, mostly of the light-water type, generated 10 percent of the commercial electricity used in the United States. Outside the United States 21 countries operated 166 reactors.

2. *The Computer*

The world's first high-speed electronic digital computer was dedicated at the University of Pennsylvania in 1946. To control and amplify its electronic signals it used bulky, heat-generating, power-consuming vacuum tubes. The first major advance was John von Neumann's idea of storing computer programs in a memory. The second was the replacement of the vacuum tube by the more dependable transistor, invented at the Bell Laboratories in 1947. The third major advance was to make the crystal of the transistor serve as its own circuit board—"the chip."

Introduced in 1959, the chip is a small piece of silicon—small enough to be carted off by an ant! It contains a complete integrated circuit capable of storing information and of executing instructions all in the form of two alternative signals: a high-voltage electric pulse represents the digit 1, a low-voltage pulse the digit 0; no other digits are needed. Because of the compact size of the chip, such signals travel short paths. Because signals travel at nearly the speed of light, a very large number of instructions per second are executed. A computer on a chip executes one million of them, or 200 times more than did the 1946 computer—and costs 1/30,000 of the latter. As for power consumption, "it draws the power of a night-light instead of a hundred lighthouses" [Boraiko (1982: 421)].

3. Nonneutral Technological Progress?

The breakthrough of inexpensive high-speed computation is having scientific, military, and commercial consequences as fundamental as those following the steam engine, electric power, the internal combustion engine, and nineteenth-century chemistry. The wider implications for blue-collar and white-collar workers alike are becoming visible towards the end of our period. Many people are doing dirty, hard, and hazardous blue-collar jobs that robots could do. Many people are doing clean, easy, and safe white-collar jobs that computers could do. Is technological progress becoming nonneutral, i.e., labor-saving—as Ricardo thought it was in his chapter 31 added to his third edition of *Principles*?

Technological progress is said to be neutral if it leaves the relative marginal productivities of labor and physical capital stock unchanged. A Cobb-Douglas production function $X = aL^\alpha S^\beta$ has the property that technological progress is neutral. Take its marginal productivities $\partial X/\partial L$ and $\partial X/\partial S$, divide one by the other, and find

$$\frac{\partial X/\partial L}{\partial X/\partial S} = \frac{\alpha S}{\beta L}$$

Here the multiplicative factor a, whose growth represents technological progress, was canceled, meaning that the relative marginal productivities depend solely on the relative exponents α/β and the relative inputs S/L. If as in the United States in the century ending in 1970, physical capital stock S was growing at roughly three percent per annum, employment L at roughly one percent per annum, and the marginal productivity $\partial X/\partial S$ not growing at all, then the marginal productivity of labor and with it the real wage rate should be growing, and did, at roughly two percent per annum.

Will what was true of the century ending in 1970 not be true of the century beginning in 1970?

4. *Government*

The first half of the twentieth century was shaken by two world wars in short succession but separated by a major depression. Warfare was no longer tactical, as it had been in the Napoleonic Wars, aiming merely at the destruction of the enemy's armed forces. As it had been in the American Civil War, warfare became strategic, aiming at the destruction of his economy.

Such large-scale strategic warfare assigned major roles to government and greatly expanded the public sector—as did the measures taken against the Great Depression. At the end of the First World War the capitalist order had been questioned in the defeated nations. By contrast, after the Second World War neither West Germany nor Japan questioned capitalist principles and proved capable of repairing the massive damage sooner and more completely than did communist regimes imposed by conquest in Eastern Europe.

5. *Developing Nations*

The end of the Second World War brought independence to former colonies and with it ambitions to industrialize and catch up. Models of interindustry equilibrium and intertemporal resource allocation might have been helpful in satisfying such ambitions. But mainstream economic thinking in the West was dominated by static short-run macroeconomics allowing saving and investment to be positive but failing to consider their effect upon capital stock. Had a longer run been considered, the expansion of capital stock resulting from positive saving and investment could no longer have been ignored. As it was, capital theory was temporarily out of favor, and Third World students clustering at the leading universities of the West must have felt frustrated by the mid-century gap between what was taught and what they needed.

Help was on its way. The computer revolution spread to our own little province of human knowledge and brought large-scale operational and empirical work within reach. Nonmainstream economics already possessed the necessary framework in the form of Leontief's interindustry equilibrium. Some fifty countries have since compiled input-output tables in an effort to plan their economic development.

6. *The Oil Shock*

Our period closed with the Great Inflation interrupting a quarter-century of nearly steady-state growth. Successful cartelization of crude oil raised its price tenfold from 1973 to 1980.

Once again, microeconomics considered finite natural resources and asked Cantillon's and Ricardo's question about the size of sustainable population. Macroeconomics finally abandoned Keynesian models of no inflation, augmented the Phillips curve by inflationary expectations, asked if breaking such expectations could reverse the oil shock, and examined the effects of large fiscal deficits.

II. NOTATION

1. *Variables*

C $\equiv$ physical consumption
c $\equiv$ cost (in microeconomic models)
η_i $\equiv$ elasticity of demand with respect to ith input coefficient a_i
G $\equiv$ physical government purchase of goods and services
g_v $\equiv$ proportionate rate of growth of variable v
I $\equiv$ physical investment
κ_{ij} $\equiv$ physical marginal productivity of ith capital stock in jth good
L $\equiv$ labor employed
P $\equiv$ price of output
p $\equiv$ price of input
Π $\equiv$ price of bonds
q $\equiv$ probability of an outcome of a random draw
R $\equiv$ government net receipts *before* interest paid by government
r $\equiv$ rate of interest
S $\equiv$ physical capital stock
U, V $\equiv$ utility indices
W $\equiv$ wage bill
w $\equiv$ money wage rate
X $\equiv$ physical output
x $\equiv$ physical input
Y $\equiv$ money national income
Z $\equiv$ profits bill

2. *Parameters*

A $\equiv$ constant term of a linear transformation
a $\equiv$ input coefficient
B $\equiv$ coefficient of a linear transformation
b $\equiv$ capital coefficient
c $\equiv$ propensity to consume (in macroeconomic models)
F $\equiv$ available labor force
g_v $\equiv$ proportionate rate of growth of parameter v
i $\equiv$ interest payment per bond

M $\equiv$ supply of money
Q $\equiv$ supply of bonds: physical quantity of government bonds outstanding

III. NONPURE COMPETITION

1. *The Years of High Theory*

Three fundamental breakthroughs burst upon economic theory
within the single decade of the thirties, i.e., nonpure competition represented by Chamberlin (1933), unemployment equilibrium by Keynes
(1936), and the existence proof of general equilibrium by von Neumann
(1937).

2. *Pure and Nonpure Competition*

Competition is said to be "pure" if every seller in a market is producing on the assumption that any output can be disposed of at the prevailing market price. Competition may then be nonpure because of either
fewness of sellers or differentiated products. Fewness had been treated by
Cournot (1838) and Bertrand (1883), and the giant corporation, as we saw
in our introduction to part IV, had been around since the second industrial revolution yet took another half-century to catch the attention of
mainstream economic theory then still residing in Cambridge, England:
Sraffa (1926: 542) found it "necessary . . . to abandon the path of free
competition". The differentiated products of the giant corporation remained untreated until the thirties.

Schumpeter (1954: 1048) asked why results were established in and
after 1930 that might easily have been established by 1890—and had in
1930 himself expressed his impatience. "There is . . . no other chapter [of
general theory]," he said in his preface to Zeuthen (1930: ix), "so full of
inconclusive controversy and uncertainty of results as the treatment of all
those cases which cover the whole of the phenomena between the limiting
cases of perfect competition and 'pure' monopoly, i.e., practically the
whole of the reality of markets . . . It is here, if anywhere, that our teach-
ing should not be left as it is."

Six new answers were offered in rapid succession around 1930, by
Bowley (1924), Hotelling (1929), Zeuthen (1929), (1930), Chamberlin
(1929), (1933), Robinson (1933), and von Stackelberg (1934).

3. *Bowley*

The nature of the duopoly problem is that each duopolist is trying to
maximize a function of which he does not control all variables. This is no

ordinary maximum problem, and Cournot (1838) could turn it into one only by letting each duopolist maximize his profits under the assumption that the quantity sold by his rival would stay put. Abandoning Cournot's assumption, Bowley (1924) introduced perceived reaction functions showing how the other duopolist's decision variable was expected to react to a duopolist's own. Bowley never asked whether such reaction functions were consistent and hence could both materialize. If not, each duopolist would see with his own eyes a consistent violation of his assumption, and no improvement upon Cournot would have been accomplished.

4. Hotelling

Hotelling (1929) was the first to treat one aspect of product quality, the geographical location of duopolist-retailers, as a decision variable. Hotelling developed a model in which consumers located along a main street choose between two duopolist-retailers, carry their produce home at a cost in proportion to the distance carried, and have no preference for either duopolist-retailer except on the grounds of the distance carried. Assuming, first, the price elasticity of demand to be "at the extreme of inelasticity" and, second, each duopolist-retailer to be free to choose his own location and to consider that of the other as given, Hotelling (1929: 54) concluded that the duopolist-retailers would cluster in the center. He generalized his clustering result:

> Instead of sellers of an identical commodity separated
> geographically we might have considered two competing cider
> merchants side by side, one selling a sweeter liquid than the
> other.... The measure of sourness now replaces distance.... The
> foregoing considerations apply, particularly the conclusion that
> competing sellers tend to become much too alike.

Under Hotelling's own assumptions, his full price-and-location equilibrium may have been incorrect [Friedman (1983: 94-99)], but those assumptions were soon to be relaxed. Poaching on rival preserve, a duopolist-retailer would, first, be losing no customers at the far end of his market only as long as demand were at the extreme of inelasticity and, second, be winning new customers in the center only as long as his rival stayed put. Instead, Smithies (1941) assumed, first, some elasticity of demand and, second, each duopolist-retailer to expect his rival to match any move of price or location. In that case the duopolist-retailers would locate themselves one at each quartile of the main street. No clustering!

5.   *Zeuthen*

Under the assumption that the quantity sold by his rival would stay put, a Cournot duopolist had maximized his profits by manipulating his quantity sold. A Cournot duopolist, in other words, had a quantity policy. Bertrand had posed a different problem. Under the assumption that the price charged by his rival would stay put, a Bertrand duopolist maximized his profits by manipulating his price.

Like Bertrand, Zeuthen (1929), (1930: 24-45) assumed his duopolists to have a price policy but cautiously removed Cournot's and Bertrand's assumption of "qualité identique." Zeuthen's product differentiation consisted of differences in product quality, geographical location, or advertising-generated image. Such product differentiation was not strong enough to protect a duopolist failing to match a price cut. Consequently, like Cournot and Bertrand duopolists, Zeuthen's duopolists would always sell at a common price. But Zeuthen's product differentiation was strong enough to allow a duopolist matching any price cut to keep his old customers. New customers would be attracted by a lower common price. A "coefficient of expansion" measured a duopolist's ability to attract them by differences in product quality, geographical location, or advertising-generated image. Zeuthen's market shares would reflect the two coefficients of expansion, hence—unlike Cournot or Bertrand market shares—would not be equal.

6.   *Chamberlin*

Fewness was treated in Chamberlin (1929), reprinted as chapter III in Chamberlin (1933). But Chamberlin's main contribution was his treatment of differentiated products. He treated them within the framework of a theory of the firm as well as within the framework of group equilibrium.

7.   *The Theory of the Firm*

All early pioneers except Hotelling and Chamberlin treated product differentiation as given among the data of their problem. Just as Hotelling had asked where two duopolist-retailers would locate themselves, Chamberlin asked which selling effort and which product quality a firm would decide upon.

Chamberlin [1933 (1948: 140-149)] began with selling effort, assumed product quality and price to be given, and asked how far selling-effort expenditure would be carried under such circumstances. An average-selling-cost curve was superimposed upon an average-production-cost curve, and the combined curve would show average production *plus* selling cost as a function of physical output sold. From such a combined average cost curve a combined marginal cost curve could be derived and the most profitable selling-effort expenditure found by the condition that combined marginal cost equals price. Still assuming product quality to be given, Chamberlin then considered both price and selling-effort expenditure free to vary. Repeating his reasoning for each possible price, he could then find "the most advantageous selling outlay for that price, and one of this series would be the best of all, thus revealing both optimum price and optimum selling outlay."

Summarizing, then, Chamberlin used not selling effort itself but selling-effort expenditure, which is always quantitative, as the variable to be optimized. If this were a satisfactory approach, it could obviously be used for nonquantitative aspects of product quality, too, especially since an early Chamberlin (1933) saw little scope for quantifying quality—a later Chamberlin (1953) was less pessimistic. But expenditure is a satisfactory proxy for neither selling effort nor product quality. Both are multidimensional, and there may be substitution among different dimensions of product quality or among different dimensions of selling effort. Somebody in the firm must know exactly how far to go in each particular dimension of quality and selling effort.

The multidimensionality of both quality and selling effort remained ignored in the literature. Von Stackelberg (1939) and Dorfman-Steiner (1954) assumed one-dimensional quality or selling effort but did see and solve the substitution problem between quality as a whole and selling effort as a whole. Nerlove-Arrow (1962) dynamized Dorfman-Steiner's use of selling-effort expenditure as a proxy for selling effort itself: demand was made a function of price and a stock of goodwill. The stock of goodwill was reduced by annual depreciation and augmented by annual advertising expenditure.

At this point let us interrupt our survey for a moment to ask [Brems (1957)] whether quality is quantifiable.

8. *Is Quality Quantifiable?*

The performance of a product in the hands of a consumer is obviously determined by its production process. To describe such a process, Walras introduced his "coefficient de fabrication" $a_i \equiv i$th physical input absorbed per unit of physical output. In his m-good world von Neumann used such input-output coefficients to define a process in which every physical input x_i is absorbed in proportion to physical output X:

$$x_i \equiv a_i X \tag{1}$$

where $i = 1, \ldots, m$.

Once decided upon, then, an input-output coefficient a_i by definition cannot vary with the scale of operations. Consequently we are free to let its variation define variations of product quality: a change in a labor input-output coefficient will reflect a change of workmanship; a change in some raw-material input-output coefficient will reflect a change of a product property dependent on that material, say purity, hardness, tensile strength, or heat resistance.

Thus product quality has been quantified: once all input-output coefficients have been decided upon, product quality has become uniquely determined, and at a given price P so has quantity demanded

$$X = X(a_1, \ldots, a_m, P) \tag{2}$$

Define cost as the sum of the market price of each input *times* its quantity absorbed:

$$c \equiv \sum_{i=1}^{m} (p_i x_i) \tag{3}$$

Define profits as revenue *minus* cost:

$$Z \equiv PX - c \tag{4}$$

Having quantified product quality we may optimize it. Let price p_i of *i*th input be given to the firm. Suppress price P of output as a decision variable to the firm. In other words, instead of letting price adjust to a given quality, as we used to do, let quality be adjusting to a given price. Vary the *i*th input-output coefficient, running into diminishing returns to quality, as shown in figure V-1. Take the partial derivative of profits Z with respect to the input-output coefficient a_i, using (1) through (4), and find

FIGURE V-1.
Product Quality or
Selling Effort Pushed
ad nauseam

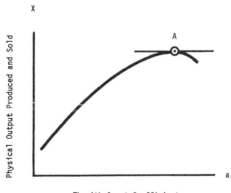

The ith Input Coefficient

$$\frac{\partial Z}{\partial a_i} = P \frac{\partial X}{\partial a_i} - \left[p_i X + \frac{\partial X}{\partial a_i} \sum_{i=1}^{m} (a_i p_i) \right] \qquad (5)$$

Let η_i be the elasticity of demand with respect to the ith input-output coefficient a_i, set the partial derivative (5) equal to zero, rearrange, and write the first-order condition for a profit maximum:

$$\eta_i \equiv \frac{\partial X}{\partial a_i} \frac{a_i}{X} = \frac{a_i p_i}{P - \sum_{i=1}^{m} (a_i p_i)} \qquad (6)$$

or, in English: the ith input should be adjusted in such a way that the per-unit expenditure on that input divided by per-unit profits equals the elasticity of demand with respect to the ith input-output coefficient.

If not one but all dimensions of quality are manipulated, the first-order condition (6) holds simultaneously for any i. Write it as

$$\frac{p_1}{\partial X/\partial a_1} = \frac{p_2}{\partial X/\partial a_2} = \cdots = \frac{p_m}{\partial X/\partial a_m} = \frac{P - \sum_{i=1}^{m} (a_i p_i)}{X} \qquad (7)$$

Consisting of m equations, one for each dimension of quality, the system (7) of simultaneous equations represents the solution of the substitution problem: how far should quality be carried in each particular one of the m possible dimensions? Quality should be improved up to the point at which the ratio between the price of an input and its marginal quality-improving productivity is the same for all m inputs.

Equation (7) is still merely a first-order condition for profit maximization. Form the Hessian determinant

$$H \equiv \begin{vmatrix} \dfrac{\partial^2 Z}{\partial a_1^2} & \cdots & \dfrac{\partial^2 Z}{\partial a_1 \partial a_m} \\ \cdots\cdots\cdots\cdots\cdots\cdots\cdots\cdots\cdots \\ \dfrac{\partial^2 Z}{\partial a_m \partial a_1} & \cdots & \dfrac{\partial^2 Z}{\partial a_m^2} \end{vmatrix}$$

The second-order conditions for profit maximization are as follows. If m is even H must be positive. If m is odd H must be negative. If the mth, the $m - 1$st, ... rows and columns are deleted, H must alternate in sign until we end up with its first element $\partial^2 Z/\partial a_1^2$, which must be negative.

Enough on quantified product quality. We must return to our survey of Chamberlinian nonpure competition.

9.   *Group Equilibrium*

As a first approximation, Chamberlin [1933 (1948: 82)] illustrated group equilibrium under his "heroic assumption" that the demand curves as well as the unit-cost curves were uniform throughout the group. Underlying the uniformity of the demand curves was an assumption of uniformity of vulnerability expressed by Chamberlin [1933 (1948: 49 and 90-91)], i.e., that the gains of a price cutter would be taken *equally* from each of his competitors: "if there were 100 sellers each loses only 1/99 of the total gained by the one who cuts his price."

But the nature of the demand curve faced by a seller would differ sharply between a large group and a small one. Chamberlin's [1933 (1948: 81-100)] large group was a group of many sellers, of polypolists. If any of them cut his price, their very multitude would make his encroachment upon each of the others so negligible that nobody would be forced to follow suit. Realizing this, each polypolist would imagine himself facing Chamberlin's so-called *dd* curve showing demand as a function of a price never matched by his rivals. Under freedom of entry and exit, an equilibrium would emerge in which such a *dd* demand curve and the unit-cost curve would have a tangent in common.

Chamberlin's [1933 (1948: 100-113)] small group was a group of few sellers, of oligopolists. If any of them cut his price, their very fewness would make his encroachment upon each of the others so apparent that everybody would be forced to follow suit. Realizing this, each oligopolist would imagine himself facing Chamberlin's so-called *DD* curve showing demand as a function of a price always matched by his rivals. Under freedom of entry and exit, an equilibrium would emerge in which such a *DD* demand curve and the unit-cost curve would have a tangent in common.

Whether the group was large or small, then, the solution was a tangency solution in which price would equal unit cost. But so it would under pure competition, so where was the difference between pure and nonpure competition? Under pure competition, the demand curve faced by the firm was horizontal, hence would have a horizontal tangent in common with a *U*-shaped unit-cost curve, and the point of tangency would be located at the minimum point of the unit-cost curve. Unit cost, then, would be at its minimum. Under nonpure competition, the demand curve faced by the firm was downward-sloping, hence would have a downward-sloping tangent in common with a *U*-shaped unit-cost curve, and the point of tangency would be located to the left of the minimum point of the unit-cost curve. Unit cost, then, would be higher than its minimum.

Is pure competition good and nonpure competition bad, then? Impossible to say. With all unit costs at their minimum, pure competition offers less variety of products than does nonpure competition. Unit costs higher than their minimum may be considered the price paid for variety. Without appointing himself a guardian of the consumer, the economist cannot say whether variety is worth its price.

A difficulty with Chamberlin's sharp distinction between large and small groups was pointed out by Chamberlin himself [1933 (1948: 103-104)] and remedied by Friedman (1983: 71-73). The difficulty was the assumed uniformity of vulnerability, that the gains of a price cutter would be taken *equally* from each of his competitors. In reality, each firm's product is a particularly close substitute for the products of only a few immediate neighbors on the quality scale and a less close substitute for the products of the more numerous and distant competitors. In other words, the large group is composed of such immediate neighborhoods, each of which must be thought of as a small group. The sharp distinction between large and small groups was in this sense too sharp!

10. *Robinson*

Robinson (1933) defined "perfect" competition as Chamberlin had defined "pure" competition and offered a model of a firm producing a differentiated product and hence facing a downward-sloping demand curve, from which Cournot's marginal-revenue function was derived and baptized. Profits were maximized by intersecting it with the marginal-cost curve.

Such use of marginal curves, Robinson said in her introduction, "contains within itself the heart of the whole matter," and such analysis of monopoly "swallowed up the competitive analysis without the smallest effort." With the "heart of the whole matter" thus disposed of, Robinson felt free to ignore, first, optimization of selling effort and product quality and, second, group equilibrium. Unlike Chamberlin, she did offer models of price discrimination and of monopsony.

11. *Von Stackelberg*

Von Stackelberg (1934) wanted a more direct visual representation of the duopoly problem than the standard demand-and-cost diagram used by Zeuthen, Chamberlin, and Robinson could offer. He gave us an iso-profits map in a diagram having the decision variables of the agents on its axes. He drew his isoprofits map for many cases. His agents could be sellers (duopolists) or buyers (duopsonists). His decision variables could be quantities or prices. His goods could be nondifferentiated or differentiated and, if differentiated, could be substitutes or complementary goods.

Of von Stackelberg's many cases we show only one, the case of substitutes offered by duopolists 1 and 2 using prices P_1 and P_2, as their decision variables, and making the profits Z_1 and Z_2, respectively. Let cost be in proportion to physical output, i.e., unit cost be constant. Let demand be such that if a common price is charged, then the sum of physical outputs sold will be higher the lower that price. From the nature of substitutes it follows, first, that at a given price of his own, a duopolist's physical output sold and hence his profits will be higher the higher the price charged by his rival and, second, that at a given price charged by his rival, the duopolist's physical output sold will be lower the higher his own price. Consequently, third, at a given price charged by his rival, the duopolist's profits will rise, pass a maximum, and then decline as his own price rises.

Let such demand and cost circumstances be identical between the duopolists. Then von Stackelberg isoprofits curves will appear as shown in figure V-2. The reaction curve OR_1 of the first duopolist is defined as the locus of all points at which his isoprofits curves Z_1 have vertical tangents. The reaction curve OR_2 of the second duopolist is defined as the locus of all points at which his isoprofits curves Z_2 have horizontal tangents. Such tangents mean that a duopolist is touching his highest possible isoprofits curve within reach as long as he can be sure that the other duopolist's price will stay put. Now consider two alternative von Stackelberg leadership equilibria.

The leadership equilibrium L_1 is defined as the point at which the second duopolist's reaction curve OR_2 and one of the first duopolist's isoprofit curves have a tangent in common. Here the first duopolist is the

FIGURE V-2.
Von Stackelberg
Leadership Equilibria

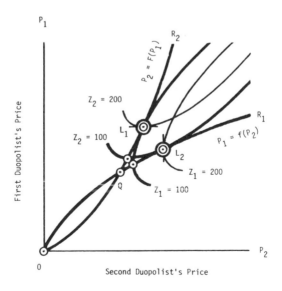

leader, knowing that the second duopolist will always react along OR_2. Under those circumstances, $Z_1 = 100$ is the highest profit the first duopolist can reach. The second duopolist is the follower, always reacting along his reaction curve OR_2, and does better: he finds himself making $Z_2 = 200$. If and only if each party accepts the role assigned to him will the other see with his own eyes a consistent confirmation of the assumptions made. Assumptions, then, are mutually consistent and expectations self-fulfilling. Next, let us reverse the roles assigned.

The leadership equilibrium L_2 is defined as the point at which the first duopolist's reaction curve OR_1 and one of the second duopolist's isoprofit curves have a tangent in common. Now the second duopolist is the leader, knowing that the first duopolist will always react along OR_1. Under those circumstances, $Z_2 = 100$ is the highest profit the second duopolist can reach. The first duopolist is the follower, always reacting along his reaction curve OR_1, and does better: he finds himself making $Z_1 = 200$. Again, if and only if each party accepts the role assigned to him will the other see with his own eyes a consistent confirmation of the assumptions made. Again, assumptions are mutually consistent and expectations self-fulfilling.

The von Stackelberg leader-follower duopoly shows that asymmetry is the price to be paid for such mutual consistency: one duopolist will have to be a leader, the other a follower, and the assignment of such roles will have to lie outside the model. Since we have assumed demand and cost circumstances to be identical between the duopolists, nothing qualifies anybody in particular for the role of leader or follower. Once assigned, would the roles be accepted? Would both duopolists try to become a leader? Hardly, because a follower always does better than a leader. Would both try to become a follower, then? The two reaction curves do have the point Q in common. Should the two duopolists somehow have landed in that point, the assumptions made would once again be seen confirmed. But either duopolist would do far worse at Q than he did at L_1 or L_2 and do worse even at L_1 or L_2 than he would have done in a von Neumann-Morgenstern coalition against the consumers. Such a coalition would maximize its combined profits $Z_1 + Z_2$ hence could make either duopolist better off without making the other worse off. For all its mutual consistency, then, the von Stackelberg leader-follower duopoly could not be the last word.

12. *Microeconometrics: Nonpure Competition*

For a long time, nonpure-competition doctrine was long on hypotheses and short on testing them, but towards the end of the present period testing began. A beginning was Telser's (1962) work on advertising and cigarettes. More comprehensive and systematic testing was offered by Lambin (1976), using 1960-1970 data on price, quality, advertising, and sales for 107 brands in 16 product classes and 8 Western European countries. The 16 product classes were: apples, auto trains, bank services, cigarettes, coffee, confectionery, deodorants, detergents, electric shavers, gasoline, hairspray, insecticides, soft drinks, suntan lotion, TV sets, and yogurt.

First, Lambin found elasticities of brand sales with respect to price, quality, and advertising. The mean of 37 significant price-elasticity estimates was -1.326; the mean of 9 significant quality-elasticity estimates was 0.521; and the mean of 37 significant long-run advertising-elasticity estimates was 0.228. In other words, pronounced diminishing returns to quality and advertising stood out.

Second, Lambin found elasticities of reaction defined as the percentage change of the rival's decision variable following a 1 percent change of the firm's own decision variable. The mean of 13 significant estimates of the elasticity of price reaction was 0.711; the mean of 18 significant estimates of the elasticity of advertising reaction was 0.471. No elasticity of quality reaction was found. Would advertising escalate? If I expand my advertising by 0.01, my rival will react by expanding his by 0.01×0.471, to which I will react by expanding mine by 0.01×0.471^2, to which he will react by expanding his by $0.01 \times 0.471^3 \ldots$ etc. Such expansions will converge to a finite equilibrium; only reaction elasticities greater than one could make escalation explosive.

We must now turn to the second of the three breakthroughs of the thirties, Keynes's unemployment equilibrium.

IV. MACROECONOMICS

1. *The Wicksellian Tradition*

The term "macroeconomics" appeared in the thirties, but the underlying concept was old. For more than a half-century, economists had been aware of the business cycle, had recorded it as a common movement of all prices, and had thought of it as a succession of transitory price disequilibria.

In 1930 such thinking was still based upon what we have called eighteenth-century assumptions: physical output was seen as bounded by supply. Demand was no problem: supply would create its own demand. There was never excess capacity. Monetary or fiscal policy might stimulate demand but to no use: monetary stimuli would merely generate inflation, fiscal stimuli merely crowding-out. There was still no doubt that, left to itself, capitalism was fully capable of utilizing its own resources.

At the opening of our period the best theorists, such as Lindahl [1930 (1939)], Keynes (1930), and Hayek (1931), had followed Wicksell (1898) in using such assumptions to build macroeconomic models of transitory price disequilibria.

2.   Hayek: Resources Fully Utilized

Wicksell [1893 (1954)] had restated a Böhm-Bawerk rate of interest, baptized it [1898 (1936)] the "natural" rate of interest, and wondered how it was related to that other rate of interest baptized the "money" rate of interest and found in markets where the supply of money met the demand for it. Wicksell examined the consequences of a discrepancy between the money and the natural rate, and Hayek (1931) followed him, with one difference. Wicksell [1898 (1936: 136)] had simplified Böhm-Bawerk by freezing the period of production at one year. Hayek wanted to treat the period of production as a variable. Within a short-run cyclical framework Hayek wanted to show how an economy could be lured out of its long-run Böhm-Bawerk equilibrium by a monetary system sending the wrong signals.

If a variable, what was the period of production a function of? It was a function of, first, the cost of capital and, second, the real wage rate. The cost of capital faced by the firm was the money rate of interest. If lowered, the money rate of interest would invite a lengthening of the period of production—more "roundaboutness." Hayek always assumed resources to be fully utilized. In that case a lengthening of the period of production would mean a reallocation of resources temporarily expanding the physical output of producers' goods at the expense of the physical output of consumers' goods.

Under a given technology, a Böhm-Bawerk natural rate could have been lowered only by a higher propensity to save. But the money rate of interest could be, and was, lowered in the absence of such a higher propensity to save. As a result, no reallocation of income between saving and consumption would be matching the reallocation of resources between physical outputs of producers' and consumers' goods. With the allocation of income out of line with the allocation of resources, a reduced supply of consumers' goods would meet the same demand for them at a higher price.

Now, still at full employment, the money wage rate would fail to catch up, so the real wage rate and hence the real wage bill and labor's physical consumption would be lower, and the allocation of income might, after all, be brought into line with the allocation of resources. Hayek's "forced saving" would do the trick. Even so, the ending was not going to be a happy one. As we saw, the period of production was a function not only of the cost of capital but also of the real wage rate. At the lower real wage rate less roundaboutness would be called for. Hayek (1939) called this "the Ricardo Effect." The ambitious investment projects, induced by a low money rate of interest and salvaged in the end by forced saving, would now turn out to be too roundabout. With their failure, bankruptcies and crisis would be at hand.

Hayek always assumed resources to be fully utilized. Offered in the year 1931, an exercise in the allocation of scarce resources was bound, however unjustly, to appear ill-timed, and the "Austrian" interlude at the London School of Economics ended with the publication of Keynes's *General Theory*. After the half-century between the Great Depression and the Great Inflation our profession became more receptive to the picture of an economy lured out of a long-run structural equilibrium by a monetary system sending the wrong signals.

3. *Resources Not Fully Utilized: Therapy before Diagnosis*

The world of the thirties was a world not unlike that of Sir William Petty, a world threatened by unemployment and imminent war. In their economic theory and policy the two periods would be expected to display similarities—and did, as we showed in our introduction to the period 1630-1730. As for the thirties, mass unemployment cried out for diagnosis and therapy. Indeed, in the United States and Germany the cry was so insistent that therapy came *before* diagnosis.

U.S. therapy consisted of what Hicks (1974: 2) calls "the rather wild collection of measures introduced by the Roosevelt administration in April 1933." Unionization of labor and cartelization by industry were encouraged. Social security at long last came to the United States. Whether intended or not, large federal deficits emerged, [see U.S. Department of Commerce (1982) and U.S. Government Printing Office (1983)]. Indeed as a percent of the gross national product, they were of the same order of magnitude as those incurred fifty years later:

1934	5.56
1935	3.85
1936	5.35
1937	3.06
1938	1.38

Ill-aimed, Roosevelt's measures failed to hit: at the end of the thirties 17 percent of the U.S. labor force remained unemployed.

What is more surprising, simultaneous German therapy scored a bull's eye: unemployment was eliminated in a couple of years. Guillebaud (1939) and Kindleberger (1973) have recorded the facts in English, and they read as a classroom example of a Keynes-Hansen model having only one equilibrating variable, physical output. Here the adjustment of saving to a fiscal deficit and autonomous investment will have to be brought about by adjustment of physical output alone. No inflation, no crowding-out! What was the therapy scoring such a bull's eye? Over the three years 1933-1936 the Hitler government deployed a three-armed fiscal policy. The first arm was a succession of fiscal deficits: federal debt increased by 50 percent over the three years. The second arm was tax reduction: tax credit for investment in import-substituting processes, tax credit for indirect taxes paid, accelerated depreciation of machines, tools, and utility vehicles, and excise-tax exemption for motor vehicles and other items of military interest. The third arm was public works in the form of a system of interstate expressways meeting, almost perfectly, Sir William Petty's prescription from 1662: they were "works of much labor and little art"; they were "without expense of Foreign Commodities"; and they were "High-wayes so broad, firm, and eaven, as whereby the charge and tedium of travelling and Carriages may be greatly lessened"—and mobilization for a two-front war greatly facilitated! After 1935 the emphasis shifted to open rearmament.

As Guillebaud (1939: 38) points out, some of the tools available for use by the Hitler government had been forged by its predecessors. The man using them so consistently was the pragmatist Hjalmar Horace Greeley Schacht (1877-1970), president of the central bank and equipped with powers that only a dictatorship, however distasteful, could bestow. Not until—almost belatedly as it were—Keynes (1936) appeared in both German and English did labor shortages, crowding-out, and upward pressure upon prices and money wage rates become noticeable. As soon as they did, Schacht (1956) refused to go along with further deficits and was removed from office. In 1945 he was liberated from a concentration camp by U.S. forces and in 1946 acquitted at the Nuremberg trials.

4.   Ohlin: Resources Not Fully Utilized

Ohlin abandoned eighteenth-century assumptions in favor of what we have called seventeenth-century ones: physical output was seen as bounded by demand. Supply was no problem. There was always excess capacity; consequently, demand would create its own supply. Monetary or fiscal policy might stimulate demand, and the result would be larger physical output and better utilization of resources.

Ohlin (1934) used four Keynesian tools of analysis, i.e., physical output as a variable, the propensity to save, liquidity preference, and the multiplier. His Keynesian tools led him to Hansenian policy conclusions: in times of excess capacity, the government should undertake investment projects—say highway construction or the electrification of state railroads—that would not compete with private investment and that should be allowed to generate fiscal deficits. Tax financing would reduce consumption and thus defeat the purpose of public works. Ohlin wrote the verbal counterpart to our government budget constraint: deficits may be financed by expanding either the bond or the money supply. Sale of government bonds, Ohlin said, would depress bond prices and thus discourage private investment, again defeating the purpose of public works. That left central-bank discounting of treasury bills as the only way that would not deprive private investment of finance. Thus financed, public works would generate income, and the income generation would be magnified by the multiplier.

In the sense that his physical output was a variable, Ohlin did anticipate Keynes. He had to: his assignment was to examine possible measures against unemployment and report to a royal commission. But Ohlin was inspired by Wicksell in the sense that his feedback between physical output and aggregate demand was not telescoped into an instant static equilibrium along a physical-output axis. Like the Wicksellian one, Ohlin's feedback unfolded in a cumulative process along a time axis and was a succession of disequilibria: expectations and plans were forever being revised in the light of new experience. In short, where Keynes used a static equilibrium, Ohlin used dynamic disequilibria. In this sense Ohlin did not anticipate Keynes.

5. *Keynes*

As for Keynes himself, as soon as he had finished his *Treatise*, he realized that the Great Depression would not fit into its framework. Being the kind of man that he was, he resolutely started from scratch, replaced the idea of transitory price disequilibria by the idea of a chronic unemployment equilibrium, and saw a future of capitalism in an oxygen tent— government supplying the oxygen. The model was at least as special as the ones it replaced: physical output was unfrozen and became a variable; in return price was frozen and became a parameter. The unemployment equilibrium was static; the price disequilibria it replaced had at least been dynamic. Yet Keynes called his model "general" and all his predecessors "classical." We shall devote our chapter 9 to Keynes's unemployment equilibrium and chapter 10 to Hansen's.

V. KEYNES IN RETROSPECT

1. *Say's Law*

The question to which Keynes's *General Theory* offered an answer was as old as economic theory itself: under flexible prices and money wage, interest, and exchange rates will a capitalist economy left to itself generate an aggregate demand sufficient to fully utilize available resources?

Say's [1803 (1830)] affirmative answer offers a convenient point of departure for Keynes's negative answer. Say's Law came in two parts. The first part was noncontroversial and consisted of the national product-national income identity: generation of product was generation of value added, and value added was somebody's earnings. Thus generated, did income become demand? The second part of Say's Law was controversial and consisted of the statement that the savings, import, and tax leakages would always be stopped by investment, export, and government expenditure, respectively, so income did become demand.

General Theory concentrated on the savings leakage, assumed a closed economy, and said nothing about fiscal policy—a subject taken up five years later by Hansen (1941).

2. The Savings Leakage

Income saved does not demand output. Will the leakage be stopped by a price mechanism? Specifically, will a well-functioning capital market exist in which a flexible rate of interest serves as an equilibrating variable between saving and investment—as Turgot [1769-1770 (1922: 74)] had suggested and Smith [1776 (1805: 78-79)] repeated?

Keynes (1936) did not think so. The savings leakage would be stopped alright, but income rather than interest would be the equilibrating variable. Income would always adjust until the amount of it saved was no more and no less than what could be invested. How did Keynes eliminate the rate of interest as an equilibrating variable?

3. The Rate of Interest Not Equilibrating Savings and Investment

As Patinkin (1976: 99) observed, Keynes always believed that his rate of interest equilibrated the supply of and the demand for money but never savings and investment. Income took care of savings and investment!

Such tidy compartmentalization misunderstands the nature of general equilibrium—but Keynes's tradition was Marshallian partial equilibrium rather than Walrasian general equilibrium. Normally, all equilibrating variables must help satisfy *all* equilibrium conditions. That the Keynesian system is no exception is seen most easily in the celebrated *IS-LM* diagram, drawn under the assumption of frozen prices.

Such a diagram, shown in figure V-3, has two equilibrating variables: the rate of interest r, plotted on the vertical axis, and physical output X, plotted on the horizontal one. The diagram also has two equilib-

FIGURE V-3.
A Keynesian
Interest-Output
Equilibrium Found by
Intersecting *IS* and *LM*
Curves

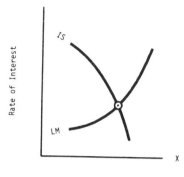

Physical Output

rium conditions. The first is that supply of and demand for goods are equal, and the *IS* curve is the locus of all interest-output combinations satisfying that condition. Physical investment is higher the lower the rate of interest. Physical consumption is higher the higher the physical output. As a result, aggregate demand for goods will be high at a low rate of interest and a high output. In other words, the *IS* curve is negatively sloped.

The second equilibrium condition is that supply of and demand for money are equal, and the *LM* curve is the locus of all interest-output combinations satisfying that condition. Demand for money is higher the lower the rate of interest. Demand for money is also higher the higher output to be transacted. The *LM* curve is drawn for given money and bond supplies. As a result, at a high rate of interest—forcing people to economize with their money holdings—such a given money supply will go farther and transact a higher output than it could have done at a low rate of interest. In other words, the *LM* curve is positively sloped.

Complete equilibrium must satisfy both equilibrium conditions, and only the intersection point between the *IS* and *LM* curves will do that. In other words, both equilibrating variables help satisfy *both* equilibrium conditions, and Keynes's neat compartmentalization of his own system was a misunderstanding.

4.   *The Rate of Interest as a Weak Equilibrating Variable*

There was, however, more to Keynes than his misunderstanding the nature of his own general equilibrium. His *IS* and *LM* curves could have such special forms that the rate of interest would not be of much help in stopping the savings leakage. Our curvatures of chapter 9 are the key.

First, owing to a low interest elasticity of investment at low interest rates it would become increasingly difficult to encourage additional investment by depressing the interest rate. The lower end of our *IS* curve would become nearly vertical! And, second, owing to a high interest elasticity of the demand for money at low interest rates, it would also become increasingly difficult to depress the interest rate by expanding the money supply. The lower end of our *LM* curve would become nearly horizontal! All in all, investment would have little give in it, and saving would have to adjust to it via Keynes's income mechanism. Indeed, as Kaldor (1966) put it: "The whole dispute between Keynesian and non-Keynesian theories is whether investment determines savings, or vice versa."

How realistic are such special forms of the *IS* and *LM* curves? Tinbergen (1939: 46, 184) found the long-term interest elasticity of investment in durable producers' goods to be "moderate." Of the low interest elasticity of investment Keynes himself may have been less convinced than were some of his followers. To the high interest elasticity of his demand for money he (1936: 207) referred as a "possibility." However that may be, later empirical work from Bronfenbrenner and Mayer (1960) to Barth, Kraft, and Kraft (1976) has not confirmed it.

So far we have mentioned neither price nor wage. Might price and wage flexibility restore full employment?

5. *Price and Wage Flexibility*

Let there be excess supply in the labor market in the form of unemployment. Let price and money wage rates be flexible and decline in response to such excess supply. The declining price will be raising the real value of money balances—the more so the farther price declines. Modify the Keynesian consumption function by adding such real balances to it and give them a chance to stimulate consumption. Then price will keep declining until the real-balance effect has stimulated demand enough to restore full employment. The stimulus is the result of adding real wealth to the consumption function and will play its role even when the rate of interest can play no role.

The real-balance effect was introduced by Pigou (1943), (1945) and Patinkin (1956) but was no part of Keynes's own system. To Keynes, price and wage flexibility would have to work, if at all, via the rate of interest as follows.

The declining price would reduce the transaction demand for money, hence release money for asset holding, and asset holders would hold it only at a reduced rate of interest. The reduced rate of interest would stimulate investment: by the detour of price and wage flexibility we are back at the rate of interest equilibrating saving and investment.

But, then, Keynes argued, would it not be much simpler to accomplish the same thing by an expansionary monetary policy at frozen prices and money wage rates? That brings us to Keynes's labor standard of money.

6. Keynes's Labor Standard of Money

By freezing his money wage rate Keynes chose what Hicks (1983: 18) called a labor standard of money. Let an expansionary monetary policy buy bonds in the open market, thus reducing the rate of interest and with it the rate of unemployment. Will Keynes's labor standard hold up?

A central bank adopts the *gold* standard of money by announcing, first, the price of gold and, second, its willingness to buy and sell gold in unlimited quantities at the announced price. But labor unions will not buy and sell *labor* in unlimited quantities at an announced money wage rate. A reduced rate of unemployment will put upward pressure on the money wage rate. The nonaugmented Phillips (1958) curve was born and asked the embarrassing question: Could an expansionary monetary policy only reduce the rate of unemployment by increasing the rate of inflation?

Keynes's labor standard assumed labor to bargain for a money, not a real, wage rate—in other words to harbor a money illusion. Experience showed labor to have inflationary expectations manifesting themselves in escalator clauses of collective agreements. The expectations-augmented Phelps (1967) version of the Phillips curve was born and asked an even more embarrassing question: Might an expansionary monetary policy fail to reduce the rate of unemployment and simply exhaust itself in a higher rate of inflation? Was there such a thing as a "natural" rate of unemployment, suggested by Friedman (1968) and Phelps (1970) but anticipated by Cannan, Clay, and Pigou, as Casson (1984) has shown? We shall return to it in section XIX,1 below.

7. The Import Leakage

Income spent on imports does not demand domestic output. Keynes's assumption of a frozen money wage rate—his labor standard—was much older than *General Theory* and explained his attack on Britain's 1925 return to a gold standard—"a barbarous relic"—based on pre-1914 parity. At 1925 money wage rates such a parity overvalued the pound, encouraged import, discouraged export, and made it impossible to stop the import leakage.

Keynes welcomed the devaluation of the pound in 1931 and of the dollar in 1933: they made it possible to stop the import leakage. No longer worrying about it and trusting his labor standard, Keynes could now go to work on his *General Theory* and write it as if his economy were a closed one.

The U.S. economy very nearly was one, both because of its sheer size and because the dollar became the world's reserve currency. For almost four decades to come, Americans could view their balance of payments with what became known as "benign neglect." Even the U.S. labor market was different: less than one-fifth of it was unionized, and Keynes's labor standard might stand a better chance here than in highly unionized Britain. Perhaps for such reasons, it was on the North American continent that advances in the Keynesian art largely took place, as Samuelson (1983: 20-21) has suggested.

But even in the United States all good things come to an end. The 1971 floating of the dollar and the 1974 oil and food shocks were a rude awakening. For domestic and international reasons alike, Keynes's labor standard had failed and could be salvaged by neither price and wage controls, "incomes policies," nor "social compacts." Half a century had taken us from the Great Depression to the Great Inflation.

VI. HANSEN IN RETROSPECT

1. *Early Dynamization*

Paradoxically the earliest improvement of Hansen (1941) had been accomplished even before the book was published. Familiar with the Continental ideas of investment demand, Hansen was never quite happy with Keynesian ones. First, he saw physical investment as the change in desired physical capital stock or $I(t) \equiv S(t) - S(t - 1)$. Second, Hansen saw desired physical capital stock in direct proportion to physical output of consumers' goods, or $S(t) = bC(t)$, where the factor of proportionality b was the accelerator. Hansen could then work out the arithmetic of an interaction between the multiplier and the accelerator. Bewildered by the multitude of possibilities thus opening up, he turned to his brightest student for help. Ignoring taxes but not government purchase of goods and services, Samuelson (1939) wrote out Hansen's system as the lagged consumption function $C(t) = cX(t - 1)$, the lagged investment function $I(t) = b[C(t) - C(t - 1)]$, and the goods-market equilibrium condition $X(t) = C(t) + I(t) + G(t)$.

Solving his system, Samuelson found the second-order linear difference equation in physical output:

$$X(t) = (1 + b)cX(t - 1) - bcX(t - 2) + G(t) \qquad (8)$$

where $G(t)$ was a constant. The corresponding characteristic equation would be a quadratic. If its roots were complex, physical output would display oscillations but otherwise either converge to the multiplier $1/(1 -$ c) *times* the constant level of government purchase $G(t)$ or be growing smoothly.

Thus, paradoxically, dynamization of Hansen (1941) had been accomplished by Samuelson (1939) two years before Hansen's book was published. Otherwise, Hansen's followers stayed static for some time, and the key to what they did was the government budget constraint.

2. The Government Budget Constraint

Ignoring the government interest bill, Hansen himself (1941), (1949), (1951) had thought of his fiscal deficit simply as the money value of government purchase of goods and services *minus* government net receipts. On the financing of it he said little but did (1951: 231-236) report Lauderdale's views on debt retirement. Lauderdale (1804) may have been the first to use a government budget constraint but did so implicitly. So did Ohlin (1934). The first to write an algebraic government budget constraint was probably the other Hansen, Bent Hansen [1955: 58 (1958), (1967)]. In the United States it was first written by Ott and Ott (1965) and Christ (1967) but without the payment of interest on government bonds. The complete constraint was offered by Christ (1969), Blinder-Solow (1974), and Turnovsky (1977). The government budget constraint could then be written as follows.

Define the fiscal deficit as the money value of government purchase of goods and services *plus* the payment of interest on government bonds *minus* government net receipts before interest paid by government, or $GP + iQ - R$. Pure money financing of it would mean that the government issued noninterest-bearing claims upon itself called money. Pure bond financing of the deficit would mean that the government issued interest-bearing claims upon itself called bonds and sold them to households and industry. The general case should allow for both money and bond financing, so we write the government budget constraint as

$$GP + iQ - R = \frac{dM}{dt} + \Pi \frac{dQ}{dt} \tag{9}$$

Writing such a government budget constraint had far-reaching consequences, which we must now set out.

3. Tying Monetary and Fiscal Policy Together

A government budget constraint was a reminder that in a closed economy, money and bonds could come into existence in no other way than by financing a fiscal deficit. Vice versa a fiscal deficit could be financed in no other way than by expanding the money or bond supplies. Their rates of growth could indeed be considered the policy instruments of monetary and fiscal policy, respectively. Such a choice of policy instruments would remind the reader of the connection between monetary and fiscal policy. Did the connection reduce monetary policy to subservience to fiscal policy, then? Not quite. Given the rates of growth of the money and bond supplies, monetary policy might still take corrective action in two forms. By open-market operations in already existing old bonds, monetary policy might readjust the money and bond supplies, but always in a seesaw manner, i.e., always expanding one at the expense of the other. Also, by varying reserve ratios, monetary policy might make Federal Reserve money go farther or less far.

4.   *The Rate of Interest as an Equilibrating Variable: Crowding-Out*

Whatever the equilibrating variables are, they will make the sum of all leakages equal zero. In a closed economy, then, saving *plus* government net receipts before interest paid by government must equal investment *plus* government purchase of goods and services *plus* interest paid by government. In short, saving must equal investment *plus* the fiscal deficit. Consequently, in a closed economy investment and saving will be equal if and only if the government balances its budget. Under a fiscal deficit, investment must fall short of saving, and a higher rate of interest might help accomplishing such crowding-out.

The extent to which it will do so will depend upon the way the fiscal deficit is financed. To see how, let us once again deploy the Hicksian (1937) *IS-LM* diagram and consider pure bond and pure money financing in turn.

5.   *Pure Bond Financing: Complete Crowding-Out*

Let government expand its demand G but fail to raise taxes accordingly. Pure bond financing of the resulting fiscal deficit would mean that the government issued interest-bearing claims upon itself called bonds and sold them to households and industry. As a result of the expanded government demand G, the IS curve will shift to the right. Furthermore, to the households the addition to the stock of government bonds is additional wealth. Perhaps, as Pigou and Patinkin suggested, such wealth should be added to the consumption function. If it is, the IS curve will shift further to the right: at a given rate of interest, the aggregate demand $C + I + G$ would be up.

Complete crowding-out would mean zero sensitivity of physical output to such a purely bond-financed fiscal deficit. Could this happen? If an *IS* curve pushed to the right must intersect an *LM* curve at a point whose abscissa remains the same as before, then the *LM* curve must stay put and be vertical, as shown in the upper case of figure V-4. A vertical *LM* curve would mean that the demand for money was insensitive to the rate of interest: no rise in the latter would induce households and industry to hold any less cash and thus release any money to transact a larger output! Such complete insensitivity of the demand for money to the rate of interest was in fact accepted by an early Friedman (1959) but abandoned by a later one (1966), (1972) and was an extreme and very special case—as extreme and special as the Keynesian opposite assumption of a complete sensitivity of the demand for money to the rate of interest.

FIGURE V-4. *IS-LM* Analysis of Deficit Financing

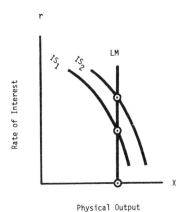

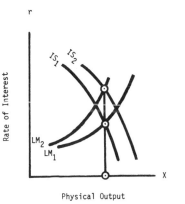 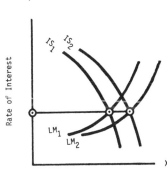

6. *Pure Bond Financing: Incomplete Crowding-Out*

In a less special case of pure bond financing let the *LM* curve stay put but have a finite positive slope. Then an *IS* curve pushed to the right would intersect an unchanged *LM* curve at a point whose abscissa and ordinate were both higher than before. The lower left-hand case of our figure V-4 would then show a larger physical output, hence incomplete crowding-out.

But will the *LM* curve stay put? In his stock equilibrium Keynes had ignored the flows of addition to and subtraction from the stock of bonds. Accordingly, we drew our *LM* curve for given money and bond supplies. Under our pure bond financing the money supply *M* does remain the same, but the bond supply *Q* is up. At a given rate of interest and a larger stock of bonds to hold, an unchanged money supply would leave less money available for transactions. As a result, under pure bond financing the *LM* curve will shift to the left. The net effect of such opposite shifts of the *IS* and *LM* curves upon the left-hand case of our figure V-4 might be an unchanged physical output, hence complete crowding-out once again.

7. *Pure Money Financing: No Crowding-Out or Inflation?*

As we just saw, in his stock equilibrium Keynes ignored the flows of addition to and subtraction from the stock of bonds. Accordingly, we drew our *LM* curve for given money and bond supplies. Under pure money financing the bond supply *Q* does remain the same, but the money supply *M* is up. At a given rate of interest and an unchanged stock of bonds to hold, a larger money supply would leave more money available for transactions. As a result, under pure money financing the *LM* curve will shift to the right. Conceivably it might shift enough to the right to keep the rate of interest from rising at all. In that extreme case there would be no crowding out at all, as shown in the lower right-hand case of figure V-4. Furthermore, in that happy case the higher output and income would boost tax revenue and thus reduce the deficit itself.

But the ending of the full story may be less happy. As we saw in our retrospect in section V,6, under an expansionary monetary policy inflation would rear its ugly head. An *IS-LM* diagram cannot, as we shall see in a moment, accommodate continuous inflation. What it can accommodate is a once-and-for-all price increase, and its effect will be twofold.

First, there may be an effect upon the *IS* curve. A price increase will reduce the real value of stocks of money and bonds, and perhaps such capital losses should be included in the consumption function. If they are, the *IS* curve will shift to the left.

Second, there may be an effect upon the *LM* curve. The original *IS-*

LM diagram, we said, was drawn under the assumption of frozen prices. At a given rate of interest and an unchanged stock of bonds to hold, the new money supply can transact a smaller physical output after the once-and-for-all price increase than before. Consequently, the *LM* curve will reverse itself and shift to the left.

As a result of such leftward shifts of both the *IS* and the *LM* curves there may be more crowding-out, and the fiscal multiplier may be smaller, than Hansen and the mercantilists believed. But a once-and-for-all price increase is one thing, inflation another, to which we now turn.

8.   *Inflation and the IS-LM Diagram*

Keynes (1936: 142-143 and 222-229) knew and discussed Fisher's distinction between a nominal and a real rate of interest but, like Wicksell, remained unconvinced. Happily, he and Hansen (1941), (1949), (1951), and (1953) ignored inflation.

One Hansen ignored inflation, but the other, Bent Hansen [1955 (1958), (1967)], did not and could not: His work was a Swedish government assignment ordering him to examine how the value of money could be stabilized at full employment. In the United States Christ (1969) offered a "Keynesian" approach with physical output as a variable at frozen price as well as an alternative, "classical," approach with price as a variable at frozen full-employment physical output. Keynesians were slow to unfreeze price: in the cores of their fiscal-policy models neither Blinder-Solow (1974) nor Tobin-Buiter (1976) did.

Once inflation was admitted as an equilibrating variable, the *IS-LM* diagram ran into two difficulties. The first was that the diagram had a single rate of interest on its vertical axis but that the *IS* curve would now be a function of the real rate of interest, while the *LM* curve would be a function of the nominal one.

The second difficulty was that the *IS-LM* diagram was static and hence could accommodate only the equilibrium levels of variables—never their time paths. But the rate of inflation defined as

$$g_P \equiv \frac{dP}{dt} \frac{1}{P} \tag{10}$$

contains a derivative with respect to time, hence is homeless in an *IS-LM* diagram. Still, Friedman (1970) heroically tried to analyze inflation within the framework of an *IS-LM* diagram. In chapter 16 we shall try to do better.

VII. MACROECONOMETRICS

1. *The Beginning*

One of the useful things that the League of Nations did before its demise was to sponsor a survey of business-cycle theories. Haberler (1937), (1941) was asked to restate and classify them and found a bewildering array of models, equally plausible from a logical point of view. But which ones were realistic? Clearly, as Leontief (1948: 390) has put it, "a new contact with reality had to be established." For establishing that contact, new tools had recently become available. The Econometric Society had been organized in 1930 and had published the first issue of *Econometrica* in 1933. By a happy choice, a pioneer in the development of the new tools was asked to test on measurable facts the business-cycle theories that Haberler had restated and classified so carefully. Tinbergen (1939) did it by accepting and rejecting explanatory variables on the basis of high or low coefficients of correlation, respectively. Macroeconometrics was born. Like the high-speed electronic digital computer itself that was to become its base, macroeconometrics outgrew its academic birthplace and became marketable!

Eckstein (1978: 185-205) distinguished three generations of macroeconometric models.

2. *The First Generation*

First-generation models by Klein (1950) and Klein-Goldberger (1955) were Keynesian, used the large aggregates of the new national income accounts, and were severely constrained by computational facilities. Klein's original model had 12 equations! Soon computational facilities made much larger models possible, and macroeconometrics rose to the challenge.

3. *The Second Generation*

The Brookings model [Duesenberry-Fromm-Klein-Kuh (1965)], the Wharton model [Evans-Klein (1967)], the Federal Reserve-M.I.T. model [De Leeuw-Gramlich (1969)], and the Data Resources model [Eckstein, Green, and Sinai (1974)] represent second-generation models. Here, room was found for Arrow-Hoffenberg's (1959) use of Leontief interindustry-equilibrium models, Ando-Modigliani's (1963) life-cycle hypothesis of saving, Jorgenson's (1967) neoclassical model of investment, and De Leeuw and Gramlich's (1969) introduction of the money and bond supplies and a variety of interest rates.

Such disaggregation and use of new explanatory variables had consequences for both the conception and the size of the models. Conceptually, the second-generation models were less Keynesian than their predecessors. As Eckstein (1978: 191) put it, income elasticities and multipliers were shrinking, and sensitivities to inflation and the rate of interest were expanding. As for size, the original Federal Reserve-M.I.T. model had 66 equations, the Brookings model 150, and the Data Resources model about 300.

4.   *The Third Generation*

Fitted to a data sample of a quarter-century of almost steady-state domestic growth, second-generation models turned out to be less vulnerable to foreign impulse and cyclical propagation than the U.S. economy that they were supposed to simulate. Helped by the scale and speed of new computers, the Data Resources model perhaps went furthest in its revision of second-generation frameworks. Sources and uses of funds were specified for households and nonfinancial corporations, and more attention was given to the structure of U.S. foreign trade, world wholesale prices, inventory hoarding, and such supply-side variables as capacity utilization and length of delivery periods.

Once again conception and size were affected. Even less Keynesian than second-generation models, third-generation models had even weaker fiscal multipliers, displayed even more crowding-out, were even more sensitive to inflation and the rate of interest, and were more cyclical. As for size, towards the end of our period the Data Resources model is approaching a thousand equations, ever more of them simultaneous rather than recursive.

Keynes's choice of equilibrating variable, i.e., physical output, was new. But his method was old. Schumpeter (1936: 792) called it Ricardian. Clower (1975: 4) suggested that Keynes must have intended to offer what Marshall might have formulated had he ever felt a need to model the economy as a whole.

We must now turn to the last of the three breakthroughs of the thirties, i.e., the existence proof of general equilibrium by von Neumann. Here, we shall find a method more original, more rigorous, and more powerful than Keynes's. We shall find it applied to the very foundations of economics.

VIII. FIRST SADDLE POINT: EXISTENCE OF DYNAMIC GENERAL EQUILIBRIUM

1. The Mathematical Austrians

The eighth and ninth decades of the nineteenth century had seen two flourishing Vienna schools, one of surgery, founded by Billroth (1819-1894), and one of economics, founded by Carl Menger (1840-1921). The third and fourth decades of the twentieth century were to see a third one, logical positivism, inspired by Wittgenstein (1889-1951). Among its members were the mathematicians Kurt Gödel and Karl Menger, the son of Carl Menger. Under Menger's chairmanship, they and other mathematicians, Viennese and foreign, met informally about every other week in a mathematical colloquium. Amidst the Great Depression and civil war, this colloquium happened to devote some of its time to the very foundations of economic theory. Schumpeter (1954: 587) calls it "a lucky chance" that our problems happened to attract the attention of some of the best mathematical minds of the time.

It all began with the seemingly pedestrian distinction between free and economic goods.

2. Free and Economic Goods

By Walras's definition of a_{ij} the number of physical units of the ith input demanded by industry must equal the sum of all the m outputs, each multiplied by its input-output coefficient with respect to that input:

$$x_i \equiv \sum_{j=1}^{m} (a_{ij}X_j)$$

But could one be sure that the number of physical units of the ith input thus demanded would equal the sum of all physical units of that input supplied? Might there not be leftovers, "excess supply," of some inputs? Zeuthen (1928: 27), (1932-1933: 2-3) saw that there might indeed:

Since one does not know in advance which inputs are free, one should insert into these equations a last term allowing for a possible unused portion. At the same time one should impose the condition that either this unused portion or the price of the input be equal to zero (my translation).

In a short paper Schlesinger [1935 (1968)] arrived at the same condition and in proof added a footnote quoting Zeuthen's passage. Neither Zeuthen nor Schlesinger attempted to prove the existence of a general equilibrium, but the economist Schlesinger persuaded the mathematician Wald to try. Wald [1935 and 1936 (1968)] succeeded but in the process did less than full justice to Walras—unnecessarily as it turned out.

3. *Wald*

In his existence proof Wald took two liberties with Walras. First, Wald always inverted Walrasian demand equations. Walras saw quantity as a function of prices, Wald saw price as a function of quantities. Second, only the prices P_j and the quantities X_j of outputs, never the prices p_i and the quantities x_i of inputs, appeared in Wald's demand equations thus inverted. Discussing Wald's [1936 (1968: 293)] second paper, Kurt Gödel made the Walrasian observation that "the demand of each individual depends also on his income," hence on the missing p_i. Gödel's observation prompted Wald [1936 (1951)] to explicitly assume away any influence of income distribution upon market demand.

In two respects Wald's existence proof did follow Walras's original assumptions. First, the economy was a stationary one, hence had no saving, no investment, and no interest rate. Second, an output could be produced in only one way, specified by its input-output coefficients a_{ij}. In his expository paper [1936 (1951: 379)] Wald promised to publish a paper on dynamic general equilibrium with substitution in production. Such a paper was written but lost, and the job was done by von Neumann.

4. *Existence of Dynamic General Equilibrium: von Neumann*

We shall devote our chapter 11 to the von Neumann [1937 (1968)] model of a dynamic general equilibrium. The model was slow in reaching print. According to Weintraub (1983: 13n), recollections by Jacob Marschak suggest the genesis of the model to be roughly contemporary with von Neumann's early work on game theory (1928). The model was presented to a Princeton mathematics seminar in 1932.

Von Neumann abandoned the Walras-Cassel-Zeuthen-Schlesinger-Wald distinction between inputs and outputs. A von Neumann good might at the same time be absorbed as an input and supplied as an output. The heart of the von Neumann model was its saddle point, and von Neumann saw it before anybody else. He saw it in the form of a primal maximum problem and a dual minimum problem.

5. *Excess Demand Must Be Nonpositive*

Feasibility requires that the sum of all inputs of any good absorbed in all processes must be smaller than or equal to the sum of all outputs of it supplied in all processes. We can always make the rate of growth high enough to generate positive excess demand for at least one good. But how high can we make it *without* doing that? When the rate of growth reaches its highest possible value, its equilibrium value, excess demand will be zero for at least one good.

Thus von Neumann had formulated his primal problem: maximize the rate of growth subject to the constraint that excess demand for any good must be nonpositive. That constraint was what Zeuthen and Schlesinger had seen.

6. *Profits Must Be Nonpositive*

Under pure competition and freedom of entry and exit, profits must be nonpositive, hence for any time-consuming process, the sum of all input cost at time t with interest added must be greater than or equal to the sum of all revenue at time $t + 1$. We can always make the rate of interest low enough to generate positive profits in at least one process. But how low can we make it *without* doing that? When the rate of interest reaches its lowest possible value, its equilibrium value, profits will become zero in at least one process.

Thus von Neumann had formulated his dual problem: minimize the rate of interest subject to the constraint that in any time-consuming process profits must be nonpositive. That constraint was seen by neither Zeuthen, Schlesinger, nor Wald.

Taking his primal and his dual together, von Neumann proved the existence of an equilibrium solution displaying a saddle point: the maximized rate of growth equals the minimized rate of interest.

7. *Von Neumann's Absence of Consumer Preferences*

But how did von Neumann treat consumption? Who consumed? Assuming all his goods to be reproducible, von Neumann excluded natural resources, their owners, and the consumption by such owners. Like Walrasian ones von Neumann's entrepreneurs didn't consume anything, because their income qua entrepreneurs was zero—pure competition and freedom of entry and exit saw to that. Capitalists did have an income, but their propensity to consume it was zero. That left labor as the only consumer in a von Neumann model. Labor was a good like any other, hence was reproducible: labor was simply the output of one or more processes whose inputs were consumers' goods. Labor might occur as an output in more than one process and thus be produced in more than one way—by being fed, so to speak, alternative menus. The alternative menus did represent substitution in consumption, but how was the choice among them made? Labor-producing processes displaying zero loss margins would be operated at positive levels representing the consumption choice of the economy. But that choice did not express anybody's preference; it merely minimized the cost, including interest, of breeding labor. Labor was bred as cattle!

IX. MICROECONOMETRICS: INTERINDUSTRY EQUILIBRIUM

On the eve of the computer revolution, Leontief (1941, 1953) revived Quesnay's idea of an interindustry equilibrium. Leontief built an interindustry model whose parameters could be estimated empirically but condensed it to ten sectors to fit the capacity of the available facilities. Only after the computer revolution could models with hundreds of sectors be estimated and solved. Even so, drastic simplification was necessary. One might think of a Leontief model as a von Neumann model collapsed in five dimensions.

First, von Neumann processes represented joint demand as well as joint supply. A Leontief model knew only joint demand. Each industry produced only one good.

Second, a von Neumann good might be produced in more than one way. A Leontief industry knew of only one way of producing its good.

Third, von Neumann labor was reproducible and might be produced by being fed alternative menus. Leontief labor was not reproducible, and its consumption was autonomous.

Fourth, in a von Neumann model all processes had a period of production of one time unit. In a static Leontief model inputs and outputs were simultaneous, and time was never mentioned. In a dynamic Leontief model, however, industries did invest in durable capital stock, and time paths of output were found.

Fifth, inequalities played a decisive role in a von Neumann model but no role at all in Leontief models, whether static or dynamic ones.

The computer revolution brought large-scale operational and empirical work within the reach of economics. The first model to which such work was applied was the open static Leontief model. Some fifty countries have used it in an effort to plan their economic development. By contrast, as Dorfman (1973: 440) points out, "dynamic input-output analysis has remained, largely, a textbook theory."

We shall devote our chapter 12 to the static and dynamic versions of a Leontief interindustry equilibrium.

X. SECOND SADDLE POINT: EXISTENCE OF STATIC GENERAL EQUILIBRIUM

1. *The Walras Grandchildren*

We shall devote our chapter 13 to those Walras grandchildren who proved the existence of a static general equilibrium with consumer preferences in it. We shall define the group as Wald [1935 (1968)], [1936 (1968)], and [1936 (1951)], Samuelson (1938), (1947), Koopmans (1951),

(1957), Arrow-Debreu (1954), Arrow-Hurwicz (1958), Dorfman-Samuelson-Solow (1958), McKenzie (1959), and Debreu (1959).

Instead of using a utility function, we shall find that revealed preference will do: given its price-budget configuration, a household will reveal its preferred consumption set. But we shall avoid taking the liberties that Wald took with Walrasian demand equations and shall see preferred consumption as a function of prices—all prices, including prices of outputs and inputs alike. Unlike Wald, we shall distinguish clearly between individual and aggregate preferred consumption and show explicitly how they depend—via input prices—upon income distribution, a dependence assumed away by Wald.

2. Excess Demand Must Be Nonpositive

As far as any input is concerned, the sum of all of it absorbed in all industries must be smaller than or equal to the quantity available. We can always make industry outputs high enough to generate positive excess demand for at least one input. But how high can we make them *without* doing that? When the industry outputs reach their highest possible value, the equilibrium value, excess demand will become zero for at least one input.

We may now formulate our primal problem: maximize the value of all output subject to the constraint that excess demand for any input must be nonpositive.

3. Profits Must Be Nonpositive

Under pure competition and freedom of entry and exit, input prices must be such that at unit level the money value of all inputs absorbed in any industry is greater than or equal to the price of that industry's product. We can always make input prices low enough to generate positive profits in at least one industry. But how low can we make them *without* doing that? When the input prices reach their lowest possible value, the equilibrium value, profits will become zero in at least one industry.

We may now formulate our dual problem: minimize the value of all input subject to the constraint that in any industry profits must be nonpositive.

Taking the primal and the dual together, we may find a saddle point—our second—at which the maximized value of all output equals the minimized value of all input.

XI. THIRD SADDLE POINT: GAME THEORY

The essence of a game is that the payoff to each player depends upon the strategy choices of all players. Each player is thus trying to maximize a function of which he does not control all variables. This is no ordinary maximum problem and could be turned into one only by making special assumptions. One such special assumption is pure competition. Here the number of players is so large that each of them may safely ignore the influence of his own strategy choice upon the payoffs, hence strategy choices, of all the other players. As a result, the pure competitor is maximizing a function of which he does control its only variable, i.e., his own quantity sold. Cournot discovered nonpure competition but still tried to think of it as an ordinary maximum problem by letting the *j*th producer maximize his profits under the assumption that the quantity sold by his rivals would stay put. In effect, Cournot solved his problem by killing it. Not until our present period did economists try to break away from Cournot and admit the reaction function. Its ultimate consequence, the von Stackelberg (1934) leader-follower duopoly, showed that asymmetry was the price to be paid for mutually consistent behavior assumptions: one duopolist would have to be a leader, the other a follower, and the assignment of such roles would have to lie outside the model.

On the eve of our present period von Neumann (1928) had built and solved a mathematical model of a game in its simplest and purest form, i.e, the zero-sum, two-person game: what the winner wins the loser loses. Sixteen years later von Neumann and Morgenstern had extended the original analysis in the hope of coming to grips with bilateral monopoly, duopoly, and oligopoly.

The extension from zero-sum to constant-sum games was easy: every constant-sum, *n*-person game turned out to be strategically equivalent to a zero-sum, *n*-person game.

We shall devote our chapter 14 to a constant-sum, two-person game played with mixed strategies. A mixed-strategy game is one in which the players choose between probabilities with which to play strategies rather than between those strategies themselves.

In such a game, as in any other, each player is trying to maximize a function of which he does not control all variables. But knowing his payoff matrix, the first player knows the lowest mathematical expectation of his own payoff for any probability choice of his. Call that lowest mathematical expectation his "floor". Always prepared for the worst that may happen to him, the first player will choose his probabilities such as to maximize that floor.

In a constant-sum game with the sum *K* any element in the second player's payoff matrix is always equal to *K* *minus* the corresponding element of the first player's payoff matrix. In that case, we need to write no separate payoff matrix for the second player but may simply let him try to minimize the same number that the first player is trying to maximize. Knowing, then, the first player's payoff matrix, the second player will know the highest mathematical expectation of the first player's payoff for any probability choice of his own. Call that highest mathematical expectation his "ceiling". Always prepared for the worst that may happen to him, the second player will choose his probabilities such as to minimize that ceiling.

Von Neumann and Morgenstern then proved that a constant-sum game with mixed strategies always had a saddle point at which the minimized ceiling equaled the maximized floor.

Friedman (1983: 210) pointed out that typical real-life games are n-person rather than two-person games. The extension from two to n players was not so easy. As soon as the number of players rises above two, coalitions become possible. By selecting every possible subset of players among the n players and thinking of it as a possible coalition, von Neumann and Morgenstern could reduce a zero-sum, n-person game to a zero-sum, two-coalition game, to which all their zero-sum, two-person results would apply.

Friedman (1983: 210) also pointed out that typical real-life games are variable-sum rather than constant-sum games. Von Neumann and Morgenstern [1944 (1947: chapter 11)] interpreted a variable-sum, n-person game as a zero-sum, $n + 1$-person game, where the $n + 1$st player was a fictitious player losing the amount won by the totality of the n real players. The fictitious player was allowed neither any influence on the moves of the game nor any participation in the interplay of coalitions and compensations.

The first to apply such an abstract framework to industrial reality, creating what he called "mathematical institutional economics," was Shubik (1959). Shubik restated and solved conventional oligopoly models in terms of game theory and built unconventional games of economic survival using such variables as initial assets, financial structure, cost of entry, and value of liquidation.

XII. A NEW UTILITY INDEX

1. A Measurable but Nonadditive Utility Index

Pareto had defined a class of utility indices that agreed on preference or indifference as long as any index was a monotonic transformation of any other. Von Neumann and Morgenstern [1944 (1947: 15-31)] defined a subclass of such indices within which any index was a linear transformation of any other. However measurable such an index was when referring to an individual consumer, von Neumann and Morgenstern [1944 (1947: 29)] considered it neither comparable nor additive among different consumers. Consequently they [1944 (1947: 47, 605)] never made any game-theoretical use of it. Still let us restate it for its own sake.

Let a consumer facing two events of consumption a and b prefer b to a. Let us assign the otherwise arbitrary indices $V(a)$ and $V(b)$ to the events a and b, respectively, such that the index assigned to b is higher than that assigned to a:

$$V(b) > V(a) \tag{11}$$

Now introduce a third event c which is preferred to both a and b. Offer the consumer the choice between the sure prospect of getting b and the uncertain prospect of getting either a or c. Whether in fact he gets a or c depends upon the outcome of a random draw in which the probability for a is q, the probability for c is $1 - q$, and $0 < q < 1$. Let the consumer reveal that value of q that leaves him indifferent between the two prospects.

Indifference can mean nothing else than equality of attractiveness between the two prospects, each multiplied by its probability. Hence an index $V(c)$ may be assigned to the event c such that

$$V(b) = qV(a) + (1 - q)V(c)$$

or after rearranging:

$$V(c) = \frac{V(b) - qV(a)}{1 - q} \tag{12}$$

2.   *The Utility Index Determined up to a Linear Transformation*

Just as Celcius and Fahrenheit measurements represent numerical valuations of heat up to a linear transformation, so a von Neumann-Morgenstern utility index represents numerical valuations of utility up to a linear transformation. Let us show this as follows.

Initially the arbitrary indices $V(a)$ and $V(b)$ were assigned to the events a and b, respectively, subject to (11). Now let us assign a different arbitrary pair of indices $U(a)$ and $U(b)$ to the same two events subject to

$$U(b) > U(a) \tag{13}$$

Then define the constants

$A \equiv$ the arbitrary constant term of a linear transformation
$B \equiv$ the arbitrary, positive coefficient of a linear transformation

and show that, subject to (13), no matter which pair of indices $U(a)$ and $U(b)$ we choose, we may always write them as

$$U(a) = A + BV(a) \tag{14}$$

$$U(b) = A + BV(b) \tag{15}$$

To see this, simply think of (14) and (15) as two equations in the two unknowns A and B, having the parameters $U(a)$, $U(b)$, $V(a)$, and $V(b)$. Solve the system (14) and (15) for A and B:

$$A = \frac{U(a)V(b) - U(b)V(a)}{V(b) - V(a)} \tag{16}$$

$$B = \frac{U(b) - U(a)}{V(b) - V(a)} \tag{17}$$

From our constraints (11) and (13) it follows that A and B are both meaningful and unique. In addition, it follows that B is always positive. So no matter which pair of indices $U(a)$ and $U(b)$ we choose, the pair $U(a)$ and $U(b)$ would be a linear transformation of the pair $V(a)$ and $V(b)$.

With our new arbitrary indices $U(a)$ and $U(b)$ safely written as (14) and (15), let us repeat the interrogation of our consumer, assumed to have remained in exactly the same state. Since the events a, b, and c haven't changed, and since he hasn't changed, his q hasn't changed either. Hence, a new index $U(c)$ may be assigned to the event c such that

$$U(b) = qU(a) + (1 - q)U(c)$$

or after rearranging:

$$U(c) = \frac{U(b) - qU(a)}{1 - q} \tag{18}$$

How does our new index (18) compare with our old one (12)? Insert (14) and (15) into (18), use (12) upon the result, and find

$$U(c) = A + BV(c) \tag{19}$$

So for the event c according to (19), a U-scale index is the same linear transformation of a V-scale index as it was for the events a and b according to (14) and (15), respectively.

The procedure applied to event c may now be applied to further events $d, e, \ldots$ For each new event, a U-scale index will be the same linear transformation of a V-scale index as it was for the events a and b according to (14) and (15), respectively:

$$U(d) = A + BV(d) \qquad\qquad (20)$$

$$U(e) = A + BV(e)$$

.

.

.

The axioms underlying the von Neumann-Morgenstern utility index, set out at length [1944 (1947: 26-29)], rule out any positive or negative utility of the act of gambling itself. This is a price that we must pay for such an index.

XIII. FOURTH SADDLE POINT: LINEAR PROGRAMMING

1. *Theory and Practice*

The first use of duality and proof of the existence of a saddle point was found in von Neumann's (1928) theory of games. The second was found in von Neumann's (1937) dynamic general equilibrium model—a seemingly very different subject. Of both one might say with Weintraub (1983: 37) that the story was "one in which empirical work, ideas of facts and falsification, played no role at all." In stark contrast, linear programming grew out of urgent work on eminently practical problems.

Kantorovich (1939), a Leningrad mathematician, was trying to solve an elementary problem of Soviet industrial planning: let there be *n* machine tools available for production of articles each of which consists of *m* components. Allocate available machine-tool time among components such as to maximize the number of completed articles. Kantorovich saw the symmetry between a primal and a dual problem. His dual was a set of accounting prices labeled "resolving multipliers" or "ratings." Such accounting prices were the only prices known in interindustry transactions: where producers' goods are not subject to private ownership there can be neither private demand for them, private supply of them, nor a market price.

Koopmans [1942 (1970)] served as a statistician for the wartime Combined Shipping Adjustment Board, whose task was to allocate scarce merchant marine tonnage among global shipping routes such as to win the war. Koopmans, too, saw duality and used his dual in the form of opportunity costs labeled "potentials."

Dantzig (1948), (1951) served as a statistician for the U.S. Air Force in 1941-1945 and at its Controller's Office in 1945-1962, "administering," as Dorfman (1951: preface) put it, "one of the largest integrated organizations in the world."

What the three settings had in common was the problem of allocation within a large organization to whose transactions market prices did not apply. Originally designed for Soviet industrial planning or Allied military allocation, linear programming soon proved itself useful in the theory of the firm, as first shown by Dorfman (1951).

2.   *Linear Programming in A Theory of the Firm*

Applied to a theory of the firm, linear programming is short-run economics making a sharp distinction between inputs available in fixed quantities and inputs available in any quantities desired. Let us call the former "fixed" inputs. Plant and equipment are examples. Such fixed inputs are already owned by the firm, and the market prices at which they were acquired in the past are of no consequence for their current use. Still, the firm may wish to impute a price to a fixed input. If the fixed input is not scarce, its imputed price should be zero: to all intents and purposes the fixed input is then a free good to the firm. If the fixed input is scarce, its imputed price should be positive, should reflect the value of the fixed input in its best use, and thus should keep it away from lesser uses.

3.   *Excess Demand Must Be Nonpositive*

As far as a fixed input is concerned, the sum of all of it absorbed in all processes must be smaller than or equal to the fixed quantity available. We can always make our process levels high enough to generate positive excess demand for at least one fixed input. But how high can we make them *without* doing that? When the process levels have been optimized, excess demand will become zero for at least one fixed input. Such fixed inputs should have positive prices imputed to them, the rest should have zero prices imputed to them.

Thus we have formulated our linear-programming primal problem: maximize gross profits subject to the constraint that excess demand for any fixed input must be nonpositive.

4.   *Net Profits Must Be Nonpositive*

The imputed prices of fixed inputs must be such that the imputed values of all the fixed inputs absorbed in any process will at least absorb the gross profits of that process. We can always make our imputed prices low enough to generate positive net profits in at least one process. But how low can we make them *without* doing that? When the imputed prices have been optimized, net profits will become zero in at least one process.

Such processes should be operated at positive levels, the rest should remain unused.

Thus we have formulated our linear-programming dual problem: minimize the sum of imputed value of all fixed inputs subject to the constraint that net profits of any process must be nonpositive.

5. A Fourth Saddle Point

Taking the primal and the dual together we may find a saddle point—our fourth—at which the maximized gross profits equal the minimized sum of imputed value of all fixed inputs—thus leaving net profits zero.

As in the von Neumann model, proving the existence of a saddle point is only a first step. The second step is to find its coordinates, i.e., to solve for the underlying physical quantities and prices. Neoclassicists rarely bother to actually compute their solutions. Linear programming *is* such computation—taking advantage of the fact that the optimum is always hiding among a finite number of solutions. Thus linear programming added new rigor, depth, and practical usefulness to Wieser's "imputation."

After the turmoil of the Great Depression and the Second World War followed a quarter-century of almost steady-state growth. Soon economists began to theorize about long-run growth, and let us see what they did.

XIV. KNIFE-EDGE GROWTH: CASSEL AND HARROD

1. Harrod

What troubled Harrod was that Keynes had allowed saving and investment to be positive and yet had failed to consider their effect upon capital stock. Had a longer run been considered, the expansion of capital stock resulting from positive saving and investment could no longer have been ignored. Harrod decided to consider such a longer run and (1948: 77, 82, 78, and 80) expressed his basic idea in a single dynamic equation saying nothing more than that the fraction of income invested would equal the fraction of income saved:

> I write the equation as follows: $GC = s$. G, which stands for growth, is the increment of total production in any unit period expressed as a fraction of total production. ... C ... is the requirement for new capital divided by the increment of output to sustain which the new capital is required. ... s is the fraction of income saved. ... I know of no alternative formulation, in the

world of modern economic theory, of any dynamic principle of comparable generality.

2. *Cassel*

Harrod was clearly unaware that his equation had been written thirty years before. Cassel [1918 (1932: 61)], too, expressed the equality between saving and investment:

Let this capital be called C and suppose that it increases annually by p per cent., p being constant. . . . Let the annual income be called I, and suppose that annually the proportion $1/s$—in absolute amount I/s—is saved. Call this quotient, which represents the community's thrift, the "degree of saving." Clearly $I/s = (p/100)C$.

Cassel and Harrod wrote in different languages and used different notation, and we ourselves shall use yet another one, see our dictionary in table V-1.

TABLE V-1. Dictionary of Three Notations

Concept	Cassel (1932:61)	Harrod (1948:80)	Our Own
Capital Coefficient	C/I	$C \equiv I/\Delta Y$	b
Propensity to Save	$1/s$	$s \equiv S/Y$	$1 - c$
Proportionate Rate of Growth	$p/100$	$G \equiv \Delta Y/Y$	g
Physical Investment		I	I
Physical Saving		S	
Physical Capital Stock	C		S
Physical Output	I	Y	X

3. *The Full Cassel-Harrod Model*

We set out the full Cassel-Harrod model in the form of an aggregative model of six equations. Entrepreneurs produce a single good from labor and an immortal capital stock of that good, hence investment is the act of setting aside part of output for installation as capital stock. Capital stock is the result of accumulated savings under an autonomously given propensity to save, and available labor force is growing autonomously. There is no substitution between labor and capital: both labor and capital coefficients are autonomous. If there is technological progress, it is "neutral" in the sense that it does not affect the capital coefficient.

Define the proportionate rate of growth of variable v as

$$g_v \equiv \frac{dv}{dt} \frac{1}{v} \tag{21}$$

Define investment as the derivative of capital stock with respect to time:

$$I \equiv \frac{dS}{dt} \tag{22}$$

Let labor input and capital stock be in proportion to output:

$$L = aX \tag{23}$$

$$S = bX \tag{24}$$

Cassel [1918 (1932: 62)] was sure that "the total income I . . . stands in an invariable ratio to the total capital C." As always, Cassel was looking for statistical estimates and found one for the year 1908 done by a Swedish commission for national defense using tax and insurance valuations of real capital. The result was a Swedish capital coefficient $b = 6\frac{2}{3}$.

Harrod (1948: 22) offered a casual numerical example in which "outstanding capital is four times national income per annum." Four pages later he defined "a neutral stream of inventions" as one leaving the capital coefficient unaffected and finally (1948: 82) stated ". . . the assumption that the capital/income ratio is constant, i.e., that the length of the production period is unchanged, . . . that inventions are neutral and . . . that the rate of interest is constant."

Let consumption be a fixed proportion of output:

$$C = cX \tag{25}$$

where $0 < c < 1$.

According to Cassel [1918 (1932: 61)], "the degree of saving $1/s$, the relative 'thriftiness' of the people, may be assumed to be constant." Without referring to sources, Cassel estimated it to be one-fifth. Harrod (1948: 11) referred to "a steady allocation of one-tenth of income to saving" and (1948: 89) thought that "saving as a fraction of income is fairly steady in the long run."

Finally, let the system be in equilibrium. Goods-market equilibrium requires the supply of goods to equal the demand for them:

$$X = C + I \tag{26}$$

We may now solve our Cassel-Harrod system.

4. *Growth-Rate Solutions*

Insert (22) into (24) and write the pure accelerator $I = b(dX/dt)$. Use (21) to write it $I = bg_X X$. Insert the accelerator along with the consumption function (25) into the goods-market equilibrium condition (26) and find

$$(1 - c)X = bg_X X$$

All we can do here is to assume that X is not zero. We may then divide by it and find the solution for the steady-state equilibrium rate of growth of physical output:

$$g_X = (1 - c)/b \qquad (27)$$

So the proportionate rate of growth of output equals the propensity to save divided by the capital coefficient. Since both $1 - c$ and b are stationary parameters, the proportionate rate of growth of output is stationary, hence growth is steady-state.

Insert the solution (27) into the labor requirement (23), the capital requirement (24), and the consumption function (25), use the definitions (21) and (22), and find the solutions for the remaining rates of growth:

$$g_C = g_X \qquad (28)$$

$$g_I = g_X \qquad (29)$$

$$g_L = g_X \qquad (30)$$

$$g_S = g_X \qquad (31)$$

or, in Cassel's words [1918 (1932: 62)]: "We ... come to the conclusion that, in the uniformly progressive exchange economy, the total income as well as both its parts—consumption and capital accumulation—increases in the same percentage as the capital."

What will that percentage be? Insert Cassel's estimate of a Swedish propensity to save of one-fifth and capital coefficient of $6^{2}/_{3}$ into solution (27) and find a steady-state equilibrium rate of growth of 3 percent, delightfully close, Cassel [1918 (1932: 63)] observes, to the national defense commission estimate of a Swedish growth rate for the period 1885-1908 of 3.18 percent. Insert Harrod's casual estimates into (27) and find a steady-state equilibrium rate of growth of $2^{1}/_{2}$ percent.

5. *Feasibility*

In a Cassel-Harrod model no mechanism guarantees feasibility, i.e., that labor employed is less than or equal to available labor force:

$$L \leqq F \qquad (32)$$

But even if (32) were satisfied at a particular time, no mechanism guarantees continued feasibility, i.e., that labor employed is growing no more rapidly than available labor force:

$$g_L \leqq g_F \tag{33}$$

If $g_L > g_F$ there would eventually be an ever-rising labor shortage; if $g_L = g_F$ there would be continued feasibility; if $g_L < g_F$ there would be an ever-rising unemployment.

Harrod came to grips with feasibility by distinguishing between two growth rates G. The first was the "warranted" rate G_w defined (1948: 82) ". . . as that over-all rate of advance which, if executed, will leave entrepreneurs in a state of mind in which they are prepared to carry on a similar advance" or, in our notation, the steady-state equilibrium rate of growth (27).

Harrod's second rate was his "natural" rate G_n defined (1948: 87) as ". . . the rate of advance which the increase of population and technological improvements allow" or, in our notation, the parameter g_F.

Harrod used this distinction to draw an important conclusion about the role of saving in his system.

6. The Role of Saving

In a Keynesian model in which investment were either autonomous or at least insensitive to the rate of interest, a higher propensity to save would be unable to affect investment but would lower the equilibrium level of physical output. Saving was a Bad Thing, and the less of it the better for an underemployed economy.

By contrast, in a Cassel-Harrod model a higher propensity to save will permit more investment and hence more rapid growth; indeed our solution (27) shows the steady-state equilibrium rate of growth to be in direct proportion to the propensity to save. Saving is a Good Thing or, in Harrod's words (1948: 88): "Saving *is* a virtue and beneficial so long as [the warranted rate of growth] G_w is below [the natural rate of growth] G_n."

Writing almost twenty years before *General Theory*, Cassel had no Keynesian savings paradox to unlearn but did observe [1918 (1932: 61-62)] that "saving is the chief element in progress."

7. Instability

By stability of equilibrium we mean the ability of equilibrium to restore itself after a disturbance. Let an asterisk denote expectation, and let entrepreneurs expect physical output to be growing at the rate

$$^*g_X = \lambda g_X \tag{34}$$

where g_X is the steady-state equilibrium rate of growth (27) of physical output, and λ is a number in the neighborhood of one: $\lambda \lesseqgtr 1$. To maintain the stationary capital coefficient b according to (24) entrepreneurs will then plan for capital stock to be growing at the rate

$$^*g_S = {}^*g_X \tag{35}$$

But then according to (21) and (22) their investment will be

$$^*I \equiv {}^*g_S S \tag{36}$$

Into (36) insert (35), (34), (24), and (27) in that order, then add consumption demand (25) to the result, and write aggregate demand

$$C + {}^*I = [c + (1 - c)\lambda]X \tag{37}$$

How does the bracket of (37) depend on λ? Multiply $\lambda \lesseqgtr 1$ by $1 - c$, add c on both sides, and write it as

$$c + (1 - c)\lambda \lesseqgtr 1$$

Consequently, in (37) we have the following three possibilities.

A $\lambda < 1$ will generate negative excess demand, and accumulation of inventory will be read as a signal that physical output is growing more rapidly than warranted by demand. Entrepreneurs will revise their expected rate (34)—already too low—further downwards. As a result, physical output will keep decelerating.

A $\lambda = 1$ will generate zero excess demand, which will be read as a signal that physical output is growing just right. As a result, the expected rate of growth of physical output (34) will remain at its correct value g_X.

A $\lambda > 1$ will generate positive excess demand, and depletion of inventory will be read as a signal that physical output is growing less rapidly than warranted by demand. Entrepreneurs will revise their expected rate (34)—already too high—further upwards. As a result, physical output will keep accelerating.

In short: any expectation (34) other than that generated by $\lambda = 1$ will generate an aggregate demand sending the wrong signal. The initial mistake is self-magnifying rather than self-correcting. Once the Harrod-Cassel economy is pushed, however slightly, off its knife-edge equilibrium growth path, it is doomed to keep veering away from that path.

XV. POST-KEYNESIAN GROWTH: ROBINSON AND KALDOR

1. *Salvaging the Keynesian Tradition*

Harrod had restored saving to its traditional role: in his model a higher propensity to save would permit more investment and hence more rapid growth. Robinson (1956) could accept no such retreat from Keynesian doctrine but demanded unconditional surrender to it—for the long run as well as for the short. In her own words, her problem was simply how to generalize *General Theory*. Kaldor (1957), in a parallel effort, wanted to show that even in the long run it is still investment that determines savings, as Keynes had said, and not the other way around.

A long-run counterpart to the short-run Keynesian model would obviously have growth rates rather than levels as its equilibrating variables; it would be dynamic. But otherwise it would still be a simple, highly aggregated model of consumption, investment, output, and income. For the utmost simplicity, we confine ourselves to the case of one good with two uses—consumption and investment—and an immortal capital stock of that good. In a one-good economy aggregate physical capital stock and all other physical aggregates are meaningful—no disagreement between post-Keynesians and neoclassicists here.

2.   Five Equations Common to Post-Keynesian and Neoclassical Growth

Define the proportionate rate of growth of variable v as

$$g_v \equiv \frac{dv}{dt}\frac{1}{v} \tag{38}$$

Define investment as the derivative of capital stock with respect to time:

$$I \equiv \frac{dS}{dt} \tag{39}$$

Define the wage bill as the money wage rate *times* employment:

$$W \equiv wL \tag{40}$$

Define money national income as the sum of wage and profits bills:

$$Y \equiv W + Z \tag{41}$$

Equilibrium requires output to equal demand for it:

$$X = C + I \tag{42}$$

3.   Production

Like a Harrod model, the post-Keynesian model had fixed input-output coefficients:

$$L = aX \tag{43}$$

$$S = bX \tag{44}$$

The post-Keynesian production equations (43) and (44) were a simultaneous system implying simultaneous variation of L and S with X. Taking partial derivatives of X with respect to L or S was therefore impossible. Marginal productivities would be such partial derivatives. Consequently, to find their distributive shares, post-Keynesians needed something else than marginal productivities.

Robinson did not assume full employment but Kaldor did:

$$L = F \qquad (45)$$

4. Distributive Shares

As an extreme case Robinson (1956: 68) assumed that profits were not consumed. That made entrepreneurs "abstract impersonal figures" who "have no life outside office hours." We don't go to such an extreme but call the propensity to consume real profits c_Z, where $0 < c_Z < 1$. Robinson also assumed that wages are not saved. Here we follow her and let the propensity to consume real wages be $c_W = 1$. We may then write the post-Keynesian consumption function

$$C = W/P + c_Z Z/P \qquad (46)$$

Money national income defined as the aggregate earnings arising from current production is identically equal to national product defined as the market value of physical output:

$$Y \equiv PX \qquad (47)$$

Insert (41) into (47), divide by P, and write

$$X \equiv W/P + Z/P \qquad (48)$$

Subtract (46) from (48) and insert (42). Use (38) and (39) to write $I \equiv g_S S$, insert (44) into that, divide by X, and use (47) to express the profits share in terms of the capital coefficient, the proportionate rate of growth of physical capital stock, and the propensity to save real profits:

$$Z/Y = bg_S/(1 - c_Z) \qquad (49)$$

Eq. (49) is not yet a solution; it merely expresses one unknown, the profits share Z/Y, in terms of another, the rate of growth of capital stock g_S. How did post-Keynesians close their system? At this point Kaldorian and Robinsonian ways were parting.

5. Solutions

Kaldor did consider the rate of growth of capital stock g_S a variable and solved for it by assuming full employment—as neoclassicists do. Insert (45) into (43), take the derivatives of (43) and (44) with respect to time, divide by (43) and (44), and find that in the absence of technological progress steady-state proportionate rates of growth are

$$g_S = g_X = g_F \qquad (50)$$

Kaldor modified his solution by offering a "technical-progress function," ignored here. Insert (50) into (49), and you have a Kaldorian solution for the profits share Z/Y.

Robinson did not consider the rate of growth of capital stock g_S a variable. To her, g_S was autonomously given by the "animal spirits" of entrepreneurs. So (49) is already a Robinsonian solution for the profits share Z/Y.

Whether Kaldorian—with (50) inserted—or Robinsonian, our result (49) is remarkable: an economy otherwise equal but with twice the propensity to save real profits $1 - c_Z$ will have half the profits share Z/Y. In this sense the give of post-Keynesian models lies on the savings side.

6. Conclusion

By extending a Keynesian adjustment of saving to an autonomous investment from the short run to the long run, Robinson-Kaldor had salvaged a Keynesian tradition and removed saving from the pedestal erected for it by Harrod. But had they also simulated the real world? In the real world will distributive shares adjust as Robinson-Kaldor say they should? Or will the capital coefficient adjust as neoclassicists say it should?

XVI. NEOCLASSICAL GROWTH: TINBERGEN AND SOLOW

1. *The One-Good Economy*

Economic theory deals with resource allocation, and the von Neumann model was a full-fledged multi-good, multi-process, dynamic general-equilibrium model. But it was too mathematical to appeal to the mainstream of economic thought dominated by one-good models. In the Cassel-Harrod model that good could be produced in one way only; consequently, a Cassel-Harrod economy would be balancing delicately on a knife-edge equilibrium growth path. Solow's problem was to find a more robust path, and he found it. His model was still a one-good model, but at least that good could be produced in alternative ways. Which way to choose is a decision that in a capitalist economy rests with individual firms, and behind the scenes the Solow model did have profit-maximizing purely competitive firms in it hiring labor up to the point where the physical marginal productivity of labor equaled the real wage rate.

We shall devote our chapter 15 to the neoclassical growth model and find that it possessed five important properties none of which was seriously at odds with historical reality: (1) stationary distributive shares, (2) convergence to steady-state growth of output; (3) identical steady-state growth rates of output and capital stock; (4) stationary rate of return to capital; and (5) identical steady-state growth rates of the real wage rate and labor productivity.

2. *A Two-Good Economy?*

The Tinbergen-Solow neoclassical growth model was a one-good model, and post-Keynesians and neoclassicists agreed that in one-good models aggregate physical capital stock and all other physical aggregates were meaningful. Multi-good models were a different matter. Here the aggregation problem was a prominent part of post-Keynesian criticism of neoclassical thinking and was believed to be serious enough to somehow render physical capital stock and its physical marginal productivity meaningless. Would it really?

Consider resource allocation and growth in a two-good economy. If full resource allocation were to be allowed for, it would not do to let the two goods be the consumers' good and the producers' good found in Ricardo, Marx, and Uzawa (1961-1963) two-good models. Such models can have substitution between the two goods in neither consumption nor production. The simplest two-good model having such substitution in both consumption and production would be one in which each good served interchangeably as a consumers' and a producers' good. The jth good, then, would be produced from labor L_j and two physical capital stocks S_{ij} where i would be the sector of origin and j the sector of installation, $i = 1$, 2 and $j = 1, 2$. The *four* physical capital stocks S_{ij} in the model and their physical marginal productivities $\kappa_{ij} \equiv \partial X_j/\partial S_{ij}$ would be perfectly meaningful as matrices, would help determine each industry's desired capital stock maximizing present net worth, and would help solve the model for the growth rates and levels of all its variables. The reader would find such solutions in Brems (1980: chapter 10). Here growth turned out to be steady-state but unbalanced: the two goods were typically growing at two different rates.

XVII. FOR THE LAST TIME: THE SAVINGS LEAKAGE

1. *The Savings Leakage: How Is It Stopped?*

Will a well-functioning capital market exist in which a flexible rate of interest serves as an equilibrating variable between saving and investment—as Turgot had suggested and Smith repeated? Or will the savings leakage be stopped in other ways? We have now encountered four such other ways. Let us summarize and compare them.

2. Keynes

As a short-run first approximation Hansen treated investment as autonomous. Let autonomous physical investment be I and physical saving be the fraction $1 - c$ of physical output X, where c is the propensity to consume. In equilibrium investment equals saving or:

$$I = (1 - c)X \tag{51}$$

where the only variable is the equilibrating one, physical output X. Consequently, as shown in the upper left-hand case of figure V-5, investment

FIGURE V-5. Four Ways to Stop the Savings Leakage

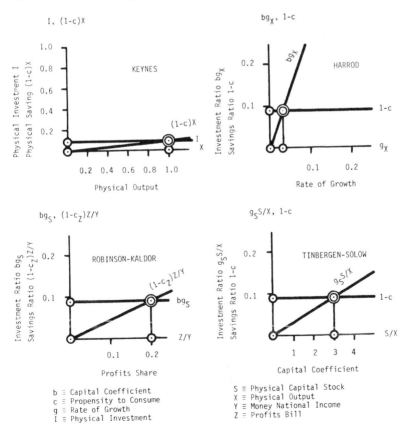

b ≡ Capital Coefficient
c ≡ Propensity to Consume
g ≡ Rate of Growth
I ≡ Physical Investment

S ≡ Physical Capital Stock
X ≡ Physical Output
Y ≡ Money National Income
Z ≡ Profits Bill

will appear as a horizontal line and saving as a straight line through the origin with the slope $1 - c$. Equilibrium will appear as the point of intersection between the two lines. The equilibrating variable will appear as the abscissa of that point, also found algebraically by rearranging (51):

$$X = I/(1 - c) \tag{52}$$

from which we see that an economy otherwise equal but with twice the propensity to save $1 - c$ will have half the level of physical output X. In this sense the adjustment lies on the savings side. Saving is a Bad Thing, and the less of it the better for an underemployed economy.

3. Harrod

In the Harrod growth model the fraction of output invested was bg_X where the capital coefficient b was a parameter and the rate of growth g_X the equilibrating variable. The fraction of output saved would be $1 - c$ where the propensity to consume c was a parameter. Now, in equilibrium the fraction of output invested would equal the fraction of it saved or:

$$bg_X = 1 - c \tag{53}$$

where the only variable is the equilibrating one, the rate of growth g_X. Consequently, as shown in the upper right-hand case of figure V-5, the fraction of output invested will appear as a straight line through the origin with the slope b and the fraction of output saved as a horizontal line. Equilibrium will appear as the point of intersection between the two lines. The equilibrating variable will appear as the abscissa of that point, also found algebraically by rearranging (53):

$$g_X = (1 - c)/b \tag{54}$$

from which we see that an economy otherwise equal but with twice the propensity to save $1 - c$ will have twice the growth rate g_X of output. In this sense the adjustment lies on the investment side. Saving is a Good Thing!

4. Robinson and Kaldor

In the Robinson-Kaldor growth model the fraction of output invested was bg_S. That fraction was autonomous, because the capital coefficient b was a parameter, and the rate of growth g_S of physical capital stock was either a parameter itself (Robinson) or equal to one (Kaldor). The adjustment of the savings fraction to an autonomous investment fraction had to be brought about by adjustment in some other equilibrating variable. Which one? Since wages were never saved and entrepreneurs had the parametric propensity to save real profits $1 - c_Z$, the fraction of output saved would be $(1 - c_Z)Z/Y$, and the only way left for the savings fraction to adjust was for the profits share Z/Y to adjust. Again, in equilibrium the fraction of output invested would equal the fraction of it saved or:

$$bg_S = (1 - c_Z)Z/Y \tag{55}$$

where the only variable is the equilibrating one, the profits share Z/Y. Consequently, as shown in the lower left-hand case of figure V-5, the fraction of output invested will appear as a horizontal line and the fraction of output saved as a straight line through the origin with the slope $1 - c_Z$. Equilibrium will appear as the point of intersection between the two lines. The equilibrating variable will appear as the abscissa of that point, also found algebraically by rearranging (55):

$$Z/Y = bg_S/(1 - c_Z) \tag{56}$$

from which we see that an economy otherwise equal but with twice the propensity to save real profits $1 - c_Z$ will have half the profits share Z/Y. In this sense the adjustment lies on the savings side.

5.   Tinbergen and Solow

Tinbergen (1942) and Solow (1956) unfroze the capital coefficient frozen by Harrod, Robinson, and Kaldor.

We shall devote our chapter 15 to the Tinbergen-Solow growth model. Here the fraction of output invested would be $g_S S/X$, where the rate of growth g_S is determined by supply-side parameters and the capital coefficient S/X, now unfrozen, has become the equilibrating variable. The fraction of output saved would be $1 - c$, where, as in the Harrod model, the overall propensity to consume c is a parameter. Again, in equilibrium the fraction of output invested would equal the fraction of it saved or:

$$g_S S/X = 1 - c \tag{57}$$

where the only variable is the equilibrating one, the capital coefficient S/X. Consequently, as shown in the lower right-hand case of figure V-5, the fraction of output invested will appear as a straight line through the origin with the slope g_S and the fraction of output saved as a horizontal line. Equilibrium will appear as the point of intersection between the two lines. The equilibrating variable will appear as the abscissa of that point, also found algebraically by rearranging (57):

$$S/X = (1 - c)/g_S \tag{58}$$

from which we see that an economy otherwise equal but with twice the propensity to save $1 - c$ will have twice the capital coefficient S/X. In this sense the adjustment lies on the investment side.

XVIII. LONG-RUN INFLATION EQUILIBRIUM: FRIEDMAN

Macroeconomic theory has made little use of the neoclassical, or any other, growth model. Dealing with short-run unemployment, Keynesians obviously have had no use for a long-run full-employment model. The monetarists, too, have ignored it, and perhaps they should not have.

Friedman wished to include the rate of inflation among his equilibrating variables and to demonstrate the crowding-out effect of a fiscal deficit. Any model admitting inflation will contain a derivative of price with respect to time, hence be intrinsically dynamic. Any model admitting inflation as an equilibrating variable will immediately have two additional ones, i.e., the nominal and the real rate of interest—as perhaps Turgot and certainly Fisher taught us. Consequently, a Friedman model must be a dynamic, two-interest-rates model.

A Friedman model must also be a long-run model. For one thing, to Friedman permanent rather than transitory income determines consumption. For another thing, to Friedman monetary policy cannot peg the rate of unemployment for more than very limited periods. Consequently, a monetarist model must dismiss and go beyond such limited periods and become a long-run model.

Such a long-run, dynamic, two-interest-rates model is clearly incompatible with the short-run, static, one-interest-rate *IS-LM* framework offered by Friedman himself (1970) as his "theoretical framework". We must do better. A good beginning would be Solow's (1956) neoclassical growth model, in which capital stock is the result of accumulated savings under an autonomously given propensity to consume. But Solow made no attempt to optimize capital stock. If we are to simulate Friedman's crowding-out we must make such an attempt. Optimizing capital stock would mean maximizing its present net worth. Here the rate of interest used in discounting the future cash flows should reflect the cost of capital faced by the firm, and that cost would be affected by taxation, as suggested by Feldstein (1976).

So we know what to do in chapter 16: we must add bonds, government, inflation, interest rates, money, and taxation to the neoclassical growth model. For the sake of the argument, we shall accept, first, a natural rate of unemployment insensitive in the long run to monetary policy, second, rational expectations in the form of self-fulfilling ones and, third, the policy rule that the money and bond supplies display steady-

state growth fully foreseen by private parties. With those three acceptances, we shall see whether Friedman's conclusions will hold.

XIX. FROM MONETARISM TO NEW CLASSICAL ECONOMICS

1. The "Natural" Rate of Unemployment

In the short run, physical capital stock may be considered frozen and
labor employed a variable. Under profit maximization and pure competition, labor employed will equalize the real wage rate and physical marginal productivity of labor. The demand curve for labor, in other words,
is labor's physical marginal productivity curve. Let the supply of labor,
too, be a function of the real wage rate. A real wage rate may be too high
in the sense that at that rate supply exceeds demand. But such unemployment may be acceptable to labor in the sense that it will not push down the
real wage rate. Friedman (1968) and Phelps (1970) defined a "natural"
rate of unemployment below which excess demand for labor would push
the real wage rate up and above which excess supply would push it down.
In that case the actual short-run rate of unemployment can differ from
the natural one only if the actual price of goods differs from what labor
expected.

For example, let an unforeseen acceleration of the money supply
stimulate demand and let goods prices respond more readily than does the
money wage rate. Consequently, at first there will be a deceleration of the
real wage rate experienced by entrepreneurs but not yet expected by labor.
That discrepancy will at first reduce the rate of unemployment below its
natural rate. Vice versa, let an unforeseen deceleration of the money supply discourage demand. Now, at first there will be an acceleration of the
real wage rate experienced by entrepreneurs but not yet expected by labor.
That discrepancy will at first raise the rate of unemployment above its
natural rate.

2. The "Natural" Supply of Goods

With short-run physical capital stock still considered frozen, physical output is uniquely determined by labor employed. Call the physical
output resulting at the natural rate of unemployment the "natural" supply of goods. In that case the actual short-run supply of goods can differ
from the natural one only if the actual price of goods differs from what
labor expected. As before, an unforeseen acceleration of the money supply would stimulate demand and lead to a rate of unemployment below its
natural rate and hence to a supply of goods above its natural rate. Vice
versa, an unforeseen deceleration of the money supply would discourage

demand and lead to a rate of unemployment above its natural rate and hence to a supply of goods below its natural rate.

In the monetarist view as expressed by Friedman such temporary discrepancies might well occur in the short run. In the new classical view they would not even occur in the short run. Such impotence of monetary policy was referred to as short-run neutrality of money, and the key to it was rational expectations.

3. Adaptive versus Rational Expectations

Adaptive expectations are partial and backward-looking: expectations of the future value of a variable are based solely upon the past performance of that variable. Systematic forecasting errors may occur, become embedded in actual performance, be given a new lease of life, and stay in the system for a long time. Meanwhile lucrative opportunities would remain open to those who knew better.

Rational expectations, first formulated by Muth (1961), are general and forward-looking: some agents are assumed to be smart enough to act as if they knew the entire structure of the model and formed their expectations accordingly. The survival of the fittest would be counted on to eliminate agents less smart from the market. If forecasting errors are admitted, they are assumed to be merely random.

A decade later the new classical economists such as Lucas (1972), Sargent (1973), and Sargent-Wallace (1975) assumed such rational expectations to hold even in the short run and hence rule out even the discrepancies described above between the actual and natural rates of unemployment and between the actual and natural supplies of goods.

4. The Long Run

The short run considered by monetarists and new classical economists is short enough to allow physical capital stock to be considered frozen.

A run long enough to consider physical capital stock a variable would be a very different matter. A long-run model must optimize physical capital stock as well as labor employed. Our long-run inflation model of chapter 16 will do that, find optimized physical capital stock to be a function of the after-tax real rate of interest, and in turn find that rate to be sensitive to monetary and fiscal policy. We must add our long-run doubts, then, to Begg's (1982) and Stein's (1982) short-run doubts about the neutrality of monetary and fiscal policy.

REFERENCES

A. Ando and F. Modigliani, "The 'Life Cycle' Hypothesis of Saving: Aggregate Implications and Tests," *Amer. Econ. Rev.*, Mar. 1963, *53*, 55-84.

K. J. Arrow and G. Debreu, "Existence of an Equilibrium for a Competitive Economy," *Econometrica*, July 1954, *22*, 265-290.

K. J. Arrow and M. Hoffenberg, *A Time Series Analysis of Interindustry Demands*, Amsterdam, 1959.

K. J. Arrow and L. Hurwicz, "On the Stability of the Competitive Economy," *Econometrica*, Oct. 1958, *26*, 522-552.

J. Barth, A. Kraft, and J. Kraft, "Estimation of the Liquidity Trap Using Spline Functions," *Rev. Econ. Stat.*, May 1976, *58*, 218-222.

D. K. H. Begg, *The Rational Expectations Revolution in Macroeconomics*, Baltimore, 1982.

J. Bertrand, "Théorie mathématique de la richesse sociale," *Journal des savants*, Sep. 1883, 499-508.

A. S. Blinder and R. M. Solow, "Analytical Foundations of Fiscal Policy," *The Economics of Public Finance*, Washington, D.C. 1974.

A. A. Boraiko, "The Chip," *National Geographic*, Oct. 1982, *162*, 421-456.

A. L. Bowley, *The Mathematical Groundwork of Economics*, Oxford, 1924.

H. Brems, "Input-Output Coefficients as Measures of Product Quality," *Amer. Econ. Rev.*, Mar. 1957, *47*, 105-118.

———, *Inflation, Interest, and Growth*, Lexington, Mass., 1980.

M. Bronfenbrenner and T. Mayer, "Liquidity Functions in the American Economy," *Econometrica*, Oct. 1960, *28*, 810-834.

G. Cassel, *Theoretische Sozialökonomie*, Leipzig, 1918, translated as *The Theory of Social Economy* by S. L. Barron, New York, 1932.

M. Casson, *Economics of Unemployment*, Cambridge, Mass., 1984.

E. H. Chamberlin, "Duopoly: Value Where Sellers Are Few," *Quart. J. Econ.*, Nov. 1929, *44*, 63-100.

———, *The Theory of Monopolistic Competition*, Cambridge, Mass., 1933, sixth ed. 1948.

———, "The Product as an Economic Variable," *Quart. J. Econ.*, Feb. 1953, *67*, 1-29.

C. F. Christ, "A Short-Run Aggregate-Demand Model of the Interdependence and Effects of Monetary and Fiscal Policies with Keynesian and Classical Interest Elasticities," *Amer. Econ. Rev.*, May 1967, *57*, 434-443.

———, "A Model of Monetary and Fiscal Policy Effects on the Money Stock, Price Level, and Real Output," *J. Money, Credit, Banking*, Nov. 1969, *4*, 683-705.

R. Clower, "Reflections on the Keynesian Perplex," *Zeitschrift für Nationalökonomie*, 1975, *35*, 1-24.

A. A. Cournot, *Recherches sur les principes mathématiques de la théorie des richesses*, Paris, 1838, translated as *Researches into the Mathematical Principles of the Theory of Wealth* by N. T. Bacon, New York, 1927.

G. B. Dantzig, *A Procedure for Maximizing a Linear Function Subject to Linear*

Inequalities, memorandum by Headquarters, U.S. Air Force, Controller, Washington, D.C., 1948.

————, "Maximization of a Linear Function of Variables Subject to Linear Inequalities," in T. C. Koopmans (ed.), *Activity Analysis of Production and Allocation*, New York, 1951, 339-347.

G. Debreu, *Theory of Value: An Axiomatic Analysis of Economic Equilibrium*, New Haven and London, 1959.

F. F. De Leeuw and E. M. Gramlich, "The Federal Reserve-M.I.T. Model," *Federal Reserve Bulletin*, June 1969.

R. Dorfman, *Application of Linear Programming to the Theory of the Firm Including an Analysis of Monopolistic Firms by Non-Linear Programming*, Berkeley, 1951.

————, "Wassily Leontief's Contribution to Economics," *The Swedish Journal of Economics*, Dec. 1973, *75*, 430-449.

R. Dorfman, P. A. Samuelson, and R. M. Solow, *Linear Programming and Economic Analysis*, New York, 1958.

R. Dorfman and P. O. Steiner, "Optimal Advertising and Optimal Quality," *Amer. Econ. Rev.*, Dec. 1954, *44*, 826-836.

J. S. Duesenberry, G. Fromm, L. R. Klein, and E. Kuh, *The Brookings Quarterly Econometric Model of the United States*, Chicago, 1965.

O. Eckstein, *The Great Recession, With a Postscript on Stagflation*, Amsterdam, 1978.

O. Eckstein, E. W. Green, and A. Sinai, "The Data Resources Model: Uses, Structure, and Analysis of the U.S. Economy," *Int. Econ. Rev.*, Oct. 1974, *15*, 595-615.

M. K. Evans and L. R. Klein, *The Wharton Econometric Forecasting Model*, Philadelphia, 1967.

M. Feldstein, "Inflation, Income Taxes, and the Rate of Interest: A Theoretical Analysis," *Amer. Econ. Rev.*, Dec. 1976, *66*, 809-820.

I. Fisher, "Appreciation and Interest," *Publications of the American Economic Association*, Aug. 1896, *II*, 331-442.

J. Friedman, *Oligopoly Theory*, New York, 1983.

M. Friedman, "The Demand for Money: Some Theoretical and Empirical Results," *J. Polit. Econ.*, Aug. 1959, *67*, 327-351.

————, "Interest Rates and the Demand for Money," *J. Law Econ.*, Oct. 1966, *9*, 71-85.

————, "The Role of Monetary Policy," *Amer. Econ. Rev.*, Mar. 1968, *58*, 1-17.

————, "A Theoretical Framework for Monetary Analysis," *J. Polit. Econ.*, Mar.-Apr. 1970, *78*, 193-238.

————, "Comments on the Critics," *J. Polit. Econ.*, Sep.-Oct. 1972, *80*, 906-950.

C. W. Guillebaud, *The Economic Recovery of Germany from 1933 to the Incorporation of Austria in March 1938*, London, 1939.

G. Haberler, *Prosperity and Depression*, Geneva, 1937 and 1941.

A. H. Hansen, *Fiscal Policy and Business Cycles*, New York, 1941.

————, *Monetary Theory and Fiscal Policy*, New York, 1949.

————, *Business Cycles and National Income*, New York, 1951.

————, *A Guide to Keynes*, New York, 1953.

B. Hansen, *Finanspolitikens ekonomiska teori*, Stockholm, 1955, translated as *The Economic Theory of Fiscal Policy*, London, 1958, and Lund, 1967.

R. F. Harrod, *Towards a Dynamic Economics*, London, 1948.

F. A. von Hayek, *Preise und Produktion*, Vienna, 1931, translated as *Prices and Production*, London, 1931.

————, *Profits, Interest, and Investment*, London, 1939.

J. R. Hicks, "Mr. Keynes and the 'Classics': A Suggested Interpretation," *Econometrica*, Apr. 1937, *5*, 147-159.

————, *The Crisis in Keynesian Economics*, Oxford, 1974.

————, "A Sceptical Follower," *The Economist*, June 18, 1983, 17-19.

H. Hotelling, "Stability in Competition," *Econ. J.*, Mar. 1929, *39*, 41-57.

L. Johansen, "Soviet Mathematical Economics," *Econ. J.*, Sep. 1966, *76*, 593-601.

————, "L. V. Kantorovich's Contribution to Economics," *Scand. J. Econ.*, 1976, *78*, 61-80.

D. W. Jorgenson, "The Theory of Investment Behavior," in R. Ferber (ed.), *Determinants of Investment Behavior*, New York, 1967, 129-155.

N. Kaldor, "A Model of Economic Growth," *Econ. J.*, Dec. 1957, *67*, 591-624.

————, "Marginal Productivity and Macroeconomic Theories of Distribution," *Rev. Econ. Stud.*, 1966, *33*, 309-319.

L. V. Kantorovich, *Mathematicheskie metody organizatsii i planirovania proizodstva*, Leningrad, 1939, translated as "Mathematical Methods in the Organization and Planning of Production, *Management Science*, July 1960, *6*, 366-422.

J. M. Keynes, *A Treatise on Money* I-II, London, 1930.

————, *The General Theory of Employment, Interest, and Money*, London, 1936, translated as *Allgemeine Theorie der Beschäftigung, des Zinses und des Geldes*, Munich and Leipzig, 1936.

C. P. Kindleberger, *The World in Depression 1929-1939*, Berkeley, 1973.

L. R. Klein, *Economic Fluctuations in the United States: 1921-1944*, New York, 1950.

L. R. Klein and A. S. Goldberger, *An Econometric Model of the United States, 1929-1952*, Amsterdam, 1955.

T. C. Koopmans, *Exchange Ratios Between Cargoes on Various Routes*, memorandum by Combined Shipping Adjustment Board, Washington, D.C., 1942, reprinted in *Scientific Papers of Tjalling C. Koopmans*, Berlin, Heidelberg, and New York, 1970.

————, "Analysis of Production as an Efficient Combination of Activities," in T. C. Koopmans (ed.), *Activity Analysis of Production and Allocation*, Cowles Commission Monograph No. 13, New York, 1951, 33-97.

————, "Allocation of Resources and the Price System," in T. C. Koopmans, *Three Essays on the State of Economic Science*, New York, 1957.

J. J. Lambin, *Advertising, Competition, and Market Conduct in Oligopoly over Time*, Amsterdam, 1976.

J. M. Lauderdale, *An Inquiry into the Nature and Origin of Public Wealth and into the Means and Causes of Its Increase*, Edinburgh and London, 1804.

W. Leontief, *The Structure of American Economy, 1919-1929*, Cambridge, Mass., 1941, enlarged edition, New York, 1951.

――, "Econometrics," in H. S. Ellis (ed.), *A Survey of Contemporary Economics*, Philadelphia and Toronto, 1948.

――, "Static and Dynamic Theory," in W. Leontief (ed.), *Studies in the Structure of the American Economy*, New York, 1953.

E. Lindahl, *Penningpolitikens medel*, Malmö, 1930, partially translated as Part Two of *Studies in the Theory of Money and Capital*, London, 1939.

R. E. Lucas, Jr., "Expectations and the Neutrality of Money," *J. Econ. Theory*, Apr. 1972, *4*, 103-124.

F. Machlup, "Friedrich von Hayek's Contribution to Economics," *Scand. J. Econ.*, 1974, *76*, 498-531.

L. W. McKenzie, "On the Existence of General Equilibrium for a Competitive Market," *Econometrica*, Jan. 1959, *27*, 54-71.

J. F. Muth, "Rational Expectations and the Theory of Price Movements," *Econometrica*, July 1961, *29*, 315-335.

M. Nerlove and K. J. Arrow, "Optimal Advertising Policy under Dynamic Conditions," *Economica*, May 1962, *29*, 129-142.

J. von Neumann, "Zur Theorie der Gesellschaftsspiele," *Mathematische Annalen*, 1928, *100*, 295-320, reprinted in J. von Neumann, *Collected Works*, VI., New York, 1963.

――, "Ueber ein ökonomisches Gleichungssystem und eine Verallgemeinerung des Brouwerschen Fixpunktsatzes," *Ergebnisse eines mathematischen Kolloquiums*, 8, Leipzig and Vienna, 1937, 73-83; translated by G. Morgenstern (Morton) in W. J. Baumol and S. M. Goldfeld (eds.), *Precursors in Mathematical Economics: An Anthology*, London, 1968, 296-306.

J. von Neumann and O. Morgenstern, *Theory of Games and Economic Behavior*, Princeton, 1944, second, corrected edition, 1947.

B. Ohlin, *Penningpolitik, offentliga arbeten, subventioner och tullar som medel mot arbetslöshet* (Monetary policy, public works, subsidies, and tariffs as measures against unemployment), Unemployment Report II, 4, Stockholm, 1934.

D. J. Ott and A. Ott, "Budget Balance and Equilibrium Income," *J. Finance*, Mar. 1965, *20*, 71-77.

D. Patinkin, *Money, Interest, and Prices*, Evanston, Ill., and White Plains, N.Y., 1956.

――, "Keynes' Monetary Thought: A Study of Its Development," *Hist. Polit. Econ.*, Spring 1976, *8*, 1-150.

E. S. Phelps, "Phillips Curves, Expectations of Inflation, and Optimal Unemployment over Time," *Economica*, Aug. 1967, *34*, 254-281.

――, "Money Wage Dynamics and Labor Market Equilibrium," in E. S. Phelps (ed.), *The Microeconomic Foundations of Employment and Inflation Theory*, New York, 1970.

A. W. Phillips, "The Relation between Unemployment and the Rate of Change of Money Wage Rates in the United Kingdom, 1861-1957," *Economica*, Nov. 1958, *25*, 283-299.

A. C. Pigou, "The Classical Stationary State," *Econ. J.*, Dec. 1943, *53*, 343-351.

――, *Lapses from Full Employment*, London, 1945.

J. Robinson, *The Economics of Imperfect Competition*, London, 1933.

———, *The Accumulation of Capital*, London, 1956.

P. A. Samuelson, "A Note on the Pure Theory of Consumer's Behavior," *Economica*, Feb. 1938, *5*, 61-71.

———, "Interactions Between the Multiplier Analysis and the Principle of Acceleration," *Rev. Econ. Stat.* May 1939, *21*, 75-78.

———, *Foundations of Economic Analysis*, Cambridge, Mass., 1947.

———, "Sympathy from the Other Cambridge," *The Economist*, June 25, 1983, 19-21.

T. J. Sargent, "Rational Expectations, the Real Rate of Interest, and the Natural Rate of Unemployment," *Brookings Papers on Economic Activity*, 1973, 429-472.

T. J. Sargent and N. Wallace, "'Rational' Expectations, the Optimal Monetary Instrument, and the Optimal Money Supply Rule," *J. Polit. Econ.*, Apr. 1975, *83*, 241-254.

J.-B. Say, *Traité d'économie politique*, Paris, 1803, translated as *A Treatise on Political Economy* by C. R. Prinsep, Philadelphia, 1830.

H. H. G. Schacht, *Confessions of "The Old Wizard,"* Boston, 1956.

K. Schlesinger, "Ueber die Produktionsgleichungen der ökonomischen Wertlehre," *Ergebnisse eines mathematischen Kolloquiums*, 6, Leipzig and Vienna, 1935, 10-11, translated as "On the Production Equations of Economic Value Theory" by W. J. Baumol in W. J. Baumol and S. M. Goldfeld (eds.), *Precursors in Mathematical Economics: An Anthology*, London, 1968, 278-280.

J. A. Schumpeter, review of *General Theory*, *J. Amer. Statist. Assoc.*, Dec. 1936, *31*, 791-795.

———, *History of Economic Analysis*, New York, 1954.

M. Shubik, *Strategy and Market Structure—Competition, Oligopoly, and the Theory of Games*, New York, 1959.

A. Smith, *An Inquiry into the Nature and Causes of the Wealth of Nations*, Edinburgh, 1776, "new" edition, Glasgow, 1805.

A. Smithies, "Optimum Location in Spatial Competition," *J. Polit. Econ.*, June 1941, *49*, 423-439.

R. M. Solow, "A Contribution to the Theory of Economic Growth," *Quart. J. Econ.*, Feb. 1956, *70*, 65-94.

P. Sraffa, "The Laws of Returns under Competitive Conditions," *Econ. J.*, Dec. 1926, *36*, 535-550.

H. von Stackelberg, *Marktform und Gleichgewicht*, Vienna and Berlin, 1934.

———, "Theorie der Vertriebspolitik und der Qualitätsvariation," *Schmollers Jahrbuch*, 1939, *63*, 43-85.

J. L. Stein, *Monetarist, Keynesian, and New Classical Economics*, New York, 1982.

L. G. Telser, "Advertising and Cigarettes," *J. Polit. Econ.*, Oct. 1962, *70*, 471-499.

J. Tinbergen, *Statistical Test of Business-Cycle Theories, I. A Method and Its Application to Investment Activities; II. Business Cycles in the United States of America, 1919-1932*, Geneva, 1939.

———, "Zur Theorie der langfristigen Wirtschaftsentwicklung," *Weltw. Ar-*

chiv, May 1942, *55*, 511-549, translated in L. H. Klaassen, L. M. Koyck, and H. J. Witteveen (eds.), *Jan Tinbergen, Selected Papers*, Amsterdam, 1959.

J. Tobin and W. Buiter, "Long-Run Effects of Fiscal and Monetary Policy on Aggregate Demand," in J. L. Stein (ed.), *Monetarism. Studies in Monetary Economics 1*, Amsterdam, 1976.

A. R. J. Turgot, "Réflexions sur la formation et la distribution des richesses," *Ephémérides du citoyen*, Nov. 1769-Jan. 1770, reprinted in E. Daire (ed.), *Oeuvres de Turgot*, Paris, 1844, translated as *Reflections on the Formation and the Distribution of Riches*, New York, 1922.

S. J. Turnovsky, *Macroeconomic Analysis and Stabilization Policy*, Cambridge, 1977.

————, "Macroeconomic Dynamics and Growth in a Monetary Economy," *J. Money, Credit, Banking*, Feb. 1978, *10*, 1-26.

————, "Monetary and Fiscal Policy in a Long-Run Macroeconomic Model," *Econ. Record*, June 1980, *56*, 158-170.

U.S. Department of Commerce, "Nominal Gross National Product—1923-1951, The National Income and Product Accounts of the United States, Statistical Tables, 1929-76," *Business Statistics 1982*, Washington, D.C., 1982.

U.S. Government Printing Office, "Federal Budget Surplus or Deficit 1923-1982," *Budget of the United States Government, Fiscal Year 1983*, Washington, D.C., 1983.

H. Uzawa, "On a Two-Sector Model of Economic Growth," I-II, *Rev. Econ. Stud.*, Oct. 1961, *29*, 40-47, and June 1963, *30*, 105-118.

A. Wald, "Ueber die eindeutige positive Lösbarkeit der neuen Produktionsgleichungen," *Ergebnisse eines mathematischen Kolloquiums*, 6, Leipzig and Vienna, 1935, 12-18, translated as "On the Unique Non-Negative Solvability of the New Production Equations" by W. J. Baumol in W. J. Baumol and S. M. Goldfeld (eds.), *Precursors in Mathematical Economics: An Anthology*, London, 1968, 281-288.

————, "Ueber die Produktionsgleichungen der ökonomischen Wertlehre," *Ergebnisse eines mathematischen Kolloquiums*, 7, Leipzig and Vienna, 1936, 1-6, translated as "On the Production Equations of Economic Value Theory" by W. J. Baumol in W. J. Baumol and S. M. Goldfeld (eds.), *Precursors in Mathematical Economics: An Anthology*, London, 1968, 289-293.

————, "Ueber einige Gleichungssysteme der mathematischen Oekonomie," *Zeitschrift für Nationalökonomie*, 5, 1936, 7, 637-670, translated as "On Some Systems of Equations of Mathematical Economics," by O. Eckstein, *Econometrica*, Oct. 1951, *19*, 368-403.

L. Walras, *Eléments d'économie politique pure*, Lausanne, Paris, and Basle, 1874-1877, translated as *Elements of Pure Economics or the Theory of Social Wealth* by W. Jaffé, Homewood, Ill., 1954.

K. F. Weaver and staff, "Energy," *National Geographic*, Feb. 1981, *159*, 1-114.

E. R. Weintraub, "On the Existence of a Competitive Equilibrium: 1930-1954," *J. Econ. Lit.*, Mar. 1983, *21*, 1-39.

L. Werin, "Tjalling Koopmans' Contribution to Economics," *Scand. J. Econ.*, 1976, *78*, 81-93.

K. Wicksell, *Ueber Wert, Kapital und Rente*, Jena, 1893, translated as *Value, Capital and Rent* by S. H. Frohwein, London, 1954.

————, *Geldzins und Güterpreise*, Jena, 1898, translated as *Interest and Prices* by R. F. Kahn with an introduction by Bertil Ohlin, published on behalf of the Royal Economic Society, London, 1936.

F. Zeuthen, *Den økonomiske Fordeling*, Copenhagen, 1928.

————, "Mellem Konkurrence og Monopol," *Nationaløkonomisk Tidsskrift*, 1929, *67*, 265-305.

————, *Problems of Monopoly and Economic Warfare*, with a preface by J. A. Schumpeter, London, 1930.

————, "Das Prinzip der Knappheit, technische Kombination und ökonomische Qualität," *Zeitschrift für Nationalökonomie*, *1*, 1932-1933, *4*, 1-24.

CHAPTER 9   Unemployment Equilibrium, Monetary Policy

KEYNES (1883-1946)

> *No man has hired us*
> *With pocketed hands*
> *And lowered faces*
> *We stand about in open places*
> T. S. Eliot, Choruses from "The Rock" (1952: 99)

I. INTRODUCTION

1. *Keynes's Problem*

In neoclassical theory, which Keynes had taught in its Marshallian form, all markets clear. Writing at the time of unemployment rates around one-fourth in Germany, the United Kingdom, and the United States, Keynes had to ask himself why the labor market didn't clear. And why was the only established form of public policy, monetary policy, so impotent?

2. *Keynes's Method*

Like Walras, Wieser, and Wicksell, Keynes separated industry from households but, like Wicksell, within a macroeconomic model. Since Wicksell, macroeconomics imagines an economy producing a single good whose physical output and price are well-defined variables expressible as single numbers. Keynes's one-good economy had three sectors, industry, households, and government, and two spheres, a real and a money sphere.

In the real sphere industry produced physical output of which it invested one part and sold the other to households earning an income equaling the money value of physical output. Part of that income was consumed, the rest saved. Government neither demanded physical output nor collected taxes, hence did not yet inhabit the real sphere: Hansen would bring it in.

In the money sphere industry and households demanded money to transact output and income and could choose to hold their assets as either money or bonds. Issuing money and bonds, government did inhabit the money sphere.

There was a threefold symmetry between Keynes's two spheres. First, in either sphere demand was composed of two parts, one a function of the level of output (the consumption function and the transaction-money function), the other a function of the rate of interest (the investment function and the liquidity-preference function). Second, the two functions whose independent variable was the level of output were linear, whereas the two functions whose independent variable was the rate of interest were nonlinear. Third, equality between supply and demand in either sphere jointly defined the equilibrating variables of the model, physical output and the rate of interest.

The three symmetries constituted an intimate interaction between the two spheres: both equilibrating variables were present in the behavior functions of either sphere, hence would both help satisfy *both* equilibrium conditions. Keynes himself did not always fully understand his own intimate interaction, as Patinkin (1976: 99) has pointed out. Keynes's tradition was Marshallian partial equilibrium, not Walrasian general equilibrium.

3.   *Our Own Restatement*

Restating Keynes's system as a simple system of seven equations solved for physical output will simulate the intimate interaction between his two spheres. Making two of those equations quadratic will dramatically simulate his policy conclusion that in certain circumstances monetary policy will be impotent. Making the two equations quadratic will give us a quartic in physical output. We shall solve it and then find the sensitivities of physical output to four important parameters of the system.

Let the notation of our restatement be as follows.

4.   *Variables*

C ≡ physical consumption
D_A ≡ demand for money for asset-holding purposes
D_T ≡ demand for money for transactions purposes
I ≡ physical investment
r ≡ rate of interest
X ≡ physical output
Y ≡ money national income

5.   *Parameters*

A ≡ autonomous consumption
c ≡ marginal propensity to consume

f ≡ parameter measuring the size of the investment ellipse
j ≡ propensity to hold transaction money
k ≡ a parameter of the investment ellipse
M ≡ supply of money
m ≡ a parameter of the liquidity-preference hyperbola
n ≡ a parameter of the liquidity-preference hyperbola
P ≡ price of goods and services

II.   THE MODEL

1.   Real-Sphere Behavior Equations

Let physical consumption be the linear function of physical output

$$C = A + cX \tag{1}$$

where $A > 0$ and $0 < c < 1$.

Hansen (1951: 133) summarized much of the debate concerning the form of an investment function by saying that it "is fairly elastic with respect to the rate of interest at *high* interest rate levels, and is fairly inelastic within a rather wide range of interest rates at the *lower* levels." An ellipse

$$I = \sqrt{f - kr^2} \tag{2}$$

would have the property described by Hansen. Here f is a positive parameter measuring the size of the ellipse. We ignore the part of the ellipse lying outside the first quadrant and assume that $r < \sqrt{f/k}$, for otherwise investment could be a complex number.

2.   The Income-Output Identity

Money national income defined as the aggregate earnings arising from current production is identically equal to national product defined as the market value of physical output:

$$Y \equiv PX \tag{3}$$

3.   Money-Sphere Behavior Equations

Neither industry nor households can fully synchronize inflow and outflow, hence need transaction money. What do they want to transact? Ignore intermediate goods transacted among firms and old paintings, used cars, used houses, etc. transacted among households and simply make the transaction demand for money the linear and homogeneous function of money national income

$$D_T = jY \tag{4}$$

where j is a positive parameter representing the reciprocal of the velocity of circulation of transaction money.

Keynesian asset holders may hold their assets in only two forms, i.e., bonds or money. Define the interest rate as the bond yield. If the interest rate is high, it is because bond prices are low, hence may be expected to rise, and assets owners will prefer to hold bonds. If the interest rate is low, it is because bond prices are high, hence may be expected to fall, and asset owners will prefer to hold money. If all asset owners were of the same opinion on future bond prices, the demand for money would be L-shaped with one branch of the L parallel to the D_A-axis. And indeed, if all asset owners are of very nearly the same opinion, the branch will be very nearly parallel to the D_A-axis or, in Keynes's own words (1936: 172): "... whilst opinion about the future of the rate of interest may be so unanimous that a small change in present rates may cause a mass movement into cash." For the demand for money to be neither L-shaped nor very nearly L-shaped, "it is important that opinions should differ," Keynes added (1936: 172).

A hyperbola

$$D_A = m/(r - n) \tag{5}$$

would have the property described by Keynes and was found in early empirical work by Tobin (1947) and others. Here, m is a positive parameter measuring the mass of assets held. We assume that $r > n$, for otherwise D_A could be meaningless or negative. The asymptotes of the hyperbola (5) are the r-axis and a line parallel to the D_A-axis at a distance n from the latter. Our four behavior equations are shown in figure 9-1.

4. *Equilibrium Conditions*

No labor-market equilibrium would require the supply of labor to equal the demand for it. But a goods-market equilibrium would require the supply of goods to equal the demand for them:

$$X = C + I \tag{6}$$

Otherwise inventory would accumulate or be depleted. And a money-market equilibrium would require the supply of money to equal the demand for it:

$$M = D_A + D_T \tag{7}$$

Otherwise either asset owners would want to hold more money than was available, and in their attempts to get it they would be selling bonds,

FIGURE 9-1. Keynes's Four Behavior Equations

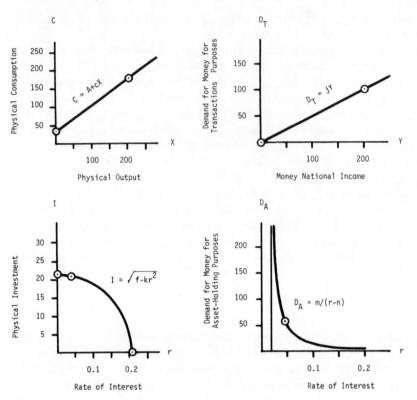

thereby depressing bond prices, raising the interest rate, and making money less attractive to hold. Or conversely, asset owners would want to hold less money than was available, and in their attempts to get rid of it they would be buying bonds, thereby raising bond prices, depressing the interest rate, and making money more attractive to hold.

III. SOLUTION

1. *Solution for Equilibrium Physical Output*

Solving for physical output X, the key variable, we obtain the quartic in X alone:

$$a_1 X^4 + a_2 X^3 + a_3 X^2 + a_4 X + a_5 = 0 \tag{8}$$

where

$$a_1 \equiv (1 - c)^2 j^2 P^2$$

$$a_2 \equiv -(1 - c)2jP[AjP + (1 - c)M]$$

$$a_3 \equiv (1 - c)M[4AjP + (1 - c)M] + j^2 P^2(A^2 - f + kn^2)$$

$$a_4 \equiv -2M[AM(1 - c) + (A^2 - f)jP] - 2jknP(m + nM)$$

$$a_5 \equiv (A^2 - f)M^2 + k(m + nM)^2$$

Let us add a bit of *Zeitgeist* to our Keynesian model by selecting the following set of values for our parameters:

$A = 30$	$j = 0.50$	$m = 1.16$
$c = 0.75$	$k = 10,000$	$n = 0.02$
$f = 457$	$M = 160$	$P = 1$

The behavior equations (1), (2), (4), and (5) will then appear as shown in figure 9-1, and our polynomial (8) will be

$$0.015625 X^4 - 13.75 X^3 + 4,111.75 X^2$$
$$- 455,752 X + 11,530,900 = 0 \qquad (9)$$

Of the four roots of the polynomial (9) only one lies within the domain acceptable for equations (2) and (5), i.e., the domain $n < r < \sqrt{f/k}$. That root is $X = 204$. Inserting it into our system (1) through (7) will give us real, positive, and unique equilibrium solutions for all variables:

$C = 183$	$I = 21$
$D_A = 58$	$r = 0.04$
$D_T = 102$	$X = Y = 204$

On each of the four curves shown in figure 9-1 a small circle indicates the location of these equilibrium solutions for the pair of variables entering it. Here is our *Zeitgeist*: our equilibrium solution $X = 204$ is roughly the U.S. national product measured in billions of 1972 dollars for the year 1933, a year for which Keynes's *General Theory* was presumably relevant.

2.   *Feasibility of Solution*

Nothing was said about inputs or a production function relating them to output. Consequently, an assumption would have to be made that our solution (8) for physical output is a feasible one, i.e., one requiring quantities of the (unspecified) inputs that are less than or equal to those available. Under this assumption, output is determined by aggregate demand alone. Demand creates its own supply!

IV. POLICY IMPLICATIONS

Let us vary each parameter A, c, f, and M in isolation, keeping the other three constant at the chosen values, and watch the effect of such isolated variations upon our key equilibrating variable, physical output X. Figure 9-2 shows our results. Each parameter is varied in both directions from the equilibrium point, again shown by a small circle. The scale of figure 9-2 is double-logarithmic—a useful visual aid, because it permits the elasticity of physical output with respect to each parameter A, c, f, and M to appear as the steepness of the curves.

The policy implications of figure 9-2 are clear: equilibrium physical output is the higher the higher any parameter A, c, f, or M. These results simulate the usual Keynesian emphasis upon the goods sphere and particularly the Keynesian emphasis upon the multiplier as derived from the marginal propensity to consume. In the money sphere the results of figure

FIGURE 9-2. Sensitivities of Physical Output to Four Parameters

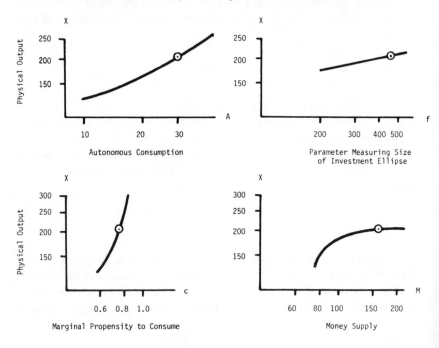

9-2 dramatically simulate the liquidity trap: physical output is extremely sensitive to the money supply if money is tight but extremely insensitive if money is easy. After 1952, monetary policy was supposed to, and did, check inflation. After 1932, monetary policy was supposed to, but didn't, check unemployment. This experience implies neither mystery nor irreversibility. All it implies is the strong curvature of the *X-M* curve in figure 9-2 or, in Samuelson's (1963) words:

> In buoyant times where interest rates are already high and credit already tight, monetary policy is quite potent enough to *both* expand and contract the system from its previous situation; in slack times when interest rates are near the floor and the system is swimming in liquidity, monetary policy is quite impotent with respect to contraction *and* expansion of the system from its previous level.

The strong curvature of the *X-M* curve in figure 9-2 is a result of our nonlinearities: owing to the low interest elasticity of the investment function (2) at low interest rates, it becomes increasingly difficult to encourage additional investment by depressing the interest rate. Owing to the high interest elasticity of the liquidity-preference function (5) at low interest rates it also becomes increasingly difficult to depress the interest rate by expanding the money supply.

V. STOCKS AND FLOWS

We saw three symmetries between the real sphere and the money sphere. But an important asymmetry was pointed out by Hicks [1956 (1965)]. In producing an equilibrium, one may choose physical quantity transacted as his equilibrating variable, which was what Keynes did in his goods sphere. The resulting equilibrium would be a flow equilibrium ensuring absence of inventory accumulation or depletion, but it would not necessarily be a stock equilibrium. The actual inventory and capital coefficients could differ from the desired ones, but in his goods sphere, Keynes ignored stock equilibrium.

Alternatively one may choose price as his equilibrating variable, which was what Keynes did in his money sphere. Here, the stock of bonds would at any moment be given, and the price of bonds would be determined by the willingness of the asset owners to hold bonds rather than money. Such a stock equilibrium would ignore the flows of addition to and subtraction from the stock of bonds, and Keynes ignored them by using a period of time so short that it would approximate a point of time.

Let us now see how Hansen opened the Keynesian model to fiscal policy.

REFERENCES

T. S. Eliot, *The Complete Poems and Plays 1909-1950*, New York, 1952.

A. H. Hansen, *Business Cycles and National Income*, New York, 1951.

J. R. Hicks, "Methods of Dynamic Analysis," *25 Essays in Honour of Erik Lindahl, 21 November 1956*, Stockholm, 1956, 139-151, further elaborated in *Capital and Growth*, Oxford, 1965, ch. 8.

J. M. Keynes, *The General Theory of Employment, Interest, and Money*, London, 1936.

D. Patinkin, "Keynes' Monetary Thought: A Study of Its Development," *Hist. Polit. Econ.*, Spring 1976, *8*, 1-150.

P. A. Samuelson, "Reflections on Central Banking," *Nat. Banking Rev.*, Sep. 1963, *1*, 15-28.

J. A. Schumpeter, *Ten Great Economists from Marx to Keynes*, New York, 1951.

J. Tobin, "Liquidity Preference and Monetary Policy," *Rev. Econ. Stat.*, May 1947, *29*, 124-131.

CHAPTER 10 Unemployment Equilibrium, Fiscal Policy

HANSEN (1887-1975)

. . . One reason to explain Hansen's importance in carrying the post-1936 ball is that America, rather than Britain, was the natural place where the Keynesian model applied: the United States was largely a closed, continental economy with an undervalued dollar that gave ample scope for autonomous macroeconomic policies; Hansen's first Harvard years of the late 1930's, when gold was flowing into this country and . . . was providing a massive controlled experiment to show the weak elasticity responses to normal easing of credit, that was the era par excellence when an approximation to Keynes's liquidity trap prevailed.

Samuelson (1976: 26)

I. INTRODUCTION

1. *Hansen's Problem*

On fiscal policy Keynes (1929), (1933) had addressed the general public. His professional address (1936), however, had no fiscal policy in it and merely tried to show the impotence of monetary policy: at a low rate of interest the demand for money was so sensitive to the rate of interest, and investment demand so insensitive to it, that the rate of interest could play no role as an equilibrating variable.

But if at a low rate of interest monetary policy was impotent, how could unemployment be reduced? This was Hansen's problem, and he (1941), (1951) solved it by adding government, taxes, and the fiscal deficit to a Keynesian model with the rate of interest left out as an equilibrating variable.

2. *Hansen's Method*

Any model of fiscal policy must deal with three magnitudes, i.e., physical government purchase of goods and services, the fiscal deficit, and the tax rate. All three cannot be parameters at the same time, or government could decide to buy all it cared for at low tax rates, yet run a fiscal surplus. A choice will have to be made: the government can fix two of the three magnitudes as parameters and let the economy determine the third as a variable. Which two? There are three different ways to select two elements from three, which gives us three alternative priority patterns. Either the government fixes government demand and fiscal deficit and lets the economy determine the necessary tax rate. Or the government fixes fiscal deficit and tax rate and lets the economy determine how much the government can afford to buy. But how can government fix the fiscal deficit? To the practical Hansen only the third priority pattern remained, i.e., the government fixes government demand and the tax rate and lets the economy determine what the fiscal deficit will be.

3. Our Own Restatement

Hansen's exposition used lucid English accompanied by variations of the celebrated 45° diagram showing an unemployment equilibrium as the point of intersection between an aggregate demand curve and a 45° line. We shall use simple algebra and calculus to derive his multipliers explicitly, and let our notation be as follows.

4. Variables

$C \equiv$ physical consumption
$d \equiv$ fiscal deficit
$R \equiv$ government net receipts
$X \equiv$ physical output
$Y \equiv$ money national income
$y \equiv$ money disposable income

5. Parameters

$A \equiv$ autonomous consumption
$c \equiv$ marginal propensity to consume real disposable income
$G \equiv$ physical government purchase of goods and services
$I \equiv$ physical investment
$P \equiv$ price of goods and services
$T \equiv$ tax rate

II. THE MODEL

Following an early Hansen, we treat investment as autonomous and leave out the rate of interest as a variable. Consider a one-good economy with industry, households, and government in it.

Money national income defined as the aggregate earnings arising from current production is identically equal to national product defined as the market value of physical output:

$$Y \equiv PX \tag{1}$$

As the mercantilists had done, ignore the government interest bill and define disposable income as money national income *minus* government net receipts:

$$y \equiv Y - R \tag{2}$$

Let consumption be a function of real disposable income:

$$C = A + cy/P \tag{3}$$

where $0 < c < 1$.

In Western tradition, as developed from the English Magna Carta of 1215, the Swedish Magna Carta at Uppsala of 1319, and the American Revolution of 1776, taxes are collected according to statute, and statute defines the tax base and the tax rate. As a good first approximation let government net receipts be in proportion to money national income:

$$R = TY \tag{4}$$

where $0 < T < 1$.

Again ignore the government interest bill and define the fiscal deficit as the money value of government purchase of goods and services *minus* government net receipts:

$$d \equiv GP - R \tag{5}$$

Goods-market equilibrium requires the supply of goods to equal the demand for them:

$$X = C + I + G \tag{6}$$

III. SOLUTIONS AND THEIR SENSITIVITIES TO POLICY INSTRUMENTS

1. *Solution for Physical Output*

To solve for our sole equilibrating variable, physical output X, insert (1) through (4) into (6) and find physical output

$$X = \frac{A + G + I}{1 - c(1 - T)} \tag{7}$$

As always in Keynesian models, our output solution (7) is assumed to be feasible: output requires quantities of the (unspecified) inputs that are less than or equal to those available. Under this assumption, output depends upon aggregate demand alone: demand creates its own supply! Under the assumptions made, our solution (7) will always be positive and unique.

Let us examine, first, the sensitivity of our output solution (7) to physical government purchase G:

$$\frac{\partial X}{\partial G} = \frac{1}{1 - c(1 - T)} \tag{8}$$

Under the assumptions made that $0 < c < 1$ and $0 < T < 1$, the derivative (8) will always be positive and larger than one: raising autonomous government demand will raise output or, in Hansen's own words (1951: 206, 487):

> In this case [in which the new government outlays are financed by borrowing] the consumption function is not depressed by any new taxes. Accordingly, the new government outlays . . . raise income . . . by the full multiplier process.

> What was urgently needed in 1939 was a powerful upward surge of autonomous investment reinforced by the multiplier and the accelerator. In the absence of this, an all-out government program was necessary. The peacetime needs of society in many areas— housing, resource development, public improvement projects, education, health—would have amply justified such an all-out effort. In the process we would have created real wealth and income for the entire population. Politically, it did not prove possible to do so; finally the necessities of war forced the expansion.

> Second, we examine the sensitivity of (7) to the tax rate T:

$$\frac{\partial X}{\partial T} = - \frac{c}{1 - c(1 - T)} X \tag{9}$$

where X stands for the output solution (7) above. Under the assumptions made, the derivative (9) is always negative: reducing the tax rate T will raise output or, in Hansen's own words (1951: 539): "One way to raise the consumption function would be to cut taxes."

2. Solution for Fiscal Deficit

Under the Hansen priority pattern the economy will determine what the fiscal deficit will be. Use (1), (4), and (5) to write it

$$d = GP - PTX \tag{10}$$

where X stands for the output solution (7) above. Let us examine the sensitivity of our fiscal-deficit solution (10) to manipulations of the same two fiscal parameters G and T.

Under the assumptions made, our solution (10) will always be unique. But nothing can be said about its sign. To see this, take the derivative

$$\frac{\partial d}{\partial G} = \frac{(1 - c)(1 - T)}{1 - c(1 - T)} P \tag{11}$$

Under the assumptions made, this derivative is always positive: a larger government demand means a larger deficit. A high enough government demand will make the deficit d positive. A low enough government demand will make it negative, i.e., will generate a surplus.

To see how the fiscal deficit depends upon the tax rate, take the derivative:

$$\frac{\partial d}{\partial T} = - \frac{1 - c}{1 - c(1 - T)} PX \tag{12}$$

where X stands for the output solution (7) above. Under the assumptions made the derivative (12) is always negative: a lower tax rate means a higher fiscal deficit. Notice that under Hansen's assumption that physical investment is autonomous, hence insensitive to the rate of interest, reducing the tax rate will never expand the tax base enough to raise the product TY of the two and thus reduce the deficit.

IV. CONCLUSION AND MODIFICATION

1. *Crowding-Out Impossible*

All solutions and multipliers were found under the assumption of an autonomous physical investment I. Being autonomous, physical investment had no give in it and could not possibly be crowded out. Since our system had only one equilibrating variable, i.e., physical output, the adjustment of saving to autonomous investment had to be brought about by adjustment of physical output alone. This is an extreme and special case that does not do full justice to Hansen.

2. *Hansen's Broader Views*

For one thing, Hansen was too much of a realist to deny that the demand for money may be less sensitive and investment demand more sensitive to the rate of interest than Keynes had imagined. A later Hansen (1953: 166) liked to think of the rate of interest as a second equilibrating variable: "The rate of interest and the national income are together mutually determined by [the consumption function; the marginal efficiency of investment schedule; the liquidity preference schedule], together with the quantity of money." If so, Hansen (1953: 104) agreed with Keynes (1936: 119) that crowding-out was possible: "The method of financing the policy [of public works] . . . may have the effect of increasing the rate of interest and so retarding investment in other directions."

For another, Hansen was too much of a realist to ignore the stock-flow distinction and its resulting dynamics. He saw physical investment (1951: ch. 11) as the change in desired physical capital stock and worked out the arithmetic of the interaction between the multiplier and the accelerator.

In all this, Hansen (1951: ix) was too well-read to ignore "the vast importance of the Continental development of the theory of investment demand and the role of investment in income formation—the work of Wicksell, Tugan-Baranowsky, Spiethoff, Schumpeter, and Cassel—a development largely overlooked by English-speaking economists until it became incorporated as a basic cornerstone of the Keynesian theory."

REFERENCES

A. H. Hansen, *Fiscal Policy and Business Cycles*, New York, 1941.
————, *Monetary Theory and Fiscal Policy*, New York, 1949.
————, *Business Cycles and National Income*, New York, 1951.
————, *A Guide to Keynes*, New York, 1953.
J. M. Keynes, *Can Lloyd George Do It?* London, 1929.
————, *The Means to Prosperity*, London, 1933.
————, *The General Theory of Employment, Interest, and Money*, London, 1936.
P. A. Samuelson, "Alvin Hansen as a Creative Economic Theorist," *Quart. J. Econ.*, Feb. 1976, *90*, 24-31.

CHAPTER 11 Existence of Dynamic General Equilibrium

VON NEUMANN (1903-1957)

> *The paper contains the first explicit statement, known to this author, of what has subsequently been called the activity analysis model of production. . . . Finally, . . . the paper contains the first rigorous, formal, and fully explicit model in nonaggregative capital theory known to this author.*
>
> Koopmans (1964: 356)

I. INTRODUCTION

1. *Von Neumann's Problem*

Walras [1874-1877 (1954: 43-44)] believed his general equilibrium to be determinate "in the sense that the number of equations entailed is equal to the number of unknowns." For the next sixty years, as pointed out by the younger Menger (1971: 50), Walras's belief remained unquestioned. Neither uniqueness nor feasibility was ever discussed.

On the European continent general equilibrium was best known in the form of Cassel's [1918 (1932: 32-41 and 152-155)] dynamized formulation of it, "the uniformly progressing state." Like Walras, Cassel had allowed for substitution in consumption but had failed to allow for it in production, had failed to treat the distinction between free and economic goods as endogenous, and had failed to prove the existence of a solution.

Such innocence lasted until the 1930s. In a new breakthrough John von Neumann [1937 (1945-1946)] first formulated a balanced and steady-state growth of a general economic equilibrium and proved the existence of a solution. The breakthrough did not lie in the subject matter, which was still allocation and relative price in general equilibrium using maxima and minima. Indeed, all economists can appreciate the simple beauty, yet high degree of generality, characterizing the von Neumann model. There is substitution in both production and consumption. The model "can handle capital goods without fuss and bother," as Dorfman-Samuelson-Solow (1958) put it. There is explicit optimization in the model: the solution weeds out all but the most profitable process or processes. There are free and economic goods, indeed the solution tells us which will be free and which economic.

299

2. Von Neumann's Method

What was new was method rather than subject matter. This time, the matter was in the hands of mathematicians from the very beginning, and the mathematics deployed was very different from the calculus deployed after 1870. The maxima and minima were handled without the use of any calculus at all. What von Neumann taught us was to use inequalities to formulate a primal and a dual problem. What von Neumann offered was a solution of his primal and dual problem displaying a saddle point.

3. Our Own Restatement

We must convey the flavor of von Neumann's method. But being one of the foremost mathematicians of the twentieth century, von Neumann used nonelementary algebra. Can the von Neumann model be solved by elementary algebra? If collapsed into two goods and two processes, it can, and let its notation be as follows.

4. Variables

g ≡ proportionate rate of growth
P_i ≡ price of ith good
p ≡ relative price
r ≡ rate of interest
u_i ≡ excess supply of ith good
v_j ≡ loss margin of jth process
X_j ≡ level of jth process
x ≡ relative process level

5. Parameters

a_{ij} ≡ input of ith good absorbed per unit of jth process level
b_{ij} ≡ output of ith good supplied per unit of jth process level

II. THE MODEL

1. Processes, Their Level, and Their Rate of Growth

A von Neumann good may be absorbed as an input as well as supplied as an output. A von Neumann process may have several inputs and several outputs, and its unit level may arbitrarily be defined as the unit of any one input or any one output per unit of time.

Let there be m goods and n processes. Operated at unit level, the jth process converts $a_{1j}, \ldots, a_{mj}$ units of the m goods absorbed as input into $b_{1j}, \ldots, b_{mj}$ units of the m goods supplied as output. The coefficients a_{ij} and b_{ij} are nonnegative technological parameters, but let each process have at least one positive a_{ij}, i.e., be absorbing at least one good as an input. And let each good have at least one positive b_{ij}, i.e., be supplied as an output in at least one process. The level of the jth process is the pure number X_j by which unit level should be multiplied in order to get actual input or output. The proportionate rate of growth g_j of the level of the jth process is defined

$$X_j(t + 1) \equiv [1 + g_j(t)] X_j(t) \tag{1}$$

A von Neumann process can handle joint supply of and demand for goods, indeed consists of such supply and demand. Yet the von Neumann model can handle substitution in both production and consumption. First, there is substitution in production, for although each process has parametric input coefficients a_{ij} and output coefficients b_{ij}, the same good may occur as an output in more than one process, hence may be produced in more than one way. Second, there is substitution in consumption, for labor is a good like any other, hence is reproducible: labor is simply the output of one or more processes whose inputs are consumers' goods. Although each such process has parametric input coefficients a_{ij} and output coefficients b_{ij}, labor may occur as an output in more than one process, hence may be produced in more than one way—by being fed, so to speak, alternative menus.

Does the von Neumann model have capital in it? It does, in fact it incorporates the time element of production in a particularly elegant way. In the von Neumann model all processes have a period of production of one time unit, but this is less restrictive than it sounds: as for circulating capital, if consumable wine has a period of production of two years, simply define two distinct processes and goods as follows. The first process absorbs zero-year-old wine and supplies one-year-old wine; the second absorbs one-year-old wine and supplies two-year-old wine. As for fixed capital, if the useful life of machines is two years, again define two distinct processes and goods. The first process absorbs zero-year-old machines and supplies one-year-old machines; the second absorbs one-year-old machines and supplies two-year-old machines!

Since a process absorbing its inputs at time t supplies its output at time $t + 1$, should the time coordinate of its level be that of its input or that of its output? Arbitrarily let it be the latter.

2.   *Excess Demand Must Be Nonpositive*

Let the level of the jth process be $X_j(t + 1)$. As a result, the input of the ith good absorbed at time t is $a_{ij}X_j(t + 1)$. Let the level of the jth process be $X_j(t)$. As a result, the output of the ith good supplied at time t is $b_{ij}X_j(t)$. We may then use (1) and write excess demand for the ith good in the jth process at time t as

$$a_{ij}X_j(t+1) - b_{ij}X_j(t) = \{a_{ij}[1 + g_j(t)] - b_{ij}\}X_j(t)$$

which will be positive, zero, or negative as the brace of the right-hand side is positive, zero, or negative. Now some processes may have positive, some zero, and some negative excess demand for the ith good. But feasibility requires overall excess demand to be nonpositive. The sum of all inputs of the ith good absorbed in all processes must be smaller than or equal to the sum of all outputs of it supplied in all processes:

$$a_{i1}X_1(t+1) + \cdots + a_{in}X_n(t+1)$$

$$\leq b_{i1}X_1(t) + \cdots + b_{in}X_n(t) \qquad (2)$$

where $i = 1, \ldots, m$. If for the ith good the less-than sign applies, that good at time t is a free good having a zero price: $P_i(t) = 0$. Rule out the uninteresting case that all goods are free and assume that at least one is not, i.e., that in the system (2) at least one equality sign applies.

3. *Profits Must Be Nonpositive*

At time $t + 1$ let the jth process be operated at unit level. The inputs absorbed at time t at unit level are a_{ij}, where $i = 1, \ldots, m$. Such inputs are purchased at the prices $P_i(t)$. Hence the input costs at unit level are $a_{ij}P_i(t)$ and their sum is $a_{1j}P_1(t) + \cdots + a_{mj}P_m(t)$. The outputs supplied at time $t + 1$ at unit level are b_{ij}. Such outputs are sold at prices $P_i(t + 1)$. Hence the revenues at unit level are $b_{ij}P_i(t + 1)$, and their sum is $b_{1j}P_1(t + 1) + \cdots + b_{mj}P_m(t + 1)$.

Now under pure competition and freedom of entry and exit, profits must be nonpositive, hence for the jth process the sum of all input cost at time t with interest added at the rate r must be greater than or equal to the sum of all revenue at time $t + 1$:

$$[1 + r(t)][a_{1j}P_1(t) + \cdots + a_{mj}P_m(t)]$$

$$\geq b_{1j}P_1(t + 1) + \cdots + b_{mj}P_m(t + 1) \qquad (3)$$

where $j = 1, \ldots, n$. If for the jth process the greater-than sign applies, that process at time $t + 1$ is a money-losing one to be operated at zero level: $X_j(t + 1) = 0$. Rule out the uninteresting case that all processes are money-losing ones and assume that at least one is not, i.e., that in the system (3) at least one equality sign applies.

4. *Equilibrium*

Cassel had thought of equilibrium growth as balanced steady-state growth of all physical outputs. Von Neumann thought of equilibrium growth as balanced steady-state growth of all process levels. Balanced growth of process levels means that the proportionate rates of growth of all process levels are equal:

$$g_1(t) = \cdots = g_n(t) \tag{4}$$

Steady-state growth of process levels means that the proportionate rates of growth of all process levels are stationary:

$$g_j(t + 1) = g_j(t) \tag{5}$$

where $j = 1, \ldots, n$.

Like Cassel, von Neumann also required the rate of interest and all prices to be stationary:

$$r(t + 1) = r(t) \tag{6}$$

$$P_i(t + 1) = P_i(t) \tag{7}$$

where $i = 1, \ldots, m$.

5. *The Primal Problem: Maximize the Rate of Growth*

In inequality (2) use (1) to express all $X_j(t + 1)$ in terms of $X_j(t)$. Use (4) to strip $g_j(t)$ of all its subscripts and (5) to strip it of its time coordinate and write (2) as

$$(1 + g)[a_{i1}X_1(t) + \cdots + a_{in}X_n(t)] \leqq b_{i1}X_1(t) + \cdots + b_{in}X_n(t) \tag{8}$$

where $i = 1, \ldots, m$. The system (8) expresses the growth pattern of goods: if the less-than sign of (8) applies, the economy more than reproduces what it absorbed one period earlier of the ith good raised by the growth rate g, hence the ith good is growing at a rate higher than g. If the equality sign of (8) applies, the ith good is growing at the rate g.

We can always make the rate of growth g high enough to generate positive excess demand for at least one good. But how high can we make it *without* doing that? When the rate of growth reaches its highest possible value, its equilibrium value, excess demand will become zero for at least one good. That good or those goods will then become economic. All other goods will be growing more rapidly and become free. Consequently, we may indeed assume, as we did, that at least one equality sign applies. The equilibrium rate of growth g will then be the rate of growth of the slowest-growing good or goods. Goods growing more rapidly than that become free.

Thus von Neumann had formulated his primal problem: maximize the rate of growth g subject to the constraint (8).

Notice that while process-level growth is balanced, goods growth is unbalanced!

6. The Dual Problem: Minimize the Rate of Interest

In inequality (3) use (6) and (7) to strip $r(t)$ and $P_i(t)$ of their time coordinates and write it as

$$(1 + r)(a_{1j}P_1 + \cdots + a_{mj}P_m) \geqq b_{1j}P_1 + \cdots + b_{mj}P_m \tag{9}$$

where $j = 1, \ldots, n$. The system (9) expresses the profitability pattern of processes: if the greater-than sign of (9) applies, revenue from the process falls short of its cost one period earlier with interest added to it at the rate r, hence the process is losing money. If the equality sign of (9) applies, the process is breaking even.

We can always make the rate of interest r low enough to generate positive profits in at least one process. But how low can we make it *without* doing that? When the rate of interest reaches its lowest possible value, its equilibrium value, profits will become zero in at least one process. That process or those processes will then break even and be operated. All other processes will be money-losing and remain unused. Consequently, we may indeed assume, as we did, that at least one equality sign applies. The equilibrium rate of interest will then be the internal rate return of the most profitable process or processes. Processes less profitable than that will remain unused.

Thus von Neumann had formulated his dual problem: minimize the rate of interest subject to the constraint (9).

III. SOLUTION: OUR FIRST SADDLE POINT

1. Collapsing the Model to Two Goods and Two Processes

Using nonelementary algebra, von Neumann proved the existence of an equilibrium solution displaying a saddle point: the maximized rate of growth equaled the minimized rate of interest. But if we collapse the von Neumann model to two goods and two processes, elementary algebra will do.

2.   Nonpositive Excess Demand Expressed as an Equality

Since in (8) all variables refer to the same time, let us suppress its time coordinates. By introducing a nonnegative auxiliary variable $u_i \geqq 0$ we may write (8) as an equality rather than as an inequality:

$$(1 + g)(a_{i1}X_1 + a_{i2}X_2) + u_i = b_{i1}X_1 + b_{i2}X_2$$

or

$$u_i = b_{i1}X_1 + b_{i2}X_2 - (1 + g)(a_{i1}X_1 + a_{i2}X_2) \tag{10}$$

from which the economic meaning of u_i is seen to be current physical output *minus* current physical input of *i*th good, or simply excess supply of *i*th good. Feasibility required excess demand for *i*th good to be nonpositive, hence requires the excess supply of it u_i to be nonnegative.

3.   Nonpositive Profits Expressed as an Equality

By introducing a nonnegative auxiliary variable $v_j \geqq 0$ we may write (9) as an equality rather than as an inequality:

$$(1 + r)(a_{1j}P_1 + a_{2j}P_2) = b_{1j}P_1 + b_{2j}P_2 + v_j$$

or

$$v_j = (1 + r)(a_{1j}P_1 + a_{2j}P_2) - (b_{1j}P_1 + b_{2j}P_2) \tag{11}$$

from which the economic meaning of v_j is seen to be unit-level cost with interest *minus* unit-level revenue, or simply loss margin of *j*th process. Freedom of entry and exit required the profit margin of the *j*th process to be nonpositive, hence requires its loss margin v_j to be nonnegative.

4.   The Saddle Point: Maximized Rate of Growth Equals Minimized Rate of Interest

Multiply the excess supply (10) of the *i*th good by its price P_i and write out the result for both goods $i = 1, 2$. Multiply the loss margin (11) of the *j*th process by its level X_j and write out the result for both processes $j = 1, 2$. The four equations are

$$P_1 u_1 = [b_{11} - (1 + g)a_{11}]P_1X_1 + [b_{12} - (1 + g)a_{12}]P_1X_2 \tag{12}$$

$$P_2 u_2 = [b_{21} - (1 + g)a_{21}]P_2X_1 + [b_{22} - (1 + g)a_{22}]P_2X_2 \tag{13}$$

$$v_1 X_1 = [(1 + r)a_{11} - b_{11}]P_1X_1 + [(1 + r)a_{21} - b_{21}]P_2X_1 \tag{14}$$

$$v_2 X_2 = [(1 + r)a_{12} - b_{12}]P_1X_2 + [(1 + r)a_{22} - b_{22}]P_2X_2 \tag{15}$$

Then add (12) through (15) and find

$$P_1 u_1 + P_2 u_2 + v_1 X_1 + v_2 X_2$$

$$= (r - g)(a_{11} P_1 X_1 + a_{12} P_1 X_2 + a_{21} P_2 X_1 + a_{22} P_2 X_2) \qquad (16)$$

But if excess supply u_i of the ith good is zero, price P_i is positive, and if excess supply u_i is positive, price P_i is zero. Consequently, the product $P_i u_i$ always has one and only one factor equaling zero and must itself be zero. Likewise, if loss margin v_j of the jth process is zero, process level X_j is positive, and if loss margin v_j is positive, process level X_j is zero. Consequently, the product $v_j X_j$, too, always has one and only one factor equaling zero and must itself be zero, and the entire left-hand side of (16) is zero.

As a result, at least one of the factors on the right-hand side must be zero. Now von Neumann ruled out the two uninteresting cases that all goods were free and all processes nonoperated. But how can a good become economic except if absorbed as an input in a process being operated? Consequently, at least one of the four terms $a_{ij} P_i X_j$ on the right-hand side of (16) will be positive, and the only way that side of (16) can be zero is if

$$g = r \qquad (17)$$

Using elementary algebra, we have proved the existence of an equilibrium solution displaying a saddle point: the maximized rate of growth equals the minimized rate of interest. So the saddle point exists, and we must find its coordinates.

5. Solutions for Process Levels and Goods Prices

We assumed that at least one good had zero excess supply u_i, hence was economic. Since the numbering of goods is arbitrary, we may let that good be the second one. So in (10) set $u_2 = 0$ and write the equation for both goods, $i = 1, 2$:

$$1 + g = \frac{b_{11} X_1 + b_{12} X_2 - u_1}{a_{11} X_1 + a_{12} X_2} \qquad (18)$$

$$1 + g = \frac{b_{21} X_1 + b_{22} X_2}{a_{21} X_1 + a_{22} X_2} \qquad (19)$$

We assumed that at least one process had zero loss margin v_j, hence was operated. Since the numbering of processes is arbitrary, we may let that process be the second one. So in (11) set $v_2 = 0$ and write the equation for both processes, $j = 1, 2$:

$$1 + r = \frac{b_{11}P_1 + b_{21}P_2 + v_1}{a_{11}P_1 + a_{21}P_2} \tag{20}$$

$$1 + r = \frac{b_{12}P_1 + b_{22}P_2}{a_{12}P_1 + a_{22}P_2} \tag{21}$$

Eqs. (18) through (21) would remain the same if process levels X_j, excess supplies u_i, goods prices, P_i, and loss margins v_j were all multiplied by an arbitrary positive constant λ. Consequently, the von Neumann system is homogeneous of degree zero in those four variables—unlike the Walras system, which was homogeneous of degree zero only in its prices, money expenditures, and money incomes. Our only hope, then, is to solve for *relative* process levels, excess supplies, goods prices, and loss margins. Like Walras, we must choose *numéraires*. We begin by choosing *numéraires* that will guarantee the meaningfulness of such relative variables.

6. *Relative Process Levels Are Meaningful*

Since the numbering of processes is arbitrary, we assumed $v_2 = 0$, hence $X_2 > 0$. In that case, division by X_2 is meaningful. Divide numerators and denominators alike of (18) and (19) by X_2, define relative process level $x \equiv X_1/X_2$, and write (18) and (19) in terms of x and u_1/X_2:

$$1 + g = \frac{b_{11}x + b_{12} - u_1/X_2}{a_{11}x + a_{12}} \tag{22}$$

$$1 + g = \frac{b_{21}x + b_{22}}{a_{21}x + a_{22}} \tag{23}$$

Set the right-hand sides of (22) and (23) equal, multiply across, and arrive at the quadratic in x:

$$x^2 + \frac{a_{11}b_{22} + a_{12}b_{21} - a_{21}b_{12} - a_{22}b_{11} + a_{21}u_1/X_2}{a_{11}b_{21} - a_{21}b_{11}} x$$

$$+ \frac{a_{12}b_{22} - a_{22}b_{12} + a_{22}u_1/X_2}{a_{11}b_{21} - a_{21}b_{11}} = 0 \tag{24}$$

7. *Relative Prices Are Meaningful*

Since the numbering of goods is arbitrary, we assumed $u_2 = 0$, hence $P_2 > 0$. In that case, division by P_2 is meaningful. Divide numerators and denominators alike of (20) and (21) by P_2, define relative price $p \equiv P_1/P_2$, and write (20) and (21) in terms of p and v_1/P_2:

$$1 + r = \frac{b_{11}p + b_{21} + v_1/P_2}{a_{11}p + a_{21}} \tag{25}$$

$$1 + r = \frac{b_{12}p + b_{22}}{a_{12}p + a_{22}} \tag{26}$$

Set the right-hand sides of (25) and (26) equal, multiply across, and arrive at the quadratic in p:

$$p^2 + \frac{a_{11}b_{22} - a_{12}b_{21} + a_{21}b_{12} - a_{22}b_{11} - a_{12}v_1/P_2}{a_{11}b_{12} - a_{12}b_{11}} p$$

$$+ \frac{a_{21}b_{22} - a_{22}b_{21} - a_{22}v_1/P_2}{a_{11}b_{12} - a_{12}b_{11}} = 0 \tag{27}$$

8. Four Possibilities

As we saw, the products $P_i u_i$ and $v_j X_j$ always have one and only one factor equaling zero and must themselves be zero. As we assumed, $P_2 > 0$ and $X_2 > 0$, hence division by them is meaningful. Consequently,

$$pu_1 = v_1 x = 0 \tag{28}$$

Our results (24), (27), and (28) represent a quadratic system in four variables, i.e., relative process level x, relative excess supply u_1/X_2, relative price p, and relative loss margin v_1/P_2. Feasibility and freedom of entry and exit require all four of them to be nonnegative. Depending upon our technology matrix a_{ij}, b_{ij} the roots of our quadratic system may or may not be nonnegative and when nonnegative, may or may not be unique. Generally we find four possibilities: (1) one free good, one unused process; (2) no free good, one unused process; (3) one free good, no unused process; and (4) no free good, no unused process. Let us examine each of these possibilities.

9. First Possibility: One Free Good, One Unused Process

For the first good to be free and the first process to be unused, we must have at the same time

$$p = x = 0 \tag{29}$$

For this to happen, relative excess supply and relative loss margin must both be positive, and we examine them in turn. A relative excess supply

$$\frac{u_1}{X_2} = -\frac{a_{12}b_{22} - a_{22}b_{12}}{a_{22}} \tag{30}$$

will make the third term of (24) zero, hence produce a root $x = 0$.

Feasibility of solutions required the relative excess supply (30) to be nonnegative, i.e., either positive or zero. As our first possibility let (30) be positive requiring

$$b_{22}/a_{22} < b_{12}/a_{12}$$

meaning that in the second process the second good is growing at a lower rate than the first good. There is no way in which the two goods could be growing at the same rate. As a result, the first good will become free.

A relative loss margin

$$\frac{v_1}{P_2} = \frac{a_{21}b_{22} - a_{22}b_{21}}{a_{22}} \tag{31}$$

will make the third term of (27) zero, hence produce a root $p = 0$.

Freedom of entry and exit required the relative loss margin (31) to be nonnegative, i.e., either positive or zero. As our first possibility let (31) be positive requiring

$$b_{21}/a_{21} < b_{22}/a_{22}$$

meaning that the second good has a lower revenue-cost ratio in the first process than in the second process. There is no way in which the two processes could be earning the same internal rate of return. As a result, the first process will remain unused.

10. Second Possibility: No Free Good, One Unused Process

The third term of (24) will still be zero, hence $x = 0$, if (30) holds. Feasibility of solutions required the relative excess supply (30) to be nonnegative, i.e., either positive or zero. As our second possibility let (30) be zero, requiring the odd piece of luck:

$$b_{22}/a_{22} = b_{12}/a_{12}$$

meaning that in the second process the second good is growing at the same rate as the first good. Now if with only one process being operated, the second, both goods are growing at the same rate in that process, then both goods may be economic and will indeed be: a zero excess supply u_1 of the first good would mean that price of that good would be positive, $p > 0$. In short, if in our second possibility relative process level x is zero, then relative price p cannot be.

11. Third Possibility: One Free Good, No Unused Process

The third term of (27) will still be zero, hence $p = 0$, if (31) holds. Freedom of entry and exit required the relative loss margin (31) to be nonnegative, i.e., either positive or zero. As our third possibility let (31) be zero, requiring the odd piece of luck:

$$b_{21}/a_{21} = b_{22}/a_{22}$$

meaning that the second good has the same revenue-cost ratio in the first process as in the second. Now if with only one economic good, the second, both processes are equally profitable in producing that good, then both processes may be operated and will indeed be: a zero loss margin v_1 of the first process would mean that the level of that process would be positive, $x > 0$. In short, if in our third possibility relative price p is zero, then relative process level x cannot be.

12. *Fourth Possibility: No Free Good, No Unused Process*

If both goods were to be economic, $p > 0$, there would have to be zero excess supply of the first good, $u_1 = 0$. If both processes were to be operated, $x > 0$, there would have to be zero loss margin of the first process, $v_1 = 0$. For $u_1 = v_1 = 0$ our system (24) and (27) collapses into the system

$$p^2 + Hp + I = 0 \tag{32}$$

$$x^2 + Jx + K = 0 \tag{33}$$

where

$$H \equiv \frac{a_{11}b_{22} - a_{12}b_{21} + a_{21}b_{12} - a_{22}b_{11}}{a_{11}b_{12} - a_{12}b_{11}}$$

$$I \equiv \frac{a_{21}b_{22} - a_{22}b_{21}}{a_{11}b_{12} - a_{12}b_{11}}$$

$$J \equiv \frac{a_{11}b_{22} + a_{12}b_{21} - a_{21}b_{12} - a_{22}b_{11}}{a_{11}b_{21} - a_{21}b_{11}}$$

$$K \equiv \frac{a_{12}b_{22} - a_{22}b_{12}}{a_{11}b_{21} - a_{21}b_{11}}$$

The roots of our quadratics will be

$$p = -H/2 \pm \sqrt{(-H/2)^2 - I} \tag{34}$$

$$x = -J/2 \pm \sqrt{(-J/2)^2 - K} \tag{35}$$

Could these roots be unique and nonnegative?

Suppose that $b_{11}/a_{11} < b_{12}/a_{12}$, meaning that the first good has a lower revenue-cost ratio in the first process than in the second, and that

$b_{22}/a_{22} < b_{21}/a_{21}$, meaning that the second good has a lower revenue-cost ratio in the second process than in the first process.

With one process thus being less profitable in producing one good but the other process being less profitable in producing the other good, a way would exist in which the two processes could be earning the same internal rate of return, i.e., if both goods were economic: $p > 0$.

Furthermore, suppose that $b_{11}/a_{11} < b_{21}/a_{21}$, meaning that in the first process the first good is growing less rapidly than the second good, and that $b_{22}/a_{22} < b_{12}/a_{12}$, meaning that in the second process the second good is growing less rapidly than the first good.

With one good thus growing less rapidly in one process but the other good growing less rapidly in the other process, a way would exist in which the two goods could be growing at the same rate, i.e., if both processes were operated: $x > 0$.

Under these four assumptions the denominator $a_{11}b_{12} - a_{12}b_{11}$ of H and I as well as the denominator $a_{11}b_{21} - a_{21}b_{11}$ of J and K would be positive. The numerators $a_{21}b_{22} - a_{22}b_{21}$ of I and $a_{12}b_{22} - a_{22}b_{12}$ of K would both be negative. As a result, I and K would both be negative, hence $-I$ in (34) and $-K$ in (35) both positive, making the absolute value of the square roots of (34) and (35) greater than the absolute value of the first terms $-H/2$ and $-J/2$, respectively. As a result, (34) for p and (35) for x would have one positive and one negative root regardless of the signs of $-H/2$ and $-J/2$, respectively. Consequently, there would exist a unique set of nonnegative solutions for relative price p and relative process level x.

With both goods being economic, what will their common rate of growth be? When we found our quadratic (24) in x, we set the right-hand sides of (22) and (23) equal and multiplied across. So we may find our equilibrium maximum rate of growth g by inserting $u_1/X_2 = 0$ and our solution (35) for x into either (22) or (23).

With both processes being operated, what will their common internal rate of return be? When we found our quadratic (27) in p, we set the right-hand sides of (25) and (26) equal and multiplied across. So we may find our equilibrium minimum rate of interest r by inserting $v_1/P_2 = 0$ as well as our solution (34) for p into either (25) or (26).

IV. CONCLUSIONS

1. *Solution*

The best way to prove the existence of a solution is to find one. By reducing the number of goods to two and the number of processes to two, we have succeeded in solving a von Neumann model by using nothing but elementary algebra—thus needing neither the game theory nor the matrix algebra applied in the excellent restatements by Kemeny, Snell, and Thompson (1957: 353-367) and Lancaster (1968: 164-168).

Since the von Neumann system is homogeneous of degree zero in its process levels, excess supplies, goods prices, and loss margins, we were able to find solutions only for *relative* process levels, excess supplies, goods prices, and loss margins. Since the numbering of goods and processes is arbitrary, we assumed that at least the second good would always become economic and that at least the second process would always be used. The first good might then be free or economic and the first process unused or used. We discussed four such possibilities and the technology generating them.

The heart of the von Neumann model is its saddle point: the maximized rate of growth equals the minimized rate of interest. An economist would make two observations on that saddle point.

2. Saving and Consumption

In a growing economy somebody must be saving. We may think of a von Neumann model as having capitalists in it who are lending money capital to the entrepreneurs to carry them over their one-time unit period of production. At the rate of interest r, capitalists at the beginning of that period lend the entrepreneurs the sum $a_{11}P_1X_1 + a_{12}P_1X_2 + a_{21}P_2X_1 + a_{22}P_2X_2$ financing the purchases of all goods absorbed as inputs.

At the end of the period of production the value of aggregate output will be $b_{11}P_1X_1 + b_{12}P_1X_2 + b_{21}P_2X_1 + b_{22}P_2X_2$, and let us express it in two different ways. First, since the product P_iu_i always has one and only one factor equaling zero, we may set (12) and (13) equal to zero, then add them and find aggregate input to have grown into aggregate output at the rate g. Second, since the product v_jX_j always has one and only one factor equaling zero, we may set (14) and (15) equal to zero, then add them and find aggregate input to have grown into aggregate output at the rate r. But in the saddle-point solution (17) the maximized rate of growth g equaled the minimized rate of interest r. Consequently, out of their sales proceeds the entrepreneurs can pay back with interest the sum they borrowed from the capitalists one time unit earlier, provided, of course, that the sale of their output can be financed. It can if for the next period of production the capitalists lend the entrepreneurs the necessary sum. New debt forever pays off old debt with interest, and the aggregate debt is a rising one, rising at the rate $g = r$. What makes it all possible is the willingness of the capitalists to save their entire interest earnings.

Thus only labor consumes in the von Neumann model. The entrepreneurs don't consume anything, because their income qua entrepreneurs is zero—pure competition and freedom of entry and exit see to that. Capitalists do have an income, but their propensity to consume it is zero.

3. Stationary or Decaying Economy

Feasibility requires nonnegative solutions such as (23) and (26) for growth and interest *factors* $1 + g$ and $1 + r$ rather than for growth and interest *rates* g and r. As a result, a von Neumann economy may be stationary[1]: $g = r = 0$, or even decaying ("unproductive"): $-1 < g = r < 0$.

REFERENCES

G. Cassel, *Theoretische Sozialökonomie*, Leipzig, 1918, translated as *The Theory of Social Economy* by S. L. Barron, New York, 1932.

R. Dorfman, P. A. Samuelson, and R. M. Solow, *Linear Programming and Economic Analysis*, New York, 1958, 381-388.

G. Haberler, "Schumpeter's Theory of Interest," in Seymour E. Harris (ed.), *Schumpeter, Social Scientist*, Cambridge, Mass., 1951, 72-78.

J. G. Kemeny, J. L. Snell, and G. L. Thompson, *Introduction To Finite Mathematics*, Englewood Cliffs, N.J., 1957.

T. C. Koopmans, "Economic Growth at a Maximal Rate," *Quart. J. Econ.*, Aug. 1964, *78*, 355-394.

K. Lancaster, *Mathematical Economics*, New York and London, 1968.

K. Menger, "Austrian Marginalism and Mathematical Economics," in J. R. Hicks and W. Weber (eds.), *Carl Menger and the Austrian School of Economics*, Vienna, 1971, 38-60.

J. von Neumann, "Ueber ein ökonomisches Gleichungssystem und eine Verallgemeinerung des Brouwerschen Fixpunktsatzes," *Ergebnisse eines mathematischen Kolloquiums*, 8, Leipzig and Vienna, 1937, 73-83, translated by G. Morgenstern (Morton) as "A Model of General Economic Equilibrium," *Rev. Econ. Stud.*, 1945-1946, *13*, 1-9. "The printing was terrible," says Weintraub (1983: 13n), and "a number of typographical errors have been corrected" by W. J. Baumol and S. M. Goldfeld (eds.), *Precursors in Mathematical Economics: An Anthology*, London, 1968, 296-306.

J. A. Schumpeter, *Theorie der wirtschaftlichen Entwicklung*, Leipzig, 1912, translated as *The Theory of Economic Development* by R. Opie, Cambridge, Mass., 1934.

[1]Schumpeter's (1912) theory of interest is validated by von Neumann: in a stationary economy $g = r = 0$. On Schumpeter's theory of interest see Haberler (1951). In a letter of December 7, 1983, Haberler is "pretty sure that Schumpeter was not aware that von Neumann validated his theory of interest."

L. Walras, *Eléments d'économie politique pure*, Lausanne, Paris, and Basle, 1874-1877, translated as *Elements of Pure Economics or the Theory of Social Wealth* by W. Jaffé, Homewood, Ill., 1954.

E. R. Weintraub, "On the Existence of a Competitive Equilibrium: 1930-1954," *J. Econ. Lit.*, Mar. 1983, *21*, 1-39.

CHAPTER 12 Interindustry Equilibrium

LEONTIEF (1906-)

*The recipes for satisfying the appetite of a blast
furnace, a cement kiln, or a thermoelectric power
station will be the same in India or Peru as it is, say, in
Italy or California. In a sense the input-coefficient
matrix derived from the U.S.-European input-output
table represents a complete cookbook of modern
technology.*

Leontief (1966)

*These input coefficients [in the open static system] do
not reflect ... the stock requirements of the economy;
they do not and cannot explain the magnitude of those
input flows which serve directly to satisfy the capital
needs of all its various sectors.*

Leontief (1953)

I. INTRODUCTION

1. Leontief's Problem

The time for empirical estimation of his general-equilibrium model must have seemed remote to Walras but did come with Leontief (1936), [1941 (1951)], (1944), (1946), and (1953). For empirical estimation drastic simplification would be necessary, and in only one respect was the Walras model simple: its input-output coefficients were technological parameters. Of such simple input-output coefficients Leontief made heavy use but in his use of them went far beyond Walras.

As we saw in chapter 5, the only inputs considered by Walras were those supplied by households, the "primary" inputs such as the various qualities of labor and the services of the various qualities of land. No interindustry transactions were considered. Interindustry transactions are the very heart of a Leontief model, and the empirical estimation of the underlying input-output coefficients is its greatest accomplishment.

An input-output coefficient may of course be zero. If $a_{ij} = 0$, then industry j does not use industry i's output for an input. Indeed, in the Bureau of Labor Statistics input-output coefficient matrix for the year

1947, in which the number of industries was 45, no less than 633 out of the 2,025 coefficients were zero [see Evans-Hoffenberg (1952: 142, table 5)].

2. Leontief's Method

The drastic simplification necessary for empirical estimation was accomplished, first of all, by ignoring all supply constraints—a parallel to Keynes. Even so, the earliest Leontief (1941) model was too ambitious. First, it was too ambitious relative to the then existing computational facilities. Leontief had compiled a 44-sector input-output table but had to condense it to ten sectors. Only with the arrival of the high-speed electronic digital computer after the Second World War could models with hundreds of sectors be estimated and solved.

But, second, the earliest Leontief (1941) model was too ambitious in being a closed one. The model had a labor-household sector selling man-hours to the industry sectors. Labor's remuneration, the wage bill, constituted the income of the labor households. The model also had an entrepreneur-household sector: the difference between an industry's revenue and its cost constituted its profits. Profits were fully distributed and constituted the income of the entrepreneur households. In a closed model, consumption demand would be in direct proportion to such incomes. But direct proportionality of all demand would make the model homogeneous of degree zero in its quantities. Consequently, like a von Neumann model, it could determine its relative quantities only. The remedy was the static open model.

3. Our Own Restatement

Closely following Leontief himself we shall, first, restate his static open model and solve it for its outputs, distributive shares, and relative price. Second, we shall restate his dynamic model and solve it in both its closed and open form.

II. THE STATIC OPEN LEONTIEF MODEL

1. Parametric Noninterindustry Demand

The static open Leontief model appeared in Leontief (1944) and (1951). Making all noninterindustry demand parametric, it proved to be more applicable to practical issues than a closed model could have been. Let its notation be as follows.

2. Variables

c_j ≡ cost of jth industry
P_j ≡ price of output of jth industry
w ≡ money wage rate
W ≡ wage bill
x_{ij} ≡ physical output of ith industry absorbed on current account by jth industry
X_j ≡ physical output of jth industry
Z_j ≡ profits bill of jth industry

3. Parameters

a_{ij} ≡ physical output of ith industry absorbed on current account per unit of physical output of jth industry
y_j ≡ final bill of goods produced by jth industry

4. The Model

Let us collapse the static open Leontief model to two industries, 1 and 2, and two household sectors, 3 and 4. Let all inputs absorbed be in proportion to output. First, let each industry absorb the other's output:

$$x_{12} = a_{12}X_2 \qquad\qquad x_{21} = a_{21}X_1 \qquad\qquad (1)$$

Second, let any industry absorb labor from labor households:

$$x_{31} = a_{31}X_1 \qquad\qquad x_{32} = a_{32}X_2 \qquad\qquad (2)$$

Third, let any industry absorb inputs of entrepreneurial services from the entrepreneur household sector. In quantitative terms, such inputs can be expressed only as the profits distributed in return to the entrepreneur households, hence:

$$x_{41} = Z_1 \qquad\qquad x_{42} = Z_2 \qquad\qquad (3)$$

Profits are defined as revenue *minus* cost:

$$Z_1 \equiv P_1X_1 - c_1 \qquad\qquad Z_2 \equiv P_2X_2 - c_2 \qquad\qquad (4)$$

Cost, in turn, is defined as the money expenditure on input:

$$c_1 \equiv P_2x_{21} + wx_{31} \qquad\qquad c_2 \equiv P_1x_{12} + wx_{32} \qquad\qquad (5)$$

"The final bill of goods" is defined as noninterindustry demand, i.e., the consumption demand of labor and entrepreneurial households:

$$y_1 \equiv x_{13} + x_{14} \qquad\qquad y_2 \equiv x_{23} + x_{24} \qquad\qquad (6)$$

which is considered autonomous.

Equilibrium in both goods markets requires the supply of goods to equal the combined demand for them:

$$X_1 = x_{12} + y_1 \qquad\qquad X_2 = x_{21} + y_2 \qquad (7)$$

5. Solutions for Output

The solutions for physical outputs are easily found:

$$X_1 = \frac{y_1 + a_{12}y_2}{1 - a_{12}a_{21}} \qquad (8)$$

$$X_2 = \frac{y_2 + a_{21}y_1}{1 - a_{12}a_{21}} \qquad (9)$$

Are the solutions (8) and (9) positive and unique? As for the numerators, assume the final bill of goods y_1 and y_2 to be positive and the coefficients a_{12} and a_{21} to be nonnegative. As for the denominators, the product $a_{12}a_{21}$ has the following economic meaning. Raise the output of the first good by one physical unit. This would require a_{21} additional units of the second good. That, in turn, would require $a_{12}a_{21}$ additional units of the first good. Now, if to produce one physical unit of the first good would take that whole unit or more, there could be nothing left for the final bill of goods. For anything to be left, $a_{12}a_{21} < 1$. This is the Hawkins-Simon (1949) condition. If the Hawkins-Simon condition is satisfied, the denominators of (8) and (9) will be positive, and the solutions (8) and (9) will be positive and unique.

Are the output equilibria (8) and (9) stable ones? The Hawkins-Simon condition can help us answer that question, too. Let us disturb equilibrium by expanding arbitrarily the output X_1 of the first good by one physical unit beyond the value determined by (8). As we saw, this expansion would require a_{21} additional units of the second good. That, in turn, would require $a_{12}a_{21}$ additional units of the first good. So when output is up by one unit, demand is up by $a_{12}a_{21}$ units. Now assume the Hawkins-Simon condition to be satisfied: $a_{12}a_{21} < 1$. In that case, additional demand falls short of additional output, hence inventory accumulation will result, and output will be induced to move back in the direction of its equilibrium value (8). Equilibrium, then, is stable.

6. Leontief Industries as Vectors

Let us illuminate our solutions (8) and (9) by a vector diagram. In a Leontief world, no good is an output *per se* or an input *per se*. All goods are at the same time outputs in some industries and inputs in others. So let the coordinates of our vector diagram be the flows of goods X_1 and X_2. A positive flow is an output, a negative flow an input. We may then show our two Leontief industries as the heavy straight lines in the second and fourth quadrants of figure 12-1. The line in the fourth quadrant represents the first Leontief industry, producing the first good and absorbing the second. The line in the second quadrant represents the second Leontief industry, producing the second good and absorbing the first.

Why the second and fourth quadrants? We wouldn't draw any industry in the first quadrant, for such an industry would have two outputs and no inputs at all, and in practice we never get something for nothing. We wouldn't draw any industry in the third quadrant either, for such an industry would have two inputs and no outputs at all and would be uninteresting.

The parameters needed for an output solution of a two-industry Leontief economy are, first, technology expressed simply as a_{12} and a_{21}, second, the final bill of goods y_1 and y_2. Assume for example:

$$a_{12} = 1/2$$

$$a_{21} = 1$$

$$y_1 = 2$$

$$y_2 = 3$$

FIGURE 12-1.
A Leontief
Interindustry
Equilibrium

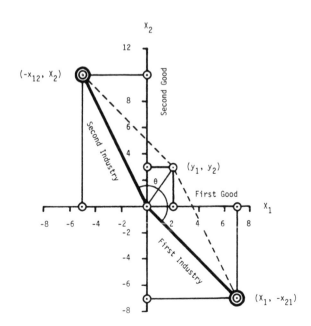

How will these parameters appear in our vector diagram? The final bill of goods is easy. It will appear as the point (2, 3) in the first quadrant. Technology a_{12}, a_{21} will determine the slope of our industry lines. The line in the fourth quadrant, representing the first industry, will have a slope equaling input per unit of output or $-x_{21}/X_1 = -a_{21} = -1$. The line in the second quadrant, representing the second industry, will have a slope equaling output per unit of input or $X_2/(-x_{12}) = -1/a_{12} = -2$.

Where will the lines end? Their end points are the variables that we must solve for: at which levels must the two industries produce in order to satisfy, first, each other's need for input and, second, the final bill of goods? To find the answer, draw through the point (y_1, y_2) two broken lines parallel to the heavy straight lines. The broken lines will intersect the heavy ones in the two points marked by double circles, and those points represent the solution to the two-industry Leontief model. Why? Because the sum of two vectors is found as the fourth vertex of a parallelogram having the origin and the end points of the vectors as the other vertices. In our own case, we have now established the parallelogram the fourth vertex of which is at the same time the final bill of goods and the sum of net output of the two Leontief industries: remember the addition-of-vectors rule that the sum of two vectors is a new vector whose abscissa is the sum of the abscissae and whose ordinate is the sum of the ordinates or, in our own case

$$(y_1, y_2) = (X_1 - x_{12}, -x_{21} + X_2)$$

which is nothing else than our goods-market equilibria (7). As they should according to (8) and (9), our double circles indicate the output solutions $X_1 = 7$ and $X_2 = 10$.

Our vector geometry gives us a vivid illumination of the Hawkins-Simon condition. In figure 12-1 the slope of the line ending in (X_1, $-x_{21}$) is $-a_{21}$. The slope of the line ending in ($-x_{12}$, X_2) is $-1/a_{12}$. Figure 12-1 is characterized by the inequality $-1/a_{12} < -a_{21}$. Multiply both sides of the inequality by -1, reverse the inequality sign, and find the Hawkins-Simon condition $a_{12}a_{21} < 1$. Geometrically speaking, only an angle $\theta < 180°$ in figure 12-1 can put the fourth vertex of our parallelogram in the first quadrant, thus satisfying a positive final bill of goods.

7. Sensitivity of Physical Output to Demand and Technology

The sensitivity of equilibrium output to changes in the final bill of goods y_1 and y_2 is expressed by the following partial derivatives:

$$\frac{\partial X_1}{\partial y_1} = \frac{1}{1 - a_{12}a_{21}} \tag{10}$$

$$\frac{\partial X_1}{\partial y_2} = \frac{a_{12}}{1 - a_{12}a_{21}} \tag{11}$$

$$\frac{\partial X_2}{\partial y_1} = \frac{a_{21}}{1 - a_{12}a_{21}} \tag{12}$$

$$\frac{\partial X_2}{\partial y_2} = \frac{1}{1 - a_{12}a_{21}} \tag{13}$$

In our vector diagram a more ambitious final bill of goods means that the point (y_1, y_2) moves east or north, thus increasing the required output of both industries within an enlarged parallelogram.

Technological progress may be thought of as a reduction of an input coefficient a_{ij} meaning that the jth industry has now organized its production or distribution process more efficiently, needing less input from industry i to maintain the same output. The sensitivity of outputs to such technological progress is expressed by the following partial derivatives or multipliers:

$$\frac{\partial X_1}{\partial a_{12}} = \frac{X_2}{1 - a_{12}a_{21}} \tag{14}$$

$$\frac{\partial X_1}{\partial a_{21}} = \frac{a_{12}X_1}{1 - a_{12}a_{21}} \tag{15}$$

$$\frac{\partial X_2}{\partial a_{12}} = \frac{a_{21}X_2}{1 - a_{12}a_{21}} \tag{16}$$

$$\frac{\partial X_2}{\partial a_{21}} = \frac{X_1}{1 - a_{12}a_{21}} \tag{17}$$

In our vector diagram technological progress means reducing the angle θ between our two industry lines, thus satisfying the same final bill of goods with less output in both industries within a diminished parallelogram.

8. *Solution for Distributive Shares*

Leontief (1946) also solved for the distributive shares and relative price. The wage and profits bills are:

$$W = w(x_{31} + x_{32}) \tag{18}$$

$$Z_1 = (P_1 - a_{21}P_2 - a_{31}w)X_1 \tag{19}$$

$$Z_2 = (P_2 - a_{12}P_1 - a_{32}w)X_2 \tag{20}$$

9. *Solution for Relative Price*

In a Leontief model there are no economies of scale, so assume all industries to be purely competitive. Also, in the long run let freedom of entry reduce all positive profits to zero, and let freedom of exit raise all negative profits to zero:

$$Z_1 = Z_2 = 0 \tag{21}$$

Hence in (19) and (20), either outputs X_1 and X_2 must be zero, which under our assumption was found to be impossible, or the profit margins must be zero:

$$P_1 - a_{21}P_2 - a_{31}w = 0 \tag{22}$$

$$P_2 - a_{12}P_1 - a_{32}w = 0 \tag{23}$$

Clearly, the two equations (22) and (23) do not suffice to determine the three absolute prices P_1, P_2, and w. Like the Walras system, the Leontief model is homogeneous of degree zero in its prices. But we may choose, say, the money wage rate w as our *numéraire*, divide (22) and (23) by it, and find the relative prices

$$\frac{P_1}{w} = \frac{a_{21}a_{32} + a_{31}}{1 - a_{12}a_{21}} \tag{24}$$

$$\frac{P_2}{w} = \frac{a_{12}a_{31} + a_{32}}{1 - a_{12}a_{21}} \tag{25}$$

Are the relative-price solutions (24) and (25) positive and unique? Let it take labor to produce both commodities: neither a_{31} nor a_{32} is zero. Let the Hawkins-Simon condition be met: $a_{12}a_{21} < 1$. Then (24) and (25) will be positive and unique.

III. THE DYNAMIC LEONTIEF MODEL

1. *Inputs on Capital Account*

In the static Leontief models all inputs were in direct proportion to output. While this is true of inputs on current account such as raw materials, fuels, electric power, and lubricants, it is not true of inputs on capital account such as the construction of durable plant and equipment. One way of handling such inputs would be to treat them as part of the final bill of goods. But the latter is a parameter, i.e., something left unexplained within the model. It would be much better to explain the demand for *all* input, whether on current account or on capital account, within the model. The dynamic Leontief (1953) model does this, thus enabling us to determine time paths, rather than mere levels, of outputs. Let us examine the closed and open versions of it and use the notation:

2. *Variables*

I_{ij} ≡ physical output of ith industry absorbed on capital account by jth industry

λ_j ≡ characteristic roots of dynamic Leontief system

S_{ij} ≡ physical capital stock produced by ith industry and held by jth industry

x_{ij} ≡ physical output of ith industry absorbed on current account by jth industry

X_j ≡ physical output of jth industry

3. *Parameters*

a_{ij} ≡ physical output of ith industry absorbed on current account per unit of physical output of jth industry

b_{ij} ≡ physical capital stock produced by ith industry and held by jth industry per unit of its physical output

c_i ≡ arbitrary numbers used to reflect initial conditions

g_{ij} ≡ coefficients of final bill of goods, policy instruments

μ_i ≡ exponents of final bill of goods, policy instruments

y_j ≡ final bill of goods produced by jth industry

The symbol e is Euler's number. The symbol t is time.

4. *The Model*

Let us collapse the dynamic Leontief model to two industries and distinguish between transactions on capital and current account. On capital account, define investment as the derivative of capital stock with respect to time:

$$I_{12} \equiv \frac{dS_{12}}{dt} \qquad\qquad I_{21} \equiv \frac{dS_{21}}{dt} \qquad (26)$$

Let physical capital stock produced by ith industry and held by jth industry be in proportion to the physical output of the jth industry:

$$S_{12} = b_{12}X_2 \qquad\qquad S_{21} = b_{21}X_1 \qquad (27)$$

On current account, let physical output of ith industry absorbed by jth industry be in proportion to the physical output of the jth industry:

$$x_{12} = a_{12}X_2 \qquad\qquad x_{21} = a_{21}X_1 \qquad (28)$$

Equilibrium in both goods markets requires the supply of goods to equal the combined demand for them:

$$X_1 = x_{12} + I_{12} + y_1 \qquad\qquad X_2 = x_{21} + I_{21} + y_2 \qquad (29)$$

5. Solution for the Time Paths of Outputs

Reduce the system (26) through (29) to a system of two simultaneous first-order differential equations, each in two variables, X_1 and X_2:

$$X_1 = a_{12}X_2 + b_{12}\frac{dX_2}{dt} + y_1 \qquad (30)$$

$$X_2 = a_{21}X_1 + b_{21}\frac{dX_1}{dt} + y_2 \qquad (31)$$

We may now see the closed and open versions of the dynamic Leontief model as special cases of (30) and (31).

6. The Closed Model

A closed model explains the demand for all input, whether on current account or on capital account, whether interindustry demand or household demand. Since nothing is left unexplained, there can be no final bill of goods y_j. Setting $y_j = 0$ in (30) and (31) leaves us with a homogeneous system—the simplest mathematically.

Solving a differential equation means recovering the primitive which gave rise to it. To solve our homogeneous version of (30) and (31) we follow Leontief (1953: 58-62 and 77-79) and try

$$X_1 = k_1 e^{\lambda t} \qquad (32)$$

$$X_2 = k_2 e^{\lambda t} \qquad (33)$$

where k_j is a constant and λ a root to be determined presently. Insert (32) and (33) as well as their derivatives with respect to time into (30) and (31), rearrange, and find

$$e^{\lambda t}[k_1 - (a_{12} + b_{12}\lambda)k_2] = 0$$

$$e^{\lambda t}[k_2 - (a_{21} + b_{21}\lambda)k_1] = 0$$

Euler's number e is not zero, hence no power of it can be. Consequently, we may divide $e^{\lambda t}$ away, find the two brackets equaling zero, and use them to find two expressions for the ratio k_1/k_2:

$$k_1/k_2 = a_{12} + b_{12}\lambda \qquad (34)$$

$$k_1/k_2 = 1/(a_{21} + b_{21}\lambda) \qquad (35)$$

which are consistent if and only if their right-hand sides are equal. Set them equal, multiply across, and find a quadratic equation in λ:

$$\lambda^2 + H\lambda + J = 0 \tag{36}$$

where

$$H \equiv (a_{12}b_{21} + a_{21}b_{12})/(b_{12}b_{21})$$

$$J \equiv (a_{12}a_{21} - 1)/(b_{12}b_{21})$$

The roots of the quadratic (36) are

$$\lambda = -H/2 \pm \sqrt{(-H/2)^2 - J}$$

In dynamic Leontief models no less than in static ones the Hawkins-Simon condition must hold that $a_{12}a_{21} < 1$. If so, J will be negative, $-J$ positive, and what is under the square-root sign always positive and greater than $(-H/2)^2$. As a result, the roots of (36) can be neither complex nor repeated.

Equations (34), (35), and (36) determine the ratio k_1/k_2 in terms of our input-output coefficients a_{ij} and our capital coefficients b_{ij}. But if (36) has two roots λ_1 and λ_2, two values of that ratio, call them k_{11}/k_{21} and k_{12}/k_{22}, will satisfy (34) and (35). Ratios remain the same if their numerator and denominator are multiplied by the same nonzero but otherwise arbitrary number, say c_1 or c_2. So if satisfied by k_{11}, k_{21}, k_{12}, and k_{22}, (34) and (35) will also be satisfied by $c_1 k_{11}$, $c_1 k_{21}$, $c_2 k_{12}$, and $c_2 k_{22}$, and (30) and (31) by the pairs

$$X_1 = c_1 k_{11} e^{\lambda_1 t}; \qquad X_1 = c_2 k_{12} e^{\lambda_2 t}$$

$$X_2 = c_1 k_{21} e^{\lambda_1 t}; \qquad X_2 = c_2 k_{22} e^{\lambda_2 t}$$

Equations (30) and (31) will be satisfied not only by those pairs taken separately but also by their weighted sum. So the primitives of our homogeneous system have been recovered and are

$$X_1 = c_1 k_{11} e^{\lambda_1 t} + c_2 k_{12} e^{\lambda_2 t} \tag{37}$$

$$X_2 = c_1 k_{21} e^{\lambda_1 t} + c_2 k_{22} e^{\lambda_2 t} \tag{38}$$

Since the weights c_1 and c_2 of the weighted sums (37) and (38) were nonzero but otherwise arbitrary numbers, we are free to let them reflect the initial conditions of the system. They may then be determined by replacing X_1 and X_2 by their initial conditions $X_1(0)$ and $X_2(0)$ on the left-hand sides of (37) and (38) and setting $t = 0$ on the right-hand sides, whereby $e^{\lambda_j t}$ will collapse into 1.

7. The Open Model

An open model leaves something unexplained, i.e., the final bill of goods y_j. A nonzero y_j in (30) and (31) leaves us with a nonhomogeneous system—a little harder to solve, but fortunately we can use everything found in the homogeneous case.

The first thing to do is to decide what we want the final bill of goods y_j to be. Let us follow Leontief (1953: 63) and adopt the exponential functions

$$y_1 = g_{11} e^{\mu_1 t} + g_{12} e^{\mu_2 t} \tag{39}$$

$$y_2 = g_{21} e^{\mu_1 t} + g_{22} e^{\mu_2 t} \tag{40}$$

where g_{ij} and μ_i are policy instruments of the open model. To solve our nonhomogeneous version of (30) and (31) we follow Leontief (1953: 63-65 and 79-81) and try

$$X_1 = h_{11} e^{\mu_1 t} + h_{12} e^{\mu_2 t} \tag{41}$$

$$X_2 = h_{21} e^{\mu_1 t} + h_{22} e^{\mu_2 t} \tag{42}$$

where h_{ij} is a constant to be determined presently. Insert (39) through (42) as well as the derivatives of (41) and (42) with respect to time into (30) and (31), rearrange, and find from (30):

$$e^{\mu_1 t}[h_{11} - (a_{12} + b_{12}\mu_1)h_{21} - g_{11}]$$
$$+ e^{\mu_2 t}[h_{12} - (a_{12} + b_{12}\mu_2)h_{22} - g_{12}] = 0 \tag{43}$$

and from (31):

$$e^{\mu_1 t}[h_{21} - (a_{21} + b_{21}\mu_1)h_{11} - g_{21}]$$
$$+ e^{\mu_2 t}[h_{22} - (a_{21} + b_{21}\mu_2)h_{12} - g_{22}] = 0 \tag{44}$$

The weights of the brackets of (43) and (44) are forever changing. So if (30) and (31), hence (43) and (44), are to hold for any time coordinate t and any policy instruments g_{ij} and μ_i we may decide on, then each of the four brackets of (43) and (44) must be zero. Setting them equal to zero will allow us to determine our coefficients h_{ij} in terms of our input-output coefficients a_{ij}, our capital coefficients b_{ij}, and our policy instruments g_{ij} and μ_i.

We are now ready for our payoff. The theory of differential equations teaches that the primitives of the nonhomogeneous version of (30) and (31) will simply be

$$X_1 = c_1 k_{11} e^{\lambda_1 t} + c_2 k_{12} e^{\lambda_2 t} + h_{11} e^{\mu_1 t} + h_{12} e^{\mu_2 t} \tag{45}$$

$$X_2 = c_1 k_{21} e^{\lambda_1 t} + c_2 k_{22} e^{\lambda_2 t} + h_{21} e^{\mu_1 t} + h_{22} e^{\mu_2 t} \tag{46}$$

Having recovered our primitives (45) and (46), we must take note of a fundamental logical problem raised by the complete absence of inequalities from the dynamic Leontief model. Leontief himself (1953: 68-76) discussed it under the label of "irreversibility."

8.   *Irreversibility*

We followed Leontief in writing (27) as an equality: physical capital stock held by the *j*th industry would always be in proportion to its physical output, neither more nor less. Now upon equalities several operations may safely be performed, and differentiation is one of them: in an equality the derivative of its left-hand side will equal the derivative of its right-hand side. Specifically, it does follow from $S_{ij} = b_{ij}X_j$ that

$$\frac{dS_{ij}}{dt} = b_{ij}\frac{dX_j}{dt}$$

of which we took advantage in deriving (30) and (31).

Could physical capital stock be less than or more than (27)? It couldn't be less as long as the capital coefficient b_{ij} is thought of as a technological necessity. But could it be more? Could there in other words be excess capacity? If so, (27) should be written as $S_{ij} \geqq b_{ij}X_{ij}$. That would raise a possibly serious problem: it does not follow from $S_{ij} > b_{ij}X_j$ that

$$\frac{dS_{ij}}{dt} > b_{ij}\frac{dX_j}{dt}$$

and indeed had better not follow. Instead, two alternative rules should be formulated. When in $S_{ij} \geqq b_{ij}X_j$ the equality sign holds and the derivative $dX_j/dt > 0$, the first rule would apply and make the capital coefficient b_{ij} the familiar technological necessity, hence $b_{ij} > 0$, thus ensuring positive investment dS_{ij}/dt. When, on the other hand, in $S_{ij} \geqq b_{ij}X_j$ the greater-than sign holds, then regardless of the sign of the derivative dX_j/dt the second rule would apply and make the capital coefficient $b_{ij} = 0$, thus ensuring zero investment dS_{ij}/dt.

Switching from one rule to the other may or may not occur. As an example of a development in which all capital stock would remain fully utilized, Leontief (1953: 71-72) mentioned a closed, i.e., homogeneous, system finding itself from the outset in its long-run equilibrium. The largest root of such a system would be positive and dominate all others. As a result, there would eventually be steady-state and balanced growth.

Dorfman, Samuelson, and Solow (1958: 343-345) agreed but also examined open, i.e., nonhomogeneous systems. Here they (1958: 340-342) found, first, that paths along which all capital stock would remain fully utilized might or might not exist and, second, if such paths did exist, they would be efficient.

IV. CONCLUSION

The Leontief model is at the same time a bold simplification of economic theory and a dramatic refinement of it. Coupled with modern large-scale computational facilities, the dramatic refinement has produced one of the most practical tools offered by economics. In its small and closed original form, the model could never have delivered a detailed analysis of the impact of such external events as industrial mobilization after 1941 and demobilization after 1945, airforce rearmament in 1949, an arms cut in the sixties, and the environmental protection and oil shocks of the seventies. Here is where the large, open, static Leontief model has triumphed. Its use has not been confined to the United States and Western Europe. Some fifty countries have compiled input-output tables in an effort to plan their economic development. Much less practical use has been found for the dynamic Leontief model.

REFERENCES

R. Dorfman, P. A. Samuelson, and R. M. Solow, *Linear Programming and Economic Analysis*, New York, 1958.
W. D. Evans and M. Hoffenberg, "The Interindustry Relations Study for 1947," *Rev. Econ. Stat.*, May 1952, *34*, 97-142.
D. Hawkins and H. A. Simon, "Some Conditions of Macroeconomic Stability," *Econometrica*, July-Oct. 1949, *17*, 245-248.
W. Leontief, "Quantitative Input and Output Relations in the Economic System of the United States," *Rev. Econ. Stat.*, Aug. 1936, *18*, 105-125.
———, *The Structure of American Economy, 1919-1929*, Cambridge, Mass., 1941, enlarged edition, New York, 1951.
———, "Output, Employment, Consumption, and Investment," *Quart. J. Econ.*, Feb. 1944, *58*, 290-313.
———, "Wages, Profits, and Prices," *Quart. J. Econ.*, Nov. 1946, *61*, 26-39.
———, "Static and Dynamic Theory," in W. Leontief (ed.), *Studies in the Structure of the American Economy*, New York, 1953.
———, *Input-Output Economics*, New York, 1966.

CHAPTER *13* Existence of Static General Equilibrium

THE WALRAS GRANDCHILDREN

> *... A model of competitive equilibrium by Abraham Wald and a model of proportional growth of a competitive economy by von Neumann ... have been at the basis of all subsequent developments.*
> Koopmans (1957: 38)

I. INTRODUCTION

1. *The Grandchildren*

To Georges Renard Walras wrote: "If one wants to harvest quickly, one must plant carrots and salads; if one has the ambition to plant oaks, one must have the sense to tell oneself: my grandchildren will owe me this shade."

Who were the Walras grandchildren? Let us think of them as Wald [1935 (1968)], [1936 (1968)], and [1936 (1951)], von Neumann [1937 (1968)], Koopmans (1951), (1957), Arrow-Debreu (1954), Arrow-Hurwicz (1958), Dorfman-Samuelson-Solow (1958), McKenzie (1959), and Debreu (1959).

Of these, von Neumann, already restated in chapter 11, stands apart in economic substance: his general equilibrium was dynamic, but he never admitted consumer preferences; his labor was bred as cattle. In mathematical method, however, von Neumann does not stand apart at all: he took economists away from calculus, handled his maxima and minima without it, and taught the other Walras grandchildren to use inequalities to formulate primal and dual problems whose solutions involved a saddle point.

2. *Our Own Restatement*

In this chapter let us see how those other grandchildren proved the existence of a static general equilibrium with consumer preferences in it. Very readable accounts are given by Baumol (1977: 549-569), Koopmans

(1957: 1-126), and Dorfman-Samuelson-Solow (1958: 346-416). Our own account, even shorter, will be in the same spirit. Instead of using a differentiable production function, we shall simply follow Walras, Cassel, and Wald in assuming each output to be produced in only one way, specified by its input-output coefficients a_{ij}. Instead of using a differentiable utility function, we shall find that Samuelson's (1938), (1947) revealed preference will do: given its price-budget configuration, a household will reveal its preferred consumption set. The beauty of revealed preference is that unlike community utility or community indifference curves, an aggregate preferred consumption set is meaningful: it is found by the perfectly harmless procedure of adding the preferred quantities of the same output.

Let the notation of our restatement be as follows.

3. Variables

C $\equiv$ money value of consumption of all households
C_k $\equiv$ money value of consumption in kth household
P_j $\equiv$ price of jth output
p_i $\equiv$ price of ith input
u_i $\equiv$ excess supply of ith input
v_j $\equiv$ loss margin of jth industry
X_j $\equiv$ jth physical output demanded by all households
X_{jk} $\equiv$ jth physical output demanded by kth household
Y $\equiv$ money value of income of all households
Y_k $\equiv$ money value of income of kth household

4. Parameters

a_{ij} $\equiv$ ith physical input demanded by industry per physical unit of jth output ("coefficient de fabrication")
x_i $\equiv$ ith physical input supplied by all households
x_{ki} $\equiv$ ith physical input supplied by kth household

II. THE MODEL

1. Output and Input: Consumption and Income

Let there be m outputs X_j supplied by industry, demanded by s households, and priced P_j, on the one hand, and n inputs x_i supplied by the s households, demanded by industry, and priced p_i, on the other. Using this distinction, define the money value of consumption in the kth household as the sum of the money values of the outputs demanded by that household:

$$C_k \equiv \sum_{j=1}^{m} (P_j X_{jk}) \tag{1}$$

Define the money value of consumption of all households as the sum of the money values of the individual consumption:

$$C \equiv \sum_{k=1}^{s} C_k \tag{2}$$

Define the number of physical units of the jth output demanded by all households as the sum of the physical units of that output demanded by each household:

$$X_j \equiv \sum_{k=1}^{s} X_{jk} \tag{3}$$

Define the money value of the income of the kth household as the sum of the money values of the inputs supplied by that household:

$$Y_k \equiv \sum_{i=1}^{n} (p_i x_{ki}) \tag{4}$$

Define the money value of the incomes of all households as the sum of the money values of the individual income:

$$Y \equiv \sum_{k=1}^{s} Y_k \tag{5}$$

Define the number of physical units of the ith input supplied by all households as the sum of the physical units of that input supplied by each household:

$$x_i \equiv \sum_{k=1}^{s} x_{ki} \tag{6}$$

As the Austrians, Cassel, and Wald did, we assume the input x_{ki} supplied by the kth household to be its entire endowment; consequently x_i is the endowment of the entire economy with the ith input, a parameter.

Our chapter 11 expressed von Neumann growth in the form of constraints on a primal maximum problem and a dual minimum problem. Let us express our present static general-equilibrium model the same way. Indeed, its constraints will be the same as those of the von Neumann model, i.e., that excess demand must be nonpositive and that profits must be nonpositive.

2. *Excess Demand Must Be Nonpositive*

Feasibility requires that the sum of all of the ith input absorbed in all industries must be smaller than or equal to the quantity x_i available:

$$a_{i1}X_1 + \cdots + a_{im}X_m \leqq x_i \tag{7}$$

where $i = 1, \ldots, n$. If for the ith input the less-than sign applies, that input is a free good having a zero price p_i. If the equality sign applies, the input will be an economic good having a positive price p_i.

For two inputs, $i = 1, 2$, the constraint (7) is shown graphically in figure 13-1. The area of nonpositive excess demand satisfying both constraints (7) appears as the area of the polygon $OABC$.

FIGURE 13-1. The Primal Problem

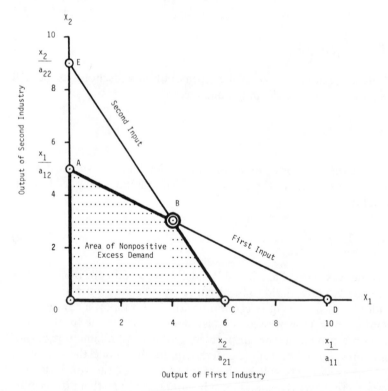

$a_{11} = 1 \qquad a_{12} = 2 \qquad a_{21} = 3 \qquad a_{22} = 2 \qquad x_1 = 10 \qquad x_2 = 18$

3.   *The Primal Problem: Maximize the Value C of All Output*

We can always make industry outputs X_j high enough to generate positive excess demand for at least one input. But how high can we make them *without* doing that? When the industry outputs X_j reach their highest possible value, the equilibrium value, excess demand will become zero for at least one input.

We may now formulate our primal problem: maximize the value C of all output subject to the constraint (7) shown in figure 13-1.

4.   *Profits Must Be Nonpositive*

Under pure competition and freedom of entry and exit, input prices p_i must be such that at unit level the money value of all inputs absorbed is greater than or equal to the price P_j of the jth industry's product:

$$a_{1j}p_1 + \cdots + a_{nj}p_n \geqq P_j \tag{8}$$

where $j = 1, \ldots, m$. If for the jth industry the greater-than sign applies, the industry will be failing to cover the costs of the resources used, hence its output X_j should be zero. If the equality sign applies, the industry will be covering the costs of the resources used, hence its output X_j should be positive.

For two outputs, $j = 1, 2$, the constraint (8) is shown graphically in figure 13-2. The area of nonpositive profits satisfying both constraints (8) appears as the area of the first quadrant lying to the northeast of the line segments *ebd*.

5.   *The Dual Problem: Minimize the Value Y of All Input*

We can always make the input prices p_i low enough to generate positive profits in at least one industry. But how low can we make them *without* doing that? When the input prices p_i reach their lowest possible value, the equilibrium value, profits will become zero in at least one industry.

We may now formulate our dual problem: minimize the value Y of all input subject to the constraint (8) shown in figure 13-2.

III.   SOLUTION: OUR SECOND SADDLE POINT

1.   *Nonpositive Excess Demand Expressed as an Equality*

By introducing a nonnegative auxiliary variable $u_i \geqq 0$ we may write (7) as an equality rather than as an inequality:

FIGURE 13-2. The Dual Problem

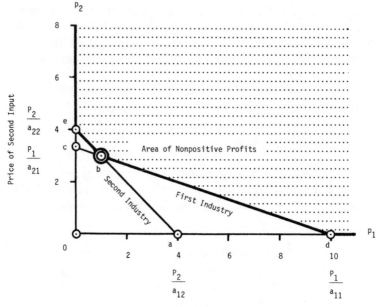

$a_{11} = 1 \qquad a_{12} = 2 \qquad a_{21} = 3 \qquad a_{22} = 2 \qquad P_1 = 10 \qquad P_2 = 8$

$$a_{i1}X_1 + \cdots + a_{im}X_m + u_i = x_i$$

or

$$u_i = x_i - (a_{i1}X_1 + \cdots + a_{im}X_m) \tag{9}$$

from which the economic meaning of u_i is seen to be available quantity of *i*th input *minus* absorption of it in all industries, or simply excess supply of *i*th input. Feasibility required excess demand for *i*th input to be nonpositive, hence requires the excess supply of it u_i to be nonnegative.

2. Nonpositive Profits Expressed as an Equality

By introducing a nonnegative auxiliary variable $v_j \geqq 0$ we may write (8) as an equality rather than as an inequality:

$$a_{1j}p_1 + \cdots + a_{nj}p_n - v_j = P_j$$

or

$$v_j = a_{1j}p_1 + \cdots + a_{nj}p_n - P_j \tag{10}$$

from which the economic meaning of v_j is seen to be unit-level cost of all inputs used in the jth industry *minus* price of its product, or simply loss margin of that industry. Freedom of entry and exit required the profit margin of the jth industry to be nonpositive, hence requires its loss margin v_j to be nonnegative.

3.   The Saddle Point: Maximized Value of All Output Equals Minimized Value of All Input

Collapsing our model to two inputs and two outputs, we write our equalities (9) and (10) as

$$u_i = x_i - (a_{i1}X_1 + a_{i2}X_2) \tag{11}$$

$$v_j = a_{1j}p_1 + a_{2j}p_2 - P_j \tag{12}$$

Now multiply (11) by the price p_i of the ith input and write out the result for both inputs $i = 1, 2$. Multiply (12) by the output X_j of the jth industry and write out the result for both industries $j = 1, 2$. The four equations are

$$p_1 u_1 = p_1 x_1 - (a_{11}p_1 X_1 + a_{12}p_1 X_2) \tag{13}$$

$$p_2 u_2 = p_2 x_2 - (a_{21}p_2 X_1 + a_{22}p_2 X_2) \tag{14}$$

$$v_1 X_1 = a_{11}p_1 X_1 + a_{21}p_2 X_1 - P_1 X_1 \tag{15}$$

$$v_2 X_2 = a_{12}p_1 X_2 + a_{22}p_2 X_2 - P_2 X_2 \tag{16}$$

Then add (13) through (16), use the definitions (1), (2), and (3) for C and (4), (5), and (6) for Y, and find

$$Y - C \equiv p_1 x_1 + p_2 x_2 - (P_1 X_1 + P_2 X_2)$$
$$= p_1 u_1 + p_2 u_2 + v_1 X_1 + v_2 X_2 \tag{17}$$

But if excess supply u_i of the ith input is zero, price p_i is positive, and if excess supply u_i is positive, price p_i is zero. Consequently, the product $p_i u_i$ always has one and only one factor equaling zero and must itself be zero. Likewise, if loss margin v_j of the jth industry is zero, its output X_j is positive, and if loss margin v_j is positive, output X_j is zero. Consequently, the product $v_j X_j$, too, always has one and only one factor equaling zero and must itself be zero, the entire right-hand side of (17) is zero, and

$$C = Y \tag{18}$$

We have found our second saddle point: the maximized value of all output equals the minimized value of all input. So the saddle point exists, and we must find its coordinates. To trap it, we shall express the price-budget configuration of households in terms of the price ratio p_1/p_2 of inputs and shall begin with the household budgets.

4. Individual and Aggregate Household Budgets

Let the kth and the $k + 1$st households be the only ones in the economy. According to the definition (1), their individual budgets are

$$C_k \equiv P_1 X_{1k} + P_2 X_{2k} \tag{19}$$

$$C_{k+1} \equiv P_1 X_{1(k+1)} + P_2 X_{2(k+1)} \tag{20}$$

which in an X_1-X_2 diagram are two parallel lines with the vertical intercepts C_k/P_2 and C_{k+1}/P_2 respectively; the horizontal intercepts C_k/P_1 and C_{k+1}/P_1, respectively; and the slope $-P_1/P_2$.

According to the definitions (2) and (3), the aggregate household budget is the sum of (19) and (20):

$$C \equiv P_1 X_1 + P_2 X_2 \tag{21}$$

which is a straight line whose vertical intercept C/P_2 is the sum of the vertical intercepts of (19) and (20); whose horizontal intercept C/P_1 is the sum of the horizontal intercepts of (19) and (20); and whose slope is the same as that of (19) and (20), i.e., $-P_1/P_2$.

5. Summing of Revealed Preference

In figure 13-3 let the point F, having the coordinates (X_{1k}, X_{2k}), represent the revealed preference of the kth household at its budget C_k and the prices P_1 and P_2. Let the point G, having the coordinates $[X_{1(k+1)}, X_{2(k+1)}]$, represent the revealed preference of the $k + 1$st household at its budget C_{k+1} and the same prices P_1 and P_2.

To F and G now apply the addition-of-vectors rule that the sum of two vectors is a new vector whose abscissa is the sum of the abscissae and whose ordinate is the sum of the ordinates. So through the points F and G draw two broken lines FH and GH which are parallel to the heavy straight lines OG and OF, respectively. The broken lines will intersect in the point H, the fourth vertex of a parallelogram having O, F, and G as its other vertices. That fourth vertex has the coordinates $[X_{1k} + X_{1(k+1)}, X_{2k} + X_{2(k+1)}]$ hence lies on the aggregate budget line (21) and represents the aggregate preferred consumption set.

To express the price-budget configuration of households in terms of the price ratio p_1/p_2 of inputs, we now turn to household incomes.

FIGURE 13-3. Addition of Individual Consumption Sets F and G of kth and $k + 1$st Households to Aggregate Consumption Set H

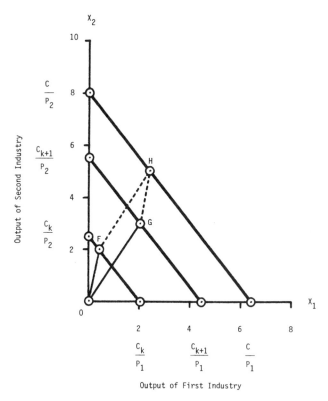

$$P_1 = 10 \qquad P_2 = 8 \qquad C_k = 20 \qquad C_{k+1} = 44 \qquad C = 64$$

6. *Income Distribution as a Function of Price Ratio of Inputs*

According to the definition (4), the incomes of our kth and $k + 1$st households are

$$Y_k \equiv p_1 x_{k1} + p_2 x_{k2} \tag{22}$$

$$Y_{k+1} \equiv p_1 x_{(k+1)1} + p_2 x_{(k+1)2} \tag{23}$$

According to definitions (5) and (6), the aggregate household income is the sum of (22) and (23):

$$Y \equiv p_1 x_1 + p_2 x_2 \tag{24}$$

Divide (22) by (23), then divide numerator and denominator alike by p_2, and write income distribution as

$$\frac{Y_k}{Y_{k+1}} = \frac{(p_1/p_2)x_{k1} + x_{k2}}{(p_1/p_2)x_{(k+1)1} + x_{(k+1)2}} \tag{25}$$

To express the price-budget configuration of households in terms of the price ratio p_1/p_2 of inputs, we finally turn to the price ratio of outputs.

7.   *Price Ratio of Outputs as a Function of Price Ratio of Inputs*

If in a two-industry economy the equality sign of the constraint (8) holds for both industries, both outputs will be produced and offered at the price tags

$$P_1 = a_{11}p_1 + a_{21}p_2 \tag{26}$$

$$P_2 = a_{12}p_1 + a_{22}p_2 \tag{27}$$

Divide (26) by (27), divide numerator and denominator of the outcome alike by p_2, and find

$$\frac{P_1}{P_2} = \frac{a_{11}p_1/p_2 + a_{21}}{a_{12}p_1/p_2 + a_{22}} \tag{28}$$

shown in figure 13-4.

We have succeeded in expressing the price-budget configuration of households in terms of the price ratio p_1/p_2 of inputs. We are now ready to put our results together as follows.

8.   *Aggregate Budget Line as a Function of Price Ratio of Inputs*

The economy is a stationary one, hence doesn't save. Indeed, let no household save, then $C_k = Y_k$, $C_{k+1} = Y_{k+1}$, and according to the definitions (2) and (5)

$$C = Y \tag{29}$$

Use (29) to write the vertical intercept C/P_2 of the aggregate household budget (21) as Y/P_2 and its horizontal intercept C/P_1 as Y/P_1. Into our intercepts Y/P_2 and Y/P_1 insert (24) for Y and (26) and (27) for P_j, then divide numerator and denominator alike of the two intercepts by p_2 and write:

$$\frac{Y}{P_2} = \frac{(p_1/p_2)x_1 + x_2}{a_{12}p_1/p_2 + a_{22}} \tag{30}$$

FIGURE 13-4. Price Ratio of Outputs as a Function of Price Ratio of Inputs

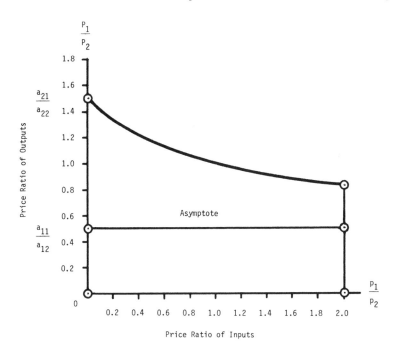

$$a_{11} = 1 \qquad a_{12} = 2 \qquad \cdot \, a_{21} = 3 \qquad a_{22} = 2$$

$$\frac{Y}{P_1} = \frac{(p_1/p_2)x_1 + x_2}{a_{11}p_1/p_2 + a_{21}} \tag{31}$$

We summarize our findings in figure 13-5 showing how a price ratio p_1/p_2 of inputs rising from zero to infinity will generate aggregate budget lines hinged, as it were, at the point B, having a vertical intercept declining from x_2/a_{22} at E to x_1/a_{12} at A, and having a horizontal intercept increasing from x_2/a_{21} at C to x_1/a_{11} at D. How do we find the intercepts (30) and (31) for p_1/p_2 approaching infinity? Simply by multiplying numerator and denominator alike by the reciprocal p_2/p_1 and realizing that if p_1/p_2 approaches infinity its reciprocal approaches zero.

9. Revealed Preference Confronted with Input Constraints

We first try the extreme value $p_1/p_2 = 0$ of the price ratio of inputs. Then figure 13-5 shows the aggregate budget line to be CE. Figure 13-1 shows that aggregate budget line to be contained in the restriction on the

FIGURE 13-5. Aggregate Budget Line as a Function of Price Ratio of Inputs

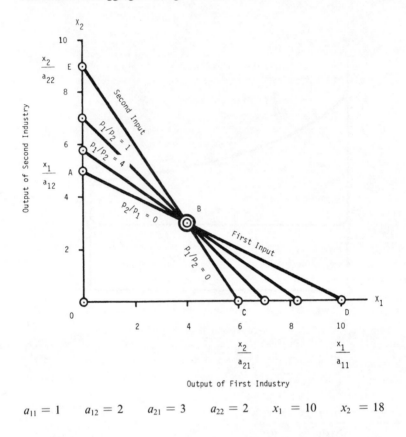

$a_{11} = 1$ $a_{12} = 2$ $a_{21} = 3$ $a_{22} = 2$ $x_1 = 10$ $x_2 = 18$

second input. On such an aggregate budget line shown in figure 13-6 there are two possibilities for revealed preference.

The first possibility is that the aggregate preferred consumption set happens to lie on the feasible part *BC* of the aggregate budget line. If so, fine! The extreme value $p_1/p_2 = 0$ will do—it has generated an aggregate preferred consumption set that is feasible in the sense that it may be satisfied without violating any of our input constraints (7). An equilibrium point exists, we have trapped it and are done.

The second possibility is that the aggregate preferred consumption set happens to lie outside the feasible part *BC* of the aggregate budget line. In that case the extreme value $p_1/p_2 = 0$ will not do—it has generated a nonfeasible aggregate preferred consumption set, say at *M*. Here the economy has enough of the second input to produce the aggregate preferred consumption set but not enough of the first input. In their

FIGURE 13-6.
Revealed Preference
Involving Positive
Excess Demand for
First Input

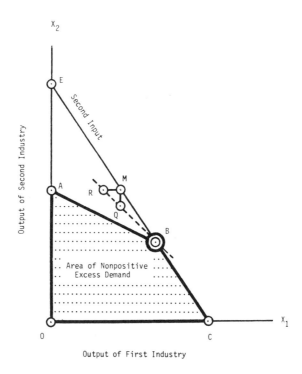

scramble to hire the first input, entrepreneurs will bid up the price ratio p_1/p_2 of inputs.

As long as endowment proportions differ between households, a different price ratio p_1/p_2 between inputs will generate a different income distribution (25), hence different intercepts of the individual budget lines (19) and (20) in figure 13-3.

As long as input proportions differ between outputs, a different price ratio p_1/p_2 between inputs will generate a different price ratio (28) between outputs, hence different slopes of the individual budget lines (19) and (20) in figure 13-3.

But if individual budget lines in figure 13-3 will have different intercepts and slopes, so will the aggregate budget line in figure 13-5.

For the resource endowments x_i and the input-output coefficients a_{ij} specified in figure 13-5 for our own particular case, a higher price ratio p_1/p_2 of inputs will lower the price ratio P_1/P_2 of outputs, thus establishing a flatter aggregate budget line in figure 13-5 passing through B, say the broken line BQR in figure 13-6 in which $p_1/p_2 = 1$.

On the new, flatter aggregate budget line an aggregate preferred consumption set Q would mean consuming the same quantity X_1 as in M but a smaller quantity X_2. An aggregate preferred consumption set R would mean consuming the same quantity X_2 as in M but a smaller quantity X_1. Or the aggregate preferred consumption set might move below and to the right of Q. Should it move all the way to B, fine! It would then be feasible, and again we would have trapped our equilibrium point. Should it still lie to the left of B, hence still not be feasible, there would be another scramble to hire the first input, the price ratio p_1/p_2 would rise still further, hence the price ratio P_1/P_2 fall still further, and our broken line BQR would be tilted still further counterclockwise around its hinge B until one of two things happens. Either the new aggregate preferred consumption set reaches B or if it doesn't the broken line BQR reaches coincidence with the restriction AB on the first input. Either way, the new aggregate preferred consumption set has become feasible, and we have trapped our equilibrium point.

IV. CONCLUSIONS

We have restated the Walras grandchildren by showing that their static general-equilibrium model of a competitive economy had a saddle point: the maximized value of all output equaled the minimized value of all input. To locate it, we first expressed the price-budget configuration of households in terms of the price ratio p_1/p_2 of inputs. That enabled us, second, to see revealed preference as a function of that ratio. It then, in turn, became possible to try out all possible price ratios p_1/p_2 of inputs and see whether the revealed preference generated by them was feasible. In short, we have followed a procedure summarized by Koopmans (1951: 10): "a preference ranking of alternatives representable by points in space is confronted with an opportunity set."

Our simple restatement has followed Walras, Cassel, and Wald in assuming each output to be produced in only one way. We have followed Cassel and Samuelson in using revealed preferences. But we have avoided Wald's inversion of Walrasian demand equations and seen preferred consumption as a function of prices—all prices, including prices of outputs and inputs alike. Unlike Wald, we have distinguished clearly between individual and aggregate preferred consumption and shown explicitly how they depend—via input prices—upon income distribution, a dependence assumed away by Wald.

Arrow-Debreu (1954) went beyond our simplicities, introduced choice among several ways of producing the same output, and derived demand functions from a maximization of utility.

We have confined ourselves to the existence of equilibrium in an institutional setting characterized by pure competition and freedom of entry and exit—ignoring the question of whether such an equilibrium could be simulated by administrative decisions in different institutional settings. The welfare aspects of a competitive equilibrium, actual or simulated, were discussed by Koopmans (1957: 66-104), Dorfman-Samuelson-Solow (1958: 390-416), and Baumol (1977: 496-536).

We have innocently assumed inputs, outputs, and consumption always to be located at the same point in space and time. Von Neumann offered the clue to dynamic general equilibrium, further discussed by Koopmans (1957: 105-126), Dorfman-Samuelson-Solow (1958: 265-346), and Baumol (1977: 597-671). Comprehensive restatements of general equilibrium in both space and time were offered by Takayama-Judge (1971).

REFERENCES

K. J. Arrow and G. Debreu, "Existence of an Equilibrium for a Competitive Economy," *Econometrica*, July 1954, *22*, 265-290.

K. J. Arrow and L. Hurwicz, "On the Stability of the Competitive Economy," *Econometrica*, Oct. 1958, *26*, 522-552.

W. J. Baumol, *Economic Theory and Operations Analysis*, Englewood Cliffs, N.J., fourth edition, 1977.

G. Cassel, *Theoretische Sozialökonomie*, Leipzig, 1918, translated as *The Theory of Social Economy* by S. L. Barron, New York, 1932.

G. Debreu, *Theory of Value: An Axiomatic Analysis of Economic Equilibrium*, New Haven and London, 1959.

R. Dorfman, P. A. Samuelson, and R. M. Solow, *Linear Programming and Economic Analysis*, New York, 1958.

T. C. Koopmans, "Analysis of Production as an Efficient Combination of Activities," in T. C. Koopmans (ed.), *Activity Analysis of Production and Allocation*, Cowles Commission Monograph No. 13, New York, 1951, 33-97.

———, "Allocation of Resources and the Price System," in T. C. Koopmans, *Three Essays on the State of Economic Science*, New York, 1957.

L. W. McKenzie, "On the Existence of General Equilibrium for a Competitive Market," *Econometrica*, Jan. 1959, *27*, 54-71.

J. von Neumann, "Ueber ein ökonomisches Gleichungssystem und eine Verallgemeinerung des Brouwerschen Fixpunktsatzes," *Ergebnisse eines mathematischen Kolloquiums*, 8, Leipzig and Vienna, 1937, 73-83, translated by G. Morgenstern (Morton) in W. J. Baumol and S. M. Goldfeld (eds.), *Precursors in Mathematical Economics: An Anthology*, London, 1968, 296-306.

P. A. Samuelson, "A Note on the Pure Theory of Consumer's Behavior," *Economica*, Feb. 1938, *5*, 61-71.

———, *Foundations of Economic Analysis*, Cambridge, Mass., 1947.

T. Takayama and G. G. Judge, *Spatial and Temporal Price and Allocation Models*, Amsterdam and London, 1971.

A. Wald, "Ueber die eindeutige positive Lösbarkeit der neuen Produktionsgleichungen," *Ergebnisse eines mathematischen Kolloquiums*, 6, Leipzig and Vienna, 1935, 12-18, translated as "On the Unique Non-Negative Solvability of the New Production Equations" by W. J. Baumol in W. J. Baumol and S. M. Goldfeld (eds.), *Precursors in Mathematical Economics: An Anthology*, London, 1968, 281-288.

————, "Ueber die Produktionsgleichungen der ökonomischen Wertlehre," *Ergebnisse eines mathematischen Kolloquiums*, 7, Leipzig and Vienna, 1936, 1-6, translated as "On the Production Equations of Economic Value Theory" by W. J. Baumol in W. J. Baumol and S. M. Goldfeld (eds.), *Precursors in Mathematical Economics: An Anthology*, London, 1968, 289-293.

————, "Ueber einige Gleichungssysteme der mathematischen Oekonomie," *Zeitschrift für Nationalökonomie*, 5, 1936, 7, 637-670, translated as "On Some Systems of Equations of Mathematical Economics," by O. Eckstein, *Econometrica*, Oct. 1951, *19*, 368-403.

L. Walras, *Eléments d'économie politique pure*, Lausanne, Paris, and Basle, 1874-1877, translated as *Elements of Pure Economics or the Theory of Social Wealth* by W. Jaffé, Homewood, Ill., 1954.

E. R. Weintraub, "On the Existence of a Competitive Equilibrium: 1930-1954," *J. Econ. Lit.*, Mar. 1983, *21*, 1-39.

C. C. von Weizsäcker, "Kenneth Arrow's Contribution to Economics," *Swed. J. Econ.*, Dec. 1972, *74*, 488-502.

CHAPTER 14 Game Theory

VON NEUMANN (1903-1957)
MORGENSTERN (1902-1977)

We had to divide the difficulties in order to overcome them.
Von Neumann and Morgenstern [1944 (1947: 608)]

I. INTRODUCTION

1. The von Neumann-Morgenstern Problem

The essence of a game is its you-or-me character. Parlor games are always zero-sum games: what the winner wins the loser loses. Economic games are sometimes constant-sum games. Duopolistic advertising may not affect the size of the market, merely the two shares of it. Zero-sum and constant-sum games have nothing else than the you-or-me essence in them.

It takes at least two to play a game, and the payoff to each player depends upon the strategy choices of both. Each player is thus trying to maximize a function of which he does not control all variables. This is no ordinary maximum problem, and Cournot (1838) could turn it into one only by letting his jth producer maximize his profits under the assumption that the quantity sold by his rivals would stay put.

2. The Method

For all his elegance and novelty, Cournot had solved his problem by virtually killing it: throughout the convergence to a Cournot equilibrium each producer would see with his own eyes a consistent violation of the assumption made, that the quantity sold by his rivals would stay put.

Not until the 1930s did economists try to break away from Cournot and admit the reaction function. Its ultimate consequence, i.e., the von Stackelberg (1934) leader-follower duopoly, showed that asymmetry was the price to be paid for mutually consistent behavior assumptions: one duopolist would have to be a leader, the other a follower, and the assignment of such roles would have to lie outside the model.

By 1944 von Neumann and Morgenstern [1944 (1947: 1)] had become convinced that "the structure of [bilateral monopoly, of duopoly, of oligopoly] problems, familiar to every student of economics, is in many respects quite different from the way in which they are conceived at the present time." But von Neumann [1928 (1963)] had by then already done the groundwork and offered an analysis of parlor games "achieved with the aid of mathematical methods which diverge considerably from the techniques applied by older or by contemporary mathematical economists."

Let the notation of our own restatement of those mathematical methods be as follows.

3. *Variables*

C ≡ ceiling to second player's mathematical expectation of payoff
E_j ≡ excess of first player's mathematical expectation above its floor assuming second player to adopt his jth strategy
F ≡ floor to first player's mathematical expectation of payoff
q_i ≡ first player's choice of probability for his ith strategy
Q_j ≡ second player's choice of probability for his jth strategy
S_i ≡ shortfall of second player's mathematical expectation below its ceiling assuming first player to adopt his ith strategy

4. *Parameters*

K ≡ constant sum of payoffs of a constant-sum game
Z_{ij} ≡ first player's payoff when he adopts his ith strategy and the second player adopts his jth strategy

II. PURE STRATEGIES

1. *Pure Strategies*

Von Neumann and Morgenstern [1944 (1947: 146)] defined a "pure" strategy as a player's choice "to play one definite strategy to the exclusion of all others." Let each of two players have two pure strategies and choose between those strategies. Call the first player's strategies $i = 1, 2$ and the second player's strategies $j = 1, 2$.

2. *Payoffs and Constant-Sum Games*

The sum, whether zero, constant, or variable, of the payoffs of all players is a crucial feature of von Neumann-Morgenstern game theory. Such a sum would be meaningless if payoffs were expressed in individual utilities. Von Neumann and Morgenstern [1944 (1947: 29)] considered such utilities to be neither comparable nor additive but [1944 (1947: 47, 605)] could "avoid all conceptual difficulties by referring . . . to a strictly monetary economy." Let the first player's payoff when he adopts his ith strategy and the second player adopts his jth strategy be, then, a sum of money Z_{ij}. In our two-player two-strategy case we write the first player's payoff as a matrix

$$\begin{bmatrix} Z_{11} & Z_{12} \\ Z_{21} & Z_{22} \end{bmatrix} \tag{1}$$

of which the first player controls the choice of row and the second player the choice of column.

A constant-sum game is a game in which the sum of the payoffs is a constant. Calling that constant K, we may then write the second player's payoff as the matrix

$$\begin{bmatrix} K - Z_{11} & K - Z_{12} \\ K - Z_{21} & K - Z_{22} \end{bmatrix} \tag{2}$$

As an example of a constant-sum game, let one duopolist's strategy choice be a green versus a red product, the other duopolist's strategy choice a blue versus an orange one. Let price and unit cost be identical between duopolists and between strategies, then profit margins will also be identical. Each duopolist's amount of profit will be in direct proportion to his physical quantity sold. Let that quantity be a function of the strategy choices of both duopolists. But let the sum of the two physical quantities sold be a constant: strategy choice cannot affect the size of the market, merely the two shares of it.

As long as the sum K is constant, the game is a you-or-me game: the second player will receive the more payoff the less the first player receives. The first player's payoff matrix (1) tells us all we need. We shall never use the second player's payoff matrix (2).

3. *Rational Behavior of Cautious Players*

Let both players know the payoff matrix (1). The first player controls the choice of its row, the second player controls the choice of its column. At the time when he makes his own choice, let no player know what the other player's choice is going to be. What, then, will be their choices?

Always expecting the worst and making the best of it, a cautious first player will choose the row whose minimum is the highest. Also always expecting the worst and making the best of it, a cautious second player will choose the column whose maximum is the lowest: putting the lowest possible ceiling on the first player's payoff is the same thing as putting the highest possible floor under his own. Let us apply these rules to some simple examples.

4. *First Simple Example*

Let our payoff matrix (1) simply consist of the first four positive integers:

$$\begin{bmatrix} 1 & 2 \\ 3 & 4 \end{bmatrix} \tag{3}$$

Here, maximizing his row minimum, the first player will choose his second strategy, for the floor 3 to its payoff is higher than the floor 1 to the payoff of his first strategy. Minimizing his column maximum, the second player will choose his first strategy, for the ceiling 3 to its payoff is lower than the ceiling 4 to the payoff of his second strategy. When the first player chooses his second row and the second player his first column, the outcome of the game is the payoff $Z_{21} = 3$.

Always looking for tidy and resilient equilibria, economists like two properties of that outcome. First, expectations come true. The outcome $Z_{21} = 3$ is both the very maximized row minimum 3 that the first player expected and the very minimized column maximum 3 that the second player expected. Both—worst!—expectations did indeed come true. Second, it would have been to nobody's advantage to have found out in advance what the adversary's choice was going to be. Had the first player known that the second player was going to choose his first column, he would still have chosen his second row. Had the second player known that the first player was going to choose his second row, he would still have chosen his first column. How sensitive is such an equilibrium to our particular choice of payoff matrix?

5. *Second Simple Example*

Let us reverse the elements of our first row of the matrix (3) and consider the matrix

$$\begin{bmatrix} 2 & 1 \\ 3 & 4 \end{bmatrix} \tag{4}$$

Here the outcome will be the same as in (3) and for the same reasons: maximizing his row minimum, the first player will still choose his second strategy. Minimizing his column maximum, the second player will still choose his first strategy, and the outcome of the game is still the payoff $Z_{21} = 3$. Both—worst!—expectations still come true, and the equilibrium is as tidy and resilient as before.

Von Neumann and Morgenstern [1944 (1947: 95)] called a point at which the maximized row minimum equals the minimized column maximum a "saddle point." Does a payoff matrix always have such a saddle point?

6. Third Simple Example

Let us finally reverse the elements of the first column of the matrix (4) and consider the matrix

$$\begin{bmatrix} 3 & 1 \\ 2 & 4 \end{bmatrix} \tag{5}$$

Here, maximizing his row minimum, the first player will still choose his second strategy, for the floor 2 to its payoff is still higher than the floor 1 to the payoff of his first strategy. Minimizing his column maximum, the second player will still choose his first strategy, for the ceiling 3 to its payoff is still lower than the ceiling 4 to the payoff of his second strategy. When the first player chooses his second row and the second player his first column, the outcome is the payoff $Z_{21} = 2$. But the saddle point is gone, and things have turned messy. To be sure, the outcome is still the maximized row minimum 2 that the first player expected but no longer the minimized column maximum 3 that the second player expected. Both—worst!—expectations can no longer come true. Surely, had the first player known that the second player was going to choose his first column, he would not have chosen his second row but his first.

With a saddle point not existing, the economist may be tempted to give up his search for tidy and resilient equilibria. But all is not lost.

III. MIXED STRATEGIES: OUR THIRD SADDLE POINT

1. Mixed Strategies

Von Neumann and Morgenstern [1944 (1947: 143-144)] observed that a moderately intelligent person playing matching pennies would decide by some fifty-fifty chance device whether to play heads or tails. The best way of protecting himself from being found out would simply be not even knowing himself what he was going to do next!

Von Neumann and Morgenstern [1944 (1947: 145)] defined a "mixed" strategy as one in which a player "plays all possible strategies and chooses only the probabilities with which he is going to play them respectively." They were able to demonstrate that, first, whether or not a game played with pure strategies has a saddle point, it will always have one when played with mixed strategies and, second, games having a saddle point when played with pure strategies may be seen as special cases of the mixed-strategy solution.

Let us restate both demonstrations. Let each of two players have two strategies and choose between the probabilities with which to play them rather than between those strategies themselves. Call the first player's probabilities q_i, $i = 1, 2$, and the second player's probabilities Q_j, $j = 1, 2$.

A primal and a dual problem may then be formulated as follows.

2.   The Primal Problem: First Player Maximizing His Floor

For his mixed strategy the first player chooses his probabilities q_1, q_2 where

$$0 \leqq q_i \leqq 1 \tag{6}$$

$$q_1 + q_2 = 1 \tag{7}$$

such as to maximize his lowest possible mathematical expectation of the payoff matrix Z_{ij}. More precisely, let F be that floor. Let the second player adopt his jth strategy, where $j = 1, 2$. Then the first player is maximizing the floor F subject to the condition that his mathematical expectation is at least F or:

$$q_1 Z_{1j} + q_2 Z_{2j} \geqq F \tag{8}$$

If to his detriment the second player should make mistakes, so much the better for the first player: then the greater-than sign of (8) would hold. But the first player counts on no such mistakes by the second player.

3.   The Dual Problem: Second Player Minimizing His Ceiling

For his mixed strategy the second player chooses his probabilities Q_1, Q_2 where

$$0 \leqq Q_j \leqq 1 \tag{9}$$

$$Q_1 + Q_2 = 1 \tag{10}$$

such as to minimize his highest possible mathematical expectation of the payoff matrix Z_{ij}. More precisely, let C be that ceiling. Let the first player adopt his ith strategy, where $i = 1, 2$. Then the second player is minimizing the ceiling C subject to the condition that his mathematical expectation is at most C, or:

$$Q_1 Z_{i1} + Q_2 Z_{i2} \leqq C \tag{11}$$

If to his detriment the first player should make mistakes, so much the better for the second player: then the less-than sign of (11) would hold. But the second player counts on no such mistakes by the first player.

4. Transforming the Primal Inequality into an Equality

As in chapters 11 and 13, by introducing a nonnegative auxiliary variable $E_j \geqq 0$ we may write (8) as an equality rather than as an inequality:

$$q_1 Z_{1j} + q_2 Z_{2j} - E_j = F$$

or

$$E_j = q_1 Z_{1j} + q_2 Z_{2j} - F \tag{12}$$

from which the economic meaning of E_j is seen to be the excess of first player's mathematical expectation above its floor when the second player adopts his jth strategy. An excess $E_j > 0$ would be to the detriment of the second player, who should therefore never adopt his jth strategy but assign the probability $Q_j = 0$ to it. An excess $E_j = 0$, on the other hand, would be acceptable to the second player, who should therefore assign a probability $Q_j > 0$ to his jth strategy.

5. Transforming the Dual Inequality into an Equality

Likewise, by introducing a nonnegative auxiliary variable $S_i \geqq 0$ we may write (11) as an equality rather than as an inequality:

$$Q_1 Z_{i1} + Q_2 Z_{i2} + S_i = C$$

or

$$S_i = C - (Q_1 Z_{i1} + Q_2 Z_{i2}) \tag{13}$$

from which the economic meaning of S_i is seen to be the shortfall of second player's mathematical expectation below its ceiling when the first player adopts his ith strategy. A shortfall $S_i > 0$ would be to the detriment of the first player, who should therefore never adopt his ith strategy but assign the probability $q_i = 0$ to it. A shortfall $S_i = 0$, on the other hand, would be acceptable to the first player, who should therefore assign a probability $q_i > 0$ to his ith strategy.

6. The Saddle Point: Minimized Ceiling C Equals Maximized Floor F

Multiply (12) by the probability Q_j that the second player adopts his jth strategy and write out the result for both strategies $j = 1, 2$. Multiply

(13) by the probability q_i that the first player adopts his ith strategy and write out the result for both strategies $i = 1, 2$. The four equations are

$$E_1 Q_1 = Q_1 q_1 Z_{11} + Q_1 q_2 Z_{21} - F Q_1 \tag{14}$$

$$E_2 Q_2 = Q_2 q_1 Z_{12} + Q_2 q_2 Z_{22} - F Q_2 \tag{15}$$

$$q_1 S_1 = C q_1 - (Q_1 q_1 Z_{11} + Q_2 q_1 Z_{12}) \tag{16}$$

$$q_2 S_2 = C q_2 - (Q_1 q_2 Z_{21} + Q_2 q_2 Z_{22}) \tag{17}$$

Then add (14) through (17), take advantage of (7) and (10), and find

$$C - F = E_1 Q_1 + E_2 Q_2 + q_1 S_1 + q_2 S_2 \tag{18}$$

But if excess E_j of first player's mathematical expectation above its floor is positive, the second player should assign a zero probability Q_j to his jth strategy, and if excess E_j is zero, the probability Q_j should be positive. Consequently, the product $E_j Q_j$ always has one and only one factor equaling zero and must itself be zero. Likewise, if shortfall S_i of second player's mathematical expectation below its ceiling is positive, the first player should assign a zero probability q_i to his ith strategy, and if shortfall S_i is zero, the probability q_i should be positive. Consequently, the product $q_i S_i$, too, always has one and only one factor equaling zero and must itself be zero, the entire right-hand side of (18) is zero, and

$$C = F \tag{19}$$

or, in English, the minimized ceiling equals the maximized floor.

Having proved the existence of our third saddle point, we must find its coordinates, i.e., solve for its underlying probabilities q_i and Q_j. We do that as follows.

7.   Basic Primal Solutions

Transforming our inequality (8) into the equality (12) meant the introduction of two new variables, E_1 and E_2. Subject to (6) and (7), the equality (12) is a system of two equations in four variables, q_i and E_j expressed in terms of F and Z_{ij}. In such a system we could arbitrarily set any two of the four variables equal to zero, solve for the remaining two, and call such a solution a "basic" one. That could be done in $\binom{4}{2} = 6$ different ways, generating six different basic primal solutions for q_i and/or E_j expressed in terms of the payoff matrix Z_{ij} alone. Let that payoff matrix be our (5).

In one of the solutions, however, the two variables arbitrarily set equal to zero would be q_1 and q_2, violating the constraint (7) and meaning that no game was being played at all. The remaining five basic primal solutions are the following, shown in table 14-1.

TABLE 14-1. Five Basic Solutions to the Primal Problem

(A) $\quad q_1 = 0; \qquad\qquad q_2 = 1; \qquad\qquad E_1 = 0; \quad E_2 = Z_{22} - Z_{21}$

(B) $\quad q_1 = \dfrac{Z_{22} - Z_{21}}{Z_{11} - Z_{12} - Z_{21} + Z_{22}}; \quad q_2 = \dfrac{Z_{11} - Z_{12}}{Z_{11} - Z_{12} - Z_{21} + Z_{22}}; \quad E_1 = 0; \qquad E_2 = 0$

(C) $\quad q_1 = 1; \qquad\qquad q_2 = 0; \qquad\qquad E_1 = Z_{11} - Z_{12}; \quad E_2 = 0$

(D) $\quad q_1 = 1; \qquad\qquad q_2 = 0; \qquad\qquad E_1 = 0; \quad' \; E_2 = Z_{12} - Z_{11}$

(E) $\quad q_1 = 0; \qquad\qquad q_2 = 1; \qquad\qquad E_1 = Z_{21} - Z_{22}; \quad E_2 = 0$

If in (12) E_1 and q_1 were equal to zero but q_2 were equal to one, then $F = Z_{21}$ and $E_2 = Z_{22} - Z_{21}$, which would be feasible because nonnegative. This is case (A).

If in (12) both E_1 and E_2 were zero, it would collapse into $q_1 Z_{11} + q_2 Z_{21} = q_1 Z_{12} + q_2 Z_{22}$, which together with (7) would give us the two solutions for q_1 and q_2 shown in case (B), both feasible because nonnegative.

If in (12) E_2 and q_2 were equal to zero but q_1 were equal to one, then $F = Z_{12}$ and $E_1 = Z_{11} - Z_{12}$, which would be feasible because nonnegative. This is case (C).

If in (12) E_1 and q_2 were equal to zero but q_1 were equal to one, then $F = Z_{11}$ and $E_2 = Z_{12} - Z_{11}$, which would be nonfeasible because negative. This is case (D).

Finally, if in (12) E_2 and q_1 were equal to zero but q_2 were equal to one, then $F = Z_{22}$ and $E_1 = Z_{21} - Z_{22}$, which would be nonfeasible because negative. This is case (E).

8. Graphical Representation of the Basic Primal Solutions

A graphical representation of the five basic primal solutions will now be useful. We have two inequalities (8), one for each strategy of the second player. Let each be represented by a straight line AD and CE in figure 14-1. The line itself is the locus of all points to which the equality sign of (8) applies. The space above it is the locus of all points to which the

FIGURE 14-1. The Primal Problem of Mixed Strategies

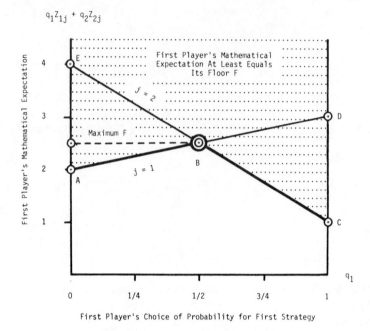

$q_1 Z_{1j} + q_2 Z_{2j}$

First Player's Mathematical Expectation

First Player's Choice of Probability for First Strategy

$Z_{11} = 3$ $Z_{12} = 1$ $Z_{21} = 2$ $Z_{22} = 4$

greater-than sign of (8) applies. As a result, the area in which the first player's mathematical expectation at least equals its floor F is represented by the shaded area above ABC in figure 14-1. The three points A, B, and C represent the basic primal solutions (A), (B), and (C) of table 14-1 and are feasible under the parameter values Z_{ij} of our matrix (5) indicated in the caption of figure 14-1: no variable q_i or E_j is negative.

The two points D and E represent the remaining basic primal solutions (D) and (E) of table 14-1 and are nonfeasible, involving negative excess E_j: in (D) $E_2 < 0$, and in (E) $E_1 < 0$.

Figure 14-1 shows that the first player will maximize his floor F by choosing the probabilities $q_1 = 1/2$, $q_2 = 1/2$ for his mixed strategy, i.e., by choosing the point B. Here his maximized floor will be $F = 2.5$.

9. *Basic Dual Solutions*

Transforming our inequality (11) into the equality (13) meant the introduction of two new variables, S_1 and S_2. Subject to (9) and (10), the equality (13) is a system of two equations in four variables, Q_j and S_i expressed in terms of C and Z_{ij}. In such a system we could arbitrarily set any two of the four variables equal to zero, solve for the remaining two, and again call such solutions basic ones. That could be done in $\binom{4}{2} = 6$ different ways, generating six different basic dual solutions for Q_j and/or S_i expressed in terms of the payoff matrix Z_{ij} alone.

In one of the solutions, however, the two variables arbitrarily set equal to zero would be Q_1 and Q_2, violating the constraint (10) and meaning that no game was being played at all. The remaining five basic dual solutions are the following, shown in table 14-2.

If in (13) S_2 and Q_2 were equal to zero but Q_1 were equal to one, then $C = Z_{21}$ and $S_1 = Z_{21} - Z_{11}$, which would be nonfeasible because negative. This is case (a).

If in (13) both S_1 and S_2 were zero, it would collapse into $Q_1 Z_{11} + Q_2 Z_{12} = Q_1 Z_{21} + Q_2 Z_{22}$, which together with (10) would give us the two solutions for Q_1 and Q_2 shown in case (b), both feasible because nonnegative.

If in (13) S_1 and Q_1 were equal to zero but Q_2 were equal to one, then $C = Z_{12}$ and $S_2 = Z_{12} - Z_{22}$, which would be nonfeasible because negative. This is case (c).

If in (13) S_1 and Q_2 were equal to zero but Q_1 were equal to one, then $C = Z_{11}$ and $S_2 = Z_{11} - Z_{21}$, which would be feasible because nonnegative. This is case (d).

Finally, if in (13) S_2 and Q_1 were equal to zero but Q_2 were equal to one, then $C = Z_{22}$ and $S_1 = Z_{22} - Z_{12}$, which would be feasible because nonnegative. This is case (e).

TABLE 14-2. Five Basic Solutions to the Dual Problem

(a)	$Q_1 = 1;$	$Q_2 = 0;$	$S_1 = Z_{21} - Z_{11};$ $S_2 = 0$
(b)	$Q_1 = \dfrac{Z_{22} - Z_{12}}{Z_{11} - Z_{12} - Z_{21} + Z_{22}};$ $Q_2 = \dfrac{Z_{11} - Z_{21}}{Z_{11} - Z_{12} - Z_{21} + Z_{22}};$	$S_1 = 0;$	$S_2 = 0$
(c)	$Q_1 = 0;$	$Q_2 = 1;$	$S_1 = 0;$ $S_2 = Z_{12} - Z_{22}$
(d)	$Q_1 = 1;$	$Q_2 = 0;$	$S_1 = 0;$ $S_2 = Z_{11} - Z_{21}$
(e)	$Q_1 = 0;$	$Q_2 = 1;$	$S_1 = Z_{22} - Z_{12};$ $S_2 = 0$

10. *Graphical Representation of the Basic Dual Solutions*

A graphical representation of the five basic dual solutions will also be useful. We have two inequalities (11), one for each strategy of the first player. Let each be represented by a straight line *ae* and *cd* in figure 14-2. The line itself is the locus of all points to which the equality sign of (11) applies. The space below it is the locus of all points to which the less-than sign of (11) applies. As a result, the area in which the second player's mathematical expectation at most equals its ceiling *C* is represented by the shaded area below *ebd* in figure 14-2. The three points *e*, *b*, and *d* represent the basic dual solutions (e), (b), and (d) of table 14-2 and are feasible under the parameter values Z_{ij} of our matrix (5) indicated in the caption of figure 14-2: no variable Q_j or S_i is negative.

The two points *a* and *c* represent the remaining basic dual solutions (a) and (c) of table 14-2 and are nonfeasible, involving negative shortfalls S_i: in (a) $S_1 < 0$, and in (c) $S_2 < 0$.

Figure 14-2 shows that the second player will minimize his ceiling *C* by choosing the probabilities $Q_1 = 3/4$, $Q_2 = 1/4$ for his mixed strategy,

FIGURE 14-2. The Dual Problem of Mixed Strategies

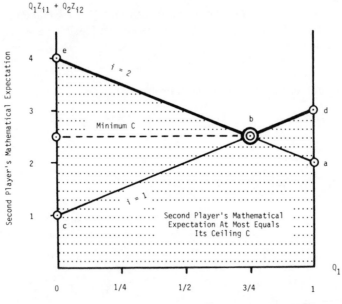

$$Z_{11} = 3 \qquad Z_{12} = 1 \qquad Z_{21} = 2 \qquad Z_{22} = 4$$

i.e., by choosing the point b. Taken together, figures 14-1 and 14-2 show that the feasible pair B and b represents the saddle point of a game characterized by the payoff matrix (5). Here $q_1 = 1/2$, $q_2 = 1/2$, $Q_1 = 3/4$, and $Q_2 = 1/4$. The maximized floor and the minimized ceiling are $F = C = 2.5$.

11. *Correspondence Between Primal and Dual Basic Solutions*

The symmetry between primal and dual manifests itself in pairs of correspondence between basic solutions. As we saw, if a primal basic solution displays a zero excess E_j, then the corresponding dual basic solution should display a positive probability Q_j. As we also saw, if a dual basic solution displays a zero shortfall S_i, then the corresponding primal basic solution should display a positive probability q_i.

Our tables 14-1 and 14-2 reflect such correspondence by using the same letter for corresponding pairs, i.e., a capital letter for the basic primal solution and a lower-case letter for the dual one.

12. *Pure Strategies as Special Cases of Mixed Ones*

Von Neumann and Morgenstern showed that whether or not a game played with pure strategies has a saddle point, it will always have one when played with mixed strategies. Indeed, applied to our simple payoff matrix (5), pure strategies possessed no saddle point but mixed ones did, i.e., the primal solution (B) and the dual solution (b).

Is the mixed-strategy solution so powerful and general that games *having* a saddle point when played with pure strategies may be seen as special cases of the mixed-strategy solution? To see if it is, let us see if our tables 14-1 and 14-2 can handle the simple payoff matrices (3) and (4), in which pure strategies did possess the saddle point $Z_{21} = 3$.

13. *The Special Case of Payoff Matrix (4)*

Let us first try our payoff matrix (4) which, as we saw, had the saddle point $Z_{21} = 3$. Tables 14-1 and 14-2 are still good and show the five basic solutions of the primal and the dual. For the payoff matrix (4), their graphical representations are shown in figure 14-3. Again, the shaded area of the primal is the locus of points at which the first player's mathematical expectation at least equals its floor F. The points A, B, and C represent the basic primal solutions (A), (B), and (C) of table 14-1 and are feasible under the parameter values Z_{ij} of matrix (4) indicated in the caption of figure 14-3: no variable q_i or E_j is negative. But the points E and

FIGURE 14-3.
Primal and Dual
Problems in the Special
Case (4) of Pure
Strategies

$Z_{11} = 2$
$Z_{12} = 1$
$Z_{21} = 3$
$Z_{22} = 4$

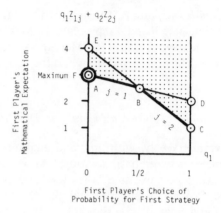

First Player's Choice of
Probability for First Strategy

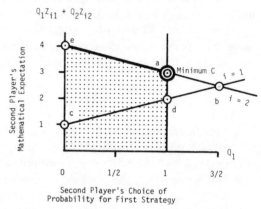

Second Player's Choice of
Probability for First Strategy

D, representing the remaining basic primal solutions (E) and (D) of table 14-1, are nonfeasible: in (E) $E_1 < 0$; in (D) $E_2 < 0$.

The shaded area of the dual is the locus of points at which the second player's mathematical expectation at most equals its ceiling C. The points a and e represent the basic dual solutions (a) and (e) of table 14-2 and are feasible under the parameter values Z_{ij} of matrix (4) indicated in the caption of figure 14-3: no variable Q_j or S_i is negative. But the points c and d, representing the basic dual solutions (c) and (d) of table 14-2, are nonfeasible: in both, $S_2 < 0$. The point b, representing the mixed-strategy basic dual solution (b), is nonfeasible: it violates the constraint (9).

Figure 14-3 shows that the feasible pair (A) and (a) represents the saddle point of a game characterized by the payoff matrix (4). Here $q_1 = 0$, $q_2 = 1$, $Q_1 = 1$, and $Q_2 = 0$. The maximized floor and the minimized ceiling are $F = C = 3$. As it happens, in the special case of our matrix (4) the optimal mixed strategies assume the form of pure ones.

14. *The Special Case of Payoff Matrix (3)*

Let us finally try our payoff matrix (3) which, as we saw, also had the saddle point $Z_{21} = 3$. Tables 14-1 and 14-2 are still good and show the five basic solutions of the primal and the dual. For the payoff matrix (3), their graphical representations are shown in figure 14-4. As usual, the shaded area of the primal is the locus of points at which the first player's mathematical expectation at least equals its floor F. The points A and D represent the basic primal solutions (A) and (D) of table 14-1 and are feasible under the parameter values Z_{ij} of matrix (3) indicated in the caption of figure 14-4: no variable q_i or E_j is negative. But the points C and E, representing the basic primal solutions (C) and (E) of table 14-1, are nonfeasible: in both $E_1 < 0$. Where is the point B, representing the mixed-strategy basic primal solution (B)? The point has disappeared: the two lines do not intersect, and the solution (B) is now meaningless, because its denominators $Z_{11} - Z_{12} - Z_{21} + Z_{22}$ are zero.

FIGURE 14-4.
Primal and Dual
Problems in the Special
Case (3) of Pure
Strategies

$Z_{11} = 1$
$Z_{12} = 2$
$Z_{21} = 3$
$Z_{22} = 4$

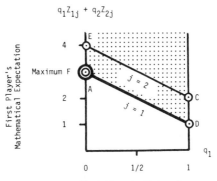

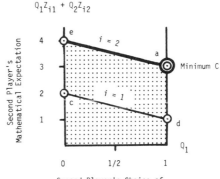

The shaded area of the dual is the locus of points at which the second player's mathematical expectation at most equals its ceiling C. The points a and e represent the basic dual solutions (a) and (e) of table 14-2 and are feasible under the parameter values Z_{ij} of matrix (3) indicated in the caption of figure 14-4: no variable Q_j or S_i is negative. But the points c and d, representing the basic dual solutions (c) and (d) of table 14-2, are nonfeasible: in both, $S_2 < 0$. The point b, representing the mixed-strategy basic dual solution (b), is absent for the same reason the point B was absent.

Figure 14-4 shows that the feasible pair (A) and (a) represents the saddle point of a game characterized by the payoff matrix (3). Here $q_1 = 0$, $q_2 = 1$, $Q_1 = 1$, and $Q_2 = 0$. The maximized floor and the minimized ceiling are $F = C = 3$. As it happens, in the special case of our matrix (3), as they did in matrix (4), the optimal mixed strategies assume the form of pure ones.

IV. CONCLUSIONS

1. *Our Third Saddle Point*

In addition to our general-equilibrium saddle points in chapters 11 and 13, we have now found a game-theory saddle point. Historically, the game-theory saddle point came first, i.e., von Neumann (1928). That von Neumann's discovery should provide the key to the solution of three problems so different and never solved before is a testimony to its power and generality.

2. *Beyond Our Restatement*

Von Neumann and Morgenstern (1944) did not think of the zero-sum, two-person game as a cut-and-dried case ready for immediate application. Rather, they thought of it as the basis of extension. The last two-thirds of their book accomplished such extension in three dimensions.

The first extension, from zero-sum to constant-sum games, was the easiest. Von Neumann and Morgenstern [1944 (1947: 245-247 and 346-348)] showed that every constant-sum game is strategically equivalent to a zero-sum game—as our own restatement has indeed considered it to be.

The second extension, from zero-sum, two-person games to zero-sum, n-person games, was not so easy. As soon as the number of players rises above two, something qualitatively new becomes possible, i.e., coalitions. Von Neumann and Morgenstern [1944 (1947: 238-240)] considered every possible subset of players selected among the n to be a possible coalition. Assuming such a coalition always to expect the worst, i.e., that the remaining players would form a countercoalition, the payoffs of such a pair of coalitions confronting each other could be calculated. Assuming each of such coalitions to be an "absolute" one, von Neumann and Morgenstern [1944 (1947: 238)] assumed full cooperation among the members within it and thus reduced the zero-sum, n-person game to a zero-sum, two-coalition game to which all their zero-sum, two-person results would apply. A new problem had, however, been introduced, i.e., how to divide the spoils. Such division was accomplished by intermember compensations determined by the opportunity of each member of the coalition to forsake it and join a different coalition.

The third extension, from zero-sum, n-person games to variable-sum, n-person games, was accomplished in the last one-sixth of the book. Von Neumann and Morgenstern [1944 (1947: 506-512)] chose to interpret a variable-sum, n-person game as a zero-sum, $n + 1$-person game. The $n + 1$st player was a fictitious one assumed to lose the amount won by the totality of the n real players. The fictitious player was allowed neither any influence on the moves of the game nor any participation in the interplay of coalitions and compensations—for the excellent reason that he did not exist.

REFERENCES

A. A. Cournot, *Recherches sur les principes mathématiques de la théorie des richesses*, Paris, 1838, translated as *Researches into the Mathematical Principles of the Theory of Wealth* by N. T. Bacon, New York, 1927.

J. von Neumann, "Zur Theorie der Gesellschaftsspiele," *Mathematische Annalen*, 1928, *100*, 295-320, reprinted in J. von Neumann, *Collected Works*, VI, New York, 1963.

J. von Neumann and O. Morgenstern, *Theory of Games and Economic Behavior*, Princeton, 1944, second, corrected edition, 1947.

H. von Stackelberg, *Marktform und Gleichgewicht*, Vienna and Berlin, 1934.

CHAPTER 15 Neoclassical Growth

TINBERGEN (1903-)
SOLOW (1924-)

The bulk of this paper is devoted to a model of long-run growth which accepts all the Harrod-Domar assumptions except that of fixed proportions.

Solow (1956: 66)

By the usual methodological standards, this is a beautiful theory, deriving a wealth of conclusions out of very few and simple assumptions, where the conclusions fit the facts they are supposed to explain.

Krelle (1977: 290)

I. INTRODUCTION

1. Solow's Problem

Cassel and Harrod had built a model of an economy delicately balancing on its knife-edge equilibrium growth path. The slightest slip would send the economy farther and farther away from such a path. Solow's problem was to find a more robust path.

2. Solow's Method

Unfreezing the frozen input-output coefficients of the Harrod model was all it took to free long-run growth from its confinement to a knife's edge. In Solow's model a production function, not necessarily of Cobb-Douglas form, permitted substitution between labor and capital stock. Capital stock was the result of accumulated savings under an autonomously given propensity to consume.

Although Solow did not know it, the model already existed. Halfway through the Second World War Tinbergen [1942 (1959)] had published it complete with econometric estimates of its parameters for four countries. But he had done it in German behind enemy lines.

3.   *Our Own Restatement*

As Cassel, Harrod, Robinson, Kaldor, Tinbergen, and Solow did, let us confine ourselves to the case of one good with two uses—consumption and investment—and an immortal capital stock of that good. In a one-good economy aggregate physical capital stock and all other physical aggregates are meaningful. We shall reproduce the Solow model using a Cobb-Douglas production function.

Let the notation of our restatement be as follows.

4.   *Variables*

C ≡ physical consumption
g_v ≡ proportionate rate of growth of variable v
I ≡ physical investment
κ ≡ physical marginal productivity of capital stock
L ≡ labor employed
P ≡ price of goods and services
S ≡ physical capital stock
W ≡ wage bill
w ≡ money wage rate
X ≡ physical output
Y ≡ money national income
Z ≡ profits bill

5.   *Parameters*

a ≡ multiplicative factor of production function
α ≡ elasticity of physical output with respect to labor employed
β ≡ elasticity of physical output with respect to physical capital stock
c ≡ propensity to consume
F ≡ available labor force
g_v ≡ proportionate rate of growth of parameter v

The symbol t is time. All parameters are stationary except a and F whose growth rates are stationary.

II.   THE NEOCLASSICAL MODEL

1.   *Five Equations Common to Post-Keynesian and Neoclassical Growth*

Define the proportionate rate of growth of variable v as

$$g_v \equiv \frac{dv}{dt}\frac{1}{v} \tag{1}$$

Define investment as the derivative of capital stock with respect to time:

$$I \equiv \frac{dS}{dt} \tag{2}$$

Define the wage bill as the money wage rate *times* employment:

$$W \equiv wL \tag{3}$$

Define money national income as the sum of the wage and profits bills:

$$Y \equiv W + Z \tag{4}$$

Equilibrium requires output to equal demand for it:

$$X = C + I \tag{5}$$

2. *Production*

Let entrepreneurs apply a Cobb-Douglas production function

$$X = aL^\alpha S^\beta \tag{6}$$

where $0 < \alpha < 1; 0 < \beta < 1; \alpha + \beta = 1;$ and $a > 0$.

Let profit maximization under pure competition equalize real wage rate and physical marginal productivity of labor:

$$\frac{w}{P} = \frac{\partial X}{\partial L} = \alpha \frac{X}{L} \tag{7}$$

Multiply by *PL* and write the wage bill

$$W \equiv wL = \alpha PX \tag{8}$$

Define physical marginal productivity of capital stock, called by Solow (1956: 80) "the commodity own-rate of interest," as

$$\kappa \equiv \frac{\partial X}{\partial S} = \beta \frac{X}{S} \tag{9}$$

Multiply by *PS* and write the profits bill

$$Z \equiv \kappa PS = \beta PX \tag{10}$$

Assume full employment:

$$L = F \tag{11}$$

3.   *Distributive Shares*

Insert (8) and (10) into (4) and find $Y = PX$ and the distributive shares $W/Y = \alpha$ and $Z/Y = \beta$. Notice that we derived this result before specifying our neoclassical consumption function

$$C = cX \tag{12}$$

where $0 < c < 1$. In the distributive shares, then, the form of the consumption function makes no difference. For example, the latter may well be a post-Keynesian one with realistic different propensities to consume real wages and real profits. In that case, we would simply have $c \equiv \alpha c_W + \beta c_Z$.

III. SOLUTIONS

1.   *Convergence to Steady-State Growth*

To solve the system, insert (11) into the production function (6), differentiate the latter with respect to time, and find

$$g_X = g_a + \alpha g_F + \beta g_S \tag{13}$$

Here, g_a and g_F are parameters but g_S a variable. Use (12), (5), (1), and (2) in that order to express it as

$$g_S = (1 - c)X/S \tag{14}$$

Differentiate (14) with respect to time, use (1) and (13), and express the proportionate rate of acceleration of physical capital stock as

$$g_{gS} = g_X - g_S = \alpha(g_a/\alpha + g_F - g_S) \tag{15}$$

In (15) there are three possibilities: if $g_S > g_a/\alpha + g_F$, then $g_{gS} < 0$. If

$$g_S = g_a/\alpha + g_F \tag{16}$$

then $g_{gS} = 0$. Finally, if $g_S < g_a/\alpha + g_F$, then $g_{gS} > 0$. Consequently, if greater than (16) g_S is falling; if equal to (16) g_S is stationary; and if less than (16) g_S is rising. Furthermore, g_S cannot alternate around (16), for differential equations trace continuous time paths, and as soon as a g_S-path touched (16) it would have to stay there. Finally, g_S cannot converge to anything than (16), for if it did, by letting enough time elapse we could make the left-hand side of (15) smaller than any arbitrarily assignable positive constant ε, however small, without the same being possible for the right-hand side. We conclude that g_S must either equal $g_a/\alpha + g_F$ from the outset or, if it does not, converge to that value.

Insert equation (16) into (13) and find the growth rate of physical output

$$g_X = g_S \tag{17}$$

Differentiate (9) with respect to time, use (17), and find the growth rate of the physical marginal productivity of capital stock

$$g_\kappa = 0 \tag{18}$$

2. Did Saving or Investment Adjust to a Higher Propensity to Save?

If the propensity to save $1 - c$ were twice as high, how would a neoclassical model adjust? Rearrange (14) and write it as

$$S/X = (1 - c)/g_S \tag{14}$$

where g_S stands for the solution (16). An economy otherwise equal but with twice the propensity to save $1 - c$ will at any time have twice the capital coefficient S/X. In this sense the adjustment lies on the investment side. In the real world, does it?

There are few advanced economies offering usable data on this matter. The two economies best known to this writer are among them. The United States 1953–1969 had a net aggregate propensity to save of 0.081 and a capital coefficient of 2.28 [Brems (1973: 35)]. Both are roughly half their Swedish counterparts: Sweden, according to Lindbeck (1972: 172), had a net aggregate propensity to save of 0.14 and, according to Lundberg (1961: 111), a capital coefficient of 4 to 5. A neoclassical observer would express no surprise at the fact that at half the capital coefficient and half the net propensity to save, the United States has managed to grow at roughly the same rate as Sweden. A post-Keynesian observer would have expected the distributive shares rather than the capital coefficient to carry the burden of adjustment. But they haven't: in his treatise on labor's share, Jungenfelt (1966) found Swedish and U.S. distributive shares to be the same.

3. The Real Wage Rate and the Wicksell Effect

To solve for the real wage rate, divide the production function (6) first by L and then by S and find

$$X/L = a(S/L)^\beta$$

$$X/S = a(L/S)^\alpha$$

Raise the latter equation to the power $-1/\alpha$, rearrange, insert into the former equation, insert the result into (7), and write the real wage rate

$$w/P = \alpha a^{1/\alpha} (S/X)^{\beta/\alpha} \tag{19}$$

Insert (14) into (19) and find the solution for the real wage rate

$$w/P = \alpha a^{1/\alpha} [(1 - c)/g_S]^{\beta/\alpha} \qquad (20)$$

Here is the Wicksell Effect. An economy otherwise equal but with twice the propensity to save $1 - c$ will, according to (14), have twice the capital coefficient S/X, hence, according to (19), a $2^{\beta/\alpha}$ *times* higher real wage rate w/P. Wicksell himself [1901 (1934: 164)] expressed his effect: "The capitalist saver is, thus, fundamentally, the friend of labour."

Notice the absence of employment L in (20): In steady-state equilibrium growth an economy otherwise equal but with twice the employment L will at any time have accumulated twice the physical capital stock S and be producing twice the physical output X. As a result, its capital coefficient S/X, and with it its real wage rate w/P, will be the same regardless of the employment L. In other words, the populous economy with twice the employment L will not be displaying a lower physical marginal productivity of labor and a lower real wage rate. No Malthusian overpopulation here. Land is ignored, and physical capital stock will accumulate as needed!

4. Mark-up Pricing

Mark-up pricing may be a deviation from neoclassical language but not from neoclassical substance. Under neoclassical pure competition, too, there are overhead costs to be covered, and freedom of entry and exit will see to it that they are. So neoclassical price, too, will exceed "prime cost." The proportion in which it does is easily found: rearrange (7) and write the neoclassical mark-up-pricing equation

$$P = \frac{wL}{\alpha X} \qquad (7)$$

saying that neoclassical price P equals per-unit labor cost wL/X marked up in the proportion $1/\alpha$. In our next chapter on a Friedman inflation equilibrium we shall make good use of such neoclassical mark-up pricing.

5. Conclusions

The solutions of the neoclassical growth model possessed five important properties: (1) stationary distributive shares; (2) convergence to steady-state growth of output; (3) identical steady-state growth rates of output and capital stock; (4) a stationary rate of return to capital; and (5) identical steady-state growth rates of the real wage rate and labor productivity. Brems (1983: ch. 7) summarized empirical findings by Christensen, Cummings, and Jorgenson (1980), Denison (1967), (1974), Kendrick et al. (1976), Kravis (1959), Kuznets (1971), and Phelps Brown (1973) and found none of the five properties to be seriously at odds with historical reality.

REFERENCES

H. Brems, *Labor, Capital, and Growth*, Lexington, Mass., 1973.
————, *Fiscal Theory*, Lexington, Mass., 1983.
L. R. Christensen, D. Cummings, and D. W. Jorgenson, "Economic Growth, 1947-1973: An International Comparison," in J. W. Kendrick and B. N. Vaccara (eds.), *New Developments in Productivity Measurement and Analysis*, Chicago and London, 1980.
E. F. Denison, *Why Growth Rates Differ: Postwar Experience in Nine Western Countries*, Washington, D.C., 1967.
————, *Accounting for United States Economic Growth, 1929-1969*, Washington, D.C., 1974.
K. G. Jungenfelt, *Löneandelen och den ekonomiska utvecklingen*, Stockholm, 1966.
J. W. Kendrick, assisted by Y. Lethem and J. Rowley, *The Formation and Stocks of Total Capital*, New York, 1976.
I. B. Kravis, "Relative Income Shares in Fact and Theory," *Amer. Econ. Rev.*, Dec. 1959, *49*, 917-949.
W. Krelle, "Basic Facts in Capital Theory—Some Lessons from the Controversy in Capital Theory," *Revue d'économie politique*, Mar.-Apr. 1977, 282-329.
S. Kuznets, *Economic Growth of Nations: Total Output and Production Structure*, Cambridge, Mass., 1971.
A. Lindbeck, *Swedish Economic Policy*, Berkeley and Los Angeles, 1972.
E. Lundberg, *Produktivitet och räntabilitet*, Stockholm, 1961.
E. H. Phelps Brown, "Levels and Movements of Industrial Productivity and Real Wages Internationally Compared, 1860-1970," *Econ. J.*, Mar. 1973, *83*, 58-71.
R. M. Solow, "A Contribution to the Theory of Economic Growth," *Quart. J. Econ.*, Feb. 1956, *70*, 65-94.
————, *Growth Theory—An Exposition*, New York and Oxford, 1970.
J. Tinbergen, "Zur Theorie der langfristigen Wirtschaftsentwicklung," *Weltw. Archiv*, May 1942, *55*, 511-549, translated in L. H. Klaassen, L. M. Koyck, and H. J. Witteveen (eds.), *Jan Tinbergen, Selected Papers*, Amsterdam 1959.
K. Wicksell, *Föreläsningar i nationalekonomi*, I, Lund, 1901, translated as *Lectures on Political Economy*, I by E. Classen and edited by Lionel Robbins, London, 1934.

CHAPTER *16* Long-Run Inflation Equilibrium

FRIEDMAN (1912-)

The monetary authority controls nominal quantities
... It cannot use its control over nominal quantities to
peg a real quantity—the real rate of interest, the rate
of unemployment, the level of real national income,
... the rate of growth of real national income.

Friedman (1968: 11)

I. INTRODUCTION

1. *Friedman's "Theoretical Framework"*

Friedman (1968: 5) dismissed and went beyond "very limited periods." His model is clearly long-run. Furthermore, he considered the rate of inflation an equilibrating variable. Containing such a derivative with respect to time, his model is intrinsically dynamic and must have two different interest rates, the nominal and the real one. A Friedman model, then, must be a long-run, dynamic, two-interest-rates model clearly incompatible with the short-run, static, one-interest-rate *IS-LM* model offered by Friedman himself (1970) as his "theoretical framework." As Thygesen (1977) observed in his Nobel article, Friedman "is clearly uncomfortable with it."

2. *Our Own Restatement*

A much more compatible framework would be a Solow (1956) model of neoclassical growth.[1] Solow made no attempt to optimize capital stock. We must do that if we are to simulate crowding-out and must, of course, add bonds, government, inflation, interest rates, money, and taxation to a Solow model. Let its tax rate and the rates of growth of its money and bond supplies be its policy instruments, and let its notation be as follows.

---

[1]Drud Hansen (1979) used a neoclassical growth model to simulate monetarism but—like Friedman himself—ignored taxation.

3. *Variables*

C ≡ physical consumption
D ≡ desired holding of money
δ ≡ ratio between fiscal deficit and money national income
G ≡ physical government purchase of goods and services
g_v ≡ proportionate rate of growth of variable v
I ≡ physical investment
k ≡ present gross worth of another physical unit of an asset
κ ≡ physical marginal productivity of capital stock
L ≡ labor employed
n ≡ present net worth of another physical unit of an asset
P ≡ price of goods and services
p ≡ coefficient in the Phillips function representing Eckstein's "shock" component
Π ≡ price of bonds
R ≡ government net receipts *before* interest paid by government
r ≡ before-tax nominal rate of interest
ρ ≡ after-tax real rate of interest
S ≡ physical capital stock
w ≡ money wage rate
X ≡ physical output
Y ≡ money national income
y ≡ money disposable income

4. *Parameters*

a ≡ multiplicative factor of production function
α ≡ elasticity of physical output with respect to labor employed
β ≡ elasticity of physical output with respect to physical capital stock
c ≡ propensity to consume
F ≡ available labor force
g_v ≡ proportionate rate of growth of parameter v
i ≡ interest payment per bond
λ ≡ fraction employed of available labor force
M ≡ supply of money
m ≡ multiplicative factor in demand-for-money function
μ ≡ exponent in demand-for-money function
π ≡ exponent in Phillips function
Q ≡ supply of bonds: physical quantity of government bonds outstanding
T ≡ tax rate
ϕ ≡ coefficient in the Phillips function representing sensitivity to inflationary expectations

The symbol e is Euler's number, the base of natural logarithms. The symbol t is general time. The symbol τ is present time. All parameters are stationary except a, F, M, and Q whose growth rates are stationary.

II. THE MODEL

1. *Rate of Growth*

Define the proportionate rate of growth of variable v as

$$g_v \equiv \frac{dv}{dt}\frac{1}{v} \tag{1}$$

2. *The Production Function and Marginal Productivities*

Monetarists have shown no interest in specifying a production function but may not object, we hope, to a Cobb-Douglas form

$$X = aL^\alpha S^\beta \tag{2}$$

where $0 < \alpha < 1$; $0 < \beta < 1$; $\alpha + \beta = 1$, and $a > 0$.

Let profit maximization under pure competition equalize real wage rate and physical marginal productivity of labor:

$$\frac{w}{P} = \frac{\partial X}{\partial L} = \alpha \frac{X}{L} \tag{3}$$

Rearrange (3) and write it as neoclassical mark-up pricing:

$$P = \frac{wL}{\alpha X}$$

or, in English: neoclassical price P equals per-unit labor cost wL/X marked up in the proportion $1/\alpha$. Differentiate with respect to time and find our price equation

$$g_P = g_w + g_L - g_X \tag{4}$$

3. *The Investment Function*

Define investment as the derivative of capital stock with respect to time:

$$I \equiv \frac{dS}{dt} \tag{5}$$

Define physical marginal productivity of capital stock as

$$\kappa \equiv \frac{\partial X}{\partial S} = \beta \frac{X}{S} \tag{6}$$

Let entrepreneurs be purely competitive ones, then price P of output is beyond their control. Let profits be taxed at the rate T. At time t, then, the after-tax marginal value productivity of capital stock is $(1 - T)\kappa(t)P(t)$.

Let there be a market in which money may be placed or borrowed at a stationary before-tax nominal rate of interest r. Let interest earnings be taxed and interest expense be tax-deductible. Then money may be placed or borrowed at the after-tax rate $(1 - T)r$. Let that rate be applied when discounting future cash flows. As seen from the present time τ, then, the after-tax marginal value productivity of capital stock is $(1 - T)\kappa(t)P(t)e^{-(1-T)r(t-\tau)}$. Define present gross worth of another physical unit of capital stock as the present worth of all future after-tax marginal value productivities over its entire useful life:

$$k(\tau) \equiv \int_\tau^\infty (1 - T)\kappa(t)P(t)e^{-(1-T)r(t-\tau)}dt \tag{7}$$

Let entrepreneurs expect physical marginal productivity of capital stock to be growing at the stationary rate g_κ:

$$\kappa(t) = \kappa(\tau)e^{g_\kappa(t-\tau)}$$

and price of output to be growing at the stationary rate g_P:

$$P(t) = P(\tau)e^{g_P(t-\tau)}$$

Insert these into (7), define

$$\rho \equiv (1 - T)r - (g_\kappa + g_P) \tag{8}$$

and write the integral (7) as

$$k(\tau) = \int_\tau^\infty (1 - T)\kappa(\tau)P(\tau)e^{-\rho(t-\tau)}dt$$

Neither $(1 - T)$, $\kappa(\tau)$, nor $P(\tau)$ is a function of t, hence all may be taken outside the integral sign. Our g_κ, g_P, and r were all said to be stationary, hence the coefficient ρ of t is stationary, too. Assume $\rho > 0$. As a result, find the integral to be

$$k = (1 - T)\kappa P/\rho$$

Define present net worth of another physical unit of capital stock as its gross worth *minus* its price:

$$n \equiv k - P = [(1 - T)\kappa/\rho - 1]P \tag{9}$$

Desired capital stock is the size of stock for which the present net worth (9) of another physical unit of capital stock equals zero. Assuming price P not to be zero, (9) can be zero if and only if

$$(1 - T)\kappa = \rho \tag{10}$$

Finally, take (6) and (10) together and find desired capital stock

$$S = (1 - T)\beta X/\rho \tag{11}$$

In a ρ-S diagram the desired-capital-stock function (11) is a rectangular hyperbola with the axes as asymptotes, exists when $\rho \neq 0$, and has branches in the first and third quadrants. Negative physical stocks are meaningless. We therefore restrict the domain of (11) to $\rho > 0$.

In accordance with the definition (5), differentiate desired capital stock (11) with respect to time and find desired investment

$$I \equiv \frac{dS}{dt} = \frac{(1 - T)\beta g_X X}{\rho} \tag{12}$$

If we think of (11) and (12) as derived for an individual entrepreneur, then everything except X on their right-hand sides is common to all entrepreneurs. Factor out all common factors and sum over all entrepreneurs, then X becomes national physical output, and (11) and (12) become national desired capital stock and investment, respectively. In the definition (8) in accordance with our solutions (28) and (38) let it be correctly foreseen that $g_\kappa = 0$. In that case, ρ collapses into the after-tax real rate of interest.

Thus our investment function (12) will neatly encompass several schools of thought. Wicksellians would expect the "natural" rate of interest and find the elasticity β of physical output with respect to capital stock. Keynesians would expect the cost of capital, have it specified for them by monetarists as the "real" rate of interest, and find it in the form ρ. Harrodians would expect incremental output and find it in the form $g_X X \equiv dX/dt$. Feldstein (1976) would expect the tax rate and find T.

4. The "Natural Rate of Unemployment"

Let labor employed be the proper fraction λ of available labor force:

$$L = \lambda F \tag{13}$$

Subtract (13) from available labor force F and find the rate of unemployment $1 - \lambda$. Friedman (1968: 8) saw a "natural" rate of unemployment below which excess demand for labor would push the real wage rate up, and above which excess supply would push it down.[2]

---

[2]Casson (1984) has demonstrated the similarity between Friedman's views and the interwar views of A. C. Pigou, H. Clay, and E. Cannan on unemployment and unemployment compensation.

5. An Expectations-Augmented Phillips Function

Natural or not, raise the rate of unemployment $1 - \lambda$ to a negative power π, multiply by a coefficient p, add a term incorporating labor's inflationary expectations, and write the expectations-augmented Phillips function

$$g_w = p(1 - \lambda)^\pi + \phi g_P \tag{14}$$

where $\phi > 0$, $\pi < 0$; and $p > 0$.

Given the inflationary expectations g_P and the sensitivity ϕ to them, the rate of unemployment $1 - \lambda$ represents Eckstein's (1981: 7-8) "state of demand" and the coefficient p his "shock." Eckstein defined his "core" as the rate of inflation "that would occur on the economy's long-term growth path, provided the path were free of shocks, and the state of demand were neutral in the sense that markets were in long-run equilibrium."

6. The Consumption Function

In a neoclassical growth model using a Cobb-Douglas production function in which $\alpha + \beta = 1$ and assuming profit maximization and pure competition, chapter 15 found money national income equaling national product defined as the market value of physical output:

$$Y = PX \tag{15}$$

Money national income in long-run steady-state neoclassical growth is purged of its transitory components, thus approaching Friedman's "permanent" income. Then define money disposable income before capital gains as money national income *plus* interest paid by government *minus* government net receipts before interest paid by government:

$$y \equiv Y + iQ - R \tag{16}$$

Since our model has wealth in it, capital gains should be considered. Wealth comes in three forms: physical capital stock S priced at P, stock of money M priced by definition at one, and stock of bonds Q priced at Π. Expressed as pure numbers per unit of time, then, the rates of nominal capital gains are g_P for physical capital stock, zero for stock of money, and g_Π for stock of bonds. The rates of real capital gains, found by subtracting the rate of inflation g_P, will be $g_P - g_P = 0$ for physical capital stock, $-g_P$ for stock of money, and $g_\Pi - g_P$ for stock of bonds. Multiply each such rate by the current value of the asset and find the flows of real capital gains expressed in current dollars per unit of time to be zero for physical capital stock, $-g_P M$ for stock of money, and $(g_\Pi - g_P)\Pi Q$ for stock of bonds. Finally, let consumption be the fraction c_1 of disposable income before capital gains *plus* the fraction c_2 of capital gains, all expressed in constant dollars per unit of time:

$$C = c_1(Y + iQ - R)/P + c_2[-g_P M + (g_\Pi - g_P)\Pi Q]/P \quad (17)$$

where $0 < c_i < 1, i = 1, 2$.

Although part of neither national product nor national income, interest iQ paid by government is still taxable and should appear in our tax function. So let government net receipts before interest paid by government be in proportion to money national income *plus* interest paid by government. Let capital gains be tax-exempt. Then our tax function is

$$R = T(Y + iQ) \quad (18)$$

where $0 < T < 1$.

7. *Demand for Money*

Interest iQ paid by government is transacted, so let the demand for money[3] be a function of money national income *plus* interest paid by government and of the after-tax nominal rate of interest

$$D = m(Y + iQ)[(1 - T)r]^\mu \quad (19)$$

where $\mu < 0$ and $m > 0$.

8. *The Government Budget Constraint*

The fiscal deficit is the money value of government purchase of goods and services *plus* interest paid by government *minus* government net receipts before interest paid by government, or $GP + iQ - R$, so we write the government budget constraint

$$GP + iQ - R = \frac{dM}{dt} + \Pi \frac{dQ}{dt} \quad (20)$$

Here the dollar proceeds of a new bond issue is price of bond Π *times* physical quantity of new bonds dQ/dt issued. What will Π be?

---

[3]On the money-market side, monetarist tradition disaggregates more than we are doing and distinguishes between money, credit, and securities markets. On the goods-market side, neither the monetarist tradition [Brunner-Meltzer (1976)] nor the rational-expectations tradition [Sargent-Wallace (1975)] distinguishes even between consumption and investment demand.

9. *The Price of Bonds*

At time t let an immortal bond be paying the interest $i(t)$ dollars per annum. Since interest earnings are taxed, the after-tax interest payment is $(1 - T)i(t)$. Since money may be placed or borrowed at the after-tax rate $(1 - T)r$, that rate should be applied when discounting future cash flows. As seen from the present time τ, then, the after-tax interest payment is worth $(1 - T)i(t)e^{-(1-T)r(t-\tau)}$. Define present gross worth of the bond as the present worth of all its future after-tax interest payments over its entire life:

$$k(\tau) \equiv \int_{\tau}^{\infty} (1 - T)i(t)e^{-(1-T)r(t-\tau)}dt$$

The interest payment is stationary:

$$i(t) = i(\tau)$$

Insert that and find the integral to be

$$k(\tau) = \int_{\tau}^{\infty} (1 - T)i(\tau)e^{-(1-T)r(t-\tau)}dt$$

Neither $(1 - T)$ nor $i(\tau)$ is a function of t, hence both may be taken outside the integral sign. Our r was said to be stationary, hence the coefficient r of t is stationary. Assume $r > 0$, take the integral, let the $(1 - T)$ in the numerator and denominator cancel, and find

$$k = i/r$$

Define present net worth of the bond as its gross worth *minus* its price:

$$n \equiv k - \Pi = i/r - \Pi$$

If $\Pi > i/r$, net worth will be negative, bondholders would wish to sell, and excess supply would lower the price. If

$$\Pi = i/r \tag{21}$$

net worth will be zero, and bondholders would be induced neither to buy nor sell. If $\Pi < i/r$, net worth will be positive, bondholders would wish to buy, and excess demand would raise the price. The price (21) alone is compatible with zero excess demand for bonds, hence is the equilibrium price.

10. *Equilibrium*

Goods-market equilibrium requires the supply of goods to equal the demand for them:

$$X = C + I + G \tag{22}$$

Money-market equilibrium requires the supply of money to equal the demand for it:

$$M = D \tag{23}$$

III. GROWTH-RATE SOLUTIONS

1. *Steady-State Growth*

For the time being, consider as given the coefficient p representing Eckstein's "shock" component. Then by applying the definition (1) to equations (2) through (23), the reader may convince himself that our system is satisfied by the following growth-rate solutions:

$$g_C = g_X \tag{24}$$

$$g_D = g_M \tag{25}$$

$$g_G = g_X \tag{26}$$

$$g_I = g_X \tag{27}$$

$$g_\kappa = g_X - g_S \tag{28}$$

$$g_L = g_F \tag{29}$$

$$g_M = g_Y \tag{30}$$

$$g_P = \frac{p(1 - \lambda)^\pi - g_a/\alpha}{1 - \phi} \tag{31}$$

$$g_p = 0 \tag{32}$$

$$g_\Pi = 0 \tag{33}$$

$$g_Q = g_Y \tag{34}$$

$$g_R = g_Y \tag{35}$$

$$g_r = 0 \tag{36}$$

$$g_\rho = 0 \tag{37}$$

$$g_S = g_X \tag{38}$$

$$g_w = \frac{p(1 - \lambda)^\pi - \phi g_a/\alpha}{1 - \phi} \tag{39}$$

$$g_{w/P} \equiv g_w - g_P = g_a/\alpha \tag{40}$$

$$g_X = g_a/\alpha + g_F \tag{41}$$

$$g_Y = g_P + g_X \tag{42}$$

$$g_y = g_Y \tag{43}$$

Our growth is steady-state growth, for the right-hand side of no growth-rate solution (24) through (43) is a function of time.

2. *Rational Expectations*

Our solutions imply self-fulfilling expectations, for we used the same symbol for the expected and realized values of any variable, implying equality between the two.

Our self-fulfilling expectations are, first, the expectations by private parties of what other private parties are going to do and, second, the expectations by private parties of what government is going to do. Our solutions (30) and (34) imply the policy rule that the money and bond supplies are growing at the same rate g_Y, a rate of steady-state growth. Private parties expect this policy rule to be upheld by the government, and it is.

Is such equality between the expected and realized values of any variable always possible? Yes, if our solutions (24) through (43) are meaningful and stable.

3. *Inflation Equilibrium: Is It Meaningful and Stable?*

To see if our inflation equilibrium (31) and (39) is meaningful and stable, insert (29) and (41) into our price equation (4), rearrange, call it (44), and confront it with our wage equation, our Phillips function (14):

$$g_w = g_a/\alpha + g_P \tag{44}$$

$$g_w = p(1 - \lambda)^\pi + \phi g_P \tag{14}$$

Both have g_w on their left-hand side, so we may plot them in figure 16-1, having g_w on the vertical axis and g_P on the horizontal axis. The price equation (44) will then appear as a single straight line with the intercept g_a/α and the slope one. The wage equation (14) will appear as a family of straight lines with the intercepts $p(1 - \lambda)^\pi$ and the slope ϕ. If a price-equation line (44) intersects a wage-equation line (14), then the coordinates of the intersection point will be our solutions (31) and (39). Such intersection points are marked by double circles in figure 16-1. Here expectations are self-fulfilling: if entrepreneurs expect labor to adopt the solution value (39) of the rate of growth of the money wage rate, then the entrepreneurs will adopt the solution value (31) of the rate of growth of price. On the other hand, if labor expects entrepreneurs to do so, then labor will adopt the solution value (39) of the rate of growth of the money

FIGURE 16-1.
The Inflation
Equilibrium: Three
Possibilities

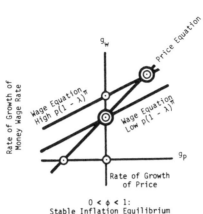

$$0 < \phi < 1:$$
Stable Inflation Equilibrium

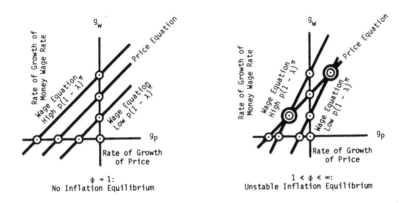

$$\phi \to 1:$$
No Inflation Equilibrium

$$1 < \phi < \infty:$$
Unstable Inflation Equilibrium

wage rate. Does such an inflation equilibrium exist and if so, is it stable? Figure 16-1 distinguishes between three possibilities.

First, let $0 < \phi < 1$. Here the wage equation (14) appears as a family of positively sloped lines whose slope ϕ is less than one, hence they intersect the price-equation line (44) from above, and the equilibria are stable. If, say, labor overshoots because it expects a g_P higher than the equilibrium value (31), then entrepreneurs will respond along their price-equation line and raise price less than labor expected. Labor will go from there and respond along its wage-equation line and overshoot less. And so it goes. The parties are moving back towards the equilibrium point.

Second, let $\phi \to 1$. Now the wage equation (14) approaches a family of lines with a unitary slope. All have the same slope as the price-equation line (44). Consequently, a wage-equation line either coincides with the price equation line or is parallel to it. Either way, no meaningful inflation equilibrium exists. If $p(1 - \lambda)^\pi = g_a/\alpha$ the limits of solutions (31) and

(39) assume the undefined form 0/0. If $p(1 - \lambda)^\pi \leqq g_a/\alpha$ the limits of (31) and (39) are

$$\lim_{\phi \to 1} g_P = \lim_{\phi \to 1} g_w = \pm \infty$$

interpreted as hyperinflation and hyperdeflation, respectively.

Third, let $1 < \phi < \infty$. The wage equation (14) appears as a family of positively sloped lines whose slope is greater than one, hence they intersect the price-equation line (44) from below, and the equilibria are unstable. If, say, labor overshoots because it expects a g_P higher than the equilibrium value (31), then entrepreneurs will respond along their price-equation line and raise price more than labor expected. Labor will go from there and respond along its wage-equation line and overshoot even more. And so it goes. The parties are now veering farther and farther away from the equilibrium point.

Our system, then, will generate hyperinflation or hyperdeflation—be "accelerationist"—only in the second case, $\phi \to 1$, in which no price-equation line (44) can intersect a wage-equation line (14). Cases in which such an intersection will occur, i.e., our first and third cases, are consistent with rational expectations: all our double-circle intersection points in figure 16-1 are located on the price-equation line (44), according to which—with much inflation or little—labor can always have and will always get a real wage rate growing at the rate (40). Our third case is unstable. But fortunately, as Eckstein (1981: 77-79) has found, our first case, $0 < \phi < 1$, is realistic. Realistically, then, our inflation equilibrium is non-accelerationist, meaningful, and stable. Is it also controllable?

4. Inflation Control

The trick of inflation control, we are told, is "to break inflationary expectations." Taken literally, the expression would merely mean reducing the g_P of the second term of our Phillips function (14). Such reduction, however, would accomplish nothing of permanence: as long as nothing had changed on the right-hand side of our solution (31), expected g_P would simply have been depressed below its equilibrium value (31). Expectations would no longer be self-fulfilling, and in the long run the equilibrium value (31) would prevail.

For anything of permanence to be accomplished, the right-hand side of our solution (31) must be reduced. How? As Friedman (1968) showed, as long as the monetary authorities kept decelerating the money supply, the rate of unemployment $1 - \lambda$ might stay above its natural rate. A temporary reduction of the right-hand side of (31) would thus have been accomplished. But once the monetary authorities stopped decelerating the money supply, the rate of unemployment $1 - \lambda$ would once again become the natural one, and no permanent reduction of the right-hand side of (31) would have been accomplished.

The only remaining hope of permanently reducing the right-hand side of our solution (31) must lie in a permanent reduction of the coefficient p, Eckstein's "shock" component. To Friedman, then, that coefficient must be a variable, and we know what to do: we can no longer consider it as given. We must solve for it.

5.   Solving for the Shock Coefficient p

Insert (30), (31), and (41) into (42) and solve for the shock coefficient p in terms of the policy instrument g_M and the structural parameters α, ϕ, g_a, g_F, $1 - \lambda$, and π:

$$p = \frac{\phi g_a/\alpha + (1 - \phi)(g_M - g_F)}{(1 - \lambda)^\pi}$$

Finally, insert our solution for the shock coefficient p into (31), assume $0 < \phi < 1$, let $1 - \phi$ cancel in the numerator and denominator of (31), and find

$$g_P = g_M - (g_a/\alpha + g_F) \tag{45}$$

Our solution (45) delivers Friedman's policy conclusion impeccably: the monetary authorities may control the rate of inflation g_P by controlling the rate of growth g_M of the money supply—but modified by the negative supply-side parenthesis of (45): a given rate of growth g_M of the money supply will generate less inflation the higher the rate g_a of technological progress and the higher the rate of growth g_F of the labor force. Notice that our inflation control (45) would turn meaningless in our second, "accelerationist," case: if $\phi = 1$, our canceling of $1 - \phi$ in the numerator and denominator of (31) would have implied division by zero!

6.   Growth-Rate Solutions: The Dichotomy Between Nominal and Real Ones

Our growth-rate solutions (24) through (45) also deliver Friedman's conclusions impeccably.

First, the growth-rate solutions for our eight nominal variables D, M, P, Q, R, w, Y, and y do have the rate of growth g_M of the money supply in them, directly or indirectly. Money does matter for nominal variables, then.

Second, no growth-rate solution for the ten real variables C, G, I, κ, L, Π, ρ, S, w/P, and X has the rate of growth g_M of the money supply in it, neither directly nor indirectly. Money doesn't matter for real variables, then.

IV. LEVELS

1. *The Level of the After-Tax Real Rate of Interest*

As we saw, the growth-rate solution for the seventh real variable, the after-tax real rate of interest ρ, had no g_M in it. But the *level* of that variable may have, as we shall now see.

Rearrange the investment function (12), insert the goods-market equilibrium condition (22) into it, and write the after-tax real rate of interest as

$$\rho = \frac{(1 - T)\beta g_X}{1 - (C/X + G/X)} \tag{46}$$

Let us express things in terms of the ratio δ between fiscal deficit and money national income. Into the government budget constraint (20) insert the definition (1) and the solutions (30) and (34), divide by money national income Y, and write that ratio

$$\delta \equiv (GP + iQ - R)/Y = g_Y(M/Y + \Pi Q/Y) \tag{47}$$

Divide the consumption function (17) by X, insert (15), (18), (33), (42), and (47), and write the ratio between physical consumption and physical output as

$$C/X = c_1(1 - T)(1 + iQ/Y) - c_2(g_Y - g_X)\delta/g_Y \tag{48}$$

Into (47) insert (15) and (18) and write the ratio between physical government purchase and physical output as

$$G/X = \delta - iQ/Y + (1 + iQ/Y)T \tag{49}$$

Finally, insert (48) and (49) into (46) and write the after-tax real rate of interest as

$$\rho = \frac{(1 - T)\beta g_X}{(1 - c_1)(1 - T)(1 + iQ/Y) - [(1 - c_2)g_Y + c_2 g_X]\delta/g_Y} \tag{50}$$

Does monetary and fiscal policy control the after-tax real rate of interest (50)? Compare two economies, both being in the steady-state growth equilibrium defined by our solutions (24) through (45) and being alike in all respects other than their monetary and fiscal policy. Let the economies have the same sum $M/Y + \Pi Q/Y$, kept stationary by our solutions (30), (33), and (34). According to (47), the two economies will then have the same ratio δ/g_Y.

But let the first economy have the more rapidly growing money and bond supplies, i.e., have the higher $g_M = g_Q = g_Y$. While the ratio δ/g_Y was the same, its coefficient $(1 - c_2)g_Y + c_2 g_X$ in (50) will not be. According to (41), g_X is unaffected by monetary and fiscal policy. Since we assumed $0 < c_i < 1$, the coefficient $1 - c_2$ of g_Y is positive. Consequently, with its higher $g_M = g_Q = g_Y$ the more inflationary economy will have the higher after-tax real rate of interest (50). The function (50) is shown in figure 16-2. Monetary and fiscal policy does control the after-tax real rate of interest!

FIGURE 16-2. After-Tax Real Rate of Interest Controlled by Monetary and Fiscal Policy

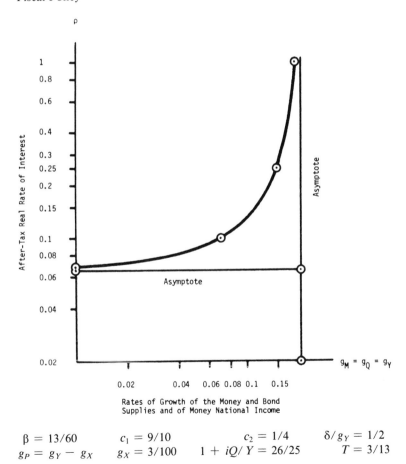

$\beta = 13/60$ $c_1 = 9/10$ $c_2 = 1/4$ $\delta/g_Y = 1/2$
$g_P = g_Y - g_X$ $g_X = 3/100$ $1 + iQ/Y = 26/25$ $T = 3/13$

2.   The Level of the After-Tax Nominal Rate of Interest

If with its higher $g_M = g_Q = g_Y$ the more inflationary economy has the higher after-tax real rate of interest (50), it must *a fortiori* have the higher after-tax nominal rate of interest $(1 - T)r$. Insert (23) into (19) and write the latter as

$$(1 - T)r = [m(1 + iQ/Y)/(M/Y)]^{-1/\mu} \tag{51}$$

It follows from (51) that to have the higher after-tax nominal rate of interest $(1 - T)r$, the first economy must have the higher bond-money mix $(1 + iQ/Y)/(M/Y)$. Whatever the bond-money mix, our solutions (30) and (34) will keep it stationary. Whatever their bond-money mix, the two economies may still, as assumed, have the same sum $M/Y + \Pi Q/Y$.

3.   The Levels of the Capital Coefficient and the Real Wage Rate

Use desired capital stock (11) to write the capital coefficient as

$$S/X = (1 - T)\beta/\rho \tag{11}$$

which is the lower the higher the after-tax real rate of interest ρ.

Next divide the production function (2) first by L and then by S and find

$$X/L = a(S/L)^\beta$$

$$X/S = a(L/S)^\alpha$$

Raise the latter equation to the power $-1/\alpha$, rearrange, insert it into the former equation, insert (11), insert the result into (3), and write the real wage rate

$$w/P = \alpha a^{1/\alpha}[(1 - T)\beta/\rho]^{\beta/\alpha} \tag{52}$$

which is the lower the higher the after-tax real rate of interest ρ. In short, in the more inflationary economy the crowding-out accomplished by the higher after-tax real rate of interest is spilling over into the capital coefficient S/X and the real wage rate w/P. Both levels will be lower than in the less inflationary economy.

V.   CONCLUSIONS

For the sake of the argument, we have accepted, first, a natural rate of unemployment insensitive in the long run to monetary policy, second, rational expectations in the form of self-fulfilling ones and, third, the policy rule that the money and bond supplies display steady-state growth fully foreseen by private parties. With those three acceptances, did Friedman's dichotomy hold?

As far as rates of growth were concerned, Friedman's dichotomy did hold: the growth-rate solutions for our eight nominal variables did have the rate of growth of the money supply in them, but the growth-rate solutions for our ten real variables did not.

As far as levels were concerned, Friedman's dichotomy did not hold. We compared two economies, both being in the steady-state growth equilibrium defined by (24) through (45) and being alike in all respects other than their monetary and fiscal policies; the first economy had the more rapidly growing money and bond supplies. As a result, Friedman's dichotomy between nominal and real broke down: the first economy had the higher after-tax real rate of interest. The higher after-tax real rate of interest crowded out physical investment and reduced the capital coefficient and the real wage rate. Thus something nominal—monetary and fiscal policies—affected something real.

REFERENCES

K. Brunner and A. H. Meltzer, "An Aggregative Theory for a Closed Economy," in J. L. Stein (ed.), *Monetarism: Studies in Monetary Economics 1*, Amsterdam, 1976.

M. Casson, *Economics of Unemployment*, Cambridge, Mass., 1984.

J. Drud Hansen, *Den Friedmanske monetarisme*, Odense, Denmark, 1979.

O. Eckstein, *Core Inflation*, Englewood Cliffs, N.J., 1981.

M. Feldstein, "Inflation, Income Taxes, and the Rate of Interest: A Theoretical Analysis," *Amer. Econ. Rev.*, Dec. 1976, *66*, 809-820.

M. Friedman, "The Role of Monetary Policy," *Amer. Econ. Rev.*, Mar. 1968, *58*, 1-17.

———, "A Theoretical Framework for Monetary Analysis," *J. Polit. Econ.*, Mar.-Apr. 1970, *78*, 193-238.

T. J. Sargent and N. Wallace, "'Rational' Expectations, the Optimal Monetary Instrument, and the Optimal Money Supply Rule," *J. Polit. Econ.*, Apr. 1975, *83*, 241-254.

R. M. Solow, "A Contribution to the Theory of Economic Growth," *Quart. J. Econ.*, Feb. 1956, *70*, 65-94.

N. Thygesen, "The Scientific Contributions of Milton Friedman," *Scan. J. Econ.*, 1, *79*, 1977, 56-98.

AFTERWORD   Was Our Journey Worth the While?

1.   *Journey's End*

We are at the end of our journey, and it has been a long one. Even so, the writer reaches his end overwhelmed by the feeling expressed by Barbara Tuchman (1962: xv) as she reached hers: "The faces and voices of all that I have left out crowd around me as I reach the end."

Was our journey worth the while? Perhaps our reader has long since had enough. Perhaps he has persevered but might have preferred "faces and voices" different from those encountered on our particular journey. Whatever the faces and voices encountered, is such a journey worth the while? Let us distinguish two views on the evolution of economic theory, i.e., the minority view that the best is behind us and the majority view that the best is ahead.

2.   *Is the Best behind Us?*

The index to Sraffa (1960) refers neither to subjects such as "consumption," "demand," "households," "preferences," "tastes," "utility," or "wants" nor to any modern writer, not even to Leontief or von Neumann. Presumably, in 1960, Sraffa considered everything happening after, say, 1817 a downhill journey from the Ricardian pinnacle. In such an extreme view a history of economic theory is vital—indeed *is* theory itself! Without sharing Sraffa's extreme view, many of us must have experienced occasional pangs of nostalgia for the innocence and simplicity of an earlier era.

3.   *Is the Best ahead of Us?*

The great majority of us believes that the best is still to come. That belief makes us push forward and try to keep up with the latest. In doing that, may we safely leave the history of our theory unopened in the attic?

Economic theory has a way of progressing in what Schumpeter (1954: 4) called a "criss-cross fashion." Whoever confines himself to the latest article, the latest survey, or the latest monograph risks being caught

in the latest cross and missing the previous criss. Forgetfulness and orthodoxy are the results of such short memories.

4. *Our Forgetfulness*

The history of our theory reminds us, first, of our long lapses into
forgetfulness. Sir William Petty wrote his *Political Arithmetick* exactly
one century before the publication of Smith's *Wealth of Nations* and
wanted "to express myself in terms of number, weight, and measure."
But his tradition "wilted," as Schumpeter (1954: 212) put it, "in the
wooden hands of the Scottish professor and was practically lost to most
economists for 250 years." Bernoulli's marginal utility was remembered
by probability theorists, experimental psychologists, and Galiani but forgotten, as we saw, by all other economists for a century and a third.

In our own keeping up with the latest, how forgetful are we ourselves?

5. *Our Orthodoxy*

The history of our theory reminds us, second, of our long lapses into
orthodoxy. How could Ricardian orthodoxy keep the British from dis-
carding the labor theory of value for so long? Mill discarded it only halfway, and Marx tried to give it another lease of life. How did Marshallian
orthodoxy succeed in keeping equilibria partial rather than general for so
long? Indeed, how could Marshallian orthodoxy keep Walras out of the
British Isles for two-thirds of a century—even denying him access to the
Economic Journal? When Hicks finally did introduce Walras, why did
he, a trained mathematician, do it by counting equations and unknowns
as Walras, a mathematical amateur, had done?

Among themselves our dissidents, too, maintained rigid ortho-
doxies. Marx was certainly afraid neither of mentioning people by name
nor of calling them names. Why did he never once mention Jevons,
Menger, or Walras, and why didn't at least his followers look for themselves? Why did a nonsocialist Walrasian like Barone have to show them
how a socialist economy might function, and why weren't they listening?

In our own keeping up with the latest, how orthodox are we ourselves?

Sciences normally progress in a criss-cross fashion, and in that respect economic theory does not differ from physics or chemistry. We all
stumble upon our ideas, sometimes prompted by accidental observations
like those of Oersted, Wöhler, Schönbein, or Perkin.

6. *Our Subject Matter Is Changing over Time*

In one respect, economic theory does differ from physics or chemistry. Ultimately, the variables of a general economic equilibrium are determined by its parameters, and we have come to think of four main categories of such parameters. First, engineering delivers our technology parameters. Second, physiology and psychology deliver our want parameters. Third, nature delivers our resource parameters. Fourth, legal institutions establish private ownership to those resources, making it possible for private persons to earn an income from them. As Menger and Wieser taught us, economics is nothing less than the full interaction of prices and quantities in a setting of given technology, wants, resources, and legal institutions. Our subject matter will be a function of time if its setting is a function of time. Is it?

The first determinant, technology, has displayed three violent industrial revolutions since Turgot, and the second determinant, human wants, has responded promptly and willingly to technology. Resources, the third determinant, were of course always there. But dormant resources are free goods. Progressing technology unlocked the dormant resources and made them economic goods. The fourth determinant, legal institutions, changed with the times. The United States abolished slavery. Bismarck's Germany adopted social security. In the United States and Britain labor unions became legal and were no longer liable for the damage caused by strikes.

Here is where economic theory differs from physics or chemistry: its very subject matter is a function of time. Cantillon's observation that "Men multiply like Mice in a barn if they have unlimited Means of Subsistence" would have been an anachronism in Keynes's century, and Keynes's observation of involuntary mass unemployment would have been an anachronism in Cantillon's century.

7. *Theory as an Inevitable Product of Its Historical Setting?*

If the setting of economic theory is a function of time, we had better visualize theories within their historical setting, and that is exactly what we have done in this book. Each of the introductions to our five periods opened with a section on the setting of the period. Did we simply see theory, then, as an inevitable product of its historical setting?

To be sure, mercantilist thinking was best understood against the background of the forces that created the nation state out of feudalism. Ricardo's chapter 31 on machinery was best understood against the background of the turmoil of the first industrial revolution. Keynesian thinking after 1930 and monetarist thinking after 1970 were best understood as explicit responses to the Great Depression and the Great Inflation, respectively. Such economists simply wrote about their time and offered to solve its problems. Their theories were products, if not inevitable products, of their setting.

8. *Theory as a Product of Logical Impulse?*

The time around 1870 happened to be a breakthrough of revolutionary new technologies, bringing with them entirely new industries, increasing returns to scale, the giant corporation, and a major reallocation of resources. The time around 1870 also happened to be a breakthrough in the way economists thought about the economy. Was our new way of thinking the result of all the hustle and bustle around us? Jevons, Menger, and Walras never mentioned it. Their olympic calm was never disturbed by it. Was it simply that economic theory was helplessly stuck in the dead-end street of the labor theory of value and began searching for logical alternatives? If so, theory was a product of logical impulse rather than setting.

9. *Both*

Good theory is often the joint product of setting and logical impulse. The idea of saddle-point duality offers a perfect example.

First, the eminently practical problems of industrial planning in early Soviet five-year plans caught the attention of a top mathematician, Leonid Kantorovich, and the eminently practical problem of allocating Allied merchant shipping tonnage among routes so as to win the Second World War caught the attention of the Dutch physicist Tjalling Koopmans.

Second, far removed from the real world, its data, and its problems, one of the foremost mathematicians of the century, John von Neumann, had applied advanced mathematics to two seemingly very different problems, i.e., optimal strategies in parlor games in 1928 and the existence of a competitive equilibrium in a growing economy in 1937.

Out of such pressures of setting and logical impulse came the common idea of duality: important economic problems may be formulated as maximization of a primal constrained by one set of inequalities and minimization of a dual constrained by another set. In particular but important cases a saddle point may be proved to exist that will at the same time maximize the primal and minimize the dual.

Was the saddle-point solution a product of setting *or* logical impulse? Both, of course.

REFERENCES

J. A. Schumpeter, *History of Economic Analysis*, New York, 1954.

P. Sraffa, *Production of Commodities by Means of Commodities*, Cambridge, 1960.

B. W. Tuchman, *The Proud Tower: A Portrait of the World before the War, 1890-1914*, New York, 1962.

AUTHOR INDEX

Note: Bibliographies are not indexed. Italicized references are the principal ones.

SUBJECT INDEX

Abstinence, in Mill, 83
Accelerationist inflation. *See* Long-run
    inflation equilibrium
Accelerator
    in Cassel-Harrod, 264
    in Hansen, 242, 298
    interaction with multiplier, 242, 298
Accounting, in Quesnay, 56-57
Activity analysis, 299, 329-343
Adaptive expectations. *See* Expectations
Allocation
    of endowments between withholding
      and supplying, in Walras, 171
    of inputs among outputs, 171, 183,
      190-191
    intertemporal, in Ramsey, 163-168
    of outputs among households, 171,
      191-192
    theory, 10, 83, 133-134, 270
American Indian, Cantillon on, 46-47
Anachronism, 69, 389
Animal spirits, in Robinson, 269
Asymmetrical duopoly. *See*
    Leader-follower equilibria
Austrian
    factor supplies (*see* Supply of factors)
    interlude in London, 235
    unifying principle, 139, 182-184
Automotive industry, 130

Baekeland's polymers, 130
Balanced budget, 66-67. *See also*
    Government budget constraint
Balanced-budget multiplier, anticipated
    by Steuart, 37-38
Balanced growth. *See* Growth

Balance of trade. *See* Export surplus;
    Import surplus
Bell's telephone, 129
Benz's automobile, 130
Birth control, 131
Bliss, in Ramsey, 168
Blood, circular flow of, 50
Bond, present net worth of, 376
Borrowers and lenders, 19, 36-37, 156
Breaking-even process
    in Cantillon, 42
    in Leontief, 322
    in Marx, 116
    in Quesnay, 56
Buddenbrooks syndrome in Marshall,
    148-149, 148n
Business cycle, 233
Business decisions under uncertainty, in
    Bernoulli, 28

Calculus
    absent in von Neumann, 300
    discovery of, 27
    unknown to Menger, 181
    unknown to Wieser, 183
    of variations, in Ramsey, 163-168
Canonical model of English classicism,
    73
Capital
    circulating
      in Böhm-Bawerk, 194
      in Mill, 84
      in von Neumann, 301
      in Ricardo, 74, 84, 96, 107
    constant, in Marx, 112
    fixed

397

The Johns Hopkins University Press

PIONEERING ECONOMIC THEORY, 1630-1980

This book was set in English Times text and display
type by Action Comp Co., Inc., from a design by
Martha Farlow. It was printed on 50-lb. Eggshell
Cream Offset paper and bound in Holliston Roxite
A by The Maple Press Company.

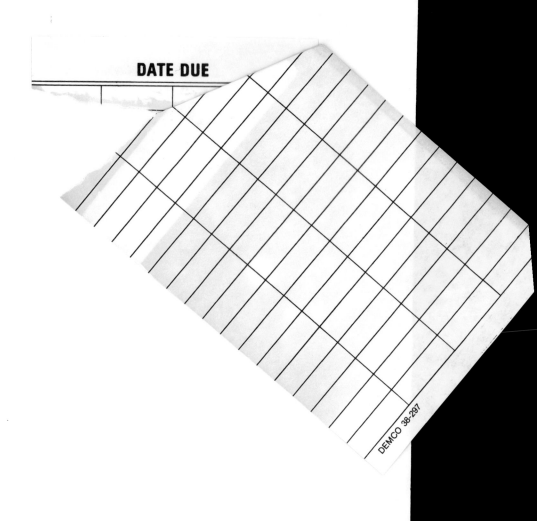

DATE DUE

DEMCO 38-297